P9-CAX-726

The Principalship

Concepts and Practices

Ralph B. Kimbrough

University of Florida

Charles W. Burkett

East Tennessee State University

ALLYN AND BACON
Boston London Toronto Sydney Tokyo Singapore

Library of Congress Cataloging-in-Publication Data

Kimbrough, Ralph B.
    The principalship : concepts and practices / Ralph B. Kimbrough,
Charles W. Burkett.
        p.   cm.
    Bibliography: p.
    Includes index.
    ISBN 0-13-700964-X
    1. School principals. 2. School management and organization.
I. Burkett, Charles W.   II. Title.
LB2831.9.K56 1990
371.2'012--dc20   89-4019
                                                       CIP

 Copyright © 1990 by Allyn and Bacon
A Division of Simon & Schuster, Inc.
160 Gould Street
Needham Heights, MA 02194

Printed in the United States of America

10 9 8 7 6 5 4 3 2   96 95 94 93 92

ISBN 0-13-700964-X

Contents

CHAPTER THREE

Using Social Systems Concepts 33

CHAPTER FOUR

The Structure of School Social Systems 51

CHAPTER FIVE

Central Office Regimes: The School District Control System 71

CHAPTER TEN

The Principal as Supervisor

CHAPTER ELEVEN

Providing Adequate Library Materials and Instructional Technology

CHAPTER TWELVE

Understanding School Law

CHAPTER THIRTEEN

Computers as Aids to Principals   *235*

CHAPTER FOURTEEN

The Personnel Function   *260*

CHAPTER FIFTEEN

Administration of Student Personnel   *273*

CHAPTER SIXTEEN

Operation of School Plant Facilities   *293*

CHAPTER SEVENTEEN

Days in the Life of Principals   *303*

Preface

Few educators and citizens will argue with the proposition that the principal of the school is the most important administrator in the American educational system. To be successful every group, even the street gang, must have a leader or face the prospect of a mob bent upon the destruction of everything in its path, including itself. Without a leader every group will move toward randomness and failure. All brutish conquerors know that the way to grasp control of a community is to destroy its leadership structure, leaving it in a temporary state of disorder, before substituting their own leaders to control the situation. There is no doubt about it: The school must have leadership and have it now when it is being so severely criticized for its shortcomings. The leadership structure of the school will seldom rise appreciably above the quality of leadership furnished by the principal.

The need for leadership knows no boundaries. Depending on the quality of their leaders, entire communities progress toward the good life or lean toward mediocrity in daily living. The primary difference between these communities is the quality of their leaders. Moreover, the quality of leadership in the community affects the efforts of educators in achieving high quality education for students.

For this reason we have emphasized how those appointed to the principalship can assume leadership with the school faculty and with the systems in which the school interacts. The reader will find in this textbook a wealth of information about how one can assume leadership of a school and how that leadership can result in the development of educational excellence. Leadership within interacting systems is the central theme of the textbook; however, we do not in any way neglect the technical aspects of running a school. The technical aspects of school administration cannot be separated from the social realm because they are intermingled; one cannot exist without the other.

Much of the current and past literature expounds on the principal as the instructional leader of the school. But in this textbook we do more than expound on this point. We help the reader learn (1) how to become a leader with the faculty and (2) how to use this position of leadership to move the school faculty toward educational excellence. Our approach to how the principal acquires a position of leadership with the faculty, parents, central office personnel, and other citizens is based on over thirty years of research about the emergence and success of community leaders. This account of how one becomes a leader is therefore superior to many small group research projects in which so many of the subjects were captive students or organizational workers. Leadership in the political crucible of the real world is vastly different from leadership in a captive group of fifth-grade students; consequently, the reader may find some of our concepts unique. But we do not in any way ignore the vast amount of empirical evidence accumulated about leadership; these concepts are explored in consistency with our approach.

Chapters 1 and 2 of this text are concerned with the background development, preparation, and means of appointment of the principal. Along with Chapter 17 (Days in the Lives of Principals), they provide an introduction to the principalship, with particular emphasis upon the principal's primary role in the scheme of things.

In Chapters 3 through 6 the reader is directed toward a systems approach to the principalship. The basic concepts of general systems theory are described and further highlighted by cases illustrative of the concepts. The educational leader who does not understand the school as a system in interaction with other systems will be severely handicapped in grasping a leadership position with the faculty, superordinates in the central office, students, and parents.

Chapters 7 through 10 discuss the difference leadership can make in the quality of education offered children and youth. This process requires knowledge of the change process, the development of a climate (or condition) for instruction and learning, and the techniques of supervision. Yet mere use of techniques is not sufficient. The principal and faculty must see in their mind's eye where the school must go to achieve excellence. Throughout this and other parts of the text we describe in considerable detail those conditions found to be associated with schools of quality.

Chapters 11 through 16 emphasize selected technical aspects of managing a school, including such leadership tasks as providing for an adequate library, understanding legal concepts, computer aids to administration, school plant facilities, and personnel management. Yet, even in these chapters we continue to support the leadership role of the principal because separating the technical from the social dimensions of administration is an arbitrary decision. These dimensions are intermingled and mutually supportive. Chapter 17 is really a source chapter for the entire book. Through the presentation of actual logs kept by principals, letters, memoranda, and other information, we present "days in the lives of principals." These materials may be used for discussing the tasks that the selected school principals performed. They are also useful for the classroom or small group discussion.

Acknowledgments

Writing the manuscript for this text required a great amount of time and energy, but this investment of energy was enhanced by the contributions of numerous persons. First, we express sincere appreciation to the school principals, librarians, supervisors, and other administrators who furnished technical information to make the book better. Appreciation is also expressed to our colleagues who furnished technical information and reviewed selected chapters during our preparation of the manuscript. Their expert inputs contributed immeasurably to the success of this project. We express special gratitude for the unswerving support and assistance of Elena Burkett and Gladys Kimbrough.

Ralph B. Kimbrough
Charles W. Burkett

The Principalship

CHAPTER ONE

About the Principal

INTRODUCTION

The school principal or head teacher was one of the first positions that emerged in the profession of educational administration. In fact, the position appeared so many years ago that an accurate history of its development is somewhat lost in antiquity. Despite current expressions about the limitations of practicing principals, the principalship has a proud, distinguished tradition. Most of us did not know much about the school superintendent or other central office administrators, but all of us remember, with varying feelings of awe, the principal of our school. Nothing could surpass the impressions made when the teacher threatened a trip to "the office."

Just who is the principal of the school? What are the principal's tasks, responsibilities, duties, and functions? These are but a few of the ideas about the principalship that are discussed in Chapters 1 and 2. Their purpose is to explore the development, tasks, leadership functions, selection processes, educational preparation, and personal demands of those who occupy the position of school principal. Along with the material in Chapter 17, which serves all chapters in the book,

Chapters 1 and 2 introduce the reader to the leadership role and function of school principal.

Excellence in education is essential for the survival of American democracy and the continued leadership of the United States among the nations of the world. We must have well-administered schools that are adequately supported by parents and other citizens. The results of research, upheld by almost unanimous opinion, have led to the widespread conclusion that strong leadership by the school principal is essential for achieving educational excellence. For example, comparative research of effective and less effective inner-city schools has highlighted strong leadership of the principal as a vital characteristic of schools of quality.[1] Yet principals are not miracle workers. The dedicated support of groups in the school's environment (such as parents, members of the central office staff, boards of education, and other officials) is essential.

The excellent school is a well-administered system interacting with a supportive environment. The strongest and most resolute principal and faculty will be severely restrained from achieving high marks of excellence if forces in the environment are at cross-purposes to the objectives of the school. Therefore, principals are accountable for the development of cooperative support among the environmental systems with which the school interacts. For example, in addition to encouraging teamwork within the school, principals must look beyond the four walls of the school for the support of the district office staff to develop good school and community relations.

In this book we emphasize the technical-knowledge and leadership aspects of the principalship. Leadership in both the technical and social subsystems is essential. The school must be thought of as a system functioning within an environment (or suprasystem). As the school interacts with the environment, the principal has the task of promoting among the faculty and support staff a self-sacrificing devotion to educating children and youth to the limits of their abilities.

DEVELOPMENT OF THE PRINCIPALSHIP

The lack of documentary evidence has clouded the early development of the position of principal; however, the position emerged as schools grew large enough to demand more than one teacher, and school trustees began to appoint "head teachers."[2] Before the appointment of head teachers or

[1]Ronald Edmonds, "Effective Schools for the Urban Poor," *Educational Leadership,* 37 (October 1979), 15–24.

[2]John S. Brubacher, *A History of the Problems of Education* (New York: McGraw-Hill, 1947), p. 588.

"principal teachers," the one-room teacher was responsible for everything. As school enrollment burgeoned in urban areas after the colonial period, the appointment of head teachers and teaching principals became accepted. With the growth in complexity of operating schools, the members of governing boards felt the need to have someone "in charge."

The term *principal* was derived from *prince* and means first in rank, degree, importance, and authority. The principal, therefore, was one with authority to make decisions about the operation of the school. According to most accounts, the formal designation of a principal was in Cincinnati about the middle of the 19th century. Yet the position of school principal is primarily a 20th-century development and was concomitant with the great growth of pupil enrollments after 1900.

The development of the principalship dims in significance compared to the rapid changes in the functions of the position in the 20th century. The position emerged as a routine administrative function. Someone had to see that the building was heated, the schedules were set, rules of procedure were followed, and strict discipline was maintained. The technology of operating a school was primitive in comparison to administering a modern comprehensive high school. Since the early schools were small and served a neighborhood, their relationships with parents and other citizens were personal.

The administrative functions of the principal have since become increasingly complex. With the development of pupil transportation capabilities and the consolidation of elementary and high schools, administrative tasks in such areas as curriculum and instruction, business management, school-plant management, pupil personnel, faculty relations, and school–community relations overburdened the principal. Additional staff became necessary, including assistant principals, deans, counselors, department heads, and directors of various activities, all especially evident in the large senior high school. The principals of large elementary and secondary schools lead large administrative staffs. The modern comprehensive school is administered by a team that must cope with many complex problem areas; in fact, many educators believe that the principalship of a large inner-city school is the most difficult administrative position in the field of education.

The emergence of the junior high school and, more recently, the middle school, added other dimensions to the principalship. The junior high school was to serve the unique developmental, emotional, and exploratory needs of students in that age bracket. During the 1950 to 1980 period many junior high schools were converted to middle schools. For years educators complained that the junior high school had become a shadow of its big brother, the senior high school. Consequently, the middle school was envisioned as an opportunity to offer a unique curriculum.

Educational philosophies have influenced the function of the principal. Beginning in the 1920s, the progressive education movement swung the pendulum toward a child-centered curriculum, away from the traditional subject-centered (basic education) emphasis. The post-World-War-II period ushered in the baby-boom growth era, which was complicated by competing educational beliefs as educators and citizens struggled with a pluralism of educational demands and philosophies. The radical left movement of the 1960s brought into focus the philosophy of existentialism and the "free school" movement. Concurrent with a political change toward the right of center, an emphasis upon the traditional basic concept of education again became popular during the early 1980s. The principal and faculty of a school still function within a pluralism of demands and issues concerning the direction of education: for example, the nature of curriculum, family education, textbooks, library holdings, and disciplinary methods.

In summary, the position of principal has developed from the appointment of head teachers, teaching principals, and full-time principals to the position of executive head of a large administrative staff, faculty, and student body. Except for small schools in rural areas, the operation of a school now requires the coordination of several members of an administrative team. The success of a school is heavily dependent upon the leadership of the principal and the competency and cooperation of the administrative team and faculty. Therefore, many of the administrative tasks for which the principal is responsible are delegated.

FUNCTIONS OF THE PRINCIPAL

As the material included in Chapter 17 illustrates, the daily life of a school principal is full of time-consuming duties and unexpected events. The best way to summarize the functions of school principals is to consider the task areas of their responsibilities. The principal is responsible for (1) instruction and curriculum, (2) pupil personnel, (3) community and school relations, (4) staff personnel, (5) organization and structure of the school, and (6) school plant facilities. Leadership responsibilities in these areas are discussed in the chapters that follow. The principal is also accountable for the performance of tasks in accounting for internal funds, management of the school lunchroom, and the loading and unloading of buses. To put it succinctly, the principal is accountable for the entire operation of the school. Since the tasks are so multitudinous, particularly in a large school, the principal must delegate authority for the performance of these tasks.

Practically everyone believes that the principal should give priority to personal leadership in curriculum and instruction. We concur with this view; however, a reasonable expectation of high performance in this area also depends on the efficient and effective performance of tasks in other areas. For example, high performance in instruction, which requires leadership in the area of staff personnel, depends on a motivated, competent faculty. Moreover, school excellence requires good school and community relations, including parents who support the school and are involved in their children's education. Obviously, the principal is accountable for the development of instructional excellence, but excellence can only be achieved through a well-functioning administrator-faculty team whose common purpose is to provide optimum opportunities for children and youth to achieve excellence. An expanded review of the principal's functions is included in Chapter 2; Chapter 17 is also devoted to this subject.

PARADOXES OF THE PRINCIPALSHIP

When persons are appointed as school principals, they usually approach their leadership task with much anticipation for developing a school of quality. Of concern to the authors is how, for some school principals, these dreams become paradoxes. Too many principals lose their unrestricted enthusiasm for leadership and become preoccupied with administrative details, or simply give up and slide along with existing conditions. Several conditions are associated with these changes in behavior.

Some beginning principals underestimate the difficulties involved in administering a large consolidated elementary, middle, junior high, or senior high school. The principalship of a large school, particularly a very large inner-city school, is a position that imposes enormous demands. Moreover, providing leadership for instructional improvement is extremely time-consuming and often frustrating; the acceptance of change by parents, members of the faculty, and students is very slow. Unfortunately, in their frustration, some principals soon lapse into taking the easy way out; they just do not try very hard, but become discouraged and lose interest.

In other situations well-meaning principals and members of their faculties suffer *goal displacement,* a condition in which the processes or means to achieve the officially prescribed goals of the school become ends in themselves and excessive energy is invested in organizational maintenance activities that are unrelated to the mission of the school. A kind of mindless administration develops in which the real purpose of the school drifts into obscurity. The principal and faculty may achieve high morale but place priority on the wrong things.

In the face of resistance to their attempts to lead the faculty and community toward excellence, some school principals simply lose courage, and the result is a failed leadership. Character (courage, honesty, dependability, generosity) is an essential mark of the successful school principal. Unfortunately, some persons are intimidated by threats when they attempt to move forward with the changes necessary to improve the instructional program of the school.

As stated earlier, strong leadership by the principal is one of the factors that differentiate effective from ineffective schools. To put it bluntly, the principalship is not a position for a wimp.

STRENGTH OF CHARACTER

One frequently hears the expression that *the principal should have strength of character,* which refers to the ethical or moral strength of the person. Each year many principals are removed from office for failure to assume their leadership obligations or for breach of ethics or moral character. Recognizing the importance of ethics, the American Association of School Administrators adopted a code of ethics in 1976, and this code was also adopted by the National Association of Elementary School Principals and the National Association of Secondary School Principals.[3]

Maintaining ethical behavior is much broader in scope than the professional code of ethics. The educational leader has two categories of administrative obligations: (1) legal obligations and (2) obligations of form. The principal is obligated to uphold the law and the policies of boards of control. Failure to act within the law or board-of-education policies (which have the effect of law) constitutes a serious breach of ethics. If one is informed about the law and operational policies, obligations in this dimension are less subject to individual interpretation than are the obligations of form. Cooper labels ethical responsibilities in this area *objective* responsibilities, whereas those obligations rooted in the conscience and not an imposed legal requirement are in the realm of *subjective* responsibilities.[4]

The ethics of form (such as use of authority, caring, character, professional commitment, formality, justice, loyalty, prudence, whistle blowing) involve obligations of a certain shape, mold, or form.[5] For example, some principals may be accused of an overbearing abuse of authority, and others of uncaring behavior. The lazy principal is as unethical as the principal who steals school funds; the student is permanently "robbed" of an oppor-

---

[3]American Association of School Administrators, *AASA Statement of Ethics for School Administrators and Procedural Guidelines* (Arlington, Va.: The Association, 1976).

[4]Terry L. Cooper, *The Responsible Administrator* (Port Washington, N.Y.: Kennikat Press, 1982).

[5]Ralph B. Kimbrough, *Ethics: A Course of Study for Educational Leaders* (Arlington, Va.: American Association of School Administrators, 1985), 8.

tunity for a good education, whereas the one who steals is usually removed from office within a short period of time and may be replaced with a competent principal.

The community and school system in which one practices have expectations about how the principal should behave; however, the ethics of form is also a matter of conscience. For example, how much the principal really cares about teachers and about students is a personal quality because the lack of caring may not constitute a basis for removal from office. Yet the caring function, the exercise of justice, prudence in making decisions, and other obligations of form are essential for well-administered schools of quality. Whether the principal practices acceptable ethics is most certainly related to student opportunity for an education.

Loyalty is a very troubling area of behavior. The principal is expected to demonstrate loyalty to superiors; however, does loyalty extend to demands to perform illegal acts or unethical behavior? Should the school principal accede to questionable edicts of an unscrupulous boss for fear of dismissal? The answer is obviously negative, yet for the principal to react ethically to these situations is very difficult. Furthermore, responding to such demands imprudently may impair the possibility for being appointed to a position in another school district. The principal has alternatives: resignation, refusal to act and taking the consequences, acting only upon written demand, and blowing the whistle. Unfortunately, blowing the whistle is often interpreted as an act of disloyalty. Space does not allow full discussion of the ethics of school principals. For further discussion of ethics, the reader is referred to a number of special publications, some of which are cited in this chapter.

In summary, dedication to high standards of ethics is essential for successful practice and for leadership in developing schools of quality. The blight on the minds of students who learn from the media that their principal is an embezzler is never removed. Yet a white-collar crime may not be as detrimental to the students as the principal who exhibits gross negligence of duty, makes unjust decisions, and exhibits intellectual dishonesty. Although these forms of unethical behavior prevent the school from achieving high marks of educational excellence, the perpetrator may remain in office for years because the unethical behavior may not be treated as criminal, supporting dismissal.

APPOINTMENT TO THE PRINCIPALSHIP

Although state requirements vary to some extent, appointment to the principalship requires state certification. Discussion of formal education and certification requirements is contained in Chapter 2.

School districts differ markedly in the appointment of persons to the principalship. Bureaucratic and community politics may be involved. The district may have some form of "cadet training" for aspirants to the position. Increased use of simulation, known as assessment centers, in selecting principals is currently a popular development.

Several staff or administrative positions may be considered entry-level positions to the principalship, such as assistant principal, dean of students, and director. Experience as department head or team leader may lay a foundation for promotions leading to the position of principal. Successful leadership of committees, task forces, and similar activities can demonstrate abilities and may be noted by higher-ups in the organization. In accepting such positions, one should perform well because evidence of leadership, even at this level, contributes to appointment to entry-level positions leading to the principalship.

THE OPEN-SYSTEMS APPROACH

Success in the principalship requires the ability to manage and provide leadership of all aspects of the school, and so requires conceptualizing the school in a holistic, systematic fashion. The school of quality is not an atomistic collection of parts; it is a totality or whole of interacting subsystems that give each school a unique quality or personality. A visit to ten schools within a three-day period reveals differences in climates, morale, and many other outward characteristics. These observed differences are not chance happenings; they are human-made systems. Therefore, to understand each school and how it became the way it is, one must analyze the interacting parts or subsystems. The open-systems approach to management, which is given emphasis in this textbook, provides a framework for empirical analysis of the whole school.

Thinking in the systems framework gives the principal a means to interpret present behavior and, to some extent, predict future behavior. In short, systems management and leadership afford the principal and faculty greater control over the processes associated with the development of school excellence. Guesswork is replaced by empirical analysis.

No concept known today will provide an incontrovertible explanation of school behavior. For example, school principals often find that the initiation of a change brings unexpected results, a condition discussed in Chapter 4 called equifinality. Yet we believe that thinking of the school as a whole system with interacting parts, or subsystems, within an environment provides the understanding essential for strong, effective leadership.

SETTING PRIORITIES, TIME MANAGEMENT, STRESS

Lest we leave the impression that the person occupying the position of principal is expected to be some kind of superperson, we should point out that principals of large consolidated schools are assisted by large staffs of assistant principals, deans, counselors, administrative assistants, secretaries, clerks, school nurses, and so on. Even the teaching principals in rural areas can expect cooperation and assistance from other teachers in the school. All effective principals delegate effectively. However, those leadership tasks that are crucial to the realization of educational excellence (such as leadership in curriculum and instruction, community leadership, leadership with the central office) must not be delegated. Moreover, it is well known that responsibility cannot be delegated; however, the principal can delegate others to be responsible for many managerial tasks for which the principal is ultimately responsible.

The authors are firm in the belief that such tasks as setting school goals, instructional leadership, leadership with parents and other citizens, and leadership with the central administrative offices must not be delegated. If, for example, the principal delegates responsibility for instructional leadership to an assistant principal for curriculum, the message to the faculty is that the instructional program has low priority; furthermore, the principal (who heads the school and approves all requests for instructional materials and equipment) will not be adequately informed about the resources needed by the faculty, nor about how to improve instructional services for students. Above all others, the principal is accountable for the education of children and youth.

Setting Priorities for Leadership. Every beginning principal must come to grips with setting leadership priorities. Which administrative tasks should be delegated to a member of the school staff? The reader might spend some time reviewing the logs of activities kept by principals given in Chapter 17. Should any of the administrative activities logged by the principals be delegated to members of the staff? Unfortunately, too many principals allow administrative details to subsume the really significant duties, and the school suffers from lack of instructional leadership. Two problems may be involved: (1) the principal has not established priorities, and (2) the principal has made inefficient use of time.

Time Management. The authors suggest that attention be given to the publications available on management of time.[6] The object of time management is to keep on task and resist those conditions that contribute to waste of the leader's time. For example, as a principal you should make a daily "to do" list of priority tasks to be completed. Use a few simple techniques to deal with those who habitually come by the office to "shoot

[6]*See,* for example, Lauren R. Januz and Susan K. Jones, *Time Management for Executives* (New York: Charles Scribner's Sons, 1981); Alan Lakein, *How to Get Control of Your Time and Your Life* (New York: Wyden, 1973).

the breeze" and thereby drain away valuable management time. Do not spend an inordinate amount of time on the telephone. Handle all correspondence only once instead of shuffling it about the piles of paper on the desk. Develop the administrative/supervisory staff of the school into a team that will step in and take care of a problem as opposed to a disorganized staff that spends an inordinate amount of time determining who is responsible. One technique for improving time management is to keep a log of activities for a few days and then review whether time is being spent wisely.

Administrative Stress. As discussed elsewhere in this text, serving as principal of a school is very demanding; consequently, the responsibilities produce stress. Prolonged stress (load or strain of the job) may for some persons create a health problem in the form of physical and mental exhaustion, anxiety, physical ailments, or "burnout." School administrators must learn how to cope with stress before it becomes a problem, by dealing personally with the many sources of extreme irritation. Overdependence on the job should be avoided. Release from the job through recreation may be indicated. Some of the problem may rest with the disposition of the person to deal with stress. For example, near the end of his program for the doctorate, a student announced to his surprised audience that he had no intention of accepting an administrative position. When asked why, he responded that people become angry with school administrators, and that he could not stand the emotional strain of having people angry at him. Some persons realize that they should not attempt to deal with the stress of the principalship. Others realize that they need help in dealing with stress. Some school districts offer centers for dealing with stress.

CHAPTER TWO

The Principalship: an Overview

The relationship of the role of the principal to effective school administration is a topic that has been subjected to close investigation. Until recently, the role of the principal was perceived as that of administrator/manager and public relations representative, but the present trend is to emphasize the principal's role as an instructional leader. Ultimately, effectiveness is determined by the impact of the principal on student learning.

Chamberlin and Cole observed, "The most important person in a school is not the principal; it is the student most in need of individual attention to his needs as a learner. However, the person most able to provide the optimum combination of staff, resources, materials, and methods for that student is the school principal."[1]

Strength in leadership and human-relations skills are essential for the development of educational excellence. Adequate formal preparation for the job is required, along with continuous personal development through in-service training programs. Moreover, the situation and placement of principals where they can best function is a critical task. In addition to the routine management and creative leadership tasks, the

[1]Leslie J. Chamberlin and Ron Roy Cole, *Administration, Education and Change* (Dubuque, Iowa: Kendall/Hunt Co., 1972).

principal must learn how to cope with some unusual demands. These aspects of the principal's job are discussed briefly in this chapter.

RESEARCH FINDINGS ON THE EFFECTIVENESS OF THE PRINCIPAL

The well-known statement *as the principal goes so goes the school* is still apropos. There have probably been more research findings to substantiate this point than for any other topic concerning the principal. Sweeney summarized numerous research studies concerning this topic and concluded that there are certain leadership behaviors and specific activities of principals that seem to make a difference. He found that effective principals made student achievement their top priority. After all, that is the primary purpose of education, but this purpose sometimes gets lost in our efforts to accomplish the many other expectations of the educational system. Sweeney further found that some of the specific activities of effective principals include scheduling faculty meetings to discuss student achievement, reducing classroom interruptions, using student assemblies and exhibits to reward student achievement, sharing information about academic achievement with students, faculty, and citizens, and highlighting the significance of achievement to students.[2]

Although not inclusive, characteristics of effective principals have been determined in many research findings. Jwaideh concluded from these findings that effective and innovative principals established goals and priorities, achieved balanced task performance and human relationships, behaved within the school norms, supported innovation and change, gained community and central office support, exhibited flexibility, and established communication with the school district. In addition, effective principals moved more often, were better educated, had more experience, and interacted frequently with other administrators.[3]

As has been alluded to before, effective principals do far more than manage schools—not that managing schools is not important; but they do a great amount of work directly involving teachers and assisting them in improving teaching methods and the teaching/learning environment of the school in general. Hord found that effective principals were especially concerned with helping teachers try innovative practices.[4] Jwaideh also

[2]Jim Sweeney, "Principals Can Provide Instructional Leadership: It Takes Commitment," *Education,* 103 (Winter 1982), 204–7.

[3]Alice R. Jwaideh, "The Principal as a Facilitator of Change," *Educational Horizons,* 63 (Fall 1984), 9–15.

[4]Shirley M. Hord, Suzanne M. Stiegelbauer, and Gene E. Hall, "How Principals Work with Other Change Facilitators," *Education and Urban Society,* 17 (November 1984), 89–109.

found that the principal's responsiveness and sensitivity to teachers and their needs was positively related to the staff's tendency to innovate. She reported on the research of others who had found that principals with innovative faculties were more in tune with their teachers' feelings and values about education, that they were better informed about their informal relationships, and that they were more professionally oriented.[5]

Studies by Reilly indicated that the most effective principals stressed student achievement. These principals provided leadership that resulted in a calm school environment, which was conducive to teaching and learning. They had high expectations of and aspirations for their faculty and students. The principals in these studies provided strong leadership in developing instructional goals and means for evaluating the outcomes.[6]

In their studies of how effective principals perform, Leithwood and Montgomery reported that they were attuned to students, teachers, and the larger school system. Effective principals' top priorities were, however, the happiness and achievement of students. The principals saw themselves as instructional leaders whose main function was to provide the best possible programs for the students, including concern for providing materials and resources for the classroom and providing leadership in implementing new practices. Other activities found in the studies by Leithwood and Montgomery related to the effectiveness of principals in selecting and delivering supplies, providing for space, scheduling planning meetings, disseminating information, developing in-service training plans, planning in-service with consultants, assessing teacher needs, and designing strategies to solve problems with the new curriculum.[7] They also determined that effective principals matched students with teachers of similar learning and teaching styles. These principals and their teachers worked together identifying instructional priorities and the means for achieving them: they employed creative means for securing materials and resources for teachers; they provided strong leadership assisting teachers in solving problems concerning implementation of new programs; and they assisted teachers in developing plans to wisely use their out-of-school planning time.[8]

Hord, Stiegelbauer, and Hall concluded that effective principals were very knowledgeable about curricular trends. They concluded that prin-

[5]Jwaideh, "Principal as a Facilitator," pp. 9–15.

[6]David H. Reilly, "The Principalship: The Need for a New Approach," *Education,* 104 (Spring 1984), 242–47.

[7]Kenneth A. Leithwood and Deborah J. Montgomery, "The Role of the Elementary School Principal in Program Improvement," *Review of Educational Research,* 52 (Fall 1982), 309–39.

[8]Leithwood and Montgomery, "Role of the School Principal," pp. 309–39.

cipals gave consideration to all components of the curriculum and particularly to its scope and sequence.[9] Sweeney reported that principals emphasized revising the curriculum based on pupil progress.[10] Not all principals, however, saw themselves as leaders in developing and improving curriculum. Baughman determined that teachers and principals disagreed on the importance of the principal's leadership in curriculum matters. Teachers thought that the principal's main role was to provide leadership in curriculum matters, but the principals thought that providing finances, developing an educational philosophy, and caring for facilities were responsibilities similar in importance to providing instructional leadership.[11] Other studies revealed that principals disagreed with central office staff as well as teachers concerning their roles as leaders in curriculum matters.[12, 13]

Three similar studies revealed that principals had important leadership roles in curriculum development, instructional programs, and developing conducive teaching/learning environments. Two of the studies revealed that principals felt that they were primarily responsible for the supervision and improvement of instruction. Two-thirds felt that they were, in fact, strong instructional leaders. Nearly all the principals in the studies felt that their importance was demonstrated by their influence on the making of decisions relevant to the instructional programs of their schools.[14, 15, 16] The National Education Association conducted a survey of principals and found that more than half believed that they were important in providing leadership to "modify and adapt" the general school curriculum.[17] Knight also discovered that principals as well as superintendents believed that providing leadership for curriculum change was a

[9]Hord, Stiegelbauer, and Hall, "How Principals Work," pp. 89–109.

[10]Sweeney, "Principals Can Provide Leadership," pp. 204–7.

[11]Myra June Baughman, "A Study of the Degree of Agreement Between Principals' and Teachers' Perceptions of the Principal's Functions and Behaviors," *Dissertation Abstracts International*, 36 (1976), 7974-A.

[12]Benjamin Ernest Spalding, "The Role of the IGE Principal as Instructional Leader," *Dissertation Abstracts International*, 43 (1982), 13.

[13]Felix John Zarlengo, "An Analysis of the Role and the Tasks of the Urban Principalship as Perceived by Principals and Central Office Administrators in the Providence, Rhode Island School Department," *Dissertation Abstracts International*, 35 (1974), 1941-A.

[14]"The Elementary School Principal in 1968: A Research Study," (Washington, D.C.: National Education Association, Department of Elementary School Principals, 1968).

[15]Edward H. Seifert and John J. Beck, "Elementary Principals: Leaders or School Managers?" *Phi Delta Kappan*, 62 (March 1981), 528.

[16]Robert Russell Agthe, "The Elementary Principals' Perception of Their Own and Teacher Roles in Curriculum Decision-Making," *Dissertation Abstracts International*, 40 (1979), 3076-A.

[17]National Education Association, *The Elementary School Principalship: A Research Study* (Washington, D.C.: Department of Elementary School Principals, *NEA*), p. 78.

major function of the administrator.[18] Findings by Blumberg and Green-field indicate that effective principals are innovators who are constantly seeking ways to improve instruction that will result in additional student learning.[19] Indications are that effective principals take responsibility for initiating and implementing new programs and then gradually turn them over to selected staff members, who are made responsible for securing the practices.[20]

Principals who provided leadership for curriculum innovation at the classroom level were found to have great respect from the teachers. Calhoun wrote that principals who gave much attention to improving the teaching/learning environment were rated very highly by the teachers.[21] Sweeney also found that principals who provided leadership for improvement were rated very high. He reported that principals ranked workshops as the main source of innovative ideas. Professional readings were ranked second, and information from other professionals was valued as the third source for innovative ideas.[22] Studies by Stoops and Marks substantiated the notion that principals were very important to and very concerned with the improvement of instruction and emphasized that this was the area to which they would most like to devote themselves.[23] Goldhammer also reported that effective principals were desirous of providing greater leadership in curriculum, and that they expressed their need for more support staff to free them so that they could devote more time to this task.[24]

Several recent studies have indicated the importance of the principal in providing leadership in all functions of the school. These studies depicted task-oriented principals as providing very effective leadership for improving the teaching/learning environment of the school. Findings in these studies did not preclude good working relationships between the principal and staff, but accomplishing the task was the principal's primary duty. These studies strongly suggested that principals who

[18]Bruce Orville Knight, "Job Functions of the Elementary Principalship," *Dissertation Abstracts International*, 43 (1982), 34A.

[19]Arthur Blumberg and William Greenfield, *The Effective Principal: Perspectives on School Leadership* (Boston: Allyn and Bacon, 1980), p. 157.

[20]Leithwood and Montgomery, "Role of the School Principal," pp. 309–39.

[21]Jan Earle Calhoun, "Leadership Behaviors of Elementary Principals that Lead to Improved Teaching-Learning Situations," *Dissertation Abstracts International*, 41 (1981), 2908-A.

[22]"The Elementary School Principalship," *NEA*, p. 86.

[23]Emory Stoops and James R. Marks, *Elementary School Supervision: Practices and Trends* (Boston: Allyn and Bacon, 1965), p. 79.

[24]Keith Goldhammer and others, *Elementary Principals and Their Schools* (Eugene, OR.: Center for Advanced Study of Educational Administration, University of Oregon, 1971), p. 52.

strive for a balance in instructional leadership, task pursuit, sound administration, and good human relations are the most effective ones.[25, 26, 27]

Most of the research findings in the literature strongly imply that the principal is *the* important person in providing leadership for improved instruction and better curricula. However, some researchers are quick to point out that there are problems with that assumption. Firestone and Wilson explain: "Research on effective schools has promoted the view that schools can be organized to improve instruction, and principals have a key role to play. Still, that optimism must be tempered by the knowledge that schools are loosely linked organizations, where the impact of the principals on instruction is limited."[28] Furthermore, there still exists a role-conflict problem for principals: "Principals daily face pressures of competing images about what their role should be, and even the best have a difficult time maintaining an appropriate balance between the tasks of managing a smooth-running school and serving as a catalyst for and facilitator of instructional improvement."[29]

There is an abundance of research to support the fact that principals have a strong leadership role in the schools. The research is much more sparse, however, on how the principal can best perform the roles of manager and leader. There are many gaps in the literature concerning these roles; many important and vast responsibilities of the principal have hardly received the attention of researchers. The research found is mostly of a descriptive nature. If the principal is so important to the effectiveness of the school, why are we not paying more attention to and spending more money on good, sound investigation of this topic? Longitudinal and experimental studies of principal effectiveness need to be conducted to shed additional light on the issue.

SKILLS NEEDED BY THE PRINCIPAL

The skills needed by an effective school principal are so extensive and diverse they almost defy any attempt to list them. The skills needed vary greatly from those required in most other leadership positions. Few, if any, middle-management positions require one individual to be responsible for so many others. The variety of skills required to deal with subordinates who have nearly as much formal education as the principal creates an

[25]Leithwood and Montgomery, "Role of the School Principal," pp. 309–39.

[26]Sweeney, "Principals Can Provide Leadership," pp. 204–7.

[27]Blumberg and Greenfield, *The Effective Principal,* p. 257.

[28]William A. Firestone and Bruce L. Wilson, "Using Bureaucratic and Cultural Linkages to Improve Instruction," *Educational Administration Quarterly,* 21 (Spring 1985), 25.

[29]Blumberg and Greenfield, *The Effective Principal,* p. 9.

unusual situation. The added dimension of providing an effective teaching/learning environment increases the list of skills needed. The principal should also have the skills to deal with hundreds of students, who have varying needs and problems. Parents, too, draw on the various human-relations skills of the principal. All things considered, the school principal does need a far greater range of skills than the ordinary middle manager in other organizations.

Hughes and Ubben identified five areas in which the principal must function effectively: school-community relations; staff personnel development; pupil personnel development; educational program development; and business and building management.[30] The abilities a principal must possess to deal with these responsibilities have also been discussed by Paul W. Hersey, Director of the Assessment Center Project of the National Association of Secondary School Principals. He emphasized problem analysis, judgment, organizational ability, decisiveness, leadership, sensitivity, range of interests, personal motivation, stress tolerance, educational values, oral communication, and written communication as the skills most needed by a principal.[31]

Hughes and Ubben as well as Hersey indicated that there are many major tasks that principals must be able to perform. Drawing on this information, we shall attempt to list some of the major professional tasks of the principal.

1. Apply administrative and/or organizational theory to practical situations
2. Convey to staff, students, and public the function of education as an essential and integral part of the total social system
3. Practice supervisory techniques that enhance an effective teaching/learning environment, promote a friendly organizational atmosphere, provide for comfortable and satisfying working relationships, and regulate the work tempo
4. Arrange working conditions such that human elements maximize the promotion of an improved teaching/learning environment
5. Promote mutual respect among the faculty, staff, and members of the community
6. Promote directed change that results in improving the teaching/learning environment of the school
7. Employ a working knowledge of statutory law, school board regulations, and precedent set by courts
8. Implement a plan for efficient utilization of financial resources
9. Demonstrate proper abilities in processes and procedures of teacher contracts and professional negotiations
10. Use a rational, deliberative, discretionary, and purposive decision-making process

[30]Larry W. Hughes and Gerald C. Ubben, *The Elementary Principal's Handbook: A Guide to Effective Action,* 2nd ed. (Boston: Allyn and Bacon, 1984), p. 4.
[31]Paul Hersey, *NASSP Assessment Handbook* (Reston, Va.: National Association of Secondary School Principals, n.d.).

11. Apply the proper technique of group process
12. Take advantage of the conditions in formal and informal settings in the schools and properly mesh the outcomes of the two in such a way as to maximize the school improvement effort
13. Develop explicit written plans based on near consensus decisions for improving the teaching/learning environment; include objectives, activities, accomplishment timeline, and person responsible
14. Develop measurement instruments and techniques adequate for evaluating objectives that have been specified for improvement
15. Implement an adequate record-keeping system
16. Outline the philosophy and history of curriculum development and apply it to the current school setting
17. Utilize psychological and sociological concepts appropriately for supporting the school improvement effort
18. Keep an updated plan for educational facilities and auxiliary services
19. Interpret research findings and apply them to the school improvement effort
20. Conduct, direct, and encourage research in the local school setting
21. Maintain discipline
22. Promote good morale
23. Provide for proper tone and school climate
24. Provide for staff development
25. Manage staff, including grievances, dismissals, recruitment, selection process of staff, orientation, interview, analysis, liability, and participatory management
26. Supervise sporting events
27. Coordinate intramural and extracurricular activities
28. Provide for special services
29. Be sensitive to neighborhood influence systems[32, 33]

The list is by no means exhaustive; neither is it discrete. The same skills may be required in more than one functional area; they may overlap within and across each of the major functions. Some recordings of actual functions of five different principals are included in Chapter 17. What do these daily logs (including the other material presented) indicate about the skills that the principal should develop?

PLACEMENT OF PRINCIPALS

There are several considerations in the selection and placement of principals. They must be formally prepared for the professional job of being principal. They must also be in the right job at the right time. A well-

[32]"Effective School Principals: A Proposal for Joint Action by Higher Education, States, and School Districts" (Atlanta: Southern Regional Education Board, 1986), ED 273–044.

[33]Don E. Brown, "Moving Toward Excellence: The Principal." A paper presented at the annual meeting of the National Association of Secondary School Principals (New Orleans: Jan. 25–29, 1985), ED 254–944.

prepared principal in the wrong job is doomed to failure; a well-prepared and well-placed principal may not succeed in a position at any given time. For example, Lyndon B. Johnson may very well have been the greatest majority leader to ever serve in the U. S. Senate. He led with much authority and respect, and history will probably treat him well concerning his performance in that role. History may not treat him so kindly in his role as U. S. President. He was probably the wrong person in the wrong job at the wrong time. He followed a charismatic and martyred president, but he was not so charismatic and certainly was not a martyr. He tried to play the role that his predecessor had played as a liberal and had some success, but was never "forgiven" by the American public for replacing their fallen hero. Even though he was well prepared for the job of president and had been a strong leader in other responsible positions, the match of place and time was wrong. Under different conditions, he might have been considered a great president.

There is no doubt that much more attention should be given to the placement of principals. Current practices for placing principals range from a studied match of person and job to a selection almost entirely based on political patronage. Some school systems do go through a search and screening process to find the best person for the position, but other systems hire principals based on how much political pull can be mustered. If the principal is as crucial an individual for educational excellence as research findings seem to indicate, then improving the selection practices for this individual would improve schools significantly. *What* the person knows would serve us better than *who* the person knows.

SELECTING THE PERSON FOR THE RIGHT POSITION

How, then, should a school system select principals in a way that will ensure success? There is no absolute right way to select principals. There have been some attempts at establishing the characteristics of successful administrators and leaders but they have not been conclusive. The Ohio State Leadership Studies,[34] conducted by Andrew W. Halpin and others at The Ohio State University, and the Prudential Study,[35] conducted by Rensis Likert and others at the University of Michigan, were some of the first studies to concentrate on how to select school leaders. As important and thorough as these studies were, they were not conclusive. There have

[34]Andrew W. Halpin, *Theory and Research in Administration* (New York: Macmillan, 1966).

[35]Rensis Likert in Daniel Kantz, Nathan Maccoby, and Nancy C. Morse, *Productivity, Supervision, and Morale in an Office Situation* (Ann Arbor: University of Michigan Institute for Social Research, 1950).

been many lesser-known studies of ways of selecting leaders by their personal traits since then with no better results. So, selecting principals by personal traits is a risky gamble at best.

We are not advocating that personal traits be ignored. Those individuals who are well prepared professionally, intelligent, hard working, sensitive, personable, energetic, honest, truthful, mentally well adjusted, and responsibly assertive seem to have the edge on those lacking some or all of these traits, although they do not assure success in a particular position at a particular time. Certainly these traits should be considered, but along with job fitness and proper timing.

People who do not have all of the traits generally associated with effective leaders often do surprisingly well when placed in leadership positions. They seem to "rise to the occasion." They appear determined to show that they have been underestimated, and, as a result, they perform their leadership roles with surprising results. For example, a few years ago we visited a small rural school in the mountainous coal-mining section of Appalachia, and to our surprise we found a very vibrant, impressive teaching/learning environment. Morale was high, the children were happy and enthused about learning, and respect for the principal was openly manifested. This school, by the way, was in a very closed school system. The principal seemed to be well prepared professionally, intelligent, hard working, sensitive, honest, truthful, and mentally well adjusted. However, he seemed to be lacking in some of the other traits we often associate with a leader, such as charisma, outgoing personality, and handsome features. In fact, he was a small man with a noticeable physical handicap, timid and unassuming. At first sight he was not what one would imagine a strong leader to be. Appearance notwithstanding, he was definitely a leader in that particular school. This was a perfect example of the right person being selected for the right job at the right time; the selection, position, and timing were right for this particular school in the conservative system in which the school operated. This is consistent with the contingency theory of leadership, which is discussed in Chapter 7.

Roueche and Baker did an extensive study on characteristics of successful principals and subsequently compared their findings to those of Peters and Waterman concerning the effectiveness of executives in what they considered to be the best-run companies in the nation. The common skills they listed were

1. Flexibility in autonomy and innovation
2. Cohesiveness within the organization
3. Commitment to school mission
4. Recognition of staff
5. Problem solving through collaboration

6. Effective delegation
7. Focus on teaching and learning[36]

When selecting principals, certainly traits such as these should be considered, but, more importantly, even though with much less certainty, their selection should be based on preparation, fit, and timing. There are and will continue to be attempts to find better ways to select principals for the right position at the right time.

Although there are no conclusive findings, there does seem to be some indication that intense assessment of potential leaders in simulated situations may be somewhat related to future success. The National Association of Secondary School Principals' Assessment Center Project, directed by Paul W. Hersey, has done some of the most significant and intense work in this area. The program assesses potential leaders in simulated situations in leaderless group activities, pressure situations, "in-basket" tasks, and structured personal interviews.[37]

The students of school administration preparing to be school principals should be very concerned about the selection process. They should not assume that, because they have a new diploma and a new certificate indicating that they are legally eligible to be principals, they should accept just any job available. Taking a principal's job that is not appropriate may be the first and last administrative job for the candidate and that job will usually be short lived. The job with the proper fit and timing is worth waiting for.

Earlier we mentioned the two extremes in selecting principals, a careful process of selection and political patronage. These two are indeed extremes and the process usually falls somewhere between the two. The fact that one has enough political influence to get the job may indeed be a plus since that kind of persuasion is often an asset in leadership positions. As a general rule, however, those principals who are selected on merit are the more productive ones. As the general public shows increasing concern about the leadership and quality of schools, it will likely demand increasing academic excellence in those selected for the principalship. As a result, the selection process will move more toward filling the position with the most appropriate leader with less concern for political persuasion.

CONTINUOUS IN-SERVICE TRAINING

We give a lot of attention to in-service training for teachers. If the principal is so important to the school why do we not give more attention to the

---

[36]John E. Roueche and George A. Baker, III, "Profiling Excellence in America's Schools," (Arlington, Va.: American Association of School Administrators, 1986), ED 274-062, pp. 52–53.
[37]Hersey, *NASSP Assessment Handbook.*

in-service training of the leader? This is a shortcoming that must be corrected if we are to improve substantially the leadership of the schools. Assess most agendas for school-wide in-service training and it will be evident that most of the items pertaining to principals appear tacked on. A continuous, well-planned in-service program for principals is a rarity.

An effective principal in-service activity will take a considerable amount of time but does not have to involve an undue amount of expense. If the system can afford the expense, an abundance of resources and resource people are available for quality principal in-service education. There should be a combining of resources from within and outside the system. However, if expense for outside expertise is a factor (and it usually is), enough expertise exists within the ranks of the principals in most school systems to solve a majority of the problems by combining their knowledge and sharing their experiences. It does take time away from the job normally considered "principaling" to participate in this kind of sharing experience, but it usually returns great dividends.

The Southern Regional Education Board (SREB) produced a publication focusing on alternatives for principal in-service training. They contended that it must be a long-range continuous project. "Research and experience show that unless there is planned follow-up and continued involvement which allows the principal to try out new behaviors and analyze results, no real change takes place in the school. If this is the desired goal of continuing education programs, then the design of the programs must include follow-up and supportive activities."[38]

We have helped organize meetings of this nature for principal in-service training that were very effective. The principals were organized to meet regularly, usually once a month, to share experiences, discuss common problems, and set personal goals. A typical monthly meeting would begin by having each principal report on the progress achieved toward a personal goal set at the previous meeting for school improvement, followed by discussions of common problems and concerns. There might even be a guest speaker. Each principal would then make a commitment to accomplish specific goals by the next meeting. The monthly meetings usually lasted approximately two hours. The principals left the in-service meeting with a high level of motivation; their future courses of action had the support of their peers, were based on the information and advice shared in the session, and needed to be fulfilled to the best of their ability since a commitment to "do their darndest" had been made. If this kind of continuous in-service training can involve several school systems, it works even better because there is a greater range of experiences from which to draw.

[38]Southern Regional Educational Board, "New Directions for Improving School Leadership," (Atlanta: Southern Regional Education Board, 1984).

PREPARATION PROGRAM

Preparation programs for principals in higher education institutions vary from institution to institution, but most of them have common elements. They usually include courses such as foundations of education and curriculum, introductions to educational administration and supervision, research, school law, school finance, school facilities, school and community relations, and a practicum. While many of these courses deal with leadership for improving the teaching/learning environment of the school, there is usually a heavy emphasis on administration. A minimum of a master's degree with emphasis on school administration is required in most states for certification as a principal. A typical preparation program at the master's degree level might look like that shown in Figure 2–1.

FIGURE 2-1. Sample Graduate Program

GRADUATE PROGRAM FOR PREPARING SCHOOL ADMINISTRATORS

COURSES	SEMESTER HOURS		
	M.A. THESIS	M.A. RESEARCH	M.Ed.
Philosophy of Education Sociology of Education History of Education Advanced Educational Psychology	3	3	3
Elementary Curriculum Middle/Junior High Curriculum Secondary School Curriculum Curriculum Development	3	3	3
Introduction to Educational Administration (Including Facilities Component)	3	3	3
Supervision Principles and Practices	3	3	3
School Law	3	3	3
Finance	3	3	3
School Community Relations	3	3	3
Methods of Research	3	3	3
Principalship	3	3	3
Research Seminar			3
Practicum	3	3	3
Thesis	3		
Electives		3	3
	33	33	36

Culbertson[39] and Farquhar[40] reported survey findings indicating that there had been four major trends in administrator-preparation programs since the 1950s. The trends were to emphasize the merging of theories that were based on social sciences with simulations, field experiences, and faculty specialization. Kimbrough and Nunnery concluded, "In our opinion, the trends identified are still fairly descriptive of the better preparation programs and are likely to remain so for the immediate future unless there are major changes in state requirements for certification."[41] They also suggested five other trends in preparation programs that have surfaced recently: (1) a growing number of women in preparation programs with a continued low representation in administrative positions; (2) specialization of preparation programs such as administration of vocational school principals; (3) making residence requirements more flexible, especially at the doctoral level; (4) computer literacy for principals; and (5) "a continuing interest in competency-based programs, where the emphasis is on identifying needed understandings, skills, and behaviors; providing for learning experiences that are individualized and reality centered; and requiring students to demonstrate their competence in relation to predetermined performance measures."[42]

There are some 500 colleges preparing school administrators at this time. It has been suggested by national study groups and major educational-administration professional organizations that the number of institutions be drastically reduced and that those remaining should only be allowed to exist if they are of very high quality.[43, 44]

The Danforth Foundation is sponsoring a project called *The Danforth Program for the Preparation of School Principals*. Its position paper states that the time appears to be right for institutions of higher education who prepare school principals and state agencies to assess the present procedures for preparing and licensing principals with the idea of possible change and improvement. Emphasis would be on experiential learning situations, such as simulated activities and self-

[39]Jack A. Culbertson, "Moving Education and its Administrations into the Microelectronics Age," Occasional Paper 8306 (Columbus, Ohio: University Council for Educational Administration, 1983), ED 239–389.

[40]Robin A. Farquhar and Michael Martin, "New Developments in the Preparation of Educational Leaders," *Phi Delta Kappan*, 54 (September 1972), pp. 26–30.

[41]Ralph B. Kimbrough and Michael Y. Nunnery, *Educational Administration: An Introduction*, 3rd ed. (New York: Macmillan, 1988), p. 13.

[42]Kimbrough, *Educational Administration: An Introduction*, pp. 14–15.

[43]National Commission on Excellence in Educational Administration: Leaders for America's Schools (Tempe, Ariz.: University Council for Educational Administration, 1987).

[44]American Association of School Administrators, *Guidelines for the Preparation of School Administrators*, 2nd ed. (Arlington, Va.: The Association, 1983).

study activities. This manner of preparation for principals would include sharing of experiences by university professors and public school administrators. "Such a partnership between universities and schools takes advantage of the practical knowledge held by practicing principals and integrates experiences in a school with academic activities at the university and internships with community leaders."[45] The objectives of the Danforth program are to identify prospective principals early in their professional careers; to provide university and public school personnel an opportunity to work together preparing principals; to develop preparation programs that combine experiences from the university, public schools, and community; to organize learning experiences taken from the university, public schools, and community; and to take advantage of experiential learning, which allows the candidate the opportunity "to demonstrate competency in schools and the community beyond those commonly expressed in schools today."[46]

The U. S. Department of Education is financing projects in all 50 states and Puerto Rico for improvement of preparation programs for school administrators (mostly principals) called Leadership in Educational Administration Development (LEAD). The funded agency in each state will use its own unique approach in preparing a select number of administrators. The idea is that the methods that work will eventually be combined to impact on all preparation programs. The eight leadership skills listed in the project are (1) creating and enhancing a school-wide environment that promotes learning and student achievement; (2) evaluating the school curriculum in order to assess and improve its effectiveness in meeting academic and other goals; (3) analyzing, evaluating, and improving instruction and teacher performance; (4) appraising and assessing student performance and other indicators of overall school performance; (5) understanding and applying the findings of research to school leadership and improvement; (6) organizing and managing school resources; (7) ensuring student discipline and a climate of order; and (8) developing human relations skills.[47]

Most of the 500 current preparation programs in this country appear to be traditional and concentrate on the administration aspect of the principalship. However, there are a few colleges and universities that are concentrating on preparing principals to lead as well as to administer. There are also a few encouraging efforts by outside agencies, such as those just described, that may very well make a significant difference in preparing the school leaders of the future.

[45]"The Danforth Program for the Preparation of School Principals," Position Paper (St. Louis: Danforth Foundation, June 1987), p. 1.

[46]Danforth, p. 2–3.

[47]U. S. Department of Education Grant Application, *Leadership in Educational Administration Development* (Washington, D.C.: U. S. Department of Education, 1986), pp. 6–7.

HUMAN-RELATIONS SKILLS

The human-relations skills needed by principals are not greatly different from those needed by leaders in business, industry, or other institutions. Teachers, students, and members of the general public with which the principal must deal have needs that are common to the rest of humanity. They want a principal who makes them feel that they belong, are secure and worthwhile, are treated fairly, are making contributions, are growing, are achieving, are respected, and are a part of the group.

Treat people as you would like to be treated is a well-worn phrase that is still apropos. Principals who have human-relations skills that permit them to treat others as they would like to be treated, everything else being equal, will succeed in their relationships with people.

Principals may not always be perceived as fair in their interactions with others, but people must believe they are trying to be fair. The milieu in which the principals work prevents them from always making decisions that are fair to all. Yet if it is generally believed that the principal is trying to be fair, the principal can survive an unintentional, unfair decision occasionally without damaging the relationships with the other persons involved.

Neither do principals have to treat everyone alike to have desirable human relations. People are not alike, so they should not be always treated the same. For example, the principal can permit one teacher to leave school early one day and deny the same request to another the next day and have general acceptance from the rest of the faculty for both decisions. If the first teacher is conscientious, always on time, never appears to cut corners and is generally respected, the decision by the principal to approve leaving school early one day for a special occasion will be accepted. On the other hand, if the second teacher is one who is constantly cutting corners, the decision on a subsequent day to deny permission to leave early will be a popular one.

The human-relations skills needed by principals are far too numerous and complex to be discussed here. The student is encouraged to study the psychology and sociology of human relations to an extent far beyond the scope of this book. There are, however, some traits that are essential to human relations, a few of which are listed here.

People with effective human relations skills

Are trustworthy

Are truthful

Feel comfortable about themselves

Help others feel comfortable about themselves

Have a tolerant, easy-going attitude toward themselves as well as others; they can laugh at themselves

Feel right about other people

Shape their environment whenever possible, adjust to it whenever necessary

Are not bowled over by their own emotions—by their fears, anger, love, jealousy, guilt or worries

Respect the many differences they find in people

Can take life's disappointments in stride

Do something about problems as they arise

Are able to meet the demands of life

Make use of their natural capacities

Can accept their own shortcomings

Are able to think by themselves and make their own decisions

Have personal relationships that are satisfying and lasting

Feel able to deal with most situations that come their way

Get satisfaction from simple, everyday pleasures

Expect to like and trust others and take for granted that others will like and trust them

Can feel they are part of a group

Have self-respect

Accept their responsibilities

Are friendly and courteous

Meet people on their own terms[48]

Principals would do well to assess periodically their human-relations skills using the foregoing as a checklist.

COPING WITH THE JOB

As discussed briefly in Chapter 1, the principal is convinced sometimes that the job is impossible; everything seems to be falling apart. It seems that there is no way to cope with all of the problems, administer the school, and, at the same time, provide leadership. Some weak principals seem to be constantly overwhelmed by the job and its accompanying problems. Strong principals, however, never give the appearance that they are overwhelmed. Principals who lose their composure in the face of adversity are comparable to health-care personnel who faint at the sight of blood.

There are many seemingly paradoxical issues with which principals must cope. For example, situations arise that appear to be sources of great conflict and seem sure to precipitate agonizing problems. Principals brace themselves and wait for the worst. They wait and wait and nothing

[48]Adapted from a Headstart document. Exact source not known.

happens. All the worrying and planning for the worst seem to be in vain. On the other hand, situations may arise that appear to be routine, and suddenly the roof falls in. It does not seem to make sense—everyone in the school and community seems to get upset about matters that appear, on the surface, to be harmless. Some minor issues with which principals must cope snowball into real problems, yet other issues that appear to be major may end up not having great social impact.

UNUSUAL ROLES OF PRINCIPALS

Principals play some unusual roles that are not usually listed in job descriptions. Indeed, some of them cannot even be imagined by the principals until unusual incidents occur that require their attention. They may have to deal with medical emergencies; they may be forced to listen to the concerns of a distraught parent who has marital problems. They will occasionally have to play the role of arbitrator between faculty members or between faculty members and irate parents. It would not be unusual for the principal to be drafted into playing the role of referee in intramural sports activities. They may be prime candidates for leaders in fund drives. The list goes on and on. Some days the principal will spend more time in unusual and unexpected roles than in the usual and expected ones. See Chapter 17 for the daily activities of five principals in current school settings.

JOB DESCRIPTION—WHAT PRINCIPALS DO, WOULD LIKE TO DO, SHOULD DO

Most principals have a list of what they should do; in other words, they have a job description. The job description may reflect some of the more important things that principals should do, but it does not always reflect what they actually do. The following is a typical job description for a school principal.
Qualifications for the position of principal are

1. Master's degree with a major in educational administration
2. A valid state certificate to practice as a school principal
3. At least five years of experience in public school administration and supervision
4. Such alternatives to these qualifications as the board may find appropriate

Specific duties of principals are

1. To be responsible for all activities occurring in the building or on the school grounds during the school day and to administer the operation of the school

2. To formulate and expedite the teaching program in the school under the direction of the curriculum division and to assist in the formulation of curriculum and other objectives for the school program

3. To be responsible for maintaining good public relations with the community and for utilizing fully the resources to enrich the learning program

4. To be responsible for school enterprises, school activities, teachers' meetings, student council, and school exhibits

5. To assist in preparing the proposed budget for departments within the school

6. To keep records of collection and expenditure of internal funds in accordance with the accounting plan adopted by law and approved by the board of education

7. To explain to teachers the policies of the board and maintain an up-to-date policy manual in the principal's office and the school library

8. To assist in evaluations and recommendations for re-election or continued employment of certificated and classified personnel in the school assigned

9. To submit recommendations to the local superintendent regarding the appointment, assignment, promotion, transfer, and dismissal of all personnel assigned to the school

10. To supervise and provide instructional leadership

11. To oversee the health and safety of students

12. To implement and administer a code of discipline and behavior within the school

13. To report any act of assault and battery or vandalism endangering life, health, or safety committed by a student on school property to the proper law enforcement officials

14. To perform such other duties which may be assigned by the superintendent pursuant to the written policies of the board of education

Principals do not always spend their time doing what they think they should be doing. Table 2–1 displays the results of a study that reflects what principals do as compared to what they think they should do. A comparison of the two columns reveals that principals would like to spend more time

TABLE 2–1. What Principals Report They Do Compared to What They Would Like to Do Concerning Curriculum Matters

		MEAN SCORES OF RANKING FROM 1 TO 5	
PHASE	*N*	TIME PRINCIPALS SPEND ON CURRICULUM MATTERS	TIME PRINCIPALS WOULD LIKE TO SPEND ON CURRICULUM MATTERS
Planning	124	1.96	2.74
Implementing	124	1.85	2.68
Evaluating	124	1.81	2.65
Total	124	1.90	2.59

TABLE 2–2. Rankings of Time Spent in Each Area by Principals in a Typical Work Week

AREAS	TIME SPENT IN EACH AREA	TIME THAT SHOULD BE SPENT IN EACH AREA
School Management	1	3
Personnel	2	2
Student Activities	3	4
Student Behavior	4	7
Program Development	5	1
District Office	6	9
Planning	7	5
Community	8	8
Professional Development	9	6

of the two columns reveals that principals would like to spend more time on curriculum matters. The results shown in Table 2-1 are from a study by Davis.[49]

A study commissioned by the National Association of Secondary School Principals[50] also dealt with how principals spend their time as compared to their perception of how they should spend their time. The results of that study are given in Table 2–2.

Both studies show that principals would prefer spending more time on leadership matters and less on administrative matters. They would especially like to spend more time improving the curriculum and teaching/learning environment. There appear to be wide differences between what the principal's job description displays, what they do, and what they would like to do.

MANAGEMENT AND LEADERSHIP

Lipham contends that there are two major functions that a principal must perform, management and leadership.[51] These two functions are at once separate and entwined—functionally, they are intermingled. Principals cannot be effective leaders without performing management functions. On the other

[49]Norman R. Davis, "Some Similarities and Differences in Selected Tennessee Elementary Principals' Perceived Allocation and Ideal Allocation of Time for Curriculum Related Activities" (Dissertation, East Tennessee State University, 1986), p. 63.

[50]"Summary Report of the Senior High School Principal," Vol. III (Reston, Va.: National Association of Secondary School Principals, 1979).

[51]James M. Lipham, "Leadership and Administration," in *Behavioral Science and Educational Administration,* Daniel E. Griffith, ed. *The Sixty-Third Yearbook of the National Society for the Study of Education* (Chicago: University of Chicago Press, 1964).

hand, principals cannot push aside leadership activities while performing as managers. Neither can they put management duties on hold while performing leadership roles.

The management part of the principal's job consists of keeping the school running in an efficient manner. It is composed of such activities as keeping records, filling out forms, procuring and directing personnel, and coordinating the resources of the entire school. Leadership, on the other hand, is more creative. It can be defined as the force that motivates people to do things they would not ordinarily do. Further discussion of the definition of leadership is provided in Chapter 7. In the case of the principal, the leadership provided motivates teachers to improve the overall teaching/learning environment of the school.

To be effective, principals must perform well in both functions. They may assign some responsibilities to assistants; however, they should not separate the jobs and have others administer while they concentrate on leading. Administration and leadership cannot be neatly separated in that way. The two functions are interdependent and must be performed in concert. Some of the activities can, however, be separated and ranked in order of importance. For example, principals can delegate the task of filling out written reports with a great degree of confidence; they cannot delegate the responsibility of providing leadership in instructional improvement with such confidence. Whether the principal does the routine work or delegates those tasks to someone else, the principal is still accountable; those administrative tasks are important to the effective operation of the school and should be performed efficiently.

The principal is responsible for the division of responsibilities in the school. The decision as to how much time should be spent in each function is a very important one; this decision determines to a great extent how effective the principal will be.

TRUTHFULNESS, TRUSTWORTHINESS, AND KNOWLEDGE AND ACCEPTANCE OF SELF

In Chapter 1 we discussed briefly the fact that the principal should have a strong ethical character. To reiterate, there are three qualities that are expected of leaders everywhere. They are truthfulness, trustworthiness, and knowledge and acceptance of self. One does not have to question whether these qualities are present or not in an individual; they are evident in every action.

It is commonly said that it is hard enough to keep the truth straight. Even when there is an effort to tell the whole truth, it may become evident in retrospect that an incident was not as it first appeared to be. Details become blurry and facts less certain. There may be times when it appears expedient to be less than truthful. Sophistry and half truths may serve for a while, but eventually the truth, the whole truth, will come out.

Principals who establish a reputation for being truthful will have credibility with teachers, students, and the general public; others will not. In a capsule, say what you mean, mean what you say, and when in doubt, do not say anything! This bit of common wisdom still serves its purpose.

Trustworthiness is similar to truthfulness in importance. To be effective, principals must be trustworthy. For example, teachers must believe that principals will always act according to their best interests and those of the school. Any acts contrary to these best interests will break that bond of trust, and trust can seldom be recovered. Principals simply cannot afford to lose the trust of their teachers. A sound relationship between principal and teacher has the same basic elements of any other relationship; trust is one of those basic elements.

To be effective, principals must know and accept themselves. Machiavelli informed the Prince that "Everybody sees what you appear to be, few feel what you are...."[52] That was wise counsel since nobody really knows you as you know yourself, especially when your innermost thoughts are concerned.

Knowledge, acceptance, and truthfulness about yourself are prerequisites to effectiveness as a leader. To know and accept the truth about yourself requires a great deal of reflection. What are your strengths and weaknesses? Which should be accepted? Which should be built upon? How honest can you be about your shortcomings? Consider the effects of a seemingly minor incident of knowledge and acceptance of self. Assume you wake up one morning and feel out of sorts. You look at yourself in the mirror and your mood is reflected on your face. You might be less than honest with yourself and put on a false smile and say to yourself "I feel great today." You go to work and make everyone around you miserable because of being out of sorts. A better approach would be to admit to the face in the mirror that you are not your usual self and to remember and compensate for this situation. You go to work aware that you must adjust your behavior because of your foul mood so that you can still contribute to a pleasant work atmosphere.

A principal does not have to possess exceptional personal attributes to succeed in the position. The principalship does require someone with sufficient strength of character to be truthful, honest, and knowledgeable about self.

---

[52]Niccolò Machiavelli, *The Prince,* rev. ed., trans. Luigi Ricci (New York: Oxford University Press, 1952), p. 94.

CHAPTER THREE

Using Social Systems Concepts

A SYSTEMS APPROACH TO THE PRINCIPALSHIP

Persons inexperienced in educational administration are often impatiently critical of the leadership ability of school principals. These persons may not realize that being an effective educational administrator is a tough job. The principal must provide leadership with complexly structured, unpredictable human systems. The mechanic who is installing a heating system is preoccupied with a physical system. This system is more likely to stay put as its elements are installed, and it may be manipulated at will. It is a highly predictable system in comparison to the human system.

As we shall see in the following chapters, the school principal is exposed to more social systems than many critics realize, namely, the community power system and its subsystems. The principal behaves within a central office system, which is in turn a subsystem of a highly structured state system. Elements of the community and state systems are tied directly to national systems. The principal is also expected to provide leadership in the social system of the individual school. Few decisions can be made without regard for the structured web of human relationships in interacting social systems.

Unless the school principal conceptualizes these systems in terms of leadership tasks, the principal will be caught in their complex structures like a fly in a spider's web. The more one struggles to exercise leadership in the absence of a conceptualized knowledge of the leadership role, the greater the entanglement and subsequent lack of success.

The material in Chapters 3 through 6 is not an encyclopedic description of all social systems with which school principals may interact, but it is presented as a way of thinking about human systems. Each social system has unique qualities. The community power system in the central area of a great city has very different qualities from the power system of an upper-middle-class, suburban school district. No two schools in the inner-city deal with community systems that are identical in every respect. These chapters, then, are written to help school principals to conceptualize the interacting social systems in which they are expected to provide leadership for a school of quality.

Practicing school principals may be somewhat suspicious of anyone who seriously advocates the use of theory. The theoretical person is often thought to be a verbalizer of fuzzy thoughts, none of which makes much difference to the operation of a school. Practical leaders are more frequently perceived as having opinions immediately useful in running a school, opinions that are down to earth and reasonable. Yet numerous writers have pointed to the error in the practical versus the theoretical dichotomy. There is nothing more practical than being theory-oriented, having a conceptual grasp of a situation that promises sound guides to action, possessing a measure of predictability about what may happen if certain actions are taken, or generating new ideas to cope with changing times. These are some of the qualities that practitioners enjoy from the use of good management theory. There is, in reality, no escape from the use of theory if one wants to be a successful principal, because theory is based on what is, rather than what ought to be.

Attempting to operate without some conception of what will happen "if I decide this" or "if I do that" would be a gamble with failure. Who wants to play Russian roulette with a professional career? To use another example, few persons would champion the guy who continually messes up every task attempted or the fellow who cannot decide what should be done. These persons lack the operational quality that theory provides, including having a grasp of the elements interacting in the situation, predicting by more than chance what will happen if certain actions are taken, and the feeling of security that goes with some control.

Even the school principal acclaimed by colleagues to be the most practical administrator is guided by a personally accepted theory or by an eclecticism of several theories. For example, the no-nonsense, demanding, efficient-minded, task-oriented school principal may well be using the traditional scientific management (Theory X) theory of running a school. If one agrees with this concept of administration, that style of leadership is viewed as very practical. On the other hand, one who accepts a humanistic view of management will not accept this style as practical. Everyone views practicality through glasses shaded by different colors of thinking, of grasping the realities of situations faced, and of predicting what will happen *if*.

Based on the discussion to this point, a manual on how to administer a school would be an incomplete text. Administering a school is too dependent on the contingencies in different situations to be reduced to a manual. The authors do indeed deal with the minutiae of running a school; however, in discussing the possible solutions to everyday problems, the principles of general systems theory (as a backdrop) and a generic way of thinking will be used. As evidenced by its inclusion in modern textbooks, systems theory, which supports contingency theory, is currently a relevant concept for integrating administrative practice.[1]

SCHOOL PRINCIPALS HAVE A CHOICE

As used here, *management theory* refers to a generalized concept of organizing, motivating, providing leadership, and making decisions; in essence, the generalized theory for running a school. School principals have a choice among at least four major theories of management that have surfaced and enjoyed popularity in this century.

Frederick W. Taylor (1856–1915) founded the scientific management theory, which achieved great popularity early in this century. This concept emphasized streamlined efficiency of organization, management control of all objectives and processes of production, rigid control of workers, the piece-rate principle for wages, a task-oriented concept of leadership, scientific study of job performance, and little, if any, concern for the psychological needs of workers. The scientific management theory encountered increasing opposition during the first half of this century, and with the completion of some rather significant management research, such as Western Electric Company studies, its popularity waned and the human-relations theory of management gained ascendancy in academe. Even in the latter part of this century, scientific management has been embraced by managers in and out of the field of school administration.

[1]See, for example, Edgar L. Morphet, Roe L. Johns, and Theodore L. Reller, *Educational Organization and Administration,* 4th ed. (Englewood Cliffs, N.J.: Prentice-Hall, 1982); Fred Luthans, *Organizational Behavior,* 4th ed. (New York: McGraw-Hill, 1985); Fremont E. Kast and James E. Rosenzweig, *Organization and Management: A Systems and Contingency Approach,* 4th ed. (New York: McGraw-Hill, 1985).

The humanistic concept of administration became very popular in educational administration during the 1940s and 1950s. Emphasis inevitably focused on what McGregor referred to as *The Human Side of Enterprise*.[2] Interest shifted away from efficiency in organizational structure to emphasis upon building faculty morale, meeting the psychological needs of the faculty, group-based administrative authority, promotion of staff harmony, and the use of concepts generated in group dynamics and the social and behavioral sciences. Most of the books dealing with the principalship emphasized variations of democratic principles of administration. Kimball Wiles' first edition of *Supervision for Better Schools* was a runaway best seller and illustrated well this new humanistic approach to school supervision and administration.[3] Although the popularity of the human-relations approach to management began to wane during the 1960s and 1970s, it is still a widely appreciated theory.

Fiedler is among those authors who feel that embracing one theory of leadership for all situations is unwise.[4] He advocated a contingency theory of management. Some school situations, for example, may call for a task-oriented principal (fixation upon the tasks to be completed), whereas in other school communities the human-relations-oriented principal may be more productive. A school that has reached leadership impasse and is experiencing goal displacement (preoccupation with group maintenance activities and inattention to educational objectives) may benefit from a task-oriented principal. On the other hand, a well-organized school in which the faculty is functioning well may be more productive with a relationship, or democratic, style of principal than under a task-oriented leader. The central idea is that *one* leadership style is not best for all schools.

We believe that systems theory offers the best possible general theory for incorporating advantages of contingency theory, humanist theory, and scientific management. Systems thinking gives the principal a handle for understanding relationships among members of the faculty, for predicting, rather than gambling on, what might happen if certain decisions are implemented, and so on. Unlike the gaps that plagued scientific management (such as neglecting the human factor) and humanistic theory (a simplistic disregard of the need for structure), systems thinking offers a realistic way of accounting for the complex process of operating a productive school.

[2]Douglas M. McGregor, *The Human Side of Enterprise* (New York: McGraw-Hill, 1960).

[3]Kimball Wiles, *Supervision for Better Schools* (Englewood Cliffs, N.J.: Prentice-Hall, 1950).

[4]Fred E. Fiedler, *A Theory of Leadership Effectiveness* (New York: McGraw-Hill, 1967).

WHAT IS A SOCIAL SYSTEM?

Rather than become bogged down in hair-splitting definitions of a social system, some everyday illustrations of systems will be discussed. The systems concept pervades practically every aspect of living. As one observes the evening weather broadcast, the meteorologist will very likely refer to weather systems while pointing to places on the weather map. The concept is predominant in the biological sciences; for example, the organism is a system of organs that are interdependent and interacting. In the healthy organism there is an adaptive balance among the component organs—malfunction in any one results in imbalance or an adaptive illness. The system has a tension level that keeps it alive. Outside pressures, or inputs, upon the system increase tension and create stress, and the system adapts to them in order to survive and maintain balance. The biological system is obviously an illustration of a living system. When one considers the social group, the family is an example of a social system.

An everyday example of a nonliving system is the heating system for a home, the parts of which are tied together (or, as systems theorists say, interrelated and interdependent) to operate as a functioning unit to keep the house temperature at a prescribed balance. The system reacts to inputs (changes in outside temperature) to retain balance; moreover, malfunction of any of the interacting elements or parts of the system results in system failure. This is only one example of nonliving systems that greatly affect society. The computer is one of the more complex systems in the information era.

Using concepts learned from these examples of systems (known as parallelism), one can conceptualize much more complex social systems, and this is where the concept begins to pay off for school principals. According to Hearn, a system "consists of *objects* which are simply the parts or components of the system; there are *attributes* which are the properties of the objects; and there are *relationships* among the objects and their attributes which tie the system together."[5]

The classroom in which a teacher has been working with students for some time develops into a system. This is particularly true of a self-contained elementary school classroom where, because of a period of interaction among the pupils and teachers (objects in Hearn's discussion), certain attributes (norms, classroom climate) and relationships (pupil cliques, leadership patterns) develop. Since most secondary schools are departmentalized, the development of an observable system takes longer and, depending on the style of the teacher, may not develop into a functioning system for some period of time. Throughout the secondary school, however, are a host of both formal and informal activities promoting the development of

---

[5]Gordon Hearn, *Theory Building in Social Work* (Toronto: University of Toronto Press, 1958).

systems. As one visits the classrooms of a school, the differences in system atmosphere, climate, or tone are striking. These differences may be even more impressive among different schools.

These atmospheres or climates of schools are variations of the outward manifestation of social systems that have developed in them. The key to using systems theory is to learn how these systems develop and how the principal can intervene to influence or change these systems. Stripping away all the superfluous explanations frequently associated with the definition of it, leadership is the ability to influence the faculty and student body, and this cannot be accomplished without an operational theory through which one can understand systems.

INTERACTING SYSTEMS

Studies of social systems by authorities in the field of group dynamics concentrated on groups of from two to twenty persons. By the 1960s, however, writers on general social systems were applying systems principles to the behavior of very large complex organizations, such as the large school faculty, the school system, and the school community. One may speak of communities as different types of systems. Iannaccone and Lutz conceptualized school district communities as sacred-type communities (emphasis on intimacy, friendship, loyalty, resistance to change) and secular-type communities (emotional recklessness, predisposition toward change, and thrill).[6] The community political systems interact with the school district organization, the individual school, and so on. Local political systems interact with state, regional, and federal systems. Although we will subsequently discuss the interaction of the school system with state and federal systems, our discussion at this time concentrates on the local systems with which the school administrator must cope. These systems are as follows:

Community political system

Central office regime

Teachers' union or organization

Social system of the school

Miller suggested the use of the terms *system, subsystem, suprasystem,* and *suprasuprasystem* for differentiating among the interacting systems.[7] One might think of the central office regime as the suprasystem of the social system of a middle school in the district. The faculty clique of a high

---

[6]Laurence Iannaccone and Frank W. Lutz, *Politics, Power and Policy: The Governing of School Districts* (Columbus, Ohio: Merrill, 1970).

[7]James G. Miller, *Living Systems* (New York: McGraw-Hill, 1978), p. 9.

school or elementary school is a subsystem of the school social system. The political power system of the school district is the suprasuprasystem of the school district system.

These component systems are interrelated into various patterns or typologies for different districts. They are separated here only for purposes of understanding and discussion. One can best conceive of each of these levels as containing interrelated sets of variables so interlaced that a change in one variable affects the conditions of other variables. Within these systems norms (expected behavior) and crystallized patterns of interactions develop. Informal subsystems (cliques) emerge with protective boundaries to cope with feedback (or inputs) and to establish an element of control over the interactions and inputs that might produce trouble or imbalance. If the principal observes these systems carefully, the basic properties of social systems (discussed operationally in Chapter 4) will come into focus (such as a hierarchy of systems, boundaries, equilibrium, feedback, and so on). A brief introductory description of the four local systems will be given at this time.

Community Political System. Interacting constantly with the school and central office systems are elements of the community political system. This interaction affects the nature of the school climate, the shaping of school policy, and the way of life in the community. One critical aspect of this community system is the community power structure. The term *community power structure* refers to the relative distribution of power among the leaders and followers of the community to influence policy—to decide "what kind of community we want." The term *power system* best expresses the uniquely arranged leadership, the norms for political participation, the use of power resources (wealth, official position, control of jobs, and so on), and other critical elements in the process of deciding community policy.

Of immediate interest to the school principal are the elements of this system that are critical to the operation of the school. For example, school riots are seldom, if ever, the result of spontaneous action of students, but are a result of the intervention of leaders both inside and outside the physical boundaries of the school. Principals cannot cope well with restive activities if they do not have a grasp of the use of power in and around their school. The exercise of power in the school district office and the community is discussed in Chapters 5 and 6.

Central Office Regime. Through the election of school board members, the appointment of a superintendent, the selection of staff, and the interaction of community leaders in this process, a complex social system develops; we shall designate it the *central office regime.* The regime of a school district includes the process of school governance, mode of administrative control, management of the decision-making process, and the use of power. The exercise of power in the regime may not be consistent with that described in the formal organizational charts for the district. We shall include within the system all the employee forces within the internal organization of the school and the arrangement of these forces in decision making and their control over the administration of system-wide policies, plans, procedures, and professional affairs. Again, these regimes are created and unique to the system, which is why one finds variance in expectations of behavior, leadership patterns, participation, and climate among different school districts. The principal must be able to conceptualize this complex system to gain power in it; to be effective, the principal must have power in the regime. The principal who is not an interacting part of the regime may become a victim of it.

Teachers' Union or Organization. Teachers' organizations have always been a source of power in the administration of secondary, middle, and elementary schools. Beginning in the 1960s, a revolution occurred in teacher participation in the form of adversary collective bargaining. For a time, school principals, the persons in the middle, did not fare well under collective bargaining because they were not always included at the table; however, this was remedied as bargaining reached maturity. Using collective bargaining, teachers forged the creation of another interacting power system and currently use political intervention to influence the central office regime and the community power structure in pursuit of teacher welfare goals. Teacher unions can and often do influence politics in the community, such as the election of school board members, members of the state legislature, and other public officials. Yet teachers' unions display the usual characteristics of social systems, including hierarchy of system and subsystems, group norms, boundary maintenance, degrees of closedness and openness to inputs, use of feedback, and desire for balance. In those districts involved in collective bargaining, principals are obligated to administer the contract negotiated by the union and the school board.

Social System of the Individual School. Our primary concern in this book is the social system of the school, because therein lies the answer to whether the faculty and administration carry out their mission. Just how do the principal and faculty create an effective system? As already discussed, the individual school system interacts with other systems and is both influenced by and influences those systems. Numerous variables are found to be important in the creation and maintenance of the social system of the school, including such elements as interaction patterns, clique or friendship groups, leadership hierarchies, group norms, and perceptions of how decisions are made. These and other elements making up the school system will be discussed in Chapter 4.

The Principal's Place in the Interacting Social Systems. In the past, professional lore presented the principal and the faculty as a big happy family with the principal serving as head of the family circle. Helping the principal in the task as the head of the family were special staff personnel (assistant principals, guidance counselors, librarians, school psychologists, directors, and so on). This simplistic concept is no longer seriously supported in the literature or in practice, except in very isolated cases. Because of current expectations associated with their positions, school principals cannot consider themselves as patriarchs of the faculty. Principals are line officers in the central office regime and, as such, are subject to the expectations (organizational norms) of this regime. These expectations of a principal's behavior are often not congruent with the need dispositions of the faculty; consequently, social distance may be created between the principal and the faculty. Thus, school principals run the risk of becoming alienated by too much identification with one or the other of the dimensions referred to by Getzels and Guba: the *nomothetic* (organizational) and *idiographic* (personal or faculty) dimensions.[8] Every time the principal is forced to carry out an administrative practice that is unpopular with the faculty, distance is created between these dimensions. Sometimes the principal may not feel much identification with either dimension. Clearly, the school principal who is at the mercy of an over-bearing central office regime has little chance to exert leadership unless a protective subsystem emerges to counteract the regime. Usually the emergence of such a subsystem is inevitable. The subsystem may be made up of a high school principal's clique, an elementary principal's clique, or other subsystems that carry out survival tactics within the regime hierarchy. Principals must constantly build their power base with groups in both the idiographic and nomothetic dimensions to replace that being chipped away by unpopular decisions.

Because understanding what is meant by the concept of social systems is so important in this text, the following section is devoted to a brief discussion of a social system by Homans.[9] Although our application of his system to the administration of a school is brief, it introduces the concept and further demonstrates the practical use of systems theory. The concept will be further developed in the remaining chapters of this text.

---

[8]Jacob W. Getzels and Egon G. Guba, "Social Behavior and the Administrative Process," *School Review*, 65 (Winter 1957), 423–41.

[9]George C. Homans, *The Human Group* (New York: Harcourt Brace Jovanovich, 1950).

THE SOCIAL SYSTEM APPLIED TO A SCHOOL

Homans' system is based on four elements: *activity, interaction, senti-ments,* and *norms.* Our discussion concerns the application of these elements in understanding the dynamics of a school. This application is very brief and may go beyond what Homans himself might have sup-ported. We believe, however, that the system is easily understood and is a practical concept that principals can use in developing an excellent school climate.

Conceptual Elements in the System

Activity refers to the things that teachers, principals, counselors, and other school personnel do. The personnel of a school engage in many activities involving participation with others in a group, such as eating lunch together, attending meetings, visiting with colleagues in the teachers' lounge, meeting with committees, participating in after-school activities of various kinds, and so on. Teachers also engage in the usual professional activities, such as preparing lessons, grading papers, lectur-ing, supervising independent study, and a host of other pursuits which may or may not involve groups. As one observes different schools, there is a noticeable difference in activities in which the faculty and administration participate. In fact, most professional shop talk involves how the activities are different among schools. Principals spend an inordinate amount of time talking about their school activities and how they differ from other schools and school districts.

Interaction includes all of the verbal and nonverbal communication among faculty members, other school personnel, students, parents, and other citizens in the community. Teachers and principals experience literally hundreds of interactions in any given day. The principal's day may begin with a phone call at home from one of the teachers, which may lead to contacts with an assistant principal, guidance counselor, or parent. The activities in which the principal is engaged have an impact upon the pattern of interactions experienced; moreover, these interactions lead to a variety of other activities. In Homans' system the elements of activity, interaction, and sentiment are interdependent or interlocked, so that any one element affects other elements in the system. If, for example, five members of the faculty develop strong sentiments for each other, their engaging in activities as a group (clique) in and out of school becomes a normal expectation, leading to many more interactions that would not have happened by chance.

Homans lumped numerous expressions of different degrees of liking or other feelings among faculty members (such as affection, sympathy, respect, pride, antagonism, anger, and scorn) under the term *sentiment*.[10] He recognized our inability to know how teacher A may really feel toward teacher B when we see teacher A smile and speak warmly to teacher B. Sentiments are inferred expressions of internal states when we observe interactions between teachers. Yet when we observe frequent warm and friendly interactions among several teachers, combined with exceptionally frequent activities together as a group in and out of school, we probably infer correctly that the members of this group have sentiments of affection for each other. On the other hand, when we hear angry statements between teacher C and teacher E, we are likely to infer correctly that teacher C and teacher E dislike each other. Their sentiments will very likely discourage interaction between them, and they will not seek further activities together.

The term *norm* is one of the most pervasive concepts in the social and behavioral sciences. It refers to the behavior that a group expects of its members. "A norm, then, is an idea in the minds of the members of a group, an idea that can be put in the form of a statement specifying what the members or other men should do, ought to do, are expected to do, under given circumstances."[11] Homans further suggested that an expectation should only be classified as a norm if the violation of the norm is followed by sanction or punishment of the violator. Yet there appears the probability of a hierarchy of norms, depending upon the extent to which one may flaunt them and still enjoy group acceptance. If one violates the most critical of group norms, punishment will surely occur and could be as severe as expulsion or worse.

Authorities studying student use of drugs have found that using drugs is an expectation for membership in certain groups. Through years of planning and working together, teachers in a given school develop norms concerning just how much subject matter students should be taught in an academic year. An energetic beginning teacher who violates this norm by teaching much more material than expected will experience gentle sanctioning at first; however, if the behavior persists, the teacher may experience rather severe punishment, such as alienation, discipline problems, loss of experienced assistance, or a bad name in the office. One beginning teacher found helpful friends among those he met during the planning period. They assisted him with various reports, problems, and routines. Without their assistance he could have looked bad in the office. On the day of the first faculty meeting the group advised the young teacher not to say much in the meeting because, as one advised, "If the old man (the beloved principal) gets excited, he will keep us there until five o'clock." Since the

[10]Homans, *The Human Group*, p. 37.
[11]Homans, *The Human Group*, p. 123.

teacher heeded this advice and the meeting was short, everyone headed home for the day; the teacher stayed in the good graces of the planning group and of "the office." When at the close of the year the principal had to give up three of the least experienced faculty members because of a student enrollment shortfall, this young teacher was not among those transferred to another school, and was described by the principal as "one of the finest young men we have had here in many years." One need not speculate what would have happened to this beginning teacher if he had insisted on violating every critical norm of his planning period group.

Function of the Conceptual Elements in the System

The conceptual elements of activity, interaction, sentiment, and norms are marked by mutual dependence. By way of illustrating, if a teacher engages in card-playing activity with other teachers in her school as recreation during evenings, she will not have the same interactions as the teacher who typically enjoys bowling with a group of businessmen. The activities and interaction patterns among first-grade teachers who are located within the same classroom wing of the building will likely not be the same as those patterns among fifth- and sixth-grade teachers who are located in a different wing of the building. Teachers who often go to the teachers' room after lunch do not have the same activities and interactions as those who frequently loiter about the office or other area. Activities affect one's interactions; moreover, interactions affect one's activities, and interactions affect sentiment just as sentiment affects activity and interaction. Extended activity, interaction, and the development of sentiment lead inevitably to the acceptance of norms. All of these mutually dependent conceptual elements are the building blocks of group activity. Of greatest significance, however, is the fact that these elements (with the possible exception of sentiment) are readily observable by the principal and can become a practical basis for leadership with the faculty.

Interdependence among activity, interaction, and sentiment can have a major influence upon persons. The proverbial statement that *birds of a feather flock together* is metaphorically true regarding the tendency toward the similarity of values of persons closely associated. Expressed another way, frequent activities among a group of persons can make *birds of a feather*. Homans made the point, "You can get to like some pretty queer customers if you go around with them long enough."[12]

---

[12]Homans, *The Human Group,* p. 115.

Interaction, sentiment, and activity form the essential, mutually interdependent elements in Homans' system. "The activities, interactions, and sentiments of the group members, together with the mutual relations of these elements with one or another during the time the group is active, constitute what we shall call the *social system*."[13]

The Operational System

The discussion here is designed to illustrate briefly how the school develops into a social system. The Fulmer Point School, which was built and opened six years ago, serves as a good illustration. At the time that the school was planned and built, certain middle-school activities were prescribed by the central office regime. For example, the building was planned within given limitations of program conceptualizations, regime policies, and traditions associated with the school system. Then the principal was appointed to begin the stream of activities and interactions and the establishment of sentiments connected with the selection of teachers, appointments, and faculty planning meetings preparatory to the school opening. Soon inquiring parents appeared, along with their gum-chewing children, carefully expressing opinions and questions in their best "professional" vocabulary. All of these conditions, and more not mentioned, constituted "the given" system when Fulmer Point opened its doors for operation.

According to Homans, most of the conditions that were given at the time the school opened were a part of the *external system*. As the aggregation of teachers, students, counselors, administrative and supervisory personnel, and other personnel began in earnest, the activities and interactions associated with the operation of the school, the internal social system, began to be manifest. One could see the development of friendships (perhaps forerunners of cliques or informal organizations). Soon leadership patterns within these informal associations began to emerge. Moreover, there was evidence of differences of opinion about operating procedures and expected behavior (norms or expectations). In time these norms became a crystallized element of the social system of Fulmer Point.

The principal was frequently "placed on trial" by direct questions involving her reactions to situations—a kind of probing to find out where she stood on issues thought to be critical. Soon the principal was the object of subtle advice offered by persons, who were persuaded by interacting groups to approach her, who used such lead-ins as "Some of us were discussing this lunchroom situation and wondered whether you thought that we should. . . . "

[13]Homans, *The Human Group,* p. 87.

Certain demands were also made upon the school from the environment. As an example of these environmental demands, a supervisor rather tersely suggested that all teachers set their objectives for the year and submit them to the principal for review. The suggestion was the subject of much discussion at the next faculty meeting and in informal group sessions in and out of school. Resentment of the supervisor's demand was expressed, and this led to increased interaction and further crystallization of sentiment. Much of this activity was informal and not visible to the supervisor. The next time this supervisor appeared on the school grounds, word was efficiently passed up and down the building to "have your objectives handy for possible discussion." These are the activities, interactions, and sentiment associated with the survival of the school faculty in the environment, the *external system.*

The Fulmer Point faculty developed a sophisticated system to survive within the community power system, especially that part of the system associated with parental demands. Parental demands that were unpopular resulted in an adjustment in the external system to protect recipients from these demands. For example, the norm of "not talking out of school" or of simply not engaging in extemporaneous discussions with those known to be "troublemakers" was supposed to be observed. Violation of these norms resulted in sanctions upon the perpetrator including, among other things, the scolding remark by the principal at the next faculty meeting that "talking out of school" was an unprofessional act. The principal was expected to protect the teachers in cases of negative criticism; failure to do this exacted severe loss of leadership among the faculty. The principal's loyalty was expected by the teachers. Such comments as "he did not back me up" could be very damaging to the character of the principal. Moreover, the Fulmer Point faculty, like any other faculty, could employ rather costly sanctions, and no one knows this better than the perceptive, experienced principal. By participating in the developing external system, the principal was in a position to make demands upon the faculty with their willing cooperation.

By the end of the first school year, the *internal social system* of Fulmer Point School was solidifying. Homans identified the *internal system* as all the activities, interactions, sentiments, and norms that emerged spontaneously within the system and not as a result of inputs from the environment, described earlier as the external system. For example, some rather persistent activities and interactions among groups of the faculty resulted in the development of informal organizations or cliques, the members of which had the sentiment of liking each other beyond that felt for other members of the faculty. Some persons in these groups were emerging to positions of leadership. As the years go by these leadership and followership patterns will become more crystallized; however, these patterns will change as persons move into and out of the groups. Also, these patterns of interaction will continue in out-of-school activities, including participation in the teachers' union and community politics. These interacting groups are really informal subsystems of the social system of the school. They express positions concerning school policy and exercise controls over the formal activities of the school. For example, a new teacher coming to the faculty was given some specific advice concerning how to conduct her classes, including things to be avoided in student behavior.

By the third year some rigid norms of production were accepted at Fulmer Point. An English teacher could express how much was to be taught in a semester, how much homework was to be expected, and so on. Anyone violating these norms might be sanctioned by an adverse reaction in "the office," experience student disciplinary problems, or face unfavorable comments in the community, including board members, not to speak of persons in a position to control promotions in the central administrative office.

The activity, interaction, sentiment, and norms developed in both the external and internal system made up the *social system* of Fulmer Point School. The system was crystallized by the end of the sixth year of operation and had great capacity to respond to forces both internal and external in attempts to maintain equilibrium. The mere addition of a few new teachers to the school no longer affected the continuity of the system—most of them were assimilated into the system as active participants.

The social system of the Fulmer Point School spilled over into the external environment and vice versa. For instance, Mrs. Forrest James, in her sixth year teaching at Fulmer Point School, is the sister of Waldo Parsons, who is president of The First National Bank and chairman of the Fulmer Point Board of Education. Another teacher, Mr. Edward Pittman, is a close friend and fishing pal of Bert Shaffer, Deputy Superintendent. Mrs. Barbara Olson is frequently spoken of as the teacher's teacher who knows everyone. When asked to explain this remark, teachers on the faculty say that Barbara and her husband, Mark Olson, associate with high society in town and are tied in closely with some of the notable persons of power and influence. Then there are heralded teachers like Anne Marie Wilkey whose reputation for excellence is built upon thirty years of outstanding service. She had taught most of the powerful leaders in Fulmer Point, and they would not want to lose credibility with her.

Thus, the social system of the faculty is tied to powerful elements in the school's environment through which certain sanctions may be placed upon the principal unless a base of influence is built beyond the legal-rational power that resides in official position. Moreover, the power of the Fulmer Point Classroom Teachers' Association, an affiliate of the American Federation of Teachers, has removed the option of operating as a paternalistic leader (or father figure) for the faculty.

USE OF SOCIAL SYSTEMS THEORY

If a theory is useful, it provides the user a means through which relationships among elements in the situation can be understood or classified and predictions can be made of what will happen *if* certain actions are initiated. The use of relevant theory is essential in taking action that will result in productive learning, adequate discipline, and adapting to changing conditions. Briefly, then, let us discuss how systems theory is useful to the principal.

Social systems theory provides a basis for understanding the dynamic relationships among the elements making up the system. Through direct study the principal can identify the subsystems, or cliques, in the school, their leaders and followers, their norms, and their sources of influence, to rise above trial-and-error behavior in attempting to manage the school. One brief example illustrates how this is useful.

The principal of a senior high school was troubled by an undertone of discord among the faculty that prevented agreement on objectives. At first the principal tried some standard group dynamics techniques (such as retreat, workshop, and social activities) suggested by a consultant, which seemed not to make things better. Abandoning these designated or specific approaches, the principal spent much time trying to understand the relationships among the system elements. The existence of two rather influential informal organizations or subsystems on the faculty became apparent, one known as the Aladdin group and the other as the Old Guard. The existence of two teachers' rooms, one frequently used by the Aladdin group and the other by the Old Guard, was obviously a complicating factor. Here was a convenient means for activity, interaction, development of sentiments, and the embracement of divergent norms concerning what schooling is all about. The principal carefully devised a strategy to convert one of the teachers' rooms to a much-needed instruction facility. He then arranged for the leaders of the groups to represent the school at a meeting to which they had to ride together for several hundred miles in a school van. Through some tedious negotiating, one of the ring leaders agreed to accept a position in another school. The principal's strategy served to change the activities, interactions, and sentiments among members of the two groups, resulting in some predictable changes in the ability of the faculty to work together.

Systems theory can be used to explain why innovations do not succeed. The social system of a faculty has a great capacity to resist forces that challenge elements of the system. The norms embraced by a faculty will not be set aside easily. The system will react in various ways to resist what it believes to be a crackpot idea of the new principal. One attribute of a social system is its constant struggle to seek a state of equilibrium; consequently, ideas about the operation of a school that may produce system disequilibrium will be resisted. Forced acceptance often fails, or worse, a superficial acceptance is displayed for fear of negative consequences.

Social-system thinking is necessary, even in such routine functions as accounting for internal funds. For example, Mary Brown's predecessor as principal of Karns Creek Elementary School had treated accounting for internal funds on an informal basis. If a teacher happened to see some instructional materials that she needed on a shopping trip to town, she purchased them with cash and presented the bill to the bookkeeper for reimbursement. Mrs. Brown explained that this was no longer acceptable and demanded an approved requisition prior to any purchase. There were no exceptions; reimbursements would not be made on the informal basis. The reverberations of faculty anguish over this "high-handed" administration caught the attention of officials high in the administration, and even the chairman of the board of education was moved to ask the superintendent about the situation. Mrs. Brown ignored the feedback from the issue and became more adamant in controlling the activities of the teachers, which ultimately cost her dearly in leadership with the faculty and very probably raised some questions about her leadership among parents and other citizens in the community.

If Mrs. Brown had been cognizant of the systems' leadership structure and had based her strategy on this understanding, she could have accomplished her goal and retained leadership with the faculty. Her strategy, handing down an edict, was perceived as a threat to system survival. Consequently, even though Mrs. Brown was technically correct, her leadership costs were heavy. *Most principals do not fail because they lack technical knowledge, but because they do not understand the political dynamics of the faculty and the interaction of that system with suprasystems.*

Likewise, classroom teachers can be successful or unsuccessful, depending upon how well they interact with the system. An illustration of the power of the system involved a young, inexperienced student who was supervised in her practice-teaching experience by one of the authors. She was placed in a school managed by a principal with a good reputation as a leader. Moreover, she was highly rated as a teaching prospect by her professors. The supervising professor was somewhat surprised when, after about three weeks, the school principal, who had not observed her teach, complained that the student was not doing well as a student teacher and was, in his words, "not working out." In conversation with the student the supervising professor found, among other things, that she was not going to the teachers' room during breaks, conspicuously left for home as soon as the final bell rang, and had never asked advice from any of the experienced teachers. The professor initiated a plan of action for the student in which she asked leaders on the faculty for advice, actively engaged in activities with the faculty in the teachers' room, and stayed around after school to hobnob with faculty members. Several weeks later the principal approached the professor and praised the student teacher for the great progress she was making as a classroom teacher: "She is going to be a great teacher—we need more like her." Thus, classroom performance in and of itself does not result in being perceived as technically excellent.

Social-system theory should be used to understand the dynamics of the central office regime because leadership in the regime is a primary obligation of school principals. Lack of success in influencing officials in the central office may deprive the individual school of opportunities to experiment with new programs or to adequately fund existing programs. Likewise, principles of social system theory are very useful in understanding the community power system with which the principal has contact daily.

Leadership can be explained as a phenomenon growing out of the dynamics of complex social systems. There is no such thing as leadership that is independent of groups. Unless there is a social system (structure of effective relations, interaction, cohesiveness, and so forth) of a given number of persons, one cannot define them as a group. They are at best an aggregation. Therefore, the prospective principal must find an effective relationship with a group to have leadership in it.

Homans makes the disturbing point that the leader of the social system is that person who most closely conforms to the norms of the group. If the principal is to be a leader of the faculty, it is necessary to support the critical norms of the system. Said another way, the principal's values will be within the central tolerance of the values held by most of the members of the faculty. Here we see a dilemma for the principal. Suppose the principal cannot accept the norms of the faculty. Must the principal superficially support the faculty norms to become a leader among the faculty? How does the principal bring about changes in undesirable norms and still retain a position of leadership in the system?

The brief discussion here indicates how system theory can help the principal understand relationships among elements in the administrative structure of the school, the central office regime, and the community power structure. In the chapters that follow we will expand upon the use of systems thinking in the administration of schools.

CHAPTER FOUR

The Structure of School Social Systems

The application of social systems to school leadership, introduced in Chapter 3, will be more concisely described at this time. Some additional concepts of the structural properties of social systems must be understood, particularly in the administration of individual schools. We have attempted to weave these abstract system properties—boundary, feedback, equifinality—into the day-to-day process of providing leadership in a school to help the principal get a handle on the job and assure enlightened leadership of the faculty and the patrons of the school. To be really successful, the person appointed principal must be able to conceptualize just how the system works and be able to intervene in it to help the faculty achieve excellence.

As we speak about the school social system in this chapter, we are not making preconceived ideas concerning what the system should be. Our task is to discuss how to use system concepts to understand the school and to exert leadership in it. Much of our discussion in this chapter involves a concrete system, which Miller identified as a "nonrandom accumulation of matter-energy, in a region in physical space-time, which is nonrandomly organized into coacting, interrelated subsystems or components."[1]

[1]James G. Miller, *Living Systems* (New York: McGraw-Hill, 1978), p. 9.

Our discussion includes the social system in interaction with the technical system or the means of production, such as teaching, equipment, facilities, or materials. In their discussion of the organization as a system, Kast and Rosenzweig explain the managerial subsystem, the technical subsystem, the structural subsystem, the psychosocial subsystem, and the goals and values subsystem.[2] The goals and values subsystem is a conceptual system that should have internal consistency. Concentration on goals is essential. As someone has said, if persons do not have goals, any road will lead to where they are going. The managerial subsystem has the coordinating function, the structural subsystem relates to the organizational structure (the organizational chart, job descriptions), and the psychosocial subsystem refers to the social system, which is one of our concerns in this chapter.

We emphasize that the school social system interacts with other social systems, such as the central office regime and the community power system. Matter, energy, and information are being exchanged among these systems. Thus the school social system must be conceptualized as interacting with, influenced by, and influencing the systems with which it is involved.

THE CONCEPT OF BOUNDARY

The *boundary* of a system is that region that divides those inside from those outside (excluded from) the system in question. Consequently, much of the energy of those in the system goes into maintaining the boundary; otherwise the system will become so open that it can no longer function and will be destroyed. The boundary is not a physical thing like the fence that surrounds an elementary school site.

To begin our discussion, suppose that you, as the principal of a high school, are walking down the hall toward the cafeteria and see four or five teachers outside Room 101 engaged in very serious conversation. Based on prior observation, you believe that the persons in the group are part of a faculty clique. Before you reach hearing distance, a member of the group glances in your direction and the demeanor of the group changes from serious exchange of information to light-hearted, how-are-things-going talk, smiles, and friendly quips about school happenings. You have just observed the manifestation of the boundary of a system; the group maintains a protective boundary not readily permeable by those outside the system. The boundary exists within the minds of those in the system, but it is just as effective as the school fence in keeping those outside the system from free exchange with those inside.

[2]Fremont E. Kast and James E. Rosenzweig, *Organization and Management: A Systems and Contingency Approach,* 4th ed. (New York: McGraw-Hill, 1985), p. 113.

The system boundary is that region wherein the interaction (exchange of matter, information, and energy) among those in the system is much more frequent, unrestricted, and open than is their interaction with those persons outside the system. In the previous example, the interaction within the faculty group was serious and unrestricted until the principal approached. Systems can be sophisticated in the strategies and techniques for boundary maintenance to the point that the casual observer may not be aware of being excluded. The family offers an excellent illustration of system boundaries. No one except the members of a family really knows what goes on in the home. As a consequence, when the members of a family that we know "wash their dirty linen" in public, we are somewhat dismayed by the things that are exposed to the public for the first time. Family skeletons seldom see the light of day.

Openness of Boundaries

Boundaries differ in permeability or exchange of information with the environment. Thus we speak of open or closed systems; however, all social systems are open to some degree. Consequently, it is more accurate to speak of degrees of closedness and openness; that is, a criminal gang may maintain a high degree of closedness, whereas a political party or a university faculty may encourage openness. What is implied, therefore, is that closed systems have an osmotic boundary through which the passage of matter, energy, and information is heavily monitored, whereas the sieve of open systems is much less restrictive. Schools differ in the degree of exchange of information with the environment, some working hard to maintain a very restrictive exchange (boundary) with the environment and others seeking freer exchange with those outside the system.

Identifying Boundaries

The boundaries of faculty cliques can be determined by observing the frequency of interaction among persons associated with each clique and by identifying the region where you have difficulty having *really serious* free-flowing communication with members of the clique, or "in-group." Almost unconsciously the members of the faculty learn about system boundaries of groups by observing the frequency of effective interaction among members of the faculty, by observing the nature of leadership influence, and through personal experience in attempting to exchange information with members of the faculty. Either you are in the system, where communication with group members about running the school is free and easy, or you are outside the group, where information transmission with members of the group is more difficult. Very soon one learns the nature of communication possible within the faculty; which is to say, one learns about the boundaries of the subsystems. We are not referring to the relaxed "how-are-you-doing" everyday conversation, but to the exchange of matter, information, and energy concerning the important policies of running the school. Everyone can exchange the niceties of conversation whether one is inside or outside the boundary; however, when the purposes, goals, and desires of the group are concerned, not everyone is privy to the conversation.

Except for the leaders, the decision concerning which teachers should be included within the boundaries of subsystems may be slightly subjective and depend on the issue at hand. Some of the teachers may be fringe members who float between cliques; however, these fringe members will not be policy leaders in the subsystem. Moreover, these persons do not communicate as effectively as do those in the inner circle of the system. If one is clannish with the persons in subsystem A, which is often in conflict with subsystem B, difficulty will be experienced in exchanging matter, energy, and information with the leaders of subsystem B.

The boundaries of systems are not fixed but are structured uniquely; consequently, school principals should not make *a priori* assumptions. The leadership, structure, goals, and processes vary among schools. School clerks, custodians, and other noncertificated personnel may perform special leadership roles in the system. Moreover, the boundary of some systems includes some parents, certain central office personnel, and so on.

DYNAMIC PROPERTIES OF THE SOCIAL SYSTEM

As suggested previously, theorists view social systems as open or closed or, more specifically, as having degrees of closedness or openness. *Closed systems* are heavily insulated from the exchange of matter, information, and energy with their environment, whereas *open systems* welcome the exchange of matter, information, and energy with their environment.

Just as there are no absolutely closed social systems, there are no absolutely open systems. A completely open system will cease to be a system, as we define system, because as it approaches complete openness the boundary disappears. The system becomes so loaded with conflicting inputs that it cannot survive. The terms open and closed are relative; schools have varying degrees of openness and closedness to the environment.

Attempts to develop organizations with rigidly impermeable boundaries are legion. Certain religious groups attempt to create a monasterial existence to resist inputs that conflict with their systems. Criminal gangs develop a sophisticated network to protect their systems. Hush-hush intelligence organizations exert great energy to prevent leaks and to protect the identity of agents. Isolated, rural areas having natural barriers to exchanges with external environments (such as mountains, oceans, and rivers) may develop closedness and provincialism. Authorities are intrigued by the persistent way in which the social systems of certain underdeveloped countries survive in the face of heavy inputs to facilitate change. Some schools and school systems also expend an extraordinary amount of energy to develop a closed organization.

Entropy and Equilibrium

All systems tend toward entropy; however, closed systems experience maximization of entropy to a higher degree than open systems. *Entropy* refers to the tendency for a social system to lean toward ineffectiveness. Miller defined entropy as the "disorder, disorganization, lack of patterning or randomness of organization in a system."[3] When entropy is maximized the energy in the system runs down and it can no longer function well— death may be at hand. If, however, the system has a high degree of openness and exchanges matter, energy, and information with its environment, the tendency toward entropy will be arrested.

When entropy is maximized, the organization passes through stages of goal displacement, structural stagnation, and death. One can see this phenomenon illustrated in provincial communities that employ only locals to operate and teach in their schools. The schools in these communities often become marked by plainness, lack of motivation, provincialism and irrelevancy. Consequently, the graduates of these schools experience much difficulty coping in the modern society.

Communities and schools with open systems that freely exchange matter, energy, and information with their environments remain highly energized and achieve what system theorists refer to as *dynamic equilibrium* or *steady state,* and entropy is arrested. Steady state or dynamic equilibrium is the balance in a system that is always changing and can never return to any previous state or reference point. An example might be a person who, while running, leans forward to the point at which a rapid pace must be maintained to keep from falling forward. Such a person has achieved a balance and will not fall so long as the running pace to keep the balance is maintained. On the other hand, maximally closed systems expend much energy maintaining equilibrium, sometimes referred to as *static equilibrium;* consequently, entropy is maximized and over time the system may reach death, which is the state in which entropy is maximized. Some historians have pointed to the fact that great nations tend to achieve

[3]Miller, *Living Systems,* p. 13.

a developmental zenith only to move toward disorganization, lack of patterning, randomness, and eventually death.

As suggested previously, since all social systems are open, one may not speak of a closed school or community, but rather of degrees of openness. The school principal cannot possibly create a closed school with boundaries impervious to the environment. However, with great effort at attaining closedness, the principal and faculty can create a school wherein the exchange of matter, energy, and information with the environment is greatly curtailed, resulting in an increase of entropy. Even the most closed schools are constantly bombarded and forced to move from one equilibrium to another and can never return to an earlier point of equilibrium—one really cannot go home again. In these schools adaptation to societal change is minimized; hence randomness, plainness, lack of energy, and goal displacement are apparent. In this book we use static equilibrium to refer to the balance or stability that characterizes closed systems and steady state and dynamic equilibrium to refer to the quality of balance in open systems.

Feedback: The Steering Mechanism

Norbert Wiener, an early leader in cybernetics, defined feedback as follows:

> This last function, as we have seen, is called feedback, the property of being able to adjust future conduct by past performance. Feedback may be as simple as that of common reflex, or it may be a higher order feedback, in which past experience is used not only to regulate specific movements, but also whole policies of behavior. Such policy feedback may, and often does, appear to be what we know under one aspect as a conditioned reflex, and under another as learning.[4]

The organization uses feedback to learn how well it is performing in its environment and as a means of control. "In the broader sense, feedback is a concept that refers to response to output, which enables a system to modify its subsequent functioning."[5] For example, suppose the school adopts a new way to report on pupil progress. When this report first goes to parents, the school may receive a positive response, negative feedback, or a mixed reaction. If the feedback is too negative, the principal and faculty will no doubt perceive that the health of the organization depends upon

---

[4]Norbert Wiener, *The Human Use of Human Beings* (Boston: Houghton Mifflin, 1954), p. 33.

[5]Ralph B. Kimbrough and Michael Y. Nunnery, *Educational Administration: An Introduction,* 3rd ed. (New York, Macmillan, 1988), p. 313.

some action to quell the parental frustration. There are many alternatives, including doing nothing and riding out the storm; however, the important concept here is that the faculty may observe how new reporting procedures can stir up a big controversy, threatening the survival of the system. In its exchange of information with the public, the faculty learns how to use its steering mechanism or control function.

In the analysis of feedback we are concerned with the inputs and outputs of information, energy, or matter across the boundary of the school social system. The example just given is an oversimplification of the process. In the first place, the school often transmits to its environment what it perceives the components of the environment will understand and accept, with the expected result of positive feedback. Furthermore, the environmental components have a mind-set concerning how they should respond to such outputs. For example, parents may hesitate to respond freely to teachers for fear that they might incriminate their children. The response of many parents may be phrased in language perceived mildly favorable to the school when, in reality, there is an undercurrent of hostility. The school, in turn, filters the feedback unconsciously; that is, the system tends to hear what it wants to hear. The failure to use feedback effectively or to hear inputs may eventually result in system malfunction or failure.

The Hierarchical Nature of Systems

Concrete systems, such as the school and school district, are *hierarchical,* or have successive levels of classification, a quality that systems theorists apply to all living systems. One can see the hierarchy of the following: cell, organ, organism, group, society. The hierarchical nature of school systems, even the most collegial, is obvious. In the individual high school, the hierarchy is integrated into classes, departments, and school faculty. Within faculty cliques is a hierarchy of leadership that interacts with higher levels of leaders in the school and school system hierarchy. As discussed in Chapter 3, one may speak of subsystem, system, and suprasystem; this also illustrates the hierarchical nature of systems. Our primary interest is the individual school as a system interacting with subsystems and suprasystems.

Equifinality and Contingency Theory

Cause-and-effect relationships can be established in closed systems, but not in open systems. If an absolutely closed elementary school existed, that is, one occupied by pupils and teachers with closed minds (robots) and walled off in a relatively closed community, then the inputs and outputs could be accurately predicted. A change in the way reading is taught to children who are conditioned to react as robots would result in a predictable change in reading behavior. When all systems are functioning well, the robot moves in a predictable direction when the right button (input) is pushed. Fortunately, humans and schools, as stated previously, are open systems—the students are not closed systems; consequently, changing the inputs to open systems does not necessarily result in predictable changes in student, faculty, or parental behavior, which brings us to the phenomenon known as equifinality.

According to Granger, *equifinality* refers to "a property of a system which permits different results from similar inputs and similar results from alternate inputs."[6] The principal soon learns that the best-laid plans for instructional change sometimes fail to produce the results expected. What was thought to be a linear relationship between a strategy (input) and a desired change produced an unexpected result. Perhaps in another instance an input thought related to another outcome produced the change desired in the prior attempt. Equifinality is a phenomenon present in all open social systems.

Open systems have too many uncontrolled variables to be expected to behave as robots. The principal must learn to live with the probability that inputs logically expected to produce certain desired results in pupil progress may produce spurious results, and that seemingly illogical strategies may sometimes produce the results preferred.

> Most experienced administrators have seen cases where two schools seemingly had similar inputs. That is, the schools were "alike" in regard to pupil population, physical facilities, size, teaching staff, support services, financial support, administrative staff, and curriculum. Yet in terms of output as measured by pupil achievement and perceptions of the school, one school was highly productive and the other was not. A person conversant with systems concepts does not have to explain the plight of the low-productive school in terms of the "wrath of the gods." Rather, such a person recognizes that schools are examples of open systems and that open systems display the property of equifinality.[7]

Before we leave this point, let us say that not even the supposedly closed systems of robotics are absolutely closed. They, too, are subject to extraneous inputs that affect expected outcomes. Even our highly developed heating systems often malfunction because of certain inputs or bugs in the system.

Equifinality supports the contingency theory of management that has gained acceptance within recent decades. *Contingency theory* presupposes that different situations may demand alternative styles of management. Traditional management theory stipulated one grand concept of management for all organizations regardless of existing conditions. Contingency theorists, however, believe that a task-oriented principal may be less productive in some schools than a relationship-oriented leader and vice versa. Davis and Newstrom observed, "Not all organizations need exactly the same amount of participation, open communication, or any other condition in order to be effective."[8] Fiedler concluded that, in what he described as "very favorable" conditions, the task-oriented leader was more effective than the human-relations style leader; yet in conditions defined as "very unfavorable" the human-relations leader tended to be more productive.[9] Leadership skills are discussed further in Chapter 7. According to Luthans, contingency theory goes one step further than systems theory and couples the environmental conditions to organizational structure.[10]

The Individual and Organizational Dimensions

In his landmark 1938 publication, *The Functions of the Executive,* Barnard identified what he referred to as the efficiency/effectiveness dimensions of organizations.[11] *Effectiveness* is the nonpersonal (organizational) dimension and refers to the productivity measure of the school, whereas *efficiency* is personal and is the extent to which the need dispositions of the faculty are satisfied. Barnard's concept of the managerial and faculty dimensions of organization has been carried forward by numerous writers.

Parsons identified three dimensions or systems: technical, managerial, and institutional.[12] The technical system is the production or task-performance system, the managerial is the coordinating system, and the institutional system connects the organization to the environment (such as the board of education). The concept of organizational and faculty dimensions is the basis of most concepts of leadership or management.

[8]Keith Davis and John W. Newstrom, *Human Behavior at Work: Organizational Behavior,* 7th ed. (New York: McGraw-Hill, 1985), p. 501.

[9]Fred E. Fiedler, *A Theory of Leadership Effectiveness* (New York: McGraw-Hill, 1967), pp. 22–32.

[10]Fred Luthans, *Organizational Behavior,* 4th ed. (New York: McGraw-Hill, 1985), pp. 565–66.

[11]Chester I. Barnard, *The Functions of the Executive* (Cambridge: Harvard University Press, 1938).

[12]Talcott Parsons, "Some Ingredients of a General Theory of Formal Organizations," in Andrew W. Halpin, ed., *Administrative Theory in Education* (New York: Macmillan, 1958), pp. 40–72.

A model widely discussed in educational administration is the one proposed by Getzels and Guba. They discussed the school as a social system with two dimensions: (1) the organizational or nomothetic dimension and (2) the faculty-need disposition or idiographic dimension.[13] The nomothetic dimension is represented by institutional roles and expectations. As numerous authors have concluded, especially with regard to the traditional bureaucratic organization, the expectations at the organizational dimension are frequently in conflict with the need dispositions of the faculty, resulting in the possibility of recurrent conflict. Thus school principals frequently find themselves in the middle or, as frequently expressed, between a rock and a hard place. These principals are frequently forced to accede to central office policies that are very unpopular with the faculty, creating distance between themselves and the faculty and staff. Consequently, the real leadership of these principals with the faculty is complicated, and they must rely upon legal/rational authority rather than group authority as a basis of leadership. If enough distance is created between the principal and faculty, the principal becomes completely isolated from the faculty social system and leadership of the faculty and staff is complicated beyond immediate repair. In this situation the school usually becomes dysfunctional; dismissal or reassignment of the principal usually follows.

ILLUSTRATIVE CASES

In this section short discussions of two different school communities are provided to further illustrate the concepts discussed. The first case is of Coleman High School, located in an incorporated city of about 100,000 citizens, which would be classified as a sacred community.[14] Sacred communities have a predisposition to resist change, emphasizing patriotism, security, maintenance of valued customs and traditions, emotional attachment to native birth, and other qualities giving rise to provincial thinking.

The second case involves Redwood Elementary School, located in a community with secular characteristics. Secular communities value change, or what the business leaders in Redwood refer to as "progress." Secular communities display neutrality to extreme patriotism, customs, traditions, emotional attachment to native birth, and, in extreme instances, display emotional recklessness, openness, and fanaticism toward

---

[13]Jacob W. Getzels and Egon Guba, "Social Behavior and the Administrative Process," *School Review,* LXV (Winter 1957), 423–41.

[14]Laurence Iannaccone and Frank W. Lutz, *Politics, Power, and Policy: The Governing of School Districts* (Columbus: Charles E. Merrill, 1970), pp. 31–32.

the thrill of change, and faddism about "progressive" changes that upon close inspection appear as phony.[15]

COLEMAN HIGH SCHOOL

As discussed previously, Coleman High School (CHS) is located in Coleman, a city that works hard to maintain closedness to change. With about four exceptions the elected officials in Coleman are native-born and most are over fifty years of age. They are prone to avoid the consideration of policies that might "rock the boat" because the leaders and their followers display a high degree of consensus about the kind of town Coleman should be. The population of Coleman increased very little during the past decade.

The Right Personnel and Administration

Mr. Richard Walsh, the superintendent of schools for the Coleman school district, can talk at length about the importance of selecting school administrators and teachers who fit in to the Coleman community and school system. School principals say that Mr. Walsh is a stickler for selecting people who, as he expresses it, "fit into our philosophy of education." As a consequence, a majority of the teachers attended nearby colleges and were native-born to Coleman or adjoining communities.

Orientation programs are emphasized for new teachers and school administrators. All new teachers attend a special meeting at which various authorities instruct them about the general operation of the school system. At Coleman High School the "big buddy" system is used. Beginning teachers are sponsored by an experienced teacher to familiarize them with standard operating procedures, usually referred to as "the Coleman way." Mr. James, the principal of CHS, also gives special supervision to teachers new to the system.

All newly appointed school administrators in the district are required to attend a meeting every two weeks, which is devoted to extolling the virtues of the Coleman schools and to learning the ongoing administrative procedures in the district. The meetings are interspersed with "what Mr. Walsh believes" expressions.

Coleman's personnel practices minimize the impact of inputs that are in conflict with the consensus in the district and maximize the maintenance of a static equilibrium. Moreover, these activities help develop a boundary that has high resistance to inputs. Teachers are brought into the

---

[15]Iannaccone and Lutz, *Politics, Power, and Policy,* p. 32.

system to replace the small turnover due to resignations, retirement, and the addition of some new programs mandated by the state legislature.

Mr. James is noted for operating a tight ship at CHS. During his twenty-year tenure as principal, he has become increasingly paternalistic in his genial leadership of the faculty. Experienced teachers express much security with his thoughtful, consistent leadership. One seldom has to guess what the next day will bring at CHS; one knows.

With a teachers' union affiliated with the state and national union, one would question how Mr. James could have so much influence. The answer to this question is not entirely clear; however, the best hypothesis is that the union in the Coleman School District is a "sweetheart union," in which the gains of the union also compliment the interests of school administrators in the system and vice versa.

The Community Power System

The political system also has an important role in maintaining a closed school regime. The power structure at Coleman is characterized as having high agreement about public policy; that is, the leaders and most followers in the structure exhibit a high degree of consensus about what kind of city Coleman should be and what kind of schools they want. There are, of course, some persons in Coleman who reject current policies; however, these are largely discounted as malcontents or "soreheads" by the mayor, who has held office for a record thirty years. Although the Coleman State Bank and the First National Bank of Coleman have been sold to state and regional banking trusts, the new managers of these banks have taken little interest in local politics. The numerous franchised fast-food restaurants, minimarkets, hardware stores, and regionally operated supermarkets have melded into the culture of Coleman, primarily because the managers, more often than not, are local persons.

As indicated previously, most elected officials are native-born citizens, fifty or more years of age. The emergence of leadership into the decision-making levels of the power structure is very slow and tends to be hereditary. The elected school board has shown much stability of membership within the past fifteen years. Mr. Richard Walsh has been superintendent of schools for over a decade. He is among the few officials in Coleman who is not native to the community; however, he has established a solid reputation as a leader in the power structure and is highly regarded. The only criticism heard is that he has built a regime so strong that the board is "nothing but a rubber stamp." Mr. Bert Peterson, the board chairman, expresses much impatience with this criticism as "the myth of a few misfits that Coleman could well do without."

The Feedback Process and Equifinality

Much of the energy of school administrators and teachers is invested in the maintenance of homogeneity. Feedback is the basis for keeping equilibrium. Those outputs known to elicit favorable feedback are employed; however, as Mr. Walsh frequently admits, "One can never predict with 100-percent accuracy whether an announcement about an operational change will be accepted by citizens." For example, last year the board announced a slight variance in attendance zones, a process often used to keep school enrollment in line. Yet, what everyone in the central office and the board thought was a routine change resulted in massive and severe criticism, which, as Mr. Walsh said, "was the biggest surprise during my career here." The board rescinded the change at a special meeting, directing the staff to study the situation.

Equifinality is illustrated here. As skilled as Mr. Walsh and his staff were in judging community sentiment, they could never explain logically why the negative feedback was so strong. As the deputy superintendent expressed it, "When you are dealing with the public, it is like the black box, and predictions of response are very difficult."

For the most part, however, the school staff of Coleman, including the principal and faculty of CHS, is often described as suave in dealing with the public. Mr. James is said to have the best PTA attendance of any high school in that region of the state. One parent explained, "His PTA meetings are very entertaining and informative." He spends much time with the faculty informing them about the strengths of CHS, and, for the most part, communication with parents shows CHS "in a good light." As Mr. James frequently explains this action, "Public-school relations is the process of selling the public on the strengths of CHS." In past years he has shown anger in faculty meetings upon hearing that a teacher has "indulged in very unprofessional behavior by making critical remarks about the school to the townspeople."

Deeply embodied in CHS is pride in membership in a high school described by local leaders as the best high school in the state. New teachers are instructed in "the Coleman way." Leaders in Coleman believe that they have the best schools in the state. A visitor might mistakenly assume that these leaders prevaricate because many of the buildings are obsolete and in much need of repair; however, one soon learns that a great majority really believes that "we are the best." Persons in a community and school system experiencing a high degree of closedness literally brainwash each other, one of the trademarks of entropy.

The result of this psychological set is that all negative feedback is either ignored or neutralized by providing additional information, scapegoating, or, in cases of extremely negative feedback, rescinding the action that has given rise to the criticism. As Mr. James often puts it, "One must be very resourceful in communicating with the public." At CHS, feedback is skillfully employed as an effective means of maintaining equilibrium. Yet, as in technical systems, bugs get in the system so that one cannot predict inputs and outputs accurately. Equifinality may be experienced in all systems; however, because the Coleman district staff and the community power structure are in control, these miscalculations are few and far between.

Summary Comments. In these paragraphs we have dealt with a minimum number of structural characteristics of the systems that keep CHS relatively closed. CHS interacts with economic, political, familial, and other social systems that make up its closed environment. Note also that the culture of Coleman embodies a traditional way of life conducive to closedness to inputs of energy, matter, and information that might place the system in imbalance or disequilibrium.

In schools like CHS, the tendency toward entropy is maximized as the system reaches a high state of homogeneity. Fortified with interacting local systems that are also highly closed to innovation and change, the inputs of energy, information, and matter from interacting systems (even the state department of education) are resisted and in most cases have minimum effect upon operations. Thus, the system experiences a decrease in energy, randomness, and disorder in its journey toward the morgue. Eventually the system will no longer possess the ability to cope with the educational needs of youth in modern society, a society that has moved into another century.

The fact that CHS is unable to meet the needs of students is borne out by state department observers who believe that CHS is one of the most backward high schools in the state. The program is irrelevant. The test scores of its graduates are among the lowest in the state, as are teachers' salaries and local financial effort. As one official expressed, "The Coleman District seems to have fallen into an orbit of low financial support, and they just stay there with no force big enough to push them out of it." Support for the school program has followed a similar orbital path of inadequate supplies, materials, textbooks, and other instructional resources. The school plant facilities are reaching an archaic stage. About the only thing that arouses the anxiety of the CHS administrators is when their best-thought-out plans for maintaining a "steady ship" result in unexpected results—equifinality—which sometimes places the system in a short period of disequilibrium.

REDWOOD ELEMENTARY SCHOOL

The case of Redwood Elementary School (RES), located in Winston, illustrates the social system characterized by a high degree of openness. Redwood Elementary is highly acclaimed by the citizens of Winston as an exemplary school, and has been frequently cited in national journals and the news media for innovative management and instruction. Unlike the city of Coleman, Winston is a very fast growing city, and the school system must employ many new teachers each year.

Personnel for a Changing Community

Winston School District maintains an aggressive personnel recruitment program in hiring new teachers and other school personnel. The teachers in RES are from several states and only one is a native of Winston. The administrators of the Winston schools emphasize finding and recruiting the best qualified teachers available, and recruiters log thousands of miles in locating viable candidates. Compliance with state certification standards by many out-of-state teachers becomes a problem and is a source of tension between the school district and the officials in the certification division of the state department of education.

The district has an organized program of orientation for new teachers. Teachers are given information about routine organizational details, such as where to obtain information, how to find and use records, and how to request instructional materials. Thad Wilkins, the principal of Redwood Elementary, works with first-year teachers to help them adjust to the new situation, but he frowns upon the use of anything like the buddy system. He encourages the adoption of new approaches to teaching and comments frequently that he never discourages innovation.

Most of the school principals in Winston are from outside the system, and the superintendent, Wilson Stevens, encourages employment of administrators with doctorate degrees. In fact, Thad Wilkins was appointed principal of Redwood Elementary after completing his degree at a nationally known university.

The visitor to Redwood Elementary is impressed with what some observers have referred to as a fetish for change and innovation. For example, Dr. Wilkins' first comment to a visitor is likely to be, "Come with me. Before I turn you over to Mrs. Johnson (the assistant principal), I want to show you our newest innovation." As this comment indicates, Dr. Wilkins has a very busy schedule. Moreover, one soon learns that he is in communication with other persons with national reputations who are located at prestigious universities. In fact, his critics characterize him as a show-off, a criticism that may not be deserved.

Inputs from Faraway Places

Two decades ago Winston was a sleepy little fishing village on the Pacific Coast. There was not much to disturb life in the community except a few tourists in season. Within a few short years Winston was transformed into a huge, technologically oriented, government-financed installation. The decision to locate in Winston was made in Washington.

The population of Winston grew at an astounding rate. It more than quadrupled within the first five-year period of rapid growth. Even more important was that the scientifically and technologically educated new residents were very different and had ideas about community living that was at great variance from the indigenous population majority. The new people soon made known their objection to existing policies, and the ruling power structure soon found itself in a struggle for existence. Within the first decade of growth political change was swift and telling—the old regime gave way to a pluralism of new forces and new ideas about government and education. Old political leaders found that they had to either swim with the tide of change or be engulfed in it. Within a few years the social system and most of its subsystems were forced into a steady state, or, as some authors prefer to say, a dynamic equilibrium.

The school system experienced phenomenal growth. Everyone wondered whether Superintendent Stevens could survive the onslaught of new pupils. Hundreds of new teachers were hired each year. Numerous administrators were employed to organize the new schools that were being opened to house the growth. Mr. Stevens proved himself more than equal to the challenge. More importantly, he and the board of education proved equal to the task of making the policy and procedural changes necessary to adjust the system to the steady state.

Creation of System Openness

The input of new energy, matter, and information to Winston resulted in system openness; the system was moved into a dynamic equilibrium. The political system and most subsystems, of which the school system was one, became a balance of forces in a state of change. The inputs to the system were used to redirect objectives and revise long-range goals. A high school like Coleman High School, in the first case discussed, could not survive in such a system.

One of the high schools in the Winston school system became so exaggerated in announced innovation that its changes appeared faddish to observers. Nevertheless, the principal of this innovative school achieved strong national recognition, and the school was visited by thousands of admirers.

Redwood Elementary School also became a mecca for visitors interested in its ungraded organization, team teaching, concept core, and other innovations that were well disseminated through the media. As one long-time observer commented, "The Winston school system was turned upside down," illustrating the theory of dynamic equilibrium or steady state.

There was a balance of inputs and outputs that maintained an equilibrium in a state of change—a steady state. Entropy was arrested.

The administration of the new program necessitated much communication among officials in the central office regime and elements of the community political system. For example, Dr. Wilkins and his faculty had to explain the program to authorities in the central office and to the board of education to elicit their approval, which necessitated planning and the development of curriculum materials. Realizing that official approval by the board was never enough to secure the successful introduction of a new program, Dr. Wilkins and his staff conducted an extensive information campaign to parents and other citizens. The school system put energy, material, and information into elements of the community power system and the central office regime. Note, however, that the regime and the community power system were also open systems and were receiving inputs of energy, material, and information from the environment. As a consequence, educational innovation was more acceptable than would have been true of Coleman. Coleman High School was confronted with a closed system that was hostile to change.

Thad Wilkins and his colleagues at RES constantly received and evaluated feedback that told them how well they were doing. Feedback was used to steer the system toward further change, whereas in Coleman High School feedback was used to resist change and maintain the system status quo. Continuous use of feedback likewise generated new outputs of energy to the community; open systems freely exchange matter, energy, and information with the environment.

What were some of the results of the development of an open system for RES? Foremost among the results was the adoption of a policy by the board of education that encouraged all elementary schools in the system to adopt the new program, which was seen as more relevant to the changing community. To facilitate the new programs, the board appropriated a sharp increase in local taxes for schools. In time the central office regime became an innovative system. The critical norm for all leaders of the system and subsystems was to be a change agent. Either the principals appointed in the system were innovative or social distance was created between them and the faculty, which might not facilitate continued tenure in the system. In summary, Redwood Elementary was propelled into a new orbital path, and this represented great distance from the days of a school in a sleepy fishing and farming town.

USE OF SYSTEMS THEORY

Knowledge and use of systems theory are strengths esential for success in the principalship. The theory is especially useful in conceptualizing the interaction of variables dealt with in the operation of a school. Our emphasis at this point is on understanding or conceptualizing. Without it the school principal cannot develop and successfully initiate strategies for supervising the operation. The use of systems theory to provide leadership in the school is discussed elsewhere in the text. For example, in Chapter 7 we discuss how systems theory may be used to promote strategies for leadership.

Systems theory should be helpful when one is seeking a position. When offered a principalship, candidates should ask themselves whether this is the school in which they can be successful. Knowledge of systems theory can help one collect and evaluate key data about the school and its environment. Instead of relying upon subjective impressions of friendliness, promises, and other social graces which are easily faked for a few hours, the candidate can consider boundaries, closedness, openness, use of feedback, entropy, and so on. Is entropy maximized or arrested? Is an out-of-touch, irrelevant school on its deathbed in a provincially minded community? If so, are you up to the task of making the changes necessary to move the school and community toward excellence? Systems framework should be used as a basis for analyzing the situation and deciding whether you are the right person for the task ahead. One does not want to experience failure too often because it builds a reputation hard to live down.

After accepting a position, the principal does not have to ponder aimlessly a big amorphous complex of people and things. Knowledge of systems theory gives a blueprint for understanding the behavior observed in the school and its interaction with subsystems and suprasystems. What interacting subsystems make up the school social system? How is feedback used by subsystems, the system, and suprasystems? How can the technical, managerial, and institutional systems of the school be harmonized in the improvement of instruction and the development of excellence? In summary, the beginning principal should know how to ask the right questions; this is one essential basis for successful leadership.

The aspects of systems theory just discussed help leaders to think intelligently about their positions and provide a means for macroscopic (holistic) and microscopic (partial) conceptualizing of organizational behavior.

> This strategy involves, first of all, locating and identifying the boundaries of the system and distinguishing the parts of it that perform each subsystem process; then identifying the important variables of each subsystem and using standard measurements or indicators to determine their values at different times; and thus discovering whether they are normal for systems of the same sort. If they are not normal, the user of this strategy will try to determine the cause of the abnormality. In order to correct it,

he [or she] will make changes in the system itself or in its relationship to other systems in its environment.[16]

The objective is not simply to conceptualize but to use systems analysis to improve the school climate, motivate the faculty, improve morale, and help the faculty and staff achieve excellence in instruction. In the process the school should be seen as interacting with other systems (such as the central office regime, community power structure, and student systems). "Because a system is characterized by interrelationships, its parts can be understood only in relation to each other and to the whole, and the whole can be understood only in relation to its component and integral parts."[17] Moreover, to use the language expressed by other authors, the technical, managerial, structural, psychosocial, and institutional subsystems must be in a harmonious relationship. Accomplishing this inevitably involves what Hoffer called the ordeal of change, in which systems theory is also helpful. In providing leadership for change, Hall and Hord suggest

> By consistently gathering information about the state of the system, facilitators can adapt and adjust their behavior to be more relevant. As they make interventions, the system state changes, affecting individuals, groups, and their interrelationships.... The effective change facilitator thinks *systemically* about how a change or alteration in one element of the system will affect other elements and subsets of the system.[18]

A Linear Concept of System

Before leaving this discussion of general systems theory, we should focus briefly on the linear concept of the systems concept as illustrated here.

Input   →   Transformation Process   →   Output

In this illustration, the inputs consist of money, people (administrators, teachers, staff), facilities, materials of instruction, and so on. The transformation process or processor, which also is referred to as the technical subsystem, includes teaching, scheduled classes, curriculum, use

[16]James G. Miller and Jessie Louise Miller, "Systems Science: An Emerging Interdisciplinary Field," *The Center Magazine*, 14 (September/October 1981), 54.

[17]Clarence A. Newell, *Human Behavior in Educational Administration* (Englewood Cliffs, N.J.: Prentice-Hall, 1978), p. 32.

[18]Gene E. Hall and Shirley M. Hord, *Change in Schools: Facilitating the Process* (Albany: State University of New York Press, 1984), p. 16.

of lesson plans, seating arrangements, and other means of providing educational services to children and youth. The output is the product of the system—the gains (or losses) in achievement, the development of citizenship, and other expected outcomes of the educational experience.

The linear concept of the school system may be useful as long as one realizes its simplistic nature. It does not account for the inputs of informal groups, the norms of the social system, the customs and traditions in the culture, entropy, energy invested in boundary maintenance, the inevitable tendency to maintain equilibrium, or other system variables that are inputs to the system. Owens wrote that by the late 1970s we realized that this linear model contributed little to understanding of school organizations function.

> For example, it presupposes that when students and teacher go to school each day, their dominant concerns are to achieve the formal, official goals of the school. Even a casual observer soon learns, however, that actually these people bring to school with them a host of their own beliefs, goals, hopes, and concerns which are more significant and more powerful to them.[19]

General systems theory represents a development light-years beyond the linear concept, because it gives the school administrator a way to understand and deal with the behavior of the school and its environment. We shall now proceed to a discussion of the central office regime, which is the suprasystem of the school and one with which the school is in constant interaction.

---

[19]Robert G. Owens, *Organizational Behavior in Education,* 3rd ed. (Englewood Cliffs, N.J.: Prentice-Hall, 1987), p. 58.

CHAPTER FIVE

Central Office Regimes: The School District Control System

The central office regime is the suprasystem of the individual school. As the central office staff interacts with individual schools to coordinate the educational process, a complex formal and informal structure or system for control develops. Since this system of control is more than that represented in the organizational chart, we use the term *regime. Central office regime* refers to a form or mode of management in the school district that includes the formal structure, the informal organization (administrator, faculty, and staff cliques), the politics of the bureaucracy, elements of the social system, and other aspects of the system of control. The complex system includes the formal organizational structure and the technical system for the production of educational services. The principal and faculty are interacting parts of this system. They have no choice in the matter so long as they practice in the district; consequently, they must learn how they can function well and achieve influence in the regime.

THE FORMAL STRUCTURE

Some form of organizational structure is essential in the operation of a school or school system. The tasks of coordinating the complex process of educating children and youth cannot be accomplished by a disordered crowd or mob. Therefore, all school systems have a structure for making decisions, selecting and placing personnel, deciding on essential objectives, coordinating task achievement, and other essential functions. School principals are confronted with a number of terms to describe organizations; for example, bureaucratic, collegial, line and staff, loosely coupled, and participative management are all used in discussing formal structures.

The Bureaucratic Model

Variations of the bureaucratic organization are employed by practically all of the school districts in the United States. Max Weber is credited with first describing the nature of this much maligned but little understood organization. The term *bureaucracy* conjures up thoughts of red tape, silly rules, and the "piling up of layer on layer of administrative authority, which makes it necessary to submit all reports with seven carbon copies,"[1] a popular perception of bureaucracy which, of course, is not what Weber proposed. The ideal bureaucratic organization has the following characteristics:

1. *Division of labor and specialization.* Since the educational process is so complex and beyond the ability of one person or a small group to master, division of labor must be accomplished to facilitate task performance. The ability to assign technically qualified administrators and teachers to perform specific tasks promotes organizational efficiency and assures excellence in the teaching and leadership processes.

2. *An integrated hierarchy of positions.* The offices in the structure are arranged into superordinate and subordinate levels of authority, providing for an integrated unity-of-command. Efficient coordination of administrators and teachers from the top to the bottom of the school system ensures that everyone knows to whom and for what to be responsible.

3. *A rationally consistent system of rules of operation.* A set of written rules to define relationships and prescribe organizational practices assures predictable behavior, facilitates the coordination of task performance, and protects subordinates from decisions based on whim. With these guidelines school principals do not have to endure the capricious demands of superordinates who are accustomed to making decisions to fit the situation.

4. *Impersonality and rationality.* The more that personal and emotional feelings, such as hate, love, and friendship, are removed from all organizational activities, the better the structure will operate. In order for

[1]Paul Woodring, "The Editor's Bookshelf," *Saturday Review,* XLV (August 20, 1966), 64.

school principals to make wise decisions about faculty, they must ignore all emotional feelings in the process of deciding. All activity based on irrational political bases is improper.

5. *Employment and promotions based on technical competence.* All school administrators, teachers, and other school employees are hired on the basis of technical competence. Promotions based on anything other than technical performance are not tolerated; they should be based on seniority or achievement or both. Consequently, all promotions in which friendship, nepotism, sexual attraction, or other irrational bases are used constitute a violation of organizational excellence.

In use the bureaucratic model becomes corrupted by nepotism and favoritism (promotions are based on personal attraction or family membership), petty politics (a process seldom rational), and rules designed to quell the offenses of a small minority that strangulates creativity and promotes inefficiency of the overwhelming majority. The extended chain-of-command in the "tall" organizations (those with many layers of authoritative positions) contributes to really big problems of communicating. Numerous authors have pointed to the possibility of becoming over-specialized in the educational process.

Another problem of bureaucracy is that it is incompatible with human nature. Numerous scholars have pointed to the inevitable conflict between bureaucratic rationality and the irrational nature of persons. From all that we have learned we are forced to conclude that much (perhaps most) of human behavior is irrational. Being in love, for example, is seldom based on rationality. A family based on the rationality proposed by Weber would soon be in trouble.

Some Alternative Models

The problem of making bureaucracy work led authorities to advocate alternative models.[2] One model often advocated during the 1950s and 1960s was the *collegial model,* which was based on the organization of the traditional university and emphasized faculty control of the curriculum and teaching process. In the collegial model the administrators function as service and coordinating agents instead of autocratic industrial tycoons.

Intermixed with the talk of collegiality during the 1950s was emphasis on "democratic administration." Books and many articles were written to extol the virtues of the *democratic organization.* Noble as the attempts to democratize education were, progress in abandoning bureaucratic orga-

---

[2]See, for example, Warren G. Bennis, *Changing Organizations* (New York: McGraw-Hill, 1966); Victor A. Thompson, *Modern Organization* (New York: Knopf, 1961); Chris Argyris, *Integrating the Individual and the Organization* (New York: John Wiley, 1964).

nizations was not fully realized. The movement did result in the abandonment of thoughtless, overbearing autocratic school principals, and teachers were given more autonomy in the educational process. Many school districts emphasized participative techniques, such as planning committees, task forces, workshops, and other means to encourage faculty and administrator participation. Since the 1960s collective bargaining has further pluralized the decision-making process, especially for those decisions concerning faculty welfare. Nevertheless, elements of the bureaucratic organization persist in education as they persist in commercial, industrial, public, and religious organizations of the nation.

Beginning in the 1970s, several writers described some organizations, particularly college and school organizations, as *loosely coupled* or *organized anarchies.* Loosely coupled organizations are characterized as having unclear goals, imprecisely understood technical processes of teaching and counseling, and loosely linked levels of authority in the hierarchy.[3] Moreover, rationality is issue-oriented (that is, what is rational for one issue is not rational for another), organizations are more pluralized than monolithic, levels of the hierarchy are more disjointed than tightly coupled, and the objectives are obscure. The result is semiautonomous schools, influenced minutely by the central office regime, and teachers influenced little by principals. Classrooms are relatively self-contained, shielded from formal influence of the community, district officials, and other teachers.

Decision making in the loosely coupled structure is described as a *garbage can* event in which there is "a collection of choices looking for problems, issues and feelings looking for decision situations in which they might be aired, solutions looking for issues to which they might be the answer, and decision makers looking for work."[4] According to proponents of this view, decision making in educational organizations is unlike the traditionally described step-by-step process of identifying the problem, collecting data, examining alternatives, and so on. Instead, it is an untidy process, the survival tactics of an organization caught in a confusion of purpose. Nevertheless, some theorists insist that the educational process should be loosely coupled.

> Some observers hold that the school is such an organization. Teachers, who are the primary operatives, function as highly trained and skilled directors of learning for the primary clients of the organization, the students....Schools that represent loosely coupled organization patterns demonstrate such

---

[3]Michael D. Cohen and James G. March, *Leadership and Ambiguity: The American College President* (New York: McGraw-Hill, 1974), pp. 1–25.

[4]Michael D. Cohen, James G. March, and Johan P. Olsen, "A Garbage Can Model of Organizational Choice," *Administrative Science Quarterly,* 17 (March 1972), 2.

characteristics as tolerance or a wide range of teaching styles, adaptability to local conditions, resistance to imposed change, and low levels of ability to mount concerted efforts, each contributing to an environment that encourages freedom and experimentation as well as individual responsibility.[5]

Evidence is not available in sufficient quantity to validate widespread existence of the loosely coupled system nor to support it as a valid alternative. Some educational organizations drift into a kind of "informal" or collegial regime; others opt for operating a "tight ship." Based on his analysis of colleges, Lutz questions whether loose coupling is an essential element in maintaining academic freedom.[6]

The loose coupling idea raises problems that have troubled authorities. A coupling problem exists in most school organizations; suggested remedies have been proposed. For example, Likert's linking-pin concept is one method to bring about more fully coupled systems.[7] Other strategies suggested are use of committees, task forces, teaching teams, and improved communication networks. In recognition of the problem of rational decision making, Simon is noted for his "satisficing model" in which the decision made is not ideal but "good enough."[8] Most experienced school administrators realize that they face making the most feasible decision within the existing restraints rather than the ideal decision. Ambiguity is, of course, a problem with all organizations, particularly with educational systems. Yet, as mentioned previously, despite all of the problems associated with its use, elements of the bureaucratic model persist throughout society and in education.

School principals can expect to practice within different versions of the bureaucratic organization, yet great variation from the ideal bureaucracy may exist. Some will be more monocratic, others more pluralistic, and still others may have some characteristics of loosely coupled systems. Nevertheless, one leadership task of the school principal is to achieve a leadership position in the politics of the bureaucracy, and that is the thrust of this chapter. The teachers and the staff have a right to expect the principal to represent them effectively in the politics of the bureaucracy, and this necessitates understanding the organization of the central office staff.

[5]William G. Monahan and Herbert R. Hengst, *Contemporary Educational Administration* (New York: Macmillan, 1982).

[6]Frank W. Lutz, "Tightening Up Loose Coupling in Organizations of Higher Education," *Administrative Science Quarterly*, 27 (December 1982), 653–69.

[7]Rensis Likert, *The Human Organization* (New York: McGraw-Hill, 1967), p. 167.

[8]Herbert A. Simon, *Administrative Behavior*, 2nd ed. (New York: Macmillan, 1957).

THE INFORMAL ORGANIZATION

The discussion to this point has been restricted to the formal organizational structure. School principals would be unwise to restrict their understanding of how the central office operates to the written description of the formal organization. If one studied in depth and described empirically the real organization of a school district and compared this with the organizational chart, the discrepancy between the formal and the real might be enormous. For example, most traditional structures employ the *line-and-staff* structure in which line officers give directives or issue orders and the staff officers serve the line officers (for example, they conduct research, provide technical assistance, advise, and provide other services). Yet every experienced school administrator knows that some staff officers may have more influence on how the organization functions than have some line officers. Formal structures are over time greatly distorted by informal organization.

> An administrative organization has an internal environment and an external environment that are largely nonrational, at least so far as the formal goals of the administrative organization are concerned. People do not come into administrative organizations as pieces of putty, as units of abstract energy, nor as mere tools sharpened to some technical or professional purpose. They bring with them their whole cultural conditioning and their personal idiosyncrasies. Each is genetically unique, and all are members of institutions—families, churches, clubs, unions, and so forth—outside the administrative organization; and within the administrative organization they form natural or adaptive groups of various kinds—friendships, cliques, car pools, and so forth—that flow across the lines of formal organization, sometimes darkening, sometimes lightening, and sometimes erasing these lines.[9]

Barnard identified as *informal organization* the informal interaction patterns of workers, such as friendship groups and cliques, that develop spontaneously and as a reaction to formal organization.[10] He pioneered the currently accepted view that informal group networks are necessary to make formal organizations function well.

> Informal groups play a significant role in the dynamics of organizational behavior. The major difference between formal and informal groups is that the formal group has officially prescribed goals and relationships, whereas the informal one does not. Despite this distinction, it is a mistake to think of formal and informal groups as two distinctly separate entities. The two types

[9]Dwight Waldo, *The Study of Public Administration* (New York: Random House, 1955), p. 13.

[10]Chester I. Barnard, *The Functions of the Executive* (Cambridge: Harvard University Press, 1938).

of groups coexist and are inseparable. Every formal organization has informal groups, and every informal organization eventually evolves some semblance of formal groups.[11]

How do formal and informal structures differ? The formal group or organization has a formally adopted and written constitution or bylaws, elected or appointed officers, a membership list, and regularly scheduled meetings guided by standard procedures. Examples of formal organizations abound in society—churches, school districts, civic organizations, businesses, professional groups, and public organizations. An informal organization (or group) has a structure of interpersonal relations, behavioral norms, a leadership hierarchy, purposes, and a leadership and action structure that, if formalized, would not be that different from the formal structure. However, its structure remains informal; for example, who ever heard an announcement that someone had been appointed president, secretary, or treasurer of a faculty clique?

Yet the power groups of informal organizations have immediate and lasting influence upon the nature of formal organizations. Some revealing studies of these structures were conducted during the late 1950s and early 1960s.[12] The results of these studies revealed well-structured subsystems of the faculty that were not temporary as organizational traditionalists had believed; in fact, some of the informal groups had transcended several administrations. The leaders and followers of these subsystems engaged in many activities together both in and outside the school. More significantly, the leaders in the informal organization were not just reacting to the formal structure; they were vitally interested in and initiating strategies to influence school policy.

> Certain groups of teachers with common beliefs concerning school issues consciously banded together and recognized informal leadership among their own ranks....These informal groupings not only recognized issues but their common points of view were focused around the major issues. When members of stable informal groupings heard teachers who were not members expressing similar points of view, other things being equal, such teachers were considered as potential new members.
> It was from this common point of view that stable informal groupings took action. If they disagreed with or were dissatisfied with formal policy, or

[11]Fred Luthans, *Organizational Behavior,* 4th ed. (New York: McGraw-Hill, 1985), p. 373.

[12]See Laurence Iannaccone, "The Social System of a School Staff" (doctoral dissertation, Teachers College, Columbia University, 1958); John N. Fleming, "An Analysis and Comparison of the Decision-Making Process in Two School Faculties" (doctoral dissertation, University of Florida, 1963).

leadership, they resorted to a number of different tactics designed to modify, change, or circumvent whatever they held in disfavor.[13]

In the years following these studies, attitudes toward cliques and other manifestations of informal organizations changed radically. The change is well expressed in the quotation given previously from Luthans. The idea that informal organization was an essential part of formal structure (in actually assisting formal structure function at higher efficiency and effectiveness) can be traced to Barnard's 1938 publication.[14] Of special significance is that some leaders in the informal structure of individual schools are closely linked with higher-ups in the central office; moreover, some of the leaders have important ties with very powerful leaders in the community power structure.

The key question is not how informal organization can be eliminated to make formal structure efficient and effective, but rather how the two can be meshed, merged, or intertwined to promote schools of quality. The first step in this process is for the principal to comprehend what we have referenced herein, the *central office regime*. The central office regime, which includes the individual schools in the school district under the central office staff, is the complex control mechanism for the school system. Principals must first understand how this exceedingly complex system functions in decision making, operation, and other functions in the administration of school programs. They must acquire power in this regime or see the schools they administer deprived of resources needed in the educational program. Secondly, resourceful leadership in the regime is clearly an obligation of the principal, and is referred to as the politics of the bureaucracy. Strategies in this process will be discussed subsequently; however, the discussion will now be focused on understanding regimes.

CENTRAL OFFICE REGIMES

In the complex interaction of formal and informal structures and, in turn, their interaction with school board members and groups in the environment of the school system, a complex social system, or central office regime, develops. Regimes vary greatly among the school systems of the nation.

How Regimes Develop

The prevailing practice in the school districts of the nation is to use bureaucratic ideas in structuring the formal organization. As this rationally prescribed model is employed under the leadership of the central

[13]Fleming, "Decision-Making Process," pp. 160–61.
[14]Barnard, *Functions of the Executive.*

administrative offices of the school district, "irrational" behavior forces structural compromises that bend the ideal structure out of proportion. As a result, one could not read the formal descriptions of an organization and predict with much accuracy the standard operating procedures in the district. For example, authority in a bureaucratic structure is based on legal and rational grounds—if you hold an office, you are clothed with a certain legal and rational authority that is not affected by informal group activity. Yet we know for certain that power in an organization is not restricted to those holding official positions. Even in the armed services, where there is great emphasis on bureaucratic authority, the staff officer can sometimes have extraordinary influence with the commanding general. Associate superintendents, directors, and supervisors in the central office engage in empire building; in fact, this becomes a passionate pastime in some organizations, and from these encounters some strange divisions of function appear in practice. The structure is further distorted by accommodations to environmental inputs.

Those at the top of the command, including the superintendent of schools, assistant superintendents, and other top officials, react in numerous ways to the leaching away of rational structure. Their aim is usually to try to retain some semblance of the bureaucracy. Yet even the most thoroughly bureaucratized mind must cope, sometimes for survival. The result is the development of a regime the likes of which is neither consciously intended by the participants nor recommended by the organizational specialists.

The crux of the discussion here is that if school principals are to achieve positions of leadership in school districts, they must comprehend the central office regime as a basis for using successful leadership strategies. What is the characteristic nature of the regime? Who are the persons having the power of decision in the regime? What are the dynamics of the system's decision making? To assist in this process, let us consider some illustrative examples of central office regimes.

The Traditional Paternalistic Regime

The paternalistic or maternalistic central office regime has been passing from the American scene and may, except for provincial or closed communities, become extinct. Nevertheless, paternalism is still found among school districts. Charisma, clothed in certain Freudian principles, is the foundation of paternalistic central office regimes. The superintendent of schools usually serves as the father or mother figure. Personal loyalty to the leaders is emphasized and highly valued. The faculty and administration are expected to be a family of professionals and to abide by strict rules of conduct, one of which is to honor the person holding the highest office. Typically, in the more blatant patriarchies of the past the rules were made to suit the situation when, as often expressed, the administrators "flew by the seats of their pants." However, such administrators are considered anachronisms in most circles today and have been replaced by very suave, urbane persons who are sophisticated in how to win over people, or by the persons supremely skilled in processes of Machiavellianism.

The superintendent must be a "good guy"; therefore, someone must play the villain role of wielding the hatchet. The so-called hatchet men perform the dirty work for the kindly head of the family. The head of the family can be sympathetic to those who have been denied by the person wielding the hatchet, which adds to the good guy image. Thus, the kindly head of the family remains unscathed by dismissals, denials of promotions, and denials of resources. The hatchet man gets the blame; interestingly, there are many persons who enjoy the villain role and are very good at it. They can use legal opinions, laws, policies, and other ways to make their actions appear impersonal.

Those top officials in the Machiavellian mold rule by suave political processes; for example, control of resources valued by administrators, teachers, and noncertificated staff. As one teacher observed in talking about a skilled superintendent, "He sleeps with a copy of *The Prince* under his pillow." Another type of patriarch comes from the sophist mold, an urbane type who is very diplomatic and polished in establishing relations with people. Being of the sophist mold these persons are not as interested in the validity of decisions as in winning people over to their point of view. A brief description will now be given of a sophist regime.

Thomas J. Stearns has served for almost two decades as superintendent of Elmtown school district. Stearns is a very engaging, mannerly person revered by the citizens as the best schoolman in the state, diligent in attention to detail and generally progressive toward school and community improvement. As one teacher expressed, "Mr. Stearns is a professional's professional."

Several underlings in Stearns' central office perform significant roles in making things go. George Livesay, his deputy superintendent, functions in numerous ways to keep the system operating with minimum disturbance; he is known as Stearns' "man Friday." The instructional supervisors are a helpful sophisticated group. Thomas Bowls, the business manager, is a past master at controlling the purse strings. He is known throughout the system as the *No* man of the system. He has a command of rules, regulations, laws, attorney generals' opinions, and budgetary allocations, and the mastery of technical language necessary to squelch any proposal not favored by the upper levels of the organization. Even though they are regarded as a negative influence, Bowls's actions seldom reflect on the popularity of Superintendent Stearns.

The Elmtown regime is a paternalistic system. Authors have dealt harshly with this system in terms of what they interpret as its undemocratic nature. Yet when one looks beneath the outward expressions of the system, it is not a tyrannical dictatorship. Although Thomas Stearns is the head of the family, he is as much a captive of the system as he is its father figure—as much its servant as its leader. The regime is held together by a complex mix of sentiments, norms, informal friendship groups, and understanding relationships that flow through the formal and informal organizations. Within the informal organization are members of the faculty and administrators who have great influence both within the system and in the community, and any policy needs support of these leaders to prevent convulsing the system. Participation in decisions is best expressed as an elite process; only those who have risen to top leadership positions in the informal and formal structure participate. Collective negotiation is viewed as a challenge to the system; however, through the years it has come to be accepted as an unwanted "family squabble" that raises tensions until they are settled in a way that leaves administrative prerogatives intact, but that also adds to the prestige of the union leaders. The emphasis upon warm personal relationships provides feelings of security; however, security is in people rather than in ideas. Morale is high and there is low teacher turnover. Promotion to leadership positions is slow and occurs only after aspirants prove that they accept the norms of the system.

What creates a paternalistic regime? In most cases the regime simply evolves; it may or may not be the result of a calculated strategy. In all probability it just drifts into existence, where persons start with the hierarchical, bureaucratic model and over time find a comfortable merger with informal organization that "works." The paternalistic model works for the district because formal structure is bent enough to contain manifestations of illegitimate behavior.

Bureaucratic Regimes

Unlike the informal personal appeals for control of irrational behavior in the paternalistic regime, the bureaucratic regime represents a rational attempt to control behavior through the proliferation of formal rules and regulations. Great energy is invested by school administrators to protect the formal structure from the casualness of informal structure. The resulting rigidity of formal structure does not dispel informal organization; however, the personal dimension is forced to make accommodation to formal structure, producing the type of person that Whyte popularized as the organization man.[15] Moreover, the administrative investment in structural maintenance activities often results in what authorities refer to as goal displacement, a condition in which the administrators lose sight of the real purpose to educate and expend most of their energy in organizational maintenance activities—mindless pursuit of keeping everything in place.

Administrators within bureaucratic regimes have an insatiable appetite for specific policies, rules, plans, and procedures designed to fit every conceivable condition and to routinize operations. The flow of formal communication from top to bottom is immense and is supplemented by an endless variety of workshops, conferences, institutes, committees, and meetings to support the system. Numerous consultants are employed to assist the principals and teachers, and there is close supervision of every function. The sheer enormity of these processes in some regimes results in a kind of conditioned impersonality not conducive to creative thinking or innovation. The decision-making process is not well understood by members of the faculty.

Presthus' analysis indicated that there were three primary accommodations to the bureaucratic regime, upward-mobiles, indifferents, and ambivalents.[16] The upward-mobiles, the organization men, thirst for power and authority and are able to synthesize personal and organizational objectives. The upward-mobiles thrive in the bureaucratic regime and perceive of higher officials as role models.

On the other hand, the indifferents, who do not desire power and authority, withdraw and find ego satisfaction in community activities outside the organization. For example, on practically every school faculty will be one or more persons who have no leadership ambition. They come to work, do their job, but keep the formal and informal activities of the faculty at arms length—they have a let-me-alone-to-do-my-job attitude.

Those who desire participation in decisions but are unable to synthesize organizational and personal goals become ambivalents. These dissidents are a "thorn in the side" of administrators. As a consequence, the ambivalent becomes a source of conflict in pressing for personal need objectives and demanding organizational change. They are easily recruited into activities opposed to the administration; from this group were recruited those who played the leadership roles to organize faculty unions during the 1950s and 1960s. Ambivalents disturb the equilibrium of the organization.

The Bay City School System serves as a good illustration of the bureaucratic regime. Paul Folsom, the popular, efficient "whiz superintendent" of Bay City, is considered to be one of the outstanding administrators

---

[15]William H. Whyte, *The Organization Man* (New York: Simon & Schuster, 1956).

[16]Robert Presthus, *The Organization Society* (New York: Knopf, 1962).

in the nation. His name is prominently mentioned in national circles, and he has served on national study groups and commissions. The system he heads is led by specialists in subject areas, administrative services, public relations, and business affairs. His aim is to have a well-organized system that is interlocked to work together like the gears in an automobile transmission.

Throughout the years Folsom has achieved an understanding with Mike Boggs, the executive secretary of the teachers' union. As Mike expressed it, "We are both leaders of an organization and understand each other."

New teachers and noncertificated employees are provided orientation material and meetings explaining operational procedures. Well-defined courses of study for all subject areas are provided. Each teacher is provided an attractively printed copy of the school board policies and a handbook containing school system operational procedures. An air of the superiority of The Bay City Plan pervades all discussions. At a recent meeting of the board of education, a citizen appeared to ask critical questions about the teaching of reading in the schools of Bay City. Dr. Folsom suggested that the board hear an explanation of the reading program from the supervisor. Upon the request of the board chairman, the supervisor of reading gave a rather involved description interspersed with technical terms concerning the teaching of reading. At the close of her statement Dr. Folsom observed, "Now, ladies and gentlemen, you see that we probably have the best reading program in the United States." No further discussion ensued.

A flow of communication downward, made up of memoranda, directives, and telecommunications, is constant; however, communication upward is more restricted. Experienced principals report that getting accurate information to the officials at the top is complicated because messages become increasingly distorted as they move through the hierarchy, and responsiveness is slow.

Those teachers critical of administrators (ambivalents) express a dislike for the way promotions are awarded to the "goody two-shoes" (the upward-mobiles). Grumbling about favoritism and cronyism is expressed. Several of the faculty and staff are apathetic (indifferents), and these, added to the upward-mobiles, leave those who express criticism a minority segment.

The Bay City system is a centralized operation, and the principals frequently feel pressured to follow directives that are not popular with the faculty, which results in suave posturing and Machiavellian strategies by principals to, as one expressed it, "keep the lid on." An inordinate amount of the principals' energy is invested in system maintenance or in trying to make things work. As a result, individual schools have little autonomy and principals can invest little time in instructional leadership.

Decentralized Regimes

Many practitioners have been dissatisfied with the dysfunctional aspects of the traditional bureaucratic structure, such as the tendency toward overspecialization, a many-layered chain of command, the proliferation of silly rules that lead to obstructive red tape, and an organization out of the control of the people. Therefore, much effort has been invested in finding an alternative structure. One approach is to decentralize or develop a flat structure to replace the traditionally tall organization. The *flat structure* is based on much delegation of authority, fewer hierarchies, short lines of communication, and more decisions made at the point of operations. Decentralization of control and operations is thought to be a means to break up centralized control and induce greater structural efficiency.

There are two major approaches to decentralization, the territorial approach and the functional basis. In the *territorial* approach, decentralization of control over the schools is based on a geographic area. For example, during the 1960s very large city school systems like New York City and Detroit decentralized the governance and control through the creation of regional boards and administrative offices. Most school districts above 75,000 student enrollment have some form of regional or area superintendents. In the area superintendent structure, principals usually are directly under the area superintendent in the chain of command.

Another approach to decentralization is on a *functional* basis. In this approach the decentralization is based on administrative function. An example would be to decentralize the personnel function so that school principals would exercise greater control over the recruitment and employment of teachers and other school personnel.

The *school-based management* approach employed in some school systems is an attempt to decentralize on both functional and territorial grounds. The objective is to, within school board and state policies, give the school principal complete managerial control of school functions, including authority over the budget, curriculum, assignment of personnel, and so on. The object is to fix accountability with the school principal for the education of children and youth. The central office becomes an information-gathering service agency of the school district.

In 1979 the board of education for the Bradbury School System, somewhat frustrated with their struggle to achieve high quality in the schools, decided to abandon centralized control and adopt school-based management. The decision was based on a two-year study of a special task force appointed by Superintendent Burton Young. Principals and central staff officials were given a full year to prepare for the change. School principals in the district were told that student achievement in each school was to match or exceed grade level on a standardized achievement test.

Principals were given an allocation of money to spend in any way that they and their faculty decided; there were no strings attached except that state law could not be violated and the citizens in the school community, especially parents, had to be reasonably satisfied with the school. Under this system the principal was accountable for the educational enterprise.

Needless to say, this was a radical change from living under a centralized bureaucracy. William Benson, the principal of East High School, was delighted with the opportunity to involve the faculty and community in a revamping of the curriculum. Within a year the decision had been made to reduce traditional vocational subjects such as the teaching of drafting, which Benson insisted was being taken over by computers. As he expressed, "We've got to move away from the skill-indus-trial-intensive subjects to the information-intensive approach." Funds previously expended in traditional industrial subjects were diverted to put heavy emphasis upon the study of computer-based systems. These changes required greater emphasis upon the basics, such as science, mathematics, and communication. Within five years East High School became the showcase innovative school of the Bradbury School System.

Yet, as Superintendent Young recently noted, about a third of the principals could not handle the freedom. These principals could not adjust to the lack of direction from the central office. As Dr. Young expressed, "They were the ones who previously used the central office as a crutch and as a convenient scapegoat if things went sour at their schools. They realized that under the new policy the buck stopped at the door of the principal." Continuing with his observation Dr. Young said, "We also had great problems with people in the central office who found that they no longer had the authority to boss people around." Under the new policy the formal structure required that central office personnel perform information-gathering duties, service, and assistance on the demand of principals. Several of the top people were, as Dr. Young put it, "lost in the power vacuum."

Although the informal organization of the district had always been fragmented into cliques of interests, it changed under the new policy into two solidified groups, one much against the school-based management system and the other group, identified as "the Superintendent's crowd," heavily in favor of the change. Both of these groups had allies among parents and other citizens and with groups outside the district. For example, professors at the nearby state university were frequently quoted, some for and some against the movement, as were officials at the state Department of Education. One former management professor, referred to by Dr. Young as a "senile old man," wrote letter after letter to the editor of the newspaper against what he referred to as "anarchy in the school system." His letters usually stimulated other citizens to write for and against the change, which kept the pot boiling to the point that two of the board members were, as Dr. Young expressed, "becoming nervous about the change because they were coming up for reelection."

Within six years after its initiation, school-based management was teetering toward the brink of disaster; moreover, Dr. Young reportedly was offered a high position in the U. S. Department of Education. Leaders in the informal structure of the school district, including school personnel and their friends in the community, were gearing up to secure the appointment of a superintendent favorable to greater centralization of control of the schools in the district.

Emphasis on Participative Management

Many authorities have expressed the need for participative management for the administration of schools, a concept that was very popular during the human-relations movement in the 1950s. The movement, further stimulated by the teacher militancy movement and the beginning of widespread collective bargaining, changed many regimes that were patterned after the bureaucratic structure. Some school districts began to practice genuine faculty, administrator, and staff participation in the decision-making process. Teacher and administrator participation through task forces, committees, team teaching, and other cooperative arrangements helped "democratize" school operation. Much interest has been expressed in differentiated staffing as a means of encouraging greater faculty participation. As a result school organizations in some school districts moved toward collegial relations; nevertheless, the authors are not aware of fully developed collegial regimes at the school-district level. We have observed collegial regimes in the operation of some individual schools and colleges.

Administrators within the collegial regime foster a feeling of egalitarianism among the faculty. Teachers feel that the administration is responsive to their feelings and that they are participants in deciding about the destiny of the enterprise. The system is kept in balance by the norms and conformity patterns created through the interaction of the leaders and followers of subsystems in the organization. Furthermore, there is a commitment to a system of ideas concerning what educating is all about rather than to the charisma of leaders or to the rulebook of a traditional bureaucracy. The collegial regime is a self-actualizing, adaptable system in which the organizational requirements are integrated with faculty need dispositions. Constructive dissent is encouraged in the interest of innovation. Communication moves freely. Although rules and regulations are present, the proliferation of restrictive rules is kept to a minimum.

The principal and faculty of Southside Middle School have operated within the collegial organization for ten years. When a school decision has to be made, Mr. Ted Alfred, the principal, refers it to the faculty. For example, an issue of promotion criteria arose last year. A member of the faculty observed that "During our faculty meeting, Mr. Alfred presented the problem, talked about it a while, and then leaned back in his chair and said in a relaxed manner, 'Well, what do you want to do about it?'" Following this, the faculty engaged in a lively debate in which all facets of the issue were vented. The discussion continued for several faculty meetings until a decision approaching a general consensus had developed.

Three years ago the board of education approved a pilot differentiated staffing project at Southside. Under this arrangement teachers achieve different ranks, through which authority for the instructional program might be shared. Resistance to the arrangement by the teachers' union has made its future tenuous. Leaders in the union are opposed to the career-ladder feature built into the continuation of the pilot project.

The Southside school faculty is not held together by the glue of a charismatic father figure or by legal/rational authority, but by the commitment of the faculty and administration to decisions cooperatively developed. Southside is an open system in which communication is transmitted with minimum distortion. Innovation is encouraged; the principal and members of the faculty are not hostage to demoralizing red tape, rigid standards of behavior, or bossism.

Is a Contingency Concept Viable?

The regimes discussed here are certainly not the only types that principals will experience. Since there are so many variables involved in the development of any management regime, much variation exists among school districts. The systems of control represent each district's way of doing things, which leads us to the consideration of the contingency theory referred to previously.

> There is little likelihood that the hope, nurtured for many years among students of administration, of discovering a set of related concepts that will lead us to the one best way of organizing, leading, motivating, and administering will be realized in the near future. Many variables seem to create contextual settings that preclude applying overly broad generalizations. One of the powerful emerging ideas in understanding organizations and the behavior of people in them is the notion of *contingency*.[17]

Contingency or situational theory is currently becoming a popular concept in the field of management and is considered to be a logical extension of systems theory. The basic idea is that there is no one univer-

[17]Robert G. Owens, *Organizational Behavior in Education,* 3rd ed. (Englewood Cliffs, N.J.: Prentice-Hall, 1987), pp. 30–31.

sally effective management style for all situations. Effective organizational structure and management practice in one school district may fail in another district. Therefore, the most effective form of management of school districts depends upon the situation and the mix of the existing conditions with management style, structure, and technology.

POLITICS OF THE BUREAUCRACY

The school principal needs to accumulate influence in the existing regime, which involves the politics of the bureaucracy. A first step in achieving power and influence is to study and conceptualize the power relationships in the organization.

Through personal observation, discussions with colleagues, and interaction with the upper levels of power in the system, much information can be collected that can be supplemented with documentary materials such as handbooks and board policy manuals. As information about the regime becomes saturated—meaning nothing new is learned from observations, discussion, and documents—the principal is ready to answer: (1) Who are the power wielders? (2) Through what processes is leadership exercised in making decisions? (3) What major formal and informal groups have influence? (4) How does the regime fit into the types discussed in this chapter?

The process of achieving power in organizations is the subject of many publications. For example, some persons claim that the way one dresses can contribute to promotion. Mintzberg suggests that organizational power accrues from control over critical resources, such as technical skill, knowledge and information, and resources needed for survival in the organization.[18] Official position, for example, does clothe one with legal/rational power that can be telescoped with certain personal resources that one controls. Illustrative resources that might be used, such as leadership skill, expertise, friendship ties, and access to those with power, are discussed in Chapters 6 and 7. Also emphasized in those chapters is using power resources within the expectations or norms of leadership and performance that legitimize the individual in the system.

In summary, to be an effective leader for the school, one must obtain and effectively use influence in the central office regime, which is not unrelated to the process of leadership in the community political system, which is the subject of Chapter 6.

---

[18]Henry Mintzberg, *Power in and Around Organizations* (Englewood Cliffs, N.J.: Prentice-Hall, 1983).

CHAPTER SIX

Community Leadership for Better School and Community Relations

The traditional doctrine of the separation of administration from politics all but disappeared in acceptance during the late 1940s and 1950s. In 1949, for example, Appleby described an intermingling of politics and administration, and by 1955 Waldo reported that the dogmatic attempts to separate the two were "almost wholly abandoned."[1] Studies since the early 1950s have shown that schools do not exist in a political vacuum; the prevailing opinion is that educational leaders should be adept at political leadership. Moreover, this opinion dictates that the school leader should see that an effective home-school partnership in the education process is developed. Thus the principal, or the person so designated by the principal, must mount strategies to establish good school-community relations, traditionally labeled public relations.

This chapter describes how to understand the community political process and how this understanding can be used to establish desirable public and school relations. A discussion is included on the personal approach to school and community relations and the use of publicity as a

[1]Paul Appleby, *Policy and Administration* (Tuscaloosa: University of Alabama Press, 1949), pp. 6–10; Dwight Waldo, *The Study of Public Administration* (New York: Random House, 1955), p. 40.

means of communicating information about the school. We believe that the principal is accountable for the development and maintenance of cooperative relations between the school and its immediate constituency.

From the systems point of view, the political structure of the community is the suprasystem of the central office regime and of the school. If educators are to provide leadership for better schools, they must understand this political process. Consequently, our discussion will begin with the political system and proceed to a consideration of the school and community-relations program.

THE PRINCIPAL IN THE POLITICAL ARENA

As discussed previously, before the 1950s educators accepted the doctrine that politics should be separated from administration. Educators often lamented that a pet school project failed because "it got mixed up in politics." Why did educators accept the proposition that the operation of schools should be separated from politics? This idea was sparked early in the 1900s by the muckraking exposés of some powerful journalists (such as Ida M. Tarbell, Thomas W. Lawson, Upton Sinclair, Ray S. Baker, David G. Phillips). The shocking exposés of these writers unveiled the startling facts of just how much certain "robber barons" controlling big oil, steel, rail, aluminum, and financial interests had control of the political processes in the United States. The authors also took aim at the sleaziness of politics, particularly at political bossism in the big cities. Their efforts initiated a broadly based governmental reform movement to separate the management of government from politics. The model school government, for example, elected the school board at special nonpartisan elections and appointed a professionally trained executive, the superintendent of schools. The policy-making process was separated from the administration of policy.

The leaders in the governmental reform movement viewed politics as a repugnant game played for keeps by selfish businessmen and self-aggrandizing, cigar-smoking, pot-bellied politicians. Thus, politics was bad. No self-respecting educational leader would admit to engaging in it. Yet, as discussed previously, few educators today would embrace the idea that school administrators are, or should be, free of participation in the educational policy-making process. When viewed in its proper role, politics is the democratic process of making significant decisions concerning public policy, including educational policy. The school principal who exercises educational leadership to improve the process of education for children and youth is inevitably involved in educational policy decisions. Even the principal who disdains politics will inevitably be drawn into it. For example, action to dismiss an incompetent teacher or to discipline a difficult student often unleashes political forces involving the principal.

Should the principal remain free of politics, even if such were possible? The answer to this question lies in whether the principal wishes to become a jellyfish, accepting any and all policies regardless of their consequences for students, or to have a part in influencing the quality of education in the school district. If the principal answers affirmatively to the first alternative, then one might rightfully ask why we need a school principal at all. Persons of relatively low training and talents can perform routine management functions. The authors reject the free-floating style of the jellyfish; principals must use their expertise to improve the operation of schools. The citizens of the community should not be deprived of the expertise of school principals in the consideration of policies for the operation of schools. Finally, principals are called upon to cope effectively with the politics of the bureaucracy or the central office regime, which was discussed at length in Chapter 5. Again, the person who exerts leadership in improving the school cannot, and should not, avoid political leadership.

Before leaving this discussion, the authors want to emphasize that we are not encouraging participation in the brand of politics that results in unethical behavior. The educational politician must at all times behave in a responsible manner that is above reproach. Unfortunately, the politics of some school districts is a sleazy process. The principal who becomes involved in this element of politics will fail the children and youth of the community. Educational leaders must never succumb to political behavior that compromises principles of professional ethics or moral behavior.

THE COMMUNITY POLITICAL PROCESS

To understand politics in the community, one must ask three important questions: (1) Who are the persons and groups that have power to influence policy concerning "what kind of town this should be"? (2) How do these persons and groups behave in the decision-making process? (What are the dynamics of the process in which community policy is established?) (3) Why, or through what beliefs or ideology, do the leaders favor this type of community (or policies)? The public schools are, of course, a vital part of any policy concerning community life; therefore, educational policy is of supreme importance to the education of children and youth as well as to the future of the community. The development of the educational program is essential if community leaders are to improve the standard of living of the school district. All attempts of leaders to improve the economic base of the district impact the educational system and, conversely, are dependent upon the quality of the school program.

Exercise of Power in the Community

The power to decide what kind of schools and community most of the people desire is unequally distributed among the citizens of a school district. Ideally, principals may feel that all of the parents of children in the school should have equal power, but the desire does not make it reality. Power to influence educational policy accrues from the perceived control of resources that people value and the legitimation of persons to use these resources as leaders. Some illustrations of these resources are wealth or the control of wealth, official position, expertise, control of credit, control of votes, leadership skills, charisma, popularity, control of jobs, kinship ties, friendship ties, personal attractiveness, control of the media, and so on. The list is long because anything material or nonmaterial that is perceived to be controlled by a leader will add to that leader's power. There are, however, constraints on how these perceived resources are used to influence others, and this involves the legitimation of the leader. If the richest woman in the community attempts to use her resources in a way that violates the critical norms of the community, she will not achieve a high power position in the existing system. She does not achieve legitimation to use her resources because she violated some of the critical norms of the power structure.

An alternative to achieving power and influence in the existing system is to displace it with a revolutionary strategy. If the educators and their friends believe that the system is preventing the development of good schools, revolution becomes a viable option to consider. Educators and their friends have successfully managed coups in some school districts with results beneficial to schools and other community agencies. On the other hand, outright attempts to overthrow the power structure frequently fail, with results not conducive to the tenure of top school administrators. Certainly the principal acting alone stands little chance of creating a revolution of the political system. Therefore, the best approach to moving the system is to obtain enough power within it to bring about a change in the existing policies.

The way in which power is accumulated can be observed among members of the school faculty. Consider as an example the renowned English teacher in her thirtieth year as a teacher in the same school. She has taught many of the parents of students now enrolled in the school (friendship ties), she is believed to be the best English teacher alive (expertise), she is from a prominent family (kinship ties), and she is president of the League of Women Voters (position), among other resources. "If you have Mrs. Inge in English, you will not have any trouble with English in college," is an opinion often expressed among parents. She is one of the most highly respected (legitimized) persons in the community. To assume that this teacher's power to participate in decisions is equal to a beginning English teacher's may be ideally correct but empirically inaccurate. Thus, as someone has expressed, although all people are equal, some people are more equal than others.

In the political arena of the school district are leaders and followers who assume unique roles. Some leaders rise to the top in influence and have a preoccupation with policy matters. Below those leaders are persons who see that the system is maintained and that policies are carried out. Others are political functionaries concerned with party or interest-group maintenance. Some persons perform "gadfly" functions; others seek the thrill of participation and media recognition, and some seek personal gain. The dynamics of the process of governing must be understood, because within that process appear the normative expectations that one must observe to become legitimized. Leaders in the process hold *procedural norms,* which illustrate how a leader should attempt to influence the process. Anyone violating these leadership norms risks loss of credibility and, if the incursions upon these expectations are capricious, the result is loss of influence and power. As discussed in Chapter 5, the political process of school districts is a mix of formal and informal group processes.

The Motivation of Community Leaders. The school principal must try to gauge the motivation of leaders in the political process. Ideology is a powerful motivator. Schools have been the object of liberal versus conservative battles involving the textbooks used in school, subjects taught, financial policy, library holdings, and so on. Litigation and political struggles for control of schools usually involve politico-religious ideology. The conflict between fundamentalist religious groups and other citizens with moderate-to-liberal ideologies is illustrative. The fundamentalists complain that some textbooks place too much emphasis upon secular humanism. When combined with religion, political beliefs can ignite a community conflict that can inflict great emotional pain on the principal and faculty. Consequently, persons aspiring to be principal must be conversant with political ideology and the function of religion in the society. A person who is completely ignorant of theology and political ideology will not understand the most basic institutions of the culture.

Not to be overlooked is self-interest as a motivator for political action. Everyone is probably guilty of being tempted by self-interest; in fact, self-interest has ideological defenders under the blanket of ethical egoism.[2] Moreover, some scholars have called attention to the situation in which projects supported by community leaders from an ideological perspective may also be consistent with their interests. In summary, educational

[2]Ayn Rand, *The Virtue of Selfishness: A New Concept of Egoism* (New York: New American Library, 1964).

leaders should pay attention to the expressed motivations of leaders to understand better the political process in the community.

The term *community power structure* has several meanings. To some it refers to a behind-the-scenes political clique, and, when it has this connotation, power structure conjures up negative thoughts of bossism and undemocratic behavior. Yet power structure also refers to the relative distribution of power among the citizens, officials, and groups in the school district to set community and educational policy. All of the people, whether they like it or not, are part of the power structure of the community in which they live. An established power structure through which community policy is established is essential; otherwise, the people are subjected to a dangerous anarchy in which the immediate future is unpredictable and very likely dangerous. The proper question is not whether we have a power structure but what kind of structure exists. Through research conducted since the early 1950s, at least four types of power structures have been identified.

The Pluralistic Power Structure. The pluralistic structure is believed to be consistent with an ideal concept of democratic thought. Some characteristics of pluralism are evident: (1) elected and appointed public officials have the most power in the establishment of community policy, including educational policy; (2) competition is waged among persons and groups concerning what kind of community they should have and, concurrently, what kind of schools they should have; (3) a high percentage of the citizens participate effectively in the political process—little apathy exists; (4) public elections are viable processes for establishing community and educational policies; and (5) the decision-making process is conducted according to a democratic creed. If there is no domination of the structure by one power bloc and the other conditions just enumerated apply, the community is governed by a pluralistic power structure that has a high degree of openness. Yet, based on research to date, pluralistic structures do not exist in numbers greater than the other types of structures described in this section.

The Competitive Elite Structure. If the school district is in the midst of a power struggle involving two or more groups about what kind of town and schools to develop and much citizen apathy exists, one may characterize the structure as *competitive elite.* In such a structure group power is wielded by elites. Yet a hard-fought power struggle is in progress among these elite groups, and regime issues are present concerning "what kind of town this is going to be." Districts so characterized are usually in the process of revolution and the changing of public policy, and very sharp differences in political ideology (or concepts of the "good community life") are apparent. Inevitably the issues involve "the good school" and very probably "the good school principal" and passionate feelings are usually expressed.

The Multigroup Noncompetitive Structure. High consensus about community policy or "what kind of town we want" is an indelible characteristic of the *multigroup noncompetitive* power structure. Two or more elite-run power groups exist in the school district; however, competition is restricted to economic advantage (for example, competing for construction, repair, service, and supply contracts with public and private agencies). Regime issues concerning policy, characteristic of the competitive elite structure, seldom surface. Competition between candidates for election to public office usually involves popularity contests rather than whether one or the other candidate seeks policy changes. For example, candidates for the city council and board of education usually emphasize personal qualifications, such as their family situation, number of children in school, military service in defense of the nation, church membership, and record of community service. One community, a high socioeconomic level suburban school district, recently interviewed for a new school superintendent. A candidate for the position reported that he interviewed with the board and at one point asked what changes or developments the board had in mind for the schools. He was told, with concurrence by every member present, that the board and community were pleased with the schools and did not desire any changes whatsoever.

Monopolistic Power Structures. The *monopolistic* structure is dominated by a single group of elites. The structure may be a political machine, a single-industry town, a powerful group of commercial, financial, or industrial tycoons, or any number of combinations of groups or persons who gain enough influence to dominate policy in the school district for two consecutive elections. Much citizen apathy and latent power (people with resources to influence who do not choose to use them) characterize the power structure. Citizen participation and elections are not viable processes. Any groups considering opposition to the elite leaders at the top of the structure usually go along with decisions as a matter of personal interest. A spirit of paternalism may characterize some structures, but there is always the possibility that coercion will be employed. On the other hand, monopolistic structures may be progressive, public-minded, and exhibit some spirit of altruism. For example, Hunter's study showed that Atlanta was dominated for many years by a behind-the-scenes group of economic elites.[3] Yet these leaders were progressive in economic development, supported cultural affairs, and have, since his study, demonstrated

[3]Floyd Hunter, *Community Power Structure* (Chapel Hill: University of North Carolina Press, 1953).

acceptance of better race relations. On the other hand, there is always the possibility that a mean-spirited motive may prevail or even the domination of a school district by a criminal element.

Principals will not have as much contact as the superintendent with the most powerful leaders of the school district, but they will interact with some of them; in fact, some of the most powerful leaders will probably reside in the attendance area of the school. Therefore, every principal should conceptualize the power structure of the district; otherwise, wisdom may not prevail in the leadership of the school. These leaders can be very helpful in the development of good community and school relations.

Studying the Power Structure. Practicing educational administrators have demonstrated ability to understand the power structure. Nunnery and Kimbrough presented some practical, informal steps that a principal can use to conceptualize the political structure.[4] Briefly, informal visits are made with leaders from different sectors of the community, such as business, politics, religion, the news media, and other areas of civic affairs. The leaders are encouraged to talk about who has the most influence in resolving community issues and to explain how these persons participate in the decision making process. Immediately after each conversation, everything one can recall that the leader said is recorded and filed. Every available source of documentary information about the leaders is reviewed, including data from the daily newspaper, and the relevant data are recorded and filed. These data are supplemented further by recording information from personal observation of leader behavior, based on the principal's participation in civic affairs. This process proceeds for several months until the saturation point is reached, which is where additional collection of information reveals nothing new. At this point the principal attempts to draft detailed answers to the questions: Who are the influential leaders? What are the dynamics of the policy making process? What is learned about the motivation of leaders and political groups? The information obtained must be updated as the leadership structure changes; one must continually be a student of the political process.

Participation in community activities provides knowledge of and access to those in the community who wield power. The principal should find ways to discuss who the leaders in other sectors of the community (such as news media, banking, law, business, general government, religion, and other areas) believe are the most influential persons in the structure. The key word is to *listen*. As other leaders discuss community problems,

[4]Michael Y. Nunnery and Ralph B. Kimbrough, *Politics, Power, Polls, and School Elections* (Berkeley: McCutchan Publishing Corporation, 1971), pp. 30–33.

who do they often mention and how much weight is given to them? What are the critical leadership norms of the structure?

The Support of Community Leaders. The support of leaders in the community power structure is a critical variable in educational development. A whisper from them about the school has greater influence upon public opinion than the shout from the rooftop of a follower. Who are the leaders among the parents of the school, and what is their relationship to the teaching staff? Who are the leaders among the student body? The answers to these questions are crucial in the event of school disturbances. For example, every school riot with which we are familiar was masterminded by neighborhood leaders and carried out by leaders among the students. In summary, knowledge of community processes for leadership and decision making is essential for school and community relations.

Keeping Up with Change

Political systems, even in communities with a high degree of closedness to inputs, are not static. All systems experience inputs. As discussed in Chapter 5, the closed or sacred communities resist inputs that might conflict with conditions, whereas open or secular communities accept inputs and make corrections in the ongoing operations. In all open and closed communities the inputs from the state, national, and even international realms create stress. The input of the federal government concerning racial integration in schools is a good illustration. In some school districts with a high degree of closedness, federal inputs (such as the courts and troops) caused stress to the point of almost destroying the system before change was realized.

Sometimes communities experience an overload of inputs; for example, the location of a huge defense installation in a rural area may result in the rapid influx of people with divergent backgrounds. If the inputs of newcomers are sufficient and if the newcomers are characteristically different from the indigenous population majority, change in the power structure is inevitable. Brevard County, Florida, experienced an overwhelming growth in population during the buildup of the Kennedy Space Center, as have rural school districts in which Strategic Air Command bases have been located. The result is very likely the development of system openness, change in governance, and revolutionary educational change.

The school principal must keep abreast of political change in the community and within the attendance area of the school. Studying the changing political structure is a never-ending task that forms the basis for maintaining leadership in the school and community.

THE SCHOOL AND COMMUNITY-RELATIONS PROGRAM

Establishing cooperative school and community relations is a complex task, but success in accomplishing this task is critical to the success of the school, not to speak of the uninterrupted tenure of the principal. Traditional public-relations programs emphasized unilateral communication of school information through the media, speeches to community organizations, printed materials distributed to parents, and other means of informing parents about the school program. Although these traditional means of communicating to external publics of the school are still a viable part of the school- and community-relations program, modern strategies also emphasize two-way communication and personal (or "flesh pressing") leadership techniques. We believe that the total process involves both the traditional publication of information and the currently popular personal leadership approach.

The principal and faculty of the individual school also have responsibilities within the public relations program of the board of education and central office. Also, school principals should draw upon the expertise of school and community relations specialists at the central office in the development of their individual strategies.

The establishment of excellent community-school relations begins with educational purpose. The purpose of the public relations program emanates from the policies and stated goals of the board of education. Knowledge of "what we are about" should undergird what we want to communicate to the external publics. The alternative to a public-relations program based on knowledge of purpose is mindlessness and the development of a credibility gap with the public.

The Personalized Process

Based on the purposes of the public-school relations program, the strategies used should be developed from empirical knowledge of the community. Included in this inventory of knowledge is the power structure, discussed previously, and the socioeconomic nature of the community. Of immediate concern in the present discussion is knowledge of the leadership and decision-making process of the school district and of the school attendance areas, which is especially critical because the support of the most influential leaders is essential for any school public-relations program. The leaders have many followers and their opinions readily become the opinions of those followers.

The principal's immediate task is to elicit the support and cooperative participation of members of the faculty and of the staff in the development of a school-community relations program. Enthusiasm must be exhibited for the program if the enthusiasm of the faculty is to be expected. One strategy would be to have a faculty committee on public relations develop ideas and strategies that can be presented to the entire faculty. Responsibility for the development and coordination of the program may be delegated; however, the personal leadership of the principal will be required. In any event, if it is to have maximum potential for success, the program must have the support and active participation of the faculty and staff of the school.

The support of students is also a key to success. If students believe that their school is bad or treats them shabbily, the most technically proficient public-relations techniques cannot change that image of the school among parents. Most polls of parents demonstrate that they obtain most of the information they have about the school from students. Therefore, in a sense good public relations begins within the school and depends on the perceived excellence of the school program. Some illustrative techniques for the personalized approach to school and community relations are included in this discussion.

Receiving Visitors and Telephone Calls at the School. The first impressions of persons contacting the school through personal visits or telephone calls may be lasting. Visitors to the school should observe attractive, clean, orderly school facilities, and should experience little difficulty finding the office, which should be the first contact of their first visit. Visitors should perceive a very attractive, well-organized, friendly, comfortable, and, above all, helpful atmosphere. All visitors should be treated with the utmost respect and dignity, even those who may be very irate who are there to complain. Returning to our original point, first impressions are powerful and very difficult to erase. If the visitor—for example, an influential newspaper editor—visits the school and observes a dirty school plant desperately in need of refurbishment, a dishevelled office, and other evidences of mismanagement, the first impression is administrative incompetency, lack of pride, and lack of quality.

All telephone calls received should be treated in a friendly, professional manner. Those answering the phone should be given thorough training and their behavior monitored regularly. They should speak distinctly, express friendliness, and be helpful. Some experts in the field warn against placing persons on hold for long periods of time. In essence, the caller should be given undivided attention and treated in a courteous manner, and this also applies to those who place irate calls.

Personal Visits with Community Leaders. Principals should seek discussions with the leaders of the parents, students, faculty, and other school and community groups. Visits to get acquainted and talk about the school serve to establish personal relationships with leaders, who communicate with followers. Establishing friendly relationships with the leaders enhances the personal leadership status of the principal. Community leaders are seldom visited by educators, yet in every program in which this approach is used the leaders appreciate the contacts. Leaders associated with retailing, governmental service, utilities, industry, and other sectors will usually welcome a visit that is planned. If students are involved in the visit, a positive reception is almost assured.

The elementary, middle (or junior high), and senior high school principals for an area might coordinate their visits to avoid the prospect of overcontact and conflict in emphasis. One of the purposes of these discussions is to discover how the school can better serve the community and how the school can assist community progress. Many leaders are interested in community development and how the school fits in with the progress of the community. For example, if businesspeople are interested in the procurement of industrial plants, they will be especially interested in the emphasis of the school program offerings in the technologies required by the commercial and industrial companies that might relocate in the area.

Parent Visits and Conferences.   The first consideration concerning conferences with parents is to gain the participation of the parents. Parents will usually come for conferences with teachers if they believe their child will benefit from the conference. The principal and members of the staff must attempt to establish a personal relationship with the parents. One successful method is to telephone parents, and in the course of the conversation drop some positive, personal information about the student, which lets the parents know that much thought has been given to each student. If parent-teacher conferences are to be marked with success, they must be carefully planned and initiated. Teachers need much help in planning and conducting conferences with parents, including practice conferences among members of the faculty that are followed by friendly critiques. Again, much individual effort may be necessary to encourage some parents to attend conferences, including some telephoning and possibly home visits.

Let's-Talk-School Discussions.   Inviting leaders to the school to talk about school in a relaxed manner can be a very good way to establish rapport with them. The principal might regularly schedule discussions in the cafeteria or conference room as an informal coffee time. The leaders and emerging leaders among parents and other citizens can have much influence upon the opinions of their followers. These leaders can also be a rich source of information for the principal and the faculty regarding people's expectations of the school. At the end of the discussion, the leaders should be given a tour of the building, and shown the positive things that are going on in the school.

The Use of Citizen-School Organizations.   Among the citizen-school organizations formed, the parent-teacher organizations (such as the National Congress of Parents and Teachers) are a mainstay. The success of the parent-teacher organization depends upon the leadership of the principal and faculty. If the principal is inept the parent-teacher organization may be reduced to a perfunctory existence with little contribution to better school and community relations. Yet if the principal and faculty provide progressive leadership, the parent-teacher organization will help to personalize communication between the school and its public.

Citizen advisory committees have also been used for many years. Some states have mandated their use either at the school or district level. Much planning is advised for the selection, size, term of office, and function of citizen committees. If the principal is unprepared or uses ill-advised procedures, citizen committees may not contribute to school-public relations. We recommend that school principals refer to the large amount of printed information available concerning how to establish and work with citizen committees.

Several other kinds of school-community groups are used to link the resources of the school with the school's constituency. For example, community clubs in some areas are strong supporters of schools. Community education programs offer opportunities for cooperative relationships between the school and community. Throughout the communities of the nation are associations that are very supportive of schools and that contribute to the establishment of warm personal relations between the school and community.

Special Invitations to Confer and Observe. Special invitations to visit the school can be very successful. For example, a few parents (possibly eight to ten) can be invited each month to tour the school and talk about its programs. Invitations may be offered on a random basis, however, as stated previously, communicating with the leaders of parents and other citizens of the community should be a priority because they communicate very effectively with their constituency. They have more influence upon the opinions of their followers than do professional educators. Invitations to attend a special school exhibit, special lecture, or open house are helpful. The variety of invitations to observe special events contributes to freer communication between school personnel and the public.

Personal Contacts through Membership in Organizations. Membership in community organizations can be a convenient means through which personal relationships may be established with community leaders. School principals should be active in civic organizations. Some school systems maintain at least one school administrator within each major civic organization in the school district.

A Cornucopia of Techniques Available to the Principal and Faculty. For additional personal leadership techniques to build communication and cooperative relationships between the home and the school, the reader is referred to texts dealing with school and community relations. For example, a successful publication in this field is published by Kindred, Bagin, and Gallagher.[5]

To summarize, what professional politicians speak of as pressing the flesh with citizens is an essential task of school principals. Obviously, the principal must enjoy meeting and talking with persons having very different backgrounds, interests, and lifestyles. Knowledge of the political power structure is essential. The best publicity program devised by the school will not substitute for a personal approach to creating better school and community relations.

Communication Processes and Techniques

Texts about school and public relations offer a great variety of techniques used to communicate information about the school to the public.[6] Some illustrative examples of these techniques are discussed here.

Organizing and Administering Publicity. Publicity about the school through the media, distribution of printed material, and speeches to community organizations are the mainstay of traditional public relations. Much is written about how to work with the press, how to prepare news information about the school, and how to release information to the media.

The media have a powerful influence upon public opinion. Many citizens are better informed about the progress of the football team at the local high school than they are about the teaching of English because of the great amount of publicity given to sports. The person charged with publicity for the school has several tasks critical to school-community relations. Publicity about the school should be enhanced by needs surveys concerning what the public wants to know. Rapport must be established with the various media available for publicity. News releases must be prepared that meet acceptable standards of quality and distributed appropriately to the media. The reporters should have available the data needed to report news events about the school. In addition to regular news releases about the school, special events, such as American Education Week, provide an opportunity to reaffirm the value of education to the community. As we have indicated previously, how to promote school publicity through the media is detailed at length

[5]Leslie W. Kindred, Don Bagin, and Donald K. Gallagher, *The School and Community Relations,* 3rd ed. (Englewood Cliffs N.J.: Prentice-Hall, 1984).

[6]Kindred, Bagin, Gallagher, *School and Community Relations.*

in a variety of publications that should be used by the person accepting primary responsibility for school publicity.

Publicity Through Speeches and Other Presentations to Community Groups. Organizations in the community are usually receptive to speeches and presentations, which provide an excellent opportunity to inform the public about schools. In cooperation with other principals, the central office staff, the faculty, and prominent laypersons in the community, consideration should be given to the establishment of a speakers' bureau. The bureau would provide ready access to persons who can communicate, through speeches and other presentations, information about the schools. We believe this affords an excellent opportunity to have leaders in the community power structure use their resources to build community support for education. For example, if a highly revered banker in the community makes an address televised to the public, his support of the schools will influence the opinions of many citizens.

Distribution of Printed Material and Letters to Parents. Printed material may be used to inform parents and other citizens about the school. Among these are newsletters, bulletins, handbooks, letters to parents, annual supplements to newspapers, and so on. The printed materials should be attractive, emphasize objectives of the school, and focus on children and youth. The language should be technically correct, appropriate to the audience, and free of complicated expression. Before any of these means of communication are distributed they should be reviewed for quality and officially approved. Distributing a statement that is sloppily prepared and full of errors can ravage positive opinions about the school.

Special School Events. The special events initiated by schools have traditionally been well attended by citizens. Among these are open house, classroom demonstrations, commencement exercises, dramatic performances, athletic contests, and other events. These performances place the school in the spotlight; therefore, they should be well organized and administered. If the commencement exercise of a high school is a disorganized mess, it reflects on the administration's ability to run a school and finally upon the oversight of the board of education.

Reacting to Public Attacks and Unfair Criticism

If the school public-relations program is successful, severe public criticism of the school should be minimal and public attacks on the school rare. Even the most competently administered school will have a few unfair critics. One lesson school administrators must learn is that some people will become angry with them for reasons not readily apparent. Moreover, a national press, critical of the schools, sometimes encourages unfounded local criticism. How to deal with public attacks and criticism becomes a judgment call among numerous alternatives. One must differentiate between constructive criticism and destructive fault-finding. Justified criticism either from within or outside the school is the basis for growth and improvement. The discussion here concerns how to meet hostile, destructive criticism and public attacks.

Expressed public criticism may be a test of school public relations. If, for example, a very critical letter to the editor results in parent unrest and dissatisfaction with the school, poor public-school relations may be indicated because ill-founded criticism should result in a reaction of public support for the school.

One's immediate reaction to unfounded critics may be to respond to each criticism in detail, which may be ill-advised because it may lead to undignified name calling, a situation in which the principal is no more respected in the eyes of the public than is the critic. If the criticism is unfounded and the school has good relations with the public, a letter to the editor, a critical statement at the PTA, or a phone call to the board chairman may best be treated with dignified silence. Persistence of hostile criticism, however, may require action to resist or otherwise deal with the critic. From experience we have learned some ways to deal with public attacks.

When confronted with the intemperate, illogical critic, one should not be drawn into an extemporaneous debate. Persistent antagonism should be met with a courteous explanation of the goals and processes of the school, with the explanation that the right to disagree is respected. Some critics are sophists, skilled at debate, and determined to create a disturbance. Attempting to debate on their terms may accomplish little but create a fire where only a smoke machine exists.[7]

The principal may not want to invest a lot of time with an inflexible critic who has the attitude, "Don't bother me with the facts—my mind is made up." But attempts should be made to reason in a pleasant, courteous manner with such a person. Critics should be included in activities that may provide insight into the school program. However, if one persists in inflexibility, it will be obvious to most persons in the community and the criticism will be neutralized.

Every attempt must be made to have a favorable press, yet educators may be victims of unscrupulous disc jockeys, editors, or other reporters bent upon increased audiences at painful cost to the object of the publicity. Again, responding to an unfavorable press is a judgment call based on knowledge of the situation. In our view, especially if good school and public

[7]Nunnery and Kimbrough, *Politics, Power, Polls,* p. 120.

relations are in place, the principal and faculty should stay with the program and not respond in great detail to outlandish criticism. If good community relationships exist, community leaders will find a way to deal with the situation without the efforts of the principal and faculty. If that is not possible, letters to the editors and responses to the editorials of television and radio stations may be used. They should be positive and not argumentative in nature.

Even in the worst of situations, school leaders should not attack personally or otherwise ridicule the critic. Any attempt to belittle a person runs the risk of creating sympathy for the critic and martyrdom.[8]

In summary, the discussion here is about unfounded, hostile public attacks that are meant to be destructive to the school. A bag of tricks does not exist that responds effectively to any and all public attacks. Rather, the principal, faculty, and friends of the school must think through unique strategies and techniques to fit each situation. The strategy that will quell a public attack in one community may not be a useful approach in another area. Consequently, after all the advice from experienced administrators and political leaders available has been considered in the light of the situation, one must mount what appears to be the best strategy. The best answer to public attacks on the school is to have the confidence of community leaders and their followers, and this comes through the establishment of good school and community relations.

[8]Nunnery and Kimbrough, *Politics, Power, Polls,* p. 120.

CHAPTER SEVEN

Developing Leadership Ability

LEADERSHIP AND SUPERVISORY FUNCTIONS

Having a position of leadership with the faculty is not enough; the educational leader must use the position to move the school toward educational excellence. Therefore, the first order of business is for the principal, administrative staff, and faculty to know "what they are becoming." If they do not have a clear vision of their goal, the faculty will dissipate its energy and not much will be accomplished. Many schools are characterized as having a lot of undisciplined energy, which says that they have lost sight of realistic goals.

Even when a school faculty has a sense of what they are becoming, they need the leadership resources of the principal to arrive at their destination. Leadership requires knowledge of how to become a leader and of the change process, an understanding of a productive school climate, and supervisory skills. Chapters 7 through 10 are devoted to the process of helping the school arrive at a high level of educational excellence.

The school principal should be a leader. A consensus exists on this statement; however, differences in opinion are expressed about the kind of leader the principal should be. Johnson and Johnson wrote that if an "influence" definition is accepted, "A *leader* may be defined as a group member who exerts more influence on other members than they exert on him."[1] Assuming that even the most calloused leaders in history were influenced by some members of their group, Attila the Hun and Mohandus Gandhi were leaders, but their styles of leadership and values were poles apart. Therefore, one consideration is what kind of leader best furthers the improvement of the instructional programs of schools.

How does the aspirant to the principalship become a strong personal leader with the faculty? The authors believe that one can learn how to become a leader, and moreover, that leaders can learn how to become better leaders.

LEADERSHIP RESEARCH

Leadership has been the subject of a tremendous amount of research effort. Between 1900 and 1950 over 500 studies about the nature of leadership were conducted in the armed services, education, industry, and government. Until about 1935 most of this effort was targeted to discover the traits that made an individual a leader. By the 1950s most authorities had become convinced that the traits theory of leadership was largely unproductive in explaining the emergence of leadership. After 1935 much effort was concentrated on the situational theory of leadership to identify those variables coming together in the dynamics of the social group to promote leadership.

In an attempt to bring some order into the multitudinous studies that were accumulating, Stogdill reviewed hundreds of research studies and in 1948 published the *Handbook of Leadership*. Following his death, a revised edition was completed by Bass.[2] In his review of theories of leadership, Bass included the following: (1) great-man theories, (2) trait theories, (3) environmental theories, (4) personal situation theories, (5) psychoanalytic theories, (6) humanistic theories, (7) exchange theories, (8) behavioral theories, and (9) perceptual and cognitive theories. Lest the reader find this long list bewildering, most of these theories standing alone are no longer major persuasions among scholars.

The great-man theory has been abandoned as a relic of the right of royalty to rule; however, the idea is still perpetuated in those nations that continue rule by a monarch. Few knowledgeable persons in the United States would endorse the idea that great persons are born to rule. As mentioned previously, the possession of a trait or a unique set of traits (for example, physical height, weight, physique, intelligence, knowledge, dom-

---

[1]David W. Johnson and Frank P. Johnson, *Joining Together: Group Theory and Group Skills,* 3rd ed. (Englewood Cliffs, N.J.: Prentice-Hall, 1987), p. 48.

[2]Bernard M. Bass, *Stogdill's Handbook of Leadership* (New York: Free Press, 1981).

inance) did not explain the nature of leadership. Some traits, such as popularity, sociability, persistence, adaptability, and interaction are associated with leadership; however, the mere possession of traits as an explanation is no longer accepted, because (1) the traits exhibited by a leader in one situation may not result in leadership status in another situation, and (2) the traits explanation does not include the interaction variable that is currently believed to be a factor in the emergence to leadership status in a group. The evidence is conclusive that the mere possession of a set of personal traits will not predict that one will emerge and function well as a leader. Likewise, the times-makes-the-man (environmental) concept is no longer considered seriously, even though being at the right place may be one among many incidents explaining how a few persons are appointed to official positions. It does not explain whether they, by the chance factor, were good or bad leaders.

Currently the most accepted explanation of the emergence of leadership incorporates the quality of interaction that emanates from the leader's association with members of a group. The frequency of satisfactory interaction, for example, is associated with status in the leadership hierarchy. Leadership is not something that is fixed; it can move about among members of the group, based on which member the group feels can contribute most to the needs of the group at the time. In other words, leadership emerges in the social system and may well be contingent upon many factors; there is not a universal set of factors that will explain the emergence of leadership in all situations.

THE SYSTEMS VIEW OF LEADERSHIP

How one emerges and functions as a leader can best be explained in a systems framework, which avoids the pitfall of explaining leadership as the possession of one or a fixed set of traits. Emergence to leadership status is the result of the interaction of multiple variables, some of which are contingent, depending upon the situation. Leadership in a school is a quality of expectation that emerges from the influence over resources and the legitimation of a person to use these resources in the leadership of the school faculty, staff, and the student body.

Theories of leadership (such as traits, exchange, and personal situation theories) may become relevant within the systems framework. For example, those persons accepting the exchange theory of leadership view the principal's leadership as the balance of behavior that produces either leadership costs or leadership rewards, expressed best as an inbasket/outbasket balance by a colleague of the authors: "When I assumed the office of superintendent in this town, no one knew me or had reason to dislike me. Every citizen was in my inbasket. But every controversial decision I had to make produced leadership costs and rewards—some citizens who were disgruntled with my decision left the inbasket and entered the outbasket. Through the years I was forced to make enough decisions that were unpopular with enough persons to deplete seriously the inbasket and to fill up the outbasket. My theory is that when the inbasket and outbasket reach an approximate balance, I had better look for another position." This is an operational explanation of exchange theory that is consistent with the systems framework. As we will see subsequently, traits of leaders also have relevancy within the systems view.

A person who is appointed principal of a school is expected to be the leader of the school and inherits certain legal/rational authority; that is, the office carries certain powers given to the person appointed or elected to it by statutes, board policies, court decisions, and traditions. But, the principal who relies solely upon this legal/rational source of leadership will not be a strong leader and, in fact, is likely to experience failure. To be the leader the school deserves, the principal must achieve personal leadership with the faculty, staff, and student body, because having the position of legal/rational authority is only one source of influence.

When viewed in the social systems framework, leadership accrues to one through the effective influence over valued resources and group legitimation of the person to use these resources to influence policy. Leadership resources may be anything material or nonmaterial valued by the faculty. For example, teachers value financial resources, a certain teaching schedule, assignment of a classroom, special assignments, humane treatment, fairness, discipline, and other material things and conditions. They also value nonmaterial ideas, ideologies, expertise, knowledge, certain religious beliefs, and, emotionally speaking, feeling good. If principals exercise control over such resources or are perceived to have control over them, they can have influence, but there is also the matter of legitimation to use those resources.

The principal must achieve legitimation (acceptability) with the faculty to use valued resources to influence, and this is where the rub comes for most persons who aspire to leadership. As discussed in Chapters 3 and 4, certain expectations or norms become accepted among the faculty concerning how faculty members should behave, including how the principal should behave. A person cannot violate the critical norms held by the members of the faculty and achieve leadership with them. This is not to say that cliques on the faculty will not have divergent expectations; divergence in opinion will always exist. Some members of the faculty may expect the principal to exercise firmness in judgment and strict discipline, whereas another group may prefer flexibility in decisions and a humane approach to discipline. Fortunately, the leader is usually given greater flexibility to deviate from the critical norms than are the marginal members of the faculty, and this can prevent loss of legitimation for the principal in situations when taking some liberties with group norms is necessary. Moreover, conflicting situations require suave leadership skills.

Illustrative Leadership Resources

Anything material or nonmaterial that is valued by the members of the faculty, staff, or student body can be a leadership resource. One of the first stages in establishing a leadership relationship with the faculty is to identify those resources valued by the faculty over which the principal may have some control.

Official position is obviously one of the resources controlled by the principal. Think for a moment about the advantages of position and how it can be expanded to include other valued resources to influence policy. The principal has greater freedom of movement than members of the faculty and can interact and communicate with more persons more frequently. Leadership tends to go to those who are at the center of communication, and leaders usually have more communication with other leaders outside the group than with followers. Inherent in the position of principal are legal/rational powers to act, and those powers and the traditions associated with them may give the principal an aura of leadership not possible for a member of the faculty. We hasten to add, however, that this aura of leadership is dependent upon legitimation to act, and the faculty, parents, and upper administration will have much to say about that. The principal who, for violation of one or more critical norms, has lost legitimation with the faculty may no longer use legal/rational powers successfully. Also, these powers should be used overtly only in extremely unsettled situations to protect the interests of the faculty or the organization. Persons who use these inherent powers arbitrarily will lose leadership with the faculty. Through their official position principals are well situated to help the faculty possess those resources valued as critical to their tasks and to the best interests of the school.

School principals should consider as rationally as possible what personal resources they possess and control that are valued by the faculty. Certain personal traits, such as physical appearance, fluency of speech, persistence, expertise, decisiveness, knowledge, and emotional control, may now become a basis for influence. No person controls all of the personal characteristics that may be valued by the faculty; furthermore, those valued by some members of the faculty may not have high priority with others.

Leadership resources may be physical, intellectual, social, political, or in a realm not easily classified, as is charisma. In the intellectual realm, being perceived as possessing superior expertise about how a school should be administered is a revered resource. Popularity, friendship ties, cooperation, and accessibility to communication are valued. In his review of hundreds of studies of traits, Bass found that the following traits had the highest correlation with leadership: originality, popularity, sociability, judgment, aggressiveness, desire to excel, humor, cooperativeness, and liveliness.[3] A person who, for whatever reason, continually makes more enemies than friends among faculty members will lose status. Although the correlation of physical characteristics such as height, weight, and physique with leadership is low, personal attractiveness may be a resource for increased leadership in the group. The reader will note that one can exercise some control over several of these personal resources. For example, persons can work at making friendships, communicating better, setting personal goals, and exuding positive cooperativeness. The ability to change certain physical characteristics, such as height, is an improbability; nevertheless, persons who are not naturally beautiful or handsome can make themselves more attractive by good grooming and dressing properly.

Charisma is an example of a resource over which one may have little control. Charisma is that elusive resource that attracts people; its basis may never be known. For those principals who have charisma it is a source of leadership with the faculty. Those who do not possess charisma—a very large majority—must compensate by developing other leadership resources.

Mintzberg identified several sources of influence, including (1) control of such valued resources as money, (2) control of a technical skill, (3) control of knowledge and information critical to the organization, (4) legal prerogatives, and (5) access to those who can use some or all of these resources.[4] In addition to the control of these resources, Mintzberg suggested willingness to use influence in a clever manner, or "will and skill."

The literature is replete with discussions of leadership skills. In our view skillful behavior with groups is a critical resource. The principal must be skillful in chairing discussion groups and be able to assist others in the process, and be skillful in helping the faculty in the problem-solving process. Skill is associated with the enhancement of a school climate conducive to improved faculty and student performance. The principal who does not possess and use acceptable social skills may contribute to faculty dissatisfaction and low morale.

In summary, anything in the material or nonmaterial realm that is valued by the faculty and over which the principal exercises some influence can contribute to leadership status. Mere control of these resources, however, does not provide personal leadership status. There is the matter

[3]Bass, *Handbook of Leadership*, p. 66.

[4]Henry Mintzberg, *Power in and Around Organizations* (Englewood Cliffs, N.J.: Prentice-Hall, 1983).

of whether the principal interacts with the faculty in ways that result in the legitimation to use the resources.

The Process of Legitimation

As discussed previously in Chapters 3 through 6, every social system develops expectations about how its members should behave, and they all have normative expectations concerning how their leader should behave. The leader who seriously violates these critical norms will not achieve legitimation. The person who fails to achieve legitimation or acceptability will be a titular principal only, not an acceptable leader authorized to use the resources controlled. The result is failure to gain *personal* leadership with the faculty. We are speaking here of legitimation in the existing system. The principal does have the alternative of attempting to crush the system and impose personal preferred norms on the faculty, but this alternative has risks that some leaders may not want to take. Yet, even in such an imposed new system, the principal must maintain legitimation.

Practically everything the rejected principal does will meet resistance, whereas the accepted, legitimized leader can do no wrong, and is currently referred to as the "teflon" leader who is not held accountable personally for questionable acts or decisions. The nonrespected principal's attempts to manipulate the school schedule will be described with such terms as selfish, Machiavellian, mean, or bumbling idiocy, but under the same circumstances the legitimized principal's action will tend to be accepted as attempts to help the faculty. The faculty will be predisposed to forgive the mistakes of the accepted principal, but the mistakes of the principal who is viewed negatively will be just more evidence that the "ogre should be fired."

Some illustrations of norms that might be critical for legitimation are in the realm of ethics. In the minds of the faculty are beliefs in justice, loyalty, character, prudence, and certain professional codes. A test of the principal's loyalty is whether to support the faculty in issues raised by irate parents. Whether the principal exhibits common sense, especially in crises, will serve as one criterion on which to judge prudence. Evaluation of teaching and handling student discipline usually raise questions of justice. The principal's character involves acceptable behavior both within and outside the school. A flawed character for whatever reason (conflict of interest, cowardice, dishonesty, infidelity, alcoholism) leads to disrespect and lack of legitimation. Some teachers may expect the principal to set a more exemplary standard of behavior than they demand for themselves. How much does the principal care about the welfare of teachers and students? The caring function is an important test of ethical behavior. Finally, just how hard does the principal work? Does the principal say, "let's all work hard" while personally lazily goofing off in the office? Nothing is more deadening to legitimation than the hypocritical principal who demands of others but loafs on the job.

The authors believe that the principal who exerts leadership in the community will have greater leadership status in the school. Within the community are expectations of leaders that can be critical for attaining leadership, and these vary greatly among school districts. Some districts may expect the principal to go to church as an indication of religious conviction. Leaders in the community may expect the principal to display interest in community service by participating in voluntary activities. In progressive communities the principal may be expected to exert positive attitudes toward community development.

The field of group dynamics offers generalizations that can guide interaction with the faculty, students, and persons in the community. From studies of street gangs, much was learned about the nature of leadership. Among other conclusions, the studies indicated that (1) leaders epitomized those behaviors valued by the group; (2) leaders met their personal obligations to the group; (3) leaders had greater respect of persons outside the group than of gang followers; and (4) within each group was a power structure, or pecking order.[5]

IN SEARCH OF THE RIGHT LEADERSHIP STYLE

Leadership style has been a prolific basis for research. A well-known seminal study of autocratic, democratic, and laissez faire styles of leadership was conducted by Lippitt and White with the assistance of Kurt Lewin, known as the father of group dynamics.[6] The results of this study were interpreted as favoring a democratic style of leadership. An overwhelming quantity of literature during the 1950s and 1960s favored the humanistic or democratic approach to management. For example, McGregor's *The Human Side of Enterprise* was a persuasive publication favoring the Theory Y style (a human-relations emphasis in management) over the traditional Theory X style (an autocratic manager).[7] The Theory X type of principal assumes that teachers dislike work, have to be coerced, controlled, and told what to do, and avoid responsibility. Theory Y leaders assume that, given a humanistic climate, teachers do not have to be coerced

[5]*See* William F. Whyte, *Street Corner Society* (Chicago: University of Chicago Press, 1943); Frederick M. Thrasher, *The Gang* (Chicago: University of Chicago Press, 1927).

[6]Kurt Lewin, Ronald Lippitt, and Ralph K. White, "Patterns of Aggressive Behavior in Experimentally Created 'Social Climates'," *Journal of Social Psychology,* 10 (May 1939), 271–99.

[7]Douglas M. McGregor, *The Human Side of Enterprise* (New York: McGraw-Hill, 1960).

to work hard, assume responsibility and self-control, and are creative. The humanistic theory of management was supported by the noted "Western Electric, Hawthorne Plant" studies.[8]

Studies in group dynamics highlighted the risks involved in the arbitrary use of authority. Except in a very few exceptional cases, the hard-boiled autocrat cannot be legitimized by most modern school faculties. Throughout the 1950s and 1960s the democratic concept of leadership was extolled as the answer to the kind of leader the principal should be and as the kind of principal that can achieve legitimation. Most students of educational administration spent an inordinate amount of time in instruction about the characteristics of a democratic leader. The central idea was that the singularly best leader had been validated through research in the social and behavioral sciences and management. The concept of administrative structure took a back seat to group process—organizational structure mattered little if the principal simply created a faculty with high morale, because a satisfied faculty having high morale would be a productive faculty.

By the 1970s the claims of the humanists began to be questioned because scholars soon learned that a school faculty could achieve high morale but have low productivity. In other words, a faculty can have a good time "teaching together," but student achievement may have a lower priority than organizational maintenance activities.

School faculties, students, and parents have widely different expectations of principals; therefore, the behavior that can result in legitimation in situation A may result in loss of status in situation B. Moreover, those aspiring to school leadership are not chameleons that can blend into any school; there are limits to how much we can adjust our personality and leadership style to different situations. Consequently, much current opinion favors a contingency theory of what kind of leader the principal should be.

The Contingency Theory of Leadership

Fiedler is noted for his research about the contingency theory of leadership. He identified two styles of leadership, the human relations or relationship style and the task-oriented style. These leadership styles are revealed by the leaders' attitudes toward their least-preferred coworkers as measured by the Least Preferred Coworker (LPC) scale. The relationship or human relations style leader sees little difference between the least-preferred and the most-preferred coworkers, whereas the task-ori-

[8]*See* Elton Mayo, *The Human Problems of an Industrial Civilization* (New York: Macmillan Publishing Co., 1933); F. J. Roethlisberger and William J. Dickenson, *Management and the Worker* (Cambridge: Harvard University Press, 1939).

ented leader perceives great difference between them. The relationship style leader views the least-preferred coworker more favorably than the task-oriented leader.[9]

The terms task-oriented and relationship- or humanistic-oriented leader have become generalized in the literature. Although different definitions are offered, the task-oriented leader is preoccupied with getting the job done with less emphasis on the development of good human relations, whereas the relationship-oriented leader places primary effort on the development of human relations. A somewhat oversimplified comparison might be that the task-oriented leader is in the autocratic tradition, whereas the humanistic leader is viewed as democratic. The difference in view today is that neither type of leader is a villain; in fact, both may be very effective in different school situations.

Fiedler predicted that the task-oriented leader would perform well in *very favorable* situations, such as when the leader is well liked, the tasks are clearly structured, and the leader holds a position of high authority, and also in *very unfavorable* situations when the tasks are ambiguous, the leader has low authority, and the leader is on poor terms with the group. On the other hand, the relationship-oriented leader would be the better choice if the situation falls between the very favorable and very unfavorable situation.[10]

Several other contingency models have been offered, with some variation in definition of the task and humanistic dimensions. Hersey and Blanchard offered a model in which leadership behavior was projected into four types: high-task/low-relationship, high-task/high-relationship, low-task/low-relationship, and low-task/high relationship.[11] Reddin developed a three-dimensional management model in which eight leadership types were identified.[12] Four of his management styles—developer, executive, bureaucrat, and benevolent autocrat—were considered effective, and four other management styles—missionary, compromiser, deserter, and autocrat—were labeled ineffective.

In summary, if one consults contingency theorists for answers concerning what kind of leader the principal should be, the answer will be "it depends." It depends on the match of the principal with the situation in which personal style is likely to produce the best results. However, the fact that not enough is known about this contingency is the problem. When a school situation deteriorates into anarchy, school boards often replace the principal with a very strong task-oriented person to "straighten out the

[9]Fred E. Fiedler, *A Theory of Leadership Effectiveness* (New York: McGraw-Hill, 1967), pp. 36–37.

[10]Fiedler, *Leadership Effectiveness,* pp. 22–32, 142–44.

[11]Paul Hersey and Kenneth H. Blanchard, *Management of Organizational Behavior: Utilizing Human Resources,* 3rd ed. (Englewood Cliffs, N.J.: Prentice-Hall, 1977).

[12]William J. Reddin, *Managerial Effectiveness* (New York: McGraw-Hill, 1970).

mess." In large school systems there are persons known to be no-nonsense benevolent autocrats who may be sent in to rescue a school that is in trouble. Conversely, the authors have observed the rescue of such schools by persons having relationship styles who were able to help the faculty and student body regain a sense of purpose and structure through persistent persuasion and participation. Finally, the authors are persuaded that contingency theory is superior to a singular style model; however, we believe that the placement of principals in situations where they can best lead is a judgment call that may be facilitated by the use of improved processes for selecting principals.

THE INSTRUCTIONAL LEADERSHIP TASKS OF THE PRINCIPAL

As principals achieve increased personal leadership status with the faculty, parents, and students, their influence should be used to inspire improvement of the instructional program of the school. As discussed in Chapter 2, research on the attainment of instructional excellence indicates that the principal must be a strong leader in the process; moreover, the entire faculty and staff of the school must gain a clear sense of where they are going by defining their educational purpose. Before we consider further skills of leadership, some of the leadership tasks essential for instructional program improvement will be discussed in this section.

As mentioned previously, considerable research effort has been invested in identifying conditions existing in effective urban schools that are not characteristic of unsuccessful urban schools. In their review of this research, Clark, Lotto, and Astuto reported a consensus on the following conditions in effective schools that were not present in less-effective schools.

1. Strong administrative leadership
2. A climate of expectation for satisfactory student achievement
3. An orderly but not oppressive school climate
4. A focus on pupil acquisition of basic school skills
5. A system for continuous monitoring of pupil progress
6. Resources that can be focused on the fundamental learning objectives of the school[13]

Until more is learned about how to achieve excellence in educational programs, the authors believe that the principal may well consider emulating these conditions in the school.

[13]David L. Clark, Linda S. Lotto, and Terry A. Astuto, "Effective Schools and School Improvement: A Comparative Analysis of Two Lines of Inquiry," *Educational Administration Quarterly,* 20 (Summer 1984), 47.

Leadership in Improving the Instructional Program

We agree with the view frequently expressed that the principal must lead in the improvement of the instructional program of the school. It is a task for which the principal alone must assume accountability, and one that should not be delegated to an assistant principal. If the head of the school does not demonstrate an enthusiastic interest in the improvement of curriculum offerings and instructional improvement, the members of the faculty and the students will assume that things other than academics have higher priority. If, for example, principals spend most of their time helping the football team win the state championship, the interscholastic sports program will have highest priority; high expectations in football, not academic achievement, will be the norm among students, and the faculty is not in a good position to counteract the misplaced goal. If the principal is not heavily engaged in the instructional program, teachers will probably not have instructional resources available when they need them.

If visitors to the school are given a tour through the building by the principal, they should leave having been impressed with the principal's grasp of the curriculum offerings and of the instructional goals and processes. Based on the authors' visits to many schools, this knowledge is not characteristic of every school principal; in fact, some principals are simply not well enough informed about the instructional program to know how to provide teachers with the resources and services they need to achieve an instructional program of quality. There is little probability that the leadership-starved school faculty will achieve excellence. The faculty and student body will soon realize where the principal's priorities lie. Some of the instructional leadership tasks of the principal are discussed next.

Leadership in Reaching Agreement on Instructional Goals. As discussed previously, a faculty that becomes absorbed with means problems to the exclusion of instructional goals suffers goal displacement. Equally disheartening is the faculty that has never seriously considered what its goals in instruction should be. One of the principal's primary leadership tasks is to guide the school faculty and students in the process of accepting and maintaining high standards of educational goal achievement. The school is an educational agency and cannot be expected to achieve its goals and be all things to all people. In the absence of well-conceived educational goals, schools are pressured into performing all kinds of social duties that are not educational in nature. Many other social, religious, and civic agencies and groups exist for the manifold social needs of the community. Since the school is in an open social system and societal change is inevitable, the decision process of setting educational objectives is a process that is never finished. However, at any given time the members of the faculty and staff should be able to define concisely "what kind of school we are becoming."

Achieving a sense of shared goals is not entirely a local endeavor free of district and state level demands. The legislature and state board of education set demands concerning educational program. Yet when the state and district mandate objectives that seem to be in conflict with sound educational goals, the principal is obligated to lead in removing those mandates. The professional Code of Ethics, which has been adopted by the two national principals' associations, states that the principal "pursues appropriate measures to correct those laws, policies, and regulations that are not consistent with sound educational goals."[14] To meet this professional standard of behavior, the principal must first, in cooperation with the school faculty, decide whether they have sound educational goals.

Leadership in Decisions About the Nature of Curriculum Content. The explosion of knowledge in this century leaves educators in a difficult situation. The schools and colleges cannot teach everything known in the arts, sciences, and vocations; in fact, only a very small amount of knowledge can be included. Educators are faced with selecting what should be taught within the enormous quantity of knowledge that continues to grow.

The decision is not the school's responsibility alone, because much of the material is given to the system in the form of state and district mandates, by publishers of textbooks, and through other external inputs. For many years curriculum specialists have emphasized the great influence that textbook authors and publishers have on what is taught in the classroom. School boards frequently make policies that influence what should or should not be taught in the schools. Moreover, the selection of curriculum content involves the principal and faculty amidst the troubled waters of philosophical and religious differences about the appropriate nature of education. Many religious issues have arisen: evolution versus the Biblical account of creation, prayer in the school, religion versus secular humanism, and so on.

Philosophical differences come into conflict in curricular decisions. Those parents and other citizens with an idealist bent come down hard in favor of the traditional subject curriculum; for example, the Paideia proposal may be favored by some.[15] Those parents with a pragmatic orientation usually favor a broadened "education is life" or reconstructionist program. On the other hand, those with a humanist or existentialist view will promote a very open, freedom-oriented program with few external

[14]American Association of School Administrators, *AASA Statement of Ethics for School Administrators and Procedural Guidelines* (Arlington, Va.: The Association, 1976).

[15]Mortimer J. Adler, *Paideia: Problems and Possibilities* (New York: Macmillan, 1983).

demands on students. To escape the quagmire of conflict and the pulling apart of the school at the seams, the principal must be a strong leader and have strong support from the faculty and leaders in the community.

One focus of the curriculum must be on student command of the fundamental processes or the basic educational skills. This should be a focus throughout all schools and all grade levels, including colleges and universities. The senior high school principal must be just as concerned about the fundamental processes as the elementary school principal.

The function of the school, however, is not limited to teaching the fundamentals of reading, writing, and arithmetic. Preparation for vocations, for post-secondary educational programs, and for citizenship are illustrations of other specific areas of the curriculum. Such areas as self-discipline, leadership skills, social interaction, and wholesome living should also be included.

The things that the school is pressured into doing that are not educational but purely governmental services should be rejected by educators. The use of school resources for day-care services is not an educational function and should be performed by other community agencies. Therefore, the school faculty and administration should reject all suggestions for services that are not educational functions.

Achieving faculty and community leader concurrence concerning the nature of curriculum offerings is a challenging task that will tax all of the leadership resources available to the principal. Yet the performance of this task is well worth the effort, because in the process the faculty and students will have internalized or "bought into" what the expectations are, and this is one of the keys to the establishment of high expectations of student achievement. The process can also contribute to the creation of a productive school climate for learning.

Leadership in Organizing Curriculum Experiences for Learning. Decisions have to be made about the organization and delivery of instruction. Some of the major decisions about the organization are given via school board policies (such as 8–4, k6–3–3, 4–4–4, 5–3–4 grade centers). Even the state legislature gets into the act by mandating lengths of the school day and year, length of periods, and so on. These mandates vary among the states. Yet, within these mandated requirements, the faculty has flexibility in the organization of instruction, including the adoption of self-contained classroom, departmental organizations, modular scheduling, traditional scheduling, large and small classroom instruction, team teaching, graded and nongraded organizations, individual instruction, and other instructional organizations. Types of classification and student grouping are areas of choice, such as whether to adopt ability grouping as a practice.

The instructional delivery system, coupled with the organization for instruction, is another area for decision making. Instructional theories have been heavily influenced by different schools of psychology in which the behaviorist, gestalt, and phenomenological schools have been prominently involved. In the traditional subject curriculum, for example, the lecture has been predominant, which is consistent with behaviorist theory. For the most part, this is also true of the broad fields or fused subject curriculum, although discovery methods may also be employed. Existential or phenomenological psychology has been popular with the humanist emphasis on curriculum content.

Leadership in Improving the Instructional Program. If teachers are to perform at maximum effectiveness and efficiency, the administrative team of the school must provide the instructional services and resources needed for a first-rate program. The enthusiastic and persistent leadership of the principal is crucial to the performance of this task.

Although there are limits to the financial and human resources available for the instructional program, the principal's attitude must be to see that teachers have instructional resources and services when they need them. Few conditions can be more discouraging and damaging to morale than having a leader who seldom responds positively to requests for instructional resources and services. If a teacher's needs are beyond the public financial resources available, the principal should be aggressive in securing additional funding. Additional funding can sometimes be found within the school district budget; if not, voluntary funding is a possibility. In any event, the teacher should know that the principal is honestly trying to find the resources requested.

Leadership in the Evaluation of School Performance. One of the most important concerns of the faculty, staff, and students is how to measure, as objectively as possible, the progress of the school. Are goals being met? Evaluation is the basis for growth and improvement. Continuous monitoring of student progress is a characteristic of effective urban schools not found in unsuccessful urban schools, and can be facilitated through the use of computer technology. Further discussion of staff and student evaluation is included in Chapters 14 and 15. The system of evaluation should include the performance of the administrative staff.

Maintaining an Orderly Climate. An orderly but not oppressive climate is characteristic of effective urban schools. The authors believe that effective student discipline is an important criterion of the principal's leadership status. Through his research using the *Leader Behavior Description Questionnaire,* Hemphill found that leaders scored high on two dimensions: (1) initiation of structure (organizing, methods of procedure, communication nets, and so on) and (2) consideration (promoting warm, friendly relations between the leader and the group and among members of the group).[16] The authors believe that these two elements of leader behavior will do much to establish an orderly but not oppressive school climate. Moreover, this climate will contribute to the maintenance of school discipline.

If, through the lack of strong leadership, the organization of the school moves toward the maximization of entropy, teachers cannot teach and students cannot learn. In the process of establishing an appropriate climate for learning, the faculty should include student participation.

LEADERSHIP SKILLS NEEDED IN TASK PERFORMANCE

Sound leadership skills are essential to the performance of the tasks involved in instructional leadership. As discussed briefly in this chapter, skill is needed in the use of leadership resources. Since the performance of the instructional leadership tasks just discussed involves working with groups of teachers, parents, and students, sensitivity to and knowledge of group dynamics is a certainty.

Leading Group Discussions

After 1930, much research was conducted in the field of group dynamics and the nature of leadership in groups. The findings of this research are of great assistance to the principal in conducting meetings with teachers, parents, and other citizens in the school district. In preparation for leadership with work-related groups, the principal may consider several questions. How should the leader function in the group? What are some variables that explain the behavior of groups? What is the role of the leader in conducting meetings and in helping the group move toward decisions?

Some of the recommendations for conducting a faculty meeting or a small faculty work group may seem somewhat routine, yet the authors have frequently observed otherwise capable people who were very unskilled in conducting meetings. The meetings could have been much more stimulating and productive through the observance of a few leadership practices that are currently routine with persons skilled in group dynamics. For example, some meetings were held in room arrangements that were not conducive to good meetings. The leader should select a meeting place with a comfortable temperature and with an arrangement conducive

---

[16] John K. Hemphill, "Patterns of Leadership Behavior in the Department of a College," *Journal of Educational Psychology,* XLVI (November 1955), 385–401.

to the tasks involved. Even the most exploratory groups should have an agenda and a reason for meeting. The leader should be skilled in encouraging individual participation and in facilitating group thinking, including the use of suave techniques for keeping the group on task. The leader should see that data that may be needed by the group are made available to participants before or during the meeting. Skillful leaders are able to sense when the group may be moving toward a decision on the alternatives being considered and thereby facilitate the decision-making process. These are only a few illustrations of practical skills for conducting small group meetings. In the case of large group meetings, the principal should have knowledge of the rules of order used so as not to appear naive. Skill in conducting large group meetings is valued by participants and is another resource that bestows leadership status.

Expressing a Positive Attitude. In all aspects of leadership functions, the principal should express a positive attitude. Teachers have enough blue Mondays and doubts of their own without the negative contributions of the principal. Studies of the most powerful community leaders of progressive communities indicate that a very negative person does not keep a strong following. The only teachers who follow a principal with a negative personality are themselves "soreheads."

Skill in Initiating and Maintaining Organization. To assume that people, if left alone, will achieve a structure appropriate to the task at hand is a fallacy. Knowledge of organizational structure and leadership is necessary if the group is to function well. It is also a fallacy to assume that good organizational arrangements are self-renewable. The leader must exercise consideration to maintain group synergy to cope with unforeseen problems. In other words, maintenance of group strength through attention to goals, reinforcing cohesiveness and morale, and keeping communication channels open are continuous tasks.

Leadership Skills in Decision Making. During the human-relations era of the 1950s, all decision making was thought to require the activity of a democratic group. Much of the preservice and in-service training of school administrators was devoted to skills related to democratic participation in decision making. As a result, some principals pressed democratic decision making to ridiculous levels. Although the authors are persuaded that participative management is a desirable approach, the method for decision making is contingent on several factors in the situation, including (1) the time available, (2) the nature of the decision facing the faculty, (3) the leadership expectations of the faculty, and (4) other situational variables. Johnson and Johnson identified seven methods for decision making: (1) decision by authority without group discussion, (2) decision by expert, (3) decision by averaging the opinions of the faculty, (4) decision by authority after group discussion, (5) decision by minority, (6) decision by majority vote, and (7) decision by consensus.[17]

If the decision has the significance of policy, participative decision making by consensus is indicated, yet if the consensus is not reached within the time limits, other methods may have to be used, all of which may not be as welcome as a consensus. For example, decision by majority vote creates winners and losers, resulting in further division of the faculty. Too frequent use of decision by authority, either with or without group discussion, risks increased social distance between the principal and members of the faculty, questionable faculty "buy-in" to decisions, depressed participation, and decreased innovation. As a deadline approaches, decision by minority may sometimes be fruitful. Legislatures and the Congress use this method by appointing conference committees to find a compromise solution that will be accepted. The principal may find helpful the use of such a committee made up of leaders on both sides of a conflict. In some very highly technical decisions, such as legal issues, health services, and computer systems, the faculty may opt to use decision by expert.

The authors find decision by authority without group discussion presumptuous. Equally overstepping due bounds is decision by averaging opinions, because that allows the principal to weasel out of accountability, and the decisions are not based on an exercise of enlightened intelligence.

In summary, the conditions existing at the time of decision will influence the method of decision used. If the faculty expects an autocratic boss, immediate use of decision by consensus may be viewed as weakness and irresponsibility, which could result in loss of leadership status. Yet, other conditions, such as time deadlines and the nature of the decision, may indicate a decision by authority followed by an explanation to the faculty. However, the principal's goal should be to develop a collegial system in which participative decision making is the norm.

Skill in Motivating the Faculty and Staff to Work Hard. Several theories of motivation have been offered, including those discussed in Chapter 10. The primary considerations here are the leadership skills and common-sense methods the principal may use to motivate members of the faculty and staff. Some of this discussion may not be consistent with some highly publicized motivation theories.

The principal should exude enthusiasm for work and the accomplishment of goals to set a role model for members of the faculty and staff. Positive enthusiasm for high levels of performance should be expressed in overt behavior. High visibility of instructional leadership and willingness to assist teachers can be a symbol of the principal's dedication to a school

[17]Johnson and Johnson, *Joining Together*, pp. 99–102.

of quality and a caring attitude. The principal's behavior should send the students the message that high standards of performance are expected. Appropriate means to recognize high achievement and effort should be employed. Thank-you notes, publication of special projects, public recognition of accomplishments, inclusion of feature stories in the media, and other means should be used.

Within the literature and common-sense knowledge of experienced educators are many techniques that encourage motivation of students and teachers. What may seem to be a small favor, such as teaching a class for a teacher or serving as a resource, indicates interest in instruction. Listen attentively to what teachers say. Organize think-tank sessions and engage appropriately in informal discussions. Responsiveness to the feelings expressed, no matter how minor, is essential. Other techniques are (1) encourage the sharing of ideas, (2) establish an open-door policy, (3) publicize the innovative ideas of the school in state and national journals, (4) use outside consultants skilled in student motivation, and (5) learn how to express appreciation to the faculty for its special effort.

The authors believe that the demonstration of ability to see that teachers have the resources they need when they need them is a powerful motivator. When teachers perceive of the principal as a person that will move heaven and earth to provide the services and resources they need, a contagion builds for working hard and for high expectations of achievement.

Leadership Skill in Communicating.   Authorities in the field of management place communication as a central factor in administration. As any experienced principal knows, skill in communicating with the faculty is essential. The typical model of communication includes sender, encoding, channel, receiver, decoding, and response elements accompanied by a feedback loop and noise factor. Diagrams of the process fall short of helping the principal know how to establish effective communication processes in the school because communication is a dynamic process.

If, for example, the principal establishes legitimacy for leadership with the faculty, the ability to communicate effectively will be enhanced. There is a psychological factor in communication—one's feelings become involved in the sending or receipt of messages. The principal who is easily angered cannot communicate well with the faculty, staff, parents, or students. When there is an element of anxiety within the faculty, the context within which the message is sent will initially have more meaning to the recipient than the message itself. For instance, the principal's written request for a conference with a teacher may immediately be interpreted to mean that the principal is displeased with the teacher, rather than that the principal wants to talk about the upcoming PTA meeting. The body language of the principal sends messages that may be inconsistent with expressed verbal symbols; congruence of the verbal and nonverbal messages is essential.

Not to be overlooked in the communication process is the ability to listen; in fact, it may be the most important skill in communication. Listen very carefully to what the faculty is saying. Their feedback can hold very important meaning for how well the school is going. The principal should not assume that all members of the faculty are good listeners; consequently, most authorities recommend the practice of redundancy in sending messages.

As discussed previously in Chapter 6, written messages to parents and other citizens should be precise and in language they understand. Likewise, written messages to the faculty and students should be expressed succinctly and with clearly understood symbols.

CHAPTER EIGHT

The Process of Change

As the leader of the school administrative staff and faculty, the principal is expected to facilitate the change process. The primary purpose of this chapter is to discuss ways in which the adoption of new ideas and practices can be facilitated in the school. Change for improvement in schools is one of the most difficult tasks faced by school principals. In his noted treatise on the accumulation and use of political power, Niccolò Machiavelli wrote, "It must be considered that there is nothing more difficult to carry out, nor more doubtful of success, nor more dangerous to handle, than to initiate a new order of things."[1] Eric Hoffer observed: "It is my impression that no one really likes the new. It is not only as Dostoyevsky put it that 'taking a new step, uttering a new word is what people fear most.' Even in slight things the experience of the new is rarely without some stirring of foreboding."[2]

Facing an impending change is like anticipating possible death. Persons who are not accustomed to change do not know what is going to happen to them—it is unsettling because they do not know what to expect.

---

[1]Niccolò Machiavelli, *The Prince,* rev. ed., trans. Luigi Ricci (New York: Oxford University Press, 1952), p. 23.

[2]Eric Hoffer, *The Ordeal of Change* (New York: Harper & Row, 1963), p. 3.

As so well expressed by Eric Hoffer, when faced with change in everyday activities, even those who perceive themselves as advocates of change feel threatened. We are secure in advocating that others change in order to improve, but the advocacy does not apply to *us*. In summary, those who choose to be change agents must suffer the consequences from those who fear and dread change. This will be discussed more later in the chapter.

Consideration of some extreme historical examples of change agents is appropriate: Socrates dared to be different and he paid the price; Christ was also an advocate of revolutionary change and paid with his life; Machiavelli was not put to death because of his ideas concerning change, but he probably suffered a more horrible grievous death because his opinions were not accepted, and he felt "wasted in inactivity."[3]

As discussed previously, the school principal has many demanding responsibilities, such as responsibility for management and leadership, and this idea is replete in all of the literature. But what does the statement mean? Trite as it may appear, it is sensible. The principal is responsible to see that the school runs smoothly and that leadership is provided that ensures its improvement; moreover, school improvement necessitates changes in ideas and practices. Sweeney contended, "Change is the very essence of educational leadership."[4]

Change can be achieved without realizing improvement, but it is impossible to have improvement without having change. Change is necessary to have improvement, painful as it may be to some persons in the school and community. We are not necessarily trying to depict change as agonizing, but the truth is that most significant change is not achieved without some resistance. The record of successful attempts at directed change in education is not reassuring. Much directed change in education has fallen short of the objectives or has failed outright, yet not all educational change has been unsuccessful, and the secret of successful improvement may be in the strategies used. The rewards are usually too small and dispensed too late. Another problem often expressed in the educational literature is timidity about innovation, especially by some leaders. In the face of so many technological and societal changes must we not have the expectation of innovation and change in education?

Technology is so awe-inspiring that its advances are hardly questioned. Technological advances and their consequences are readily accepted by millions of citizens. Most persons no longer rely on a medicine man or even a religious shaman to cure their ills; they expect technology to do it. Scientific developments in medicine are viewed as protectors of health. Yet many citizens may be satisfied by doing the same old thing in

---

[3]Hoffer, *Change*, p. 87.

[4]James Sweeney, "Training Educational Leaders as Change Agents: The Effect of the Internship," *Educational Technology* (June 1980), pp. 20, 42–45.

education. Promoting new ideas and practices in the social realm is indeed threatening. Consequently, needed change in education is lagging as other areas race for the future. The challenge to management and leadership for the adoption of new ideas and practices in the school is a heavy obligation of the principal.

THE IMPACT OF TECHNOLOGICAL DEVELOPMENT

Innovation and adaptation strategies are needed in education to cope with the impact of the technological inventions that have changed the lifestyles of citizens, such as the telephone and the automobile. Before these inventions were in common use, neighbors were the families who lived next door. Now, with these inventions, neighbors may live across town or in another town. A phone call to them is quicker than a walk next door, one of many examples of how behavior has been affected by technological developments. The development of the automobile made possible the transportation of pupils and was the forerunner of the development of large, complex schools.

More recent inventions, such as television, plastics, and intercontinental missiles, have had an even more far-reaching impact on education and society. Yet these inventions have occurred during the lifetime of many Americans, a relatively short period of time considering human history.

Television brought the world into living rooms, and many people build their daily schedule around it. The horrors of the wars in Vietnam, Iran, Iraq, and Afghanistan appear on the tube daily; the poverty of Africa and the affluence of "Dallas" focus on contrasting extremes of affluence. These visions have a tremendous impact on the perceptions of society. Wars such as Vietnam, which might have been acceptable to another generation, suddenly became unacceptable to a generation who could see the horrors of it on television. Poverty in other countries was not something that greatly stirred our emotions and drove us to action until children could be seen with their hollow eyes and bloated stomachs on the evening news. Viewers can see people from all walks of life, with their varying cultures, behavior, clothing, and mannerisms. As has been so aptly stated by Marshall McLuhan, "The medium is the message."

Synthetics (plastics) were almost unheard of until after World War II. Imagine what life would be like without synthetic materials. Look around, and see their influence everywhere. If plastics suddenly disappeared, our whole way of life would be disrupted, because most of the objects we use daily are, in whole or in part, made from synthetic materials.

According to many futurists, society is moving from the industrial or technological revolution into the information era. Just consider the impact on our daily life of computer technology, which is the basis for automation and the displacement of millions of workers. Modern desktop computers can process more information and data than a roomful of computers could barely twenty years ago. Changes in information processing within the last two decades have revolutionized the marketplace and are greatly impacting the field of educational administration. We included a complete chapter (Chapter 13) on the use of computers that would not have appeared in a text on the principalship five years ago.

IS SCHOOL CHANGE KEEPING UP?

Contrast technological advances and their impact on social behavior with changes in the schools and their impact on our education system. There have been some noticeable changes in schools, but none that compare with the impact of technology on the administration of many corporations. For the most part, and in comparison to business and industry, schools have made few substantive changes. The basic structure of school buildings has not changed noticeably. We do not use horn books or hand-held slates anymore, but the textbooks and notebooks are not radically different. A few computers are evident in most schools, but their use is minimal, primarily restricted to accelerated students, which leads us to an earlier question: Can our schools continue to function in the same old way? Many governors and other citizens say no to this question. Stimulated by the National Commission on Excellence in Education report *A Nation at Risk,* the governors, legislators, and other citizens are demanding a reform of educational programs. Yet educational leaders are not leading the reform movement in some states, which should be a source of much concern for educators.

There is an old story that when Rip Van Winkle woke up, he looked around and decided that someone had moved him while he was asleep. He did not recognize anything around him. He started walking down a road and he did not recognize anything until he came to the school. He then determined that he had not been moved because it appeared to be the same old place that it had been twenty years earlier. Compared to technological developments this must be the way schools still appear to most people. Numerous writers have sounded the warning to educators that, if the public schools do not keep up with societal changes and expectations, they will not survive. Almost daily we are confronted with demands from citizens to seek reform of the educational process. In the past educators have not been as responsive to these demands as they might have been.

THE PRINCIPAL: A CHANGE AGENT

Technological developments have been equated with goodness. We have seen how such technological developments as the automatic washing machine, microwave oven, and vacuum cleaner have taken some of the drudgery out of life. Physical labor has been reduced and there is much more time for leisure or more desirable work. The prevailing attitude in the United States seems to be that change is good; it leads to a better life. Manufacturers of products used in the home have found that the term "new" on the label increases sales.

Belief in change has been applied to our concern about education. Parents expect change in the schools and most of them equate it with goodness, even those who desire to turn back the clock. The expectation of change has put great pressure on the principal to promote changes in the school. As discussed previously, state legislators in most states are demanding educational reform. The principal's skills as a change agent will be of growing importance if education is to improve its status in the system. In the past the schools have provided persons with the skills to conduct needed research and increase technical knowledge. Economists have suggested that other countries, such as Brazil, have more natural resources than the United States, yet one great difference they single out to explain the comparative economic success of the United States is our educational system. A group of businessmen recently appointed to study the future of the economy concluded that the growth of the economy in the United States will depend greatly on the quality of the educational system and that there is a need for change.

We have been somewhat critical of the lack of innovation in public schools; however, educators are not entirely to blame for this situation. Schools are operated within a plurality of interest groups with conflicting ideas. If poor change strategies are employed, many proposed substantive innovations might embroil the principal and school faculty in a conflict with the community. Moreover, the changes desired by parental groups often result in turmoil for the principal, and too many public issues are not conducive to tenure or the job. Too many principals decide to avoid making any substantive changes rather than run the risk of being severely criticized and possibly lose their positions.

If the strategies used are well developed and administered, changes in ideas and practices in the schools need not create great problems. We believe that the leadership ideas expressed in this and other chapters of the text will make educational changes acceptable to both members of the profession and the public.

In summary, successful change agentry gives the principal and faculty more, not less, control of the school program. To use the vernacular, change agentry is not a rose garden for the principal. If principals and teachers make changes in school practices to improve them, those moves do not make life easier for them; new practices may even be more difficult. Educational leaders have to work harder if they are to implement new ideas and practices. It is much easier to let things slide along, but the easy way out is a delusion, because when parents finally learn that their children have been deprived of educational excellence, the lazy principal will reap the whirlwind. A serious question of professional ethics is involved if we do not do our best to give children and youth the best education possible with the resources available. If the development of excellence in education is the proper perspective, and we believe that it is, how can principals promote change for improvement in the schools that will keep pace with technological change? The remaining part of this chapter is devoted to explaining this concept of change agentry.

PLANNED CHANGE

Change occurs regardless of whether it is planned—it is inevitable. Unplanned change will occur randomly and often not in the best interest of the school. Planned change, however, is more likely to result in desirable outcomes, and the correct strategy is needed to promote these changes. The principal who is familiar with the research-based process of change has a great advantage in promoting new planned practices.[5] Two types of organizational change are presented: "unplanned—evolutionary change that occurs without deliberate guidance. . . [and] planned—a conscious effort to alter the status quo by affecting the function, structure, technology, and/or resources of an organization."[6]

According to Harris, change is not always planned, but planned change is preferred.[7] Bennis, Benne, and Chin stated: "Planned change entails mutual goal setting by one or both parties, an equal power-ratio, and deliberateness, eventually at least on the part of both sides."[8] Bennis and associates noted that there are several kinds of change, including indoctrination, coercive, technocratic, interactional, socialization, emulative, and natural. Indoctrination indicates deliberate and mutual goal setting. It also involves imbalance in power. Hospitals, prisons, and schools usually fall into this category. Coercive change suggests nonmutual goal setting with an imbalanced power ratio and one-sided deliberateness. Technocratic change is accomplished solely by

[5]W. A. Firestone and B. L. Wilson, "Using Bureaucratic and Cultural Linkages to Improve Instruction: The Principal's Contribution," *Educational Administration Quarterly,* 21 (Spring 1985), 7–30.

[6]"Managing Organizational Change: Dangers and Opportunities" (Atlanta: O. D. Resource, Inc., 1978).

[7]Ben M. Harris, *Supervisory Behavior in Education* (Englewood Cliffs, N.J.: Prentice-Hall, 1975), p. 82.

[8]Warren G. Bennis, Kenneth D. Benne, and Robert Chin, *The Planning of Change* (New York: Holt, Rinehart, & Winston, 1964), p. 154.

collecting data. Interactional change demands mutual goal setting, power being distributed fairly, and no deliberateness by either party. Teacher-child or parent-child relationships are examples of a socialization change. There is a direct relationship with the two parties. Emulative change is the process associated with formal organizations. The superior-subordinate relationship is clear-cut. Finally, natural change does not involve any apparent deliberateness nor does it involve goal setting by any parties to the change.[9]

Research About the Process

There has been a great deal of research on the process of planned change. It is a favorite topic of many scholars in the behavioral sciences. Many of them, especially sociologists, have devoted their life studies to it. Many volumes have been written on the topic. The principal who is serious about becoming knowledgeable of the process of planned change has much information from which to draw. We do not expect to present all the information that is available about planned change in this chapter. Our hope is to present some of the more succinct notions about the subject to give the student a basic knowledge. The primary objective is to whet the appetite of readers, and to make an impression concerning the importance of the topic.

Mort did serious studies on the process of planned change as early as the 1950s. He did basic research on the process in his well-known adaptability studies.[10] Rogers also directed early studies on the subject and reviewed hundreds of studies on the topic. Many of those studies were conducted by rural sociologists in the field of agriculture.[11] Many of the early researchers on the subject, such as Lionberger[12] and Beal and Bohlen[13] placed much emphasis on the planned-change research model used in agricultural experimental stations. The agriculture model, based on experiment stations for doing research with county agents to disseminate the findings to farmers, was very successful. Many organizations and particularly educators have given the agricultural change model a lot of attention. The National Institute of Education also made attempts to adapt the model to education.

---

[9]Bennis, Benne, and Chin, *Planning of Change*, p. 154.

[10]Paul Mort, *Educational Adaptability* (New York: Metropolitan School Study Council, 1953).

[11]Everett M. Rogers, *Diffusion of Innovations* (New York: New York Press, 1962).

[12]Herbert F. Lionberger, *Adoption of New Ideas and Practices* (Ames: Iowa State University Press, 1960), pp. 3–4.

[13]George M. Beal and Joe M. Bohlen, "The Diffusion Process" (Ames: Iowa State Univ. Agr. Ext. Ag. Ser. Spec. Rept. No. 18, March 1957).

Stages or Steps in the Adoption of New Ideas

Change theorists have investigated how the individual adopts new ideas and practices. Lionberger listed the series of stages that a person enters in the adoption of new ideas and practices.

Awareness: The first knowledge about a new idea, product or practice

Interest: The active seeking of extensive and detailed information about the idea, to determine its possible usefulness and applicability

Evaluation: Weighing and sifting the acquired information and evidence in light of the existing conditions into which the practice would have to fit

Trial: The tentative trying out of a practice or idea, accompanied by acquisition of information on how to do it

Adoption: The full-scale integration of the practice into the ongoing operation[14]

The principal may find this concept useful; however, it should be used advisedly. It is important to be aware, Lionberger points out, that one may not go through all of the above stages on every occasion that the model is applied.[15]

Lipham also listed phases of planned change as awareness, initiation, implementation, routinization, refinement, renewal, and evaluation.[16] Hall and Ford discussed the following phases of the change process.

Research: The findings of quantitative and qualitative studies lead to the suggestion that certain previously unidentified or underutilized practices or materials will be more effective

Development: New approaches or materials are created, packaged, and evaluated to achieve a particular objective

Diffusion: The natural spread of awareness and use of an innovation across a social system

Dissemination: The deliberate marketing of an innovation and encouragement of its adoption

Adoption: The decision-making process or, conversely, the decision point that leads to selection of an innovation and commitment to implementation

Implementation: The initial and early use of an innovation involving negotiation between the user system and the innovation to arrive at an amicable match

Institutionalization: The incorporation of routine use in a state of equilibrium

[14]Lionberger, *Adoption*, pp. 3–4.

[15]Lionberger, *Adoption*, p. 23.

[16]James M. Lipham, Robb E. Rankin, and James A. Hoek, Jr., *The Principalship: Concepts, Competencies, and Cases* (New York: Longman, 1985), pp. 114–17.

Refinement: Fine tuning of innovation use to maximize outcomes in the local setting

Abandonment: Discontinuance of use[17]

According to Glickman, change must be dealt with at three levels: orientation, integration, and refinement. *What* and *why* questions should be dealt with during the orientation stage. The integration stage should be devoted to the implementation of the innovation. Concern for refinement of experiences and a search for ways to make innovations better should be the central focus of the refinement stage.[18] Reilly contended that the principal has three key roles to play in the process of change: planning and developing programs, implementing and improving programs, and evaluating program effectiveness.[19]

STEPS NECESSARY TO PROMOTE CHANGE

We suggest several steps that are necessary for successfully promoting change: determining the need for change, promoting the idea, exploring the alternative practices, implementing change, evaluating, and disseminating. The steps should be taken in the order listed.

DETERMINING THE NEED FOR CHANGE

The first step to initiate change is to determine the need for change. Just what is the problem? Determining the need requires careful consideration. Assume you, as principal, have decided that there is a need for improving the teaching and learning environment of the school. If the environment is to be improved through a process of planned change, specific needs must be determined.[20] The needs must then be sorted in terms of importance, urgency, and approachability.

Change is often centered on a movement that is popular at the time. If everyone else is promoting experiential learning, it is assumed to be the real need of a particular school. Yet, when the real need for change is

---

[17]Gene E. Hall and Shirley M. Ford, *Change in Schools: Facilitating the Process* (Albany: State University of New York Press, 1987), p. 331.

[18]Carl D. Glickman, *Supervision of Instruction: A Developmental Approach* (Boston: Allyn and Bacon, 1985), p. 248.

[19]D. H. Reilly, "The Principalship: The Need for a New Approach," *Education,* 104 (Spring 1984), 242–47.

[20]K. A. Leithwood and D. J. Montgomery, "The Role of the Elementary School Principal in Program Improvements," *Review of Educational Research,* 52 (Fall 1982), 309–39.

properly assessed, the solution may be something much more basic and immediate than trendy experiential learning. It logically follows that the real need must not be determined by what everyone else is doing; that is letting faddism rule over responsible administration. The need should be determined and agreed upon by the principal and teachers of the school. It may not be the most important or urgent need, but the real need according to the teachers, the ones directly involved in the change process. The need may not be the most important one that should be addressed for the purpose of change, but it has to be the agreed-upon, feasible need.

The term *need* related to change may be a misnomer. The need for change derives from the desire of the people in the organization who will be affected by the change. No change of consequence will be implemented if it is not desired at a particular time by the persons who are directly affected by it. A friend of the authors started a consulting firm and publishing business that was intended to help elementary school teachers. According to his account, he was publishing what he knew elementary teachers needed, and his knowledge came from many years of experience as teacher, principal, and consultant. However, his materials and consulting services did not sell, and he was on the verge of bankruptcy. Out of desperation and with great reluctance he started providing services and printing educational materials that teachers wanted. His business as an educational consultant and publisher flourished, and he became a major competitor of other nationally recognized consulting firms. After he was recognized nationally he could afford to take some risks. Only then could he start providing services that he knew teachers needed. The moral of the story is that principals cannot assume that the teacher's perception of needs for improvement is in agreement with theirs. The need for significant change for improving the teaching and learning environment should be cultivated, starting with the expressed needs of the teachers. Only when this is accomplished can teachers be directed to the more global and universal needs of the school.

All individual needs are established on a personal premise. Every personal action may be initiated by a self-serving motive. This is not to say that the only motive for action is self-serving but that the basis for the act must be self-satisfying. A teacher who works long hours after school and makes great personal sacrifices to provide the best possible teaching and learning environment for the students does have the best interest of the students in mind. However, teachers must have a basic need for self-satisfaction, pride, and praise for a job well done, or they will not make the extra effort. Hence, the need for change must be based on well-thought-out, long-range planning by professional administrators, but the sequence of the needs to be established in the process of planned change must be based on the choice of those most concerned with implementing the change, the teachers.

A checklist that could be applied when determining the need for change might be like the following.

1. Is there really a need?
2. Is the need clearly defined?
3. Are other needs associated with it? If so, what are they? Must these needs be dealt with congruently or can they be factored out?
4. What kind of need is it? For example, does it involve curriculum, instruction, law, policy, human relations, organization, personnel, or technical equipment?
5. Is it a need that should be dealt with now, later, or not at all?
6. Who should decide if and when the need should be considered?
7. How threatening is this idea for change?
8. What will be the consequences if you do not deal with the need?
9. What do you hope to accomplish if you deal with the need and promote the change?
10. Do you have all of the facts to establish the particulars of the need?
11. Is it the proper time for dealing with the need?
12. What are the alternatives to dealing with the need?
13. What are the alternatives to not dealing with the need?
14. What is the best course of action for dealing with the promotion of the idea for change?

PROMOTING THE IDEA

Once the need has been determined the task of implementing the idea for change must be begun. Promoting an idea for change may be one of the most demanding responsibilities of a school principal. It will test the patience of even the most determined principal because promoting change is usually a slow, arduous process. Change agents warn that one can initially expect to invest a great amount of energy with little movement; however, as movement is achieved, the process will speed up. As Hechinger said, "Trying to bring about changes in education has been compared to moving a cemetery."[21] Words of wisdom offered by Marks, Stoops, and King-Stoops should be considered, "Many good ideas, which should have worked, have failed miserably because they were put into effect too quickly."[22] Barnard's approach based on formal and informal organizations would do much for setting the pace when promoting the idea for change.[23]

[21]F. M. Hechinger, "Where Have All the Innovators Gone?" *Today's Education,* 65 (September/October 1976), 80–83, 125.

[22]James R. Marks, Emery Stoops, and Joyce King-Stoops, *Handbook of Educational Supervision: A Guide for the Practitioner* (Boston: Allyn and Bacon, 1971), p. 80.

[23]Chester I. Barnard, *Functions of the Executive* (Cambridge: Harvard University Press, 1938), p. 232.

Barnard contended that effectiveness (the organizational dimension) is accomplished through formal organization and that efficiency (the personal side of organization) is determined by informal organization.[24] Faculty meetings are examples of formal organizations; teacher cliques are examples of informal organizations.

The principal who does not give attention to both the formal and informal organization when promoting change is courting failure. Not allowing for deliberate proceedings in promoting change is also inviting disaster. The principal who succeeds in promoting change will be patient when patience is required and assertive at the opportune moment for moving. Successfully promoting ideas for change requires engaging teachers in both the formal and informal organizations and proceeding at a deliberate but patient pace.

A principal who is promoting a change of some significance, perhaps a different teaching method, must patiently, deliberately, and wisely work through both formal and informal organizations to promote the idea. Consider this situation: Assume that a principal is promoting a change of methodology from lecture to experiential teaching. If successful change is to be achieved, the procedure for promoting the change will be pursued through both the formal and the informal organization.

The idea will likely be presented in a faculty meeting—the formal structure. An idea of such consequence should never, except in times of crisis, be presented at a faculty meeting and voted on at that same meeting. Any teacher at a particular initial meeting may be persuaded to vote one way, and yet after meeting with an informal group and discussing the idea have a completely different view of the matter. In the end the teacher might be inclined to vote just the opposite of what had been expressed at the original formal meeting. The proper process for promoting the idea starts in the meeting at which the notion is formally presented.

The teachers should then be given time to meet with their informal groups (cliques) and discuss the matter. The wise principal will sense what the teachers are really thinking about the idea. The informal groups will decide how efficiently the idea will be promoted, or if it will indeed be worthy of promoting. By the next faculty meeting, say two weeks hence, the principal who has listened to the informal network, especially its leaders, will have a good feel for the reception of the idea. Adjustments can then be made based on what has been learned from the teachers, and the principal can act accordingly by pursuing the idea in the next formal meeting. The leader should pursue this process of sifting through the formal and informal structures for as long as it is needed to achieve a near-consensus regarding the idea. When the time comes to adopt the idea, it must be done in the formal organization. The idea is brought to the

[24]Barnard, *Functions,* p. 176.

faculty meeting and the formal implementation of the idea is begun. In summary, the idea is put into effect through the formal organization, but how efficiently it is implemented is determined by the informal organization in interaction with the formal organization.

Deciding to Change

Change will take place when there is an imbalance between the forces for change and the forces for stability on the part of the teachers. Teachers cannot be expected to change until the rewards for change outweigh the need for stability. Ideas for change cannot be successfully promoted until that imbalance has been established. When the rewards are adequate and appropriate, teachers will want to change. In other words, in order to get people to change one must motivate them to want the change.

Mager and associates emphasized the importance of getting people to want to change.[25] Barnett also stressed the importance of promoting the desire to change.[26] The reasons he listed for people wanting to change were credit wants, subconscious wants, linkage wants, convergent wants, compensatory wants, entrained wants, voluntary wants, creative wants, relief and avoidance wants, the desire for quantitative variation wants, and vicarious wants.

Credit Wants

About the only thing that many principals have to offer teachers for promoting change is credit. Except for the possibility of linking merit pay with innovation, there are seldom financial rewards for suggesting innovative practices. In fact, instead of getting rewarded financially, teachers may spend some of their own money to support an idea and then experience more work by being appointed as leaders to promote and implement the idea. Small wonder that many teachers do not make more suggestions for change; they are not rewarded by being given credit for the idea. Since citizens are demanding some form of differential in salary, the educational leaders of school districts may be able to use the adoption of change as one criterion for salary.

Barnett[27] discovered that innovativeness is not rewarded in many cultures, but it is highly prized in this country. One example of the reward

[25]Robert Mager, *Analyzing Performance Problems* (Boston: Fearon, 1972).

[26]H. G. Barnett, *Innovation: The Basis of Cultural Change* (New York: McGraw-Hill, 1953), p. 105.

[27]Barnett, *Innovation*, p. 106.

system is the emphasis on patents for inventions. He stated that "in by far the majority of cases there has been relatively little possibility of assigning credit to an innovator." The lack of credit is not because such ideas have not been worthwhile, but because the concept of assigning credit has so often been weak or absent. In many societies the amount of prestige that goes with the conception of a new idea is so small, the granting of it so uncertain, and its duration so fleeting that it can hardly be expected to function as an incentive. "Our knowledge that most Americans are engaged to strive for any goal if it carries a financial reward, and our belief that they should do so are reflections of the generic cultural bias that postulated individual recognition as an essential condition for any labor."[28] In conclusion, Barnett said that "the conscious desire for credit is an important motivation to invention."[29]

It must be abundantly clear by now that the most important thing principals have to offer teachers is recognition for their ideas and efforts. Principals should make the most of that knowledge. It is not unusual for a teacher to approach the principal with what is thought to be a brilliant idea for improving the teaching and learning process in the school. The wise principal receives the idea, gives the teacher credit for the suggestion, and helps the teacher pursue the idea to its limit. Too often, however, the principal may shrug off the idea as if it is of no consequence, and then two months later consider it a great idea but present it as a personal creation. The dishonesty will be received for what it is—unethical conduct or plagiarism. How many other ideas for change will that teacher or any other teacher in the school present? Of course they will offer none. In conclusion, if one wants teachers to adopt new ideas and practices, ways must be found to encourage their initiative, not discourage it.[30]

ESTABLISHING STRATEGIES FOR TEACHER MOTIVATION

Change strategies must include attention to motivating teachers to act. In this section we approach motivation from the standpoint of wants that inspire teachers to change. There are at least four categories of wants that will be motivating factors, subconscious wants, linkage of wants, entrained wants, and compensatory wants.

[28]Barnett, *Innovation,* p. 107.

[29]Barnett, *Innovation,* p. 108.

[30]S. M. Hord, S. M. Stiegelbauer, and G. E. Hall, "How Principals Work with Other Change Facilitators," *Education and Urban Society,* 17 (November 1984), 90–109.

Subconscious Wants

There are certain wants that inspire teachers to change that are subliminal in nature. The innate desire to pursue effort after meaning is a natural bent in those who have satisfied the more basic needs of food, shelter, and safety, and who have reached a higher order of reasoning. Most teachers fall into that category. Most have advanced their thinking and creative desires to the point where they get self-satisfaction from pursuing effort after meaning for the sake of knowing. Some of these subconscious wants come about because of boredom. For example, people doodle to satisfy a subconscious, creative need when they are bored. The results of these creative wanderings should be given attention, for they can be valuable sources of ideas for improvement. Edison was reported to be toying with materials in his workshop when he accidentally discovered that carbon was the key to the mystery of the incandescent lamp filament. In the same manner, Leroy Grumman's discovery of the notion for the backward-folding airplane was supposedly a result of his tinkering with an eraser and paper clips.[31, 32]

Like Grumman, teachers make common-sense discoveries that could be valuable for improving the school. Unlike Grumman's experience, however, many of the discoveries will go unnoticed and unused unless an astute leader is aware of the benefits of their efforts. The subconscious wants inherent in teachers can be a great source of ideas for improvement if the notions are harnessed and linked to the objectives of the school.

Linkage of Wants and Expectations

Some wants for change are linked in that a certain one is dependent on another. A teacher's desire to change the content of a course may be linked to the content of the adopted text. The content of the course is, therefore, dependent on the content of the text. Just the opposite could be true. Changing a text could be linked to changing the content of the course. The teacher may want to change the content of the course but can only do so if a new text is adopted.

The best time for introducing and implementing changes in the school program is when moving into a new building or when a major alteration and refurbishment has been completed. The expectation of something new and different is prevalent since the physical environment is different. The linkage between a new building and the expectation of a new, improved program is strong.

[31]Barnett, *Innovation,* p. 132.

[32]Howard W. Blakeslee, "The Folding Wing: What it All Means to Our Carriers," *Washington Post,* April 15, 1944.

Entrained Wants

Maslow[33] and McGregor[34] discussed the desire of persons to have certain basic needs fulfilled. Maslow especially emphasized that all needs cannot be fulfilled and that there is a hierarchy of needs innate in humans. When one need is fulfilled, another need surfaces. For example, a young married couple buys a new house. They are convinced that by owning the new house, their need for shelter will be fulfilled. They may have obligated their budget to the limit. Of course, there are always the property insurance, taxes, and other incidentals that may or may not have been figured in the monthly payments—all necessities. As soon as they move in, the wife immediately discovers that the house would look so much better with new drapes, another converging want. The paint in the kitchen and master bedroom just does not blend in with the decor, and on and on. In the same vein, a boy who has just turned sixteen and obtained a new driver's license would be perfectly content if he could have a car, just a set of wheels to get around. He gets a car, and right away he discovers that it would look so much sharper with fancy hub caps. This, he believes will give him recognition, which is a higher, psychological order of need. Shortly he realizes that he needs a girlfriend to ride in the car with him, and the list of needs keeps growing bigger and bigger.

Barnett dealt with this subject when he said:

> The entrainment of wants is due in part to the dynamic quality of the physical universe. All things change under the constant interaction of natural forces: iron rusts, winds blow and subside; men are born, grow old, and die; and the seasons change. Human wants are correlated with these alterations as well as determined by their own dynamics. Human beings wish for stability or for change, for more security or less of it, as the individual case may be. The achievement of any one desire merely sets another complex of forces to work, for which again there is a demand for greater or less stability.[35]

Effective principals use the entrained-wants notion to keep the sequence for change moving. One improvement should create a desire in teachers for another and another. Promoted properly, the entrained-wants idea leads to a pyramid of improvements in the school, each one building on the other.

Compensatory Wants

Teachers can be moved to change because of compensatory wants. They want to be compensated in some way, not necessarily by money, even

[33]Abraham Maslow, *Motivation and Personality* (New York: Harper & Row, 1954).

[34]Douglas M. McGregor, "The Human Side of Enterprise," in Bennis, Benne, and Chin, *The Planning of Change* (New York: Holt, Rinehart & Winston, 1961), pp. 422–31.

[35]Barnett, *Innovation*, p. 151.

though money may serve as a strong motivator for underpaid teachers. However, the receipt of a merit award may be more important in the satisfaction of psychological wants, to the need for recognition, than in the satisfaction of basic physiological needs. Tennessee implemented a "Better Schools Program"[36] in the middle 1980s. Change came from the top; it was planned and implemented by directions of the governor and a trusted few high-ranking administrators. Local school teachers and administrators were not involved in the initial planning and implementation of the program. The act went against most rules for directed change except in one aspect: Teachers and administrators were compensated monetarily for implementing one part of the program. The one part of the program for which compensation was given was merit. A system of levels based on merit was established. On reaching Level I, the educators received an additional $1000; for Level II an additional $3000; and for Level III, $6000 was added to the salaries. The levels could be reached in a limited number of ways. One route for reaching Level I became almost universal and was attained by most of the Tennessee teachers and principals. The requirement was 40 hours of in-service training on the Tennessee Instructional Model (TIM) and the subsequent implementation of that model. TIM was the heart of the Better Schools Program and was implemented at some level by most teachers in the state. Without the additional compensation for Level I, it is unlikely that the Better Schools Program reform movement would have stood a chance of being implemented.

VARIABLES RELATED TO CHANGE

There are many variables that are related to the change process. Barnett[37] listed several of the more important ones, such as expectation of change, dependence upon authority, accumulation of ideas, collaboration of effort, conjunction of differences, competition of rivals, and deprivation of essentials. We will explore these variables because they are so closely associated with attitudes toward change.

Expectation of Change

Expectation of change may be the greatest force for change in schools in this country. As discussed earlier, many persons have come to expect change in technology and they equate it with goodness. People have also

---

[36]Better Schools Program (Tennessee, Working Document from State Department of Education).

[37]Barnett, *Innovation*, pp. 39–97.

come to expect change in schools, and they equate that with goodness. Any particular change in the school may or may not be good, but progress and change have become synonymous in our expectations; people have come to expect change as a force to reckon with, whether it is for better or for worse.

Every fall, customers anxiously wait for the new automobile models to appear in showrooms of the local dealers. Change in appearance and performance capability are expected. The dealers tout the new improved look and performance. Customers often wonder why they did not wait just one more year to buy that new car. The gas mileage capability has been increased, the car has been given new contours that decrease wind resistance and give the driver a better view from all directions, and the list of improvements continues, making older models undesirable. Never mind that the car may be recalled for deficiencies brought about by the changes— there is an atmosphere of anticipation that cars will change each year, and that with the changes will come improvement. Positive expectation is what keeps customers going back to buy new cars even while the present car is still in perfect condition, "purrs like a kitten," and still looks good. Barnett contended, "Innovation flourishes in an atmosphere of anticipation of it. If the members of a society expect something new, it is more likely to appear than if it is unforeseen and unheralded. The change frequency will be augmented in proportion to the number of expectant individuals. The greater the number of people who expect to use them, the more frequently they will be seen."[38] Principals who promote the expectation of change in schools will see change and improvement.

Dependence Upon Authority

As a general rule, the more independent people are, the more innovative they become. For example, after having lived in the same house with others, a person living alone will change habits much more readily. The adjustments will be made partly because of necessity, but, for the most part, they will be made because of the independence one has when living alone. Individuals living alone change eating, sleeping, and working habits to fit their newly found independent style. "The greater the freedom of the individual to explore his world experience and to organize its elements in accordance with his private interpretation of his sense impressions, the greater the likelihood of new ideas coming into being. Contrariwise, the more the reliance upon authoritative dictates, the less the frequency of new conceptualizations."[39] It follows that in the schools where greater independence of thinking and less dependence on authority exists, there will be

[38]Barnett, *Innovation,* p. 56
[39]Barnett, *Innovation,* p. 65..

evidence of greater change. If, in schools where there is a great dependence on authority, the authority figure is amenable to change, chances for improvement are much greater than they are in schools where the opposite is true.

Accumulation and Concentration of Ideas

A single idea for change may not move people to action, but an accumulation and concentration of ideas may. A teacher may believe that a change to individualized instruction will improve students' chances of learning but cannot conceive of how it can be done one-on-one. However, by reading about and observing other attempts at individualizing instructions, the teacher begins to acquire accumulated ideas on the subject. The teacher begins to see that individualized instruction can be accomplished in ways other than independent study. As ideas accumulate for small and large group instruction, as well as independent study, the teacher may see how the change can be managed and will subsequently change to an individualized instruction approach that incorporates all of those ideas. One idea may not move the teacher to change, but the accumulation and concentration of ideas will.

Collaboration of Effort

One teacher working alone may view a particular idea for change, such as revising all unit plans for Biology II, as too monumental to attempt. A feeling of insufficient information may appear for a project that expansive. If it is found, however, that the other two biology teachers are willing to explore the idea for revision of the units simultaneously and cooperatively, the teacher will find the idea much more palatable. The interaction among the three teachers will be mutually encouraging. The concentration not only allows for division of labor for a common task but provides an accumulation of ideas for solving the problem as well.

There is enough expertise in any school to have an outstanding teaching and learning environment if the ideas for improvement can be pooled. For every area where there is a teacher with an evident weakness, there is likely another teacher in the same school with an evident strength in that same area of competency. Getting those competencies shared is the real key to improvement. Strong principals promote a collaboration of effort among the teachers in their schools.

The results of discoveries and accomplishments by persons who receive great acclaim are, almost without exception, based on a compilation of ideas from the works of others. There is some value to being recognized for an individual accomplishment even though it may be based on the collaborative efforts of others, but most great achievements have required a combined effort. Salk received recognition for the breakthrough in the polio vaccine, but no doubt he would have acknowledged that it was not his single effort alone. Research in the treatment and cure of cancer has been done by literally thousands of researchers and has been a slow process. Without a monumental collaborative effort, there likely would be comparatively little progress in cancer research. The same can be applied to improving schools. Significant change will be the result of a collaborative effort.[40]

Conjunction of Differences

Throughout history, people have been changing because of the exchange of ideas. One person's ideas are merged with the differing views of another and the thought process of assimilation is set into action. Two teachers have similar ideas for change, but they go about initiating and implementing the ideas in different ways. When they get together and discuss an idea in an honest and professional manner, a conjunction of their differences about the idea and how it can be put into action will usually result.

Competition of Rivals

One need only to look around to see the effects of the competition of rivals. Turn on the television, and you will see and hear why you should buy a Ford truck rather than a Chevrolet or vice versa. You will also be told that one soap powder is new and improved and far superior to its rival product. The soap companies keep changing their products and so do the automobile manufacturers. The greatest reason for changing their products is the competition among rivals for sales. Teachers may change because they are in competition with a rival teacher. They want to look good. They do not want to be considered out-of-touch. School systems will change for the same reasons. We all know of school systems that take great pride in being on the cutting edge of trendy practices. They do not want someone or some system to get ahead of them in the race to be first in trying new ideas. According to Lipham, "Thus, competition between and among schools is an underestimated force for significant change."[41] The principal can appeal to the sense of competitiveness in teachers and reap great results in promoting an idea for change.

[40]Warren G. Bennis, *The Unconscious Conspiracy: Why Teachers Can't Lead* (New York: American Management Association, 1976).

[41]Lipham, *Principalship,* p. 119.

Deprivation of Essentials

Deprive persons of something they think they have a right to retain or expect and they will change in order to keep or get their rights. Essentials are whatever we define as such. Luxuries become essentials, depending on conditions. President Hoover's statement "a car in every garage and a chicken in every pot" seemed like a dream and a luxury at the time it was uttered—not so now. Most families consider more than one car a necessity during this mobile age, and chicken is considered one of the staple meats in most households. In the same vein, what is a necessity in one society or community may be a luxury in another. Principals should constantly point out to teachers the essentials of which they are deprived. When teachers realize that they are deprived of what is essential for meeting their needs, they will change.

EXPLORING ALTERNATIVE PRACTICES

Once the idea for change has been accepted and the decision to change has been made, the next step is to investigate the alternative practices. There is no point in trying to reinvent the wheel. Hechinger observed that there is never anything new in education; most ideas in education are borrowed rather than invented.[42] There are many alternative practices in effect in other schools and even other organizations that are similar. Those sources should be investigated. There are three major sources from which to draw: visits to other schools, reading about similar programs, and using resource people.

Visits to Other Schools

An investigation should first be made to develop a list of schools that seem to already have the change derived. The personnel of the department of education in individual states are usually a good source for locating those schools. When the list has been completed, a letter requesting information about each school and especially about the practice in question should be sent. Most principals are pleased to be recognized as having exemplary practices in operation and will respond with the desired information. When all of the information has been gathered, a sorting process will be helpful to determine the information that will be useful and which schools should be visited. The selection of schools to be visited will be influenced, to some extent, by the time and expense required for the visit. Time and funds spent for visiting other schools will pay handsome dividends.

[42]Hechinger, *Today's Education*, p. 35.

The visits will produce additional ideas for change and may convince the principal and faculty to adopt some of the practices observed. Keep careful notes of all visits and observations; the dimmest ink is brighter than the brightest memory. One's intention is to remember details, but they may be lost without explicit notes. Visitation of other schools when preparing for change is invaluable. The principal should not try to make a major change without it.

Read About Similar Programs

Read, read, read about similar practices. There is usually an abundance of literature on most ideas for change. A thorough literature search is essential when considering the alternatives to change. The teachers involved should choose subtopics concerning the practice to be adopted and should make a complete literature investigation of each subtopic. The combination of their efforts will yield tidbits of knowledge that will be invaluable in implementing the chosen idea.

Use Resource People

An expert is one who is at least fifty miles from home, as the saying goes. Use some of the professionals who are knowledgeable about the new idea. Usually, outsiders have the psychological advantage of being known only for their expertise in the chosen topic; they have an advantage over local experts because their weaknesses are not readily known. Outsiders are usually enough removed from the situation to be objective, but they should be chosen on the recommendation of other respected professionals. Access to resource persons is usually limited by funds and availability, so they should be chosen and used wisely.

Local resource persons should not be overlooked. As mentioned earlier, there is usually enough expertise around to solve most problems if it can be combined and properly directed.

It would be highly unlikely that an alternative practice could be found that could be exported in its entirety to another school. Ordinarily it is not desirable to attempt this move, since no two schools or their needs are alike. However, by visiting other schools, reading about similar practices, and drawing on the expertise of resource people, the results of implementing change in a new practice will be greatly enhanced.

IMPLEMENTING CHANGE

The basic rule in implementing change is to avoid implementing and planning at the same time. Almost without exception, those who try to plan and change at the same time plan themselves right back to where they started. As the implementation progresses, the change becomes threatening. If those most directly involved in the change, teachers in this case, are allowed to change plans as they implement, each time they are threatened they will change directions to a more comfortable position. That change is usually backward to the old, secure practice. Given time, they will be back where they started, in that comfortable, secure "rut."[43]

The plan for change is never complete. We know of schools that have been planning change for years and have not started implementing the changes yet because the plans are not complete. The plans will never be complete. A reasonable length of time should be given to the planning, and at some point a judgment must be made as to when to stop planning and start implementing the change. A principal who has a working knowledge of the change process and a feel for the tone of the school will know when the switch needs to be made.[44]

Before the implementation stage, the plan must be organized and written in detail.[45] There are four essentials in the written plan: (1) what is to be done, or the objectives; (2) how it is to be done, or the activities; (3) when each objective is to be accomplished; and (4) who will be responsible for the accomplishment of which objective. See the PERT and Gantt charts in Chapter 10 for further details.

The objectives for accomplishing the change must be couched in terms that will reveal some tangible evidence that they have been completed. Accomplishment of some of the objectives will naturally produce tangible evidence. For example, if one of the objectives is to produce a certain number of learning activity packets that include specified criteria, the finished, approved volumes will be tangible evidence that the objective has been completed. Some objectives will not be specific and will not produce tangible results. In that case a written statement from the person responsible for the objective may have to suffice as evidence of its accomplishment. We reemphasize that it is crucial to produce tangible evidence indicating that the objective has been accomplished, that an objective should be checked off the plan when achieved, and that written records should be kept that verify its accomplishment.

The activities developed to accomplish the objectives should be as specific as can be anticipated. Specifications are an area of the plan that may have to be modified or expanded as the need arises, but no changes should be made if they compromise the intent of the original objectives;

[43]A. R. Jwaideh, "The Principal as a Facilitator of Change," *Educational Horizons,* 63 (Fall 1984), 9–15.

[44]L. S. Chamberlin and R. R. Cote, *Administration, Education, and Change* (Dubuque, Iowa: Kendall/Hunt, 1972).

[45]Jwaideh, "Principal as a Facilitator," pp. 9–15.

changes should be made to expedite the accomplishment of the objective. The activities are simply what has to be done to accomplish the objective, and sometimes they cannot be anticipated accurately.

The period of time during which the objective is to be accomplished should be projected,[46] although this estimate cannot always be accurate. Inaccurate as it might be, it should be targeted because of the tendency to procrastinate. Sufficient time should be allotted for completion of the objectives. Lipham contends, "Most major changes take years, not months."[47]

If a target date is not set for completion, many tasks will never be completed. The projected date of accomplishment of each objective should be a written part of the plan, even though the target may be missed. It is better to explain why the objective was not completed by the projected date than not to have a deadline.

The written plan should specify who is responsible for the achievement of each objective. If at all possible, one person should be designated to accept responsibility. If two persons are made responsible for one task, each one will wait for the other and place responsibility on the other to act. If more than two persons are designated to see that something is accomplished, it probably will never get done. When everyone is in charge, no one is in charge; when everyone is responsible, no one is responsible.

Procedures for implementing the plan should be approached in an orderly manner. The written program should be followed without deviation. Teachers should work in small groups to determine what they are willing to do. If teachers decide things in "we agree sessions" they should have no latitude as to whether the ideas agreed upon will be implemented, since they went through the democratic process earlier. The principal can then be autocratic and insist that the agreed-upon ideas be implemented. Everyone's professional reputation, including the principal's, will be on the line because a formal commitment had already been made to make the specified changes.

The implementation stage of the change process is when most change is lost. It is relatively easy to plan change compared to implementing it. During the implementation stage, the stark realization dawns on the teachers, the ones most affected by the change, that this is the real thing. Before, the ideas seemed daring and the principal so cavalier in a brave approach to changing the order of things. Now, during the implementation stage, the principal seems much less of a Prince Charming, but instead seems downright threatening and like an enemy when demands are made that the earlier decisions be honored. Now the principal's character is

[46]Marks, *Handbook*, p. 80.
[47]Lipham, *Principalship*, p. 119.

tested. If a firm stand is taken, the principal is truly a leader. If vacillation is detected, the principal is a weakling who will not survive as a leader over the long run. When the going gets tough in the implementation stage of change, the principal undergoes the truest test of leadership. Those who pass the test emerge as true professionals. To be effective, principals must know what they want to do, plan carefully, and pursue the change with zeal.

EVALUATING THE RESULTS OF CHANGE

The plan for evaluating change must be developed from the beginning, because the evaluation plan becomes the action plan. The objectives, activities, timeline, and responsible individual mentioned earlier are all part of the evaluation plan. The evaluation plan should look something like Table 8–1. It should include the objectives and the activities developed to achieve them, an evaluation summary chart, and a timeline by which objectives will be accomplished.

Table 8–1.   Evaluation Design Summary Chart

OBJECTIVE	MEASUREMENT INSTRUMENTS			DATA COLLECTION PROCEDURES		
	Name/Type of Instrument	Date Instrument Completed	Baseline Data	Target Group	Scheduled Date(s)	Person Responsible

The evaluator, whether internal or external, should evaluate according to the requirements of the program; specifically, whether the objectives were accomplished according to the criteria established for them, whether they were accomplished on time, and whether the responsible persons did their jobs.

DISSEMINATION

The final step after the change has been implemented and evaluated is the dissemination of the practices to the remainder of the school, to other schools in the system, and finally, to education systems throughout the country.

Many good practices are made operational in schools and never disseminated beyond those institutions. At a lower level, many good practices are implemented in individual classrooms and never disseminated to the rest of the school. We implied earlier in this chapter that there is enough expertise in most schools to achieve excellence if the expertise is shared. Therefore, the final step in the process of change is to disseminate effective change processes to the rest of the school in which the practice was first implemented, and eventually to other schools.

Throughout this chapter we have discussed the importance of change—its impact on our daily lives, how change is brought about, some obstacles to change, the variables surrounding change that affect its accomplishment, and finally, a planned change program was discussed as the most effective way to produce change.

Change is a constant in our lives, whether at home, in school or the market place. To stand still is to fall behind, yet often we fear the unknown so strongly that we avoid it at all costs. The authors' objective has been to reduce that fear by describing the change process as thoroughly as possible within some obvious limitations and presenting ways of planning and implementing change in an orderly fashion. We emphasize that promoting the adoption of new ideas and practices is a difficult task, whereas sitting in the office as an administrator of routine details is an easy life. But the principal's obligation is to provide leadership for educational excellence. Consequently, the principal is the primary leader and change agent for achieving excellence. Anything short of great effort by the principal is gross malfeasance and immorality.

Firestone and Wilson found that "research on effective schools has promoted the view that schools can be organized to improve instruction and that principals have a key role to play."[48] Jwaideh argues that change and improvement is brought through leadership by principals.[49] Lipham also contends that the "primary responsibility for change rests with the principal" and that no major changes occur without the support of the principals.[50] Principals need to understand and have skills in implementing change so that schools can become more effective. Yet "despite considerable study of educational change, there still is no general and overarching theory of change, just as there is no comprehensive theory of administration."[51]

[48]Firestone and Wilson, "Using Bureaucratic and Cultural Linkages," pp. 7–30.

[49]Jwaideh, "Principal as a Facilitator," pp. 9–15.

[50]Lipham, *Principalship*, p. 118.

[51]Lipham, *Principalship*, p. 106.

CHAPTER NINE

Improving the Teaching and Learning Environment

School principals should be leaders in improving the teaching and learning environment; this is one of their primary functions as educational leaders. They are the leaders in defining goals for the school, developing a curriculum compatible with those goals, and promoting instructional processes that support both. This chapter is devoted to a discussion of leadership for the human support system (such as climate and atmosphere) necessary for good teaching and learning. Chapter 10 emphasizes supervisory leadership to improve the technical system for teaching.

Teachers have expressed their feelings that the environmental conditions in which they practice influence their effectiveness. The authors' perusal of the literature indicated that a number of those conditions are assumed to be associated with schools of quality.

CONDITIONS ASSOCIATED WITH SCHOOLS OF QUALITY

Numerous conditions that are believed to contribute to an effective teaching and learning environment are indicated with some consistency in the literature. For example, one encounters such expressions as *the faculty and administration must have clear and well-conceptualized instructional goals that are compatible with the overall mission of the school.* One expression is that the principal is a person of vision concerning what the school is becoming. The faculty is described as having an emotional attachment to the expressed goals or mission of the school, and priorities are established for goal attainment.

Well-Selected, Capable Teachers Committed to Excellence. Frequently found in the literature is a reference to selecting teachers with great expertise in the instructional and learning processes. Excellent teachers supported by outstanding leaders are the heartbeat of a school of quality. Thus, the recruitment and selection of teachers (see Chapter 14) are crucial to the success of the school.

Principals Are Actively Involved with the Faculty in the Instructional Program of the School. The authors encountered many references in the literature to such expressions as (1) principals visit classrooms frequently; (2) there is a thorough and ongoing assessment of instructional needs; (3) principals are well informed about teachers' strengths and weaknesses; (4) school leaders are informed about the problems of teachers; (5) principals consistently observe and counsel students; and (6) instructional resources are provided. The principal must function as the instructional leader of the school, and in this capacity is intimately involved with the faculty in the instructional process.

Strong Leadership by the Principal. The adjective *strong* does not refer to a particular style. Depending on the school situation, principals can be either strong relationship-oriented or strong task-oriented leaders and be successful in establishing an environment that maximizes learning.

The Planning Function. Numerous comments appear in the literature concerning the relationship of planning to school improvement. For example, references are made about the significance of explicit planning and a well-planned teacher evaluation process.

A Successful In-service Education Program. Establishing educational excellence begins with the selection of competent administrators and teachers; however, this must be augmented by a first-class in-service education program. Otherwise, entropy may become maximized, and in such a state the program will begin the road to antiquity. Staff development programs should be established for instructional and organizational renewal.

High Expectations of Students and Teachers. Some beneficial expectations include: (1) high academic standards, (2) the expectation that all students can and will achieve, (3) effective monitoring of student achievement, and (4) high expectations of teachers.

An Organizational Climate Conductive to Instruction.   The organizational climate of the effective school is often described as open, with high morale and emotional support for faculty and students. Incentives are provided for teachers and students. Participatory decision making is stressed by numerous authorities. Statements in this area include: (1) warm, supportive atmosphere, (2) high morale for teachers and students, (3) provision for emotional support for teachers, (4) provision for incentives for teachers, and (5) evidence of incentives for learning. Other references highlight the need for openness and the encouragement of instruction to accommodate the unique learning styles of students.

School Discipline.   One of the pervasive conditions in the literature concerning school excellence is the imperative to maintain orderly student behavior. However, references to maintaining discipline indicate that an arbitrary, boot-camp, first-sergeant atmosphere is not indicated. The authors have discussed this previously in Chapter 7 and further discussion appears in Chapter 15.

The Involvement of Parents in the Education of Their Children.   Parent involvement in the educational progress of their children is associated with student motivation. As discussed in Chapter 6, the administration and faculty of the school should find methods and techniques to establish rapport with parents and guardians of students. In this regard, the literature suggests that principals should possess a thorough knowledge of the community by being in the center of community activities.

Time on Task for Instruction.   For many years teachers have registered strong complaints about mandated duties that have little relationship to instruction. Moreover, lack of skill in classroom management and instructional processes creates classroom interruptions, which result in loss of time on instructional tasks and rob students of time for learning. One of the leadership roles of the principal must be to assist teachers in providing time on task for instruction.

The Evaluation Function.   The importance of evaluation in improving the instructional program is stressed throughout the literature. Self-evaluation of the principal and evaluation of teachers are extolled.

We chose to discuss some of these conditions in other chapters where they seemed logically to fit best. For example, the need for clear and well-conceptualized goals, the requirements for strong instructional leadership by the principal, and the high expectations of students are presented in Chapter 7. The tasks associated with the selection and evaluation of teachers and maintenance of student discipline are discussed in Chapters 14 and 15.

In this chapter we will concentrate on the principal's leadership role in (1) improving the school climate, (2) involvement with the faculty in instruction, (3) encouraging parents to become involved in the education of their children, (4) providing adequate time on task for instruction, and (5) promoting organizational maintenance activities to improve the teaching and learning environment.

MAINTAINING A CLIMATE THAT MAXIMIZES ACHIEVEMENT

The noted Western Electric Company studies during the 1920s stimulated interest in the social conditions associated with worker motivation. Considerable interest was focused on worker morale as the critical element in maximizing worker productivity. In time, authorities concentrated on *climate* or *organizational climate* to describe how productive schools are operated. In her review of over 200 studies of school climate, Anderson found considerable difference in opinion expressed about a definition of climate.[1] The problem lies in the fact that empirical definitions do not exist; consequently, present definitions tend to be intuitive and somewhat elusive. Some definitions, for example, seem very close to definitions of morale, which is also subject to varied definitions.

Nevertheless, the authors are convinced that by whatever definition used, variations of school climate exist and have influence on student achievement. Halpin and Croft characterized organizational climate: "Personality is to the individual what 'climate' is to the organization."[2] More recently, Sweeney defined climate as "a term to describe how people feel about their school."[3] He further wrote that "When a school has a 'winning climate,' people feel proud, connected, and committed. They support, help, and care for each other."[4] The right climate for the school was described as resulting in joyful pursuit of teaching and learning.

[1]Carolyn S. Anderson, "The Search for School Climate: A Review of the Research," *Review of Educational Research,* 52 (Fall 1982), 368–420.

[2]Andrew W. Halpin and Donald B. Croft, *The Organizational Climate of Schools* (Chicago: Midwest Administration Center, University of Chicago, 1963), p. 1.

[3]Jim Sweeney, *Tips for Improving Climate* (Arlington, Va.: American Association of School Administrators, 1988), p. 1.

[4]Sweeney, *Tips for Improving Climate,* p. 1.

Halpin and Croft reported the existence of six different climates from their study of elementary schools: open, autonomous, controlled, familiar, paternal, and closed climate.[5] The open climate had a well-integrated faculty marked by high consideration, flexibility, and few monitoring activities. In the autonomous climate the principal gave teachers much freedom, remained aloof from them, and ran the school in an impersonal, businesslike manner. The principal was dominating, directive, and inflexible in the controlled climate. The familiar climate was based on the "big happy family" attitude. In the paternal climate the principal assumed a "Daddy knows best" position. The closed climate was characterized by the rigid, autocratic ruler and impersonal atmosphere of "let's work harder." Halpin and Croft favored the open climate and described the closed climate as in need of radical surgery.[6]

Halpin and Croft believed that the management style of the principal was the key element producing the school climate. Yet as the subject has been pursued, other dimensions have been thought to contribute to the development of school climate, including the input (either positive or negative) of the faculty, the central office regime, the community power structure, students, and parents. For example, a public attack on the school by a community group will initiate system closedness in the school social system. An overbearing demand of an assistant superintendent who is unpopular with the faculty will also produce a change in behavior and a corresponding change in the climate of the school. Studies in the social sciences have demonstrated that the appointed leader of the group tends to move toward group expectations; consequently, the faculty will influence the principal as the principal attempts to influence it. In summary, the climate of the school emerges from multiple inputs to the social system.

At this juncture in our pursuit of the truth, we cannot describe organizational climate in objective, empirical language; nevertheless, as we have indicated previously, one can feel the difference in human relationships, commitment to educational goals, achievement expectations, cooperation, motivation, and so on, among different schools. Climate, then, is an expressed condition of the school faculty and administration that emerges from the interaction of the dynamics of the school social system with the central office regime, the community power system, and the cultural institutions, such as family, religion, government, and economics, of the society. It includes a unique gestalt of those conditions, discussed earlier, that are associated with the quality of the teaching and learning environment.

[5]Halpin and Croft, *Organizational Climate of Schools.*
[6]Halpin and Croft, *Organizational Climate of Schools,* p. 181.

Characteristics of a Healthy Climate for Learning

In the introduction to this chapter we discussed some of the conditions that are conducive to the improvement of student achievement, such as strong leadership of the principal, expectation of student achievement, orderly student behavior, and so on. Based on these conditions, one would expect that the climate of the school would radiate a feeling of confidence in its goals, high expectations of self and others, loyalty to the school and its goals, a collegial feeling of cooperation, strong motivation to succeed, an expression of challenge, an innovative attitude, and high esprit de corp. One would also expect to see democratic values expressed concerning equal opportunity, fairness, and justice. Trust would be established throughout the faculty, administration, and student body.

The Principal's Leadership Role

As we discussed in Chapter 7, we agree with the belief of many writers that the leadership of the principal can be one of the key variables influencing the nature of organizational climate. The extent of this influence depends on the principal's motivation, leadership skills, sensitivity to goals, the establishment of trust, and legitimation with the faculty. The principal's behavior should convey a sense of genuineness, loyalty, and vision. Given these basic conditions, the principal can employ certain methods and techniques, which Sweeney referred to as "tips" for the development of a productive climate.[7] Among the many tips suggested by Sweeney were emphasizing growth, promoting fun activities, fixing up the school plant facilities, maintaining standards for student conduct, promoting innovation, promoting a positive attitude, demonstrating enthusiasm, and so on. Sweeney further suggests the use of rewards, development of a sense of family, and a close relationship to parents.[8]

We reiterate, however, that the use of such techniques should be employed by a leader who is legitimized with the faculty. Use of these techniques by a person who does not have leadership status with the faculty or who is not perceived as trustworthy will very likely be viewed with suspicion, aggression, distrust, or an attitude of silent resistance. For example, if the principal lacks legitimation as a leader, the attitude might be "What is the charlatan up to now?" or "Watch out! He's out to fleece us again." The writers believe that a set of techniques in the hands of persons not trusted as leaders can only make a bad situation worse for the faculty and teachers.

[7]Sweeney, *Tips for Improving Climate*, p. 1.
[8]Sweeney, *Tips for Improving Climate*, p. 1.

INVOLVEMENT WITH TEACHERS IN INSTRUCTION

As administrative head of the school, the principal must be active in and knowledgeable about the instructional program and communicate concern to the teachers. Two of the primary purposes for visiting with teachers in the classroom are to let them know that someone cares and to be knowledgeable about the instructional processes. In observing instruction, the principal should demonstrate a positive attitude and enthusiasm about teaching. Through direct involvement with teachers in the instructional process, the principal can develop a sense of rapport and trust with the faculty, which sends the message that the development of effective instruction is a mutual task of the administrative staff and faculty.

The use of classroom visitation to improve the technical system for teaching is discussed in depth in Chapter 10. The present discussion emphasizes visitation to develop mutual trust and a helping relationship. The essential concern here is that the principal becomes personally involved with teachers in the instructional process.

Teachers are persons with dignity and worth and should be treated with respect during the monitoring process; different teachers react differently to similar inputs. The beginning teacher is likely to have deep feelings of insecurity; consequently, the slightest suggestion may be interpreted as a serious criticism. More secure teachers can accept suggestions as well as give suggestions about how the principal might better administer the school.

INVOLVEMENT OF PARENTS IN THEIR CHILDREN'S EDUCATION

The closeness of parents to the schooling process was interrupted by the elimination of the one- and two-teacher schools. Parental involvement in the education of their children further declined concomitant with the decline of the neighborhood school, the increase in the two-worker family, and the emergence of latch-key kids. Other developments in the society, including the pulling away of school personnel from community involvement, have contributed to the lack of parental involvement. Unfortunately, the seriousness of this situation was not realized before a generation of children and youth had passed through the school systems. We now realize that parental involvement is a very critical element in student achievement. If teachers lack the positive support of parents, many students will not receive a full opportunity for an education.

Some principals mistakenly assume the parents will create trouble for the school if they are involved in school affairs. The authors believe, however, that the greatest disruptions can come to the school as a result of keeping parental participation to a minimum. While it is true that a few parents will occasionally create problems, such negative involvement pales in significance to the gains in student achievement and improvement in the teaching and learning environment.

Involving Parents on an Individual Basis. Parents should be involved on an individual basis. For example, the authors recommend (see Chapter 15) that the school administration and faculty establish personal communication with each parent or guardian of each student in the school. One opportunity is the establishment of teacher-parent conferences to discuss student progress in school. Every effort should be made to enlist and maintain the assistance and cooperation of individual parents in the educational process. Establishing close cooperative relations with parents in present-day society is not easy. Burden and Whitt proposed the four *I*s: get parents *in,* get them *interested* and *involved,* and keep them *informed.*[9]

The authors recently completed a survey in two school systems concerning the attitudes of parents about the schools. Approximately 85 percent of the parents in the two systems stated that they would be willing to go to school one evening each month to learn how to better help their children with homework. Almost without exception, involved parents develop a positive attitude toward and appreciation for the school.

Involving Parents Through Group Participation. Parents and other citizens have a wealth of talent and expertise that can be very valuable in the instructional program. The involvement of influential leaders assists in convincing other parents and other citizens to assist the school in its efforts to educate.

Initially, decisions must be made by the principal and teachers concerning what kind of volunteer services parents and other citizens may perform. Many tasks can be accomplished to improve the teaching and learning environment of the school through the leadership resources of parents and other citizens. Examples of tasks include serving as volunteer teacher aides, taking care of ill children (as do the Grey Ladies), grading papers, serving as experts in class presentations, assisting with music and art lessons, serving as library assistants, and helping to beautify buildings and grounds. The attitude should be that these activities are a joint community/school effort to serve better the educational needs of children and youth.

---

[9]Larry Burden and Robert L. Whitt, *The Community School Principal: New Horizon* (East Lansing, Mich.: Pendell, 1973).

Specific, written rules and guidelines should be developed for a parent participation program. The rules and guidelines should be presented to the volunteers so that they understand their commitments. The guidelines should be presented at the initial meeting with potential volunteers. All socioeconomic groups in the school community should participate equally. For example, if all teaching aides are from the higher socioeconomic groups and all groundskeepers from the lower socioeconomic sectors, the process will not work. The principal (or assistant in charge of volunteers) should insist that those who volunteer for tasks be diligent in performance. Parents who do not keep their commitments should be asked to resign from the program. If uniforms are required or first-aid training is required for the sick room, the cost should be borne by the volunteer. The principal is ultimately responsible for the program. If a parent is causing difficulty, the principal is the person who should deal with the problem.

Bean and Clemes identified the following strategies for the initiation of volunteer programs:

1. The principal and his staff should assess the need for parent aides in their school: How many? Doing what jobs? For how long during the school day? In what classes or parts of classes?
2. Select a few dedicated parents and establish a Parent/Volunteer Committee.
3. Telephone parents and ask them to volunteer.
4. Have an event that brings the parents to the school, such as a potluck dinner, back to school night, or children's program.
5. The need for volunteers should be regularly mentioned in the school's newsletter or other communications to parents.
6. Ask parents who are presently volunteers to recruit their friends and neighbors, including those without children.
7. Ask teachers about parents who show special interest in the school.
8. Emphasize effective and positive parent relations with your staff.[10]

Bean and Clemes further dealt with how to keep the volunteers after they have been recruited. Included in their discussion was a reminder to be sure that the volunteers have manageable jobs, recognize their contributions, and realize through various means that their contributions are appreciated.

As discussed in Chapter 6, parent advisory councils can assist the administrative staff and teachers in establishing cooperative relations with the community. The members of the council can pass along the

[10]Reynold Bean and Harris Clemes, *Elementary Principal's Handbook* (New York: Parker, 1978), p. 152.

opinion that parent participation in the education of their children is welcomed.

TIME ON TASK

As stated previously, teachers resent having to perform tasks that have little relationship to instruction and that deprive students of valuable time for instruction. An assessment of these robbers of instruction time reveals that many are pure service activities, which should and could be performed by a community agency other than the school. Some are administrative in nature, such as collecting background information about children for a federal agency. Other time for instruction is lost with school programs that may have little relationship to the school objectives.

However, not all of the blame for loss of time devoted to teaching lies with externally based restraints. Part of the problem lies with the classroom management and skills of the teacher. If the teacher is disorganized in the presentation of data or not well prepared, students become bored and inattentive, and time on task is lost. Moreover, discipline problems usually arise in these classrooms, further disrupting time on task.

Educators were slow to recognize that teachers need leadership and management skills to administer a classroom. The teacher has to plan carefully and organize the students for instruction or face disorganization, disruption, and loss of time on instructional tasks. Authorities have discovered that certain skills are associated with desirable classroom management. Jones and Jones suggest that on-task teaching can be improved by observing a few simple rules of teaching to maximize time on task: provide clear instructions, which contribute to a well-managed, on-task classroom; begin each lesson with captivating skill; handle minor disruptions before they get out of hand; and use seatwork wisely.[11]

Just as the principal must be the leader in developing a school climate for learning, the teacher has to be a leader in organizing the classroom into a productive unit, and needs all of the know-how and skills discussed about leadership and change in this text. The teacher must develop trust with students, a climate of good human relations, and organization. Above all, the teacher must know how to motivate students to do their best. To reiterate, the classroom develops into a subsystem that is influenced by, and influences, the school social system. If either system is not maintained by effective leadership, the school fails in its mission.

[11]Vernon F. Jones and Louise S. Jones, *Comprehensive Classroom Management: Creating Positive Learning Environments* (Boston: Allyn and Bacon, 1986).

OTHER ORGANIZATIONAL MAINTENANCE ACTIVITIES

The leader must keep the faculty system strong and capable of coping with current and future problems, which comes under the terminology of maintenance processes. Much of what we know about group maintenance comes to us from the field of group dynamics. Some of these techniques are used in *organizational development* (OD).[12] The objectives of OD are to help administrators learn how to enhance the organizational climate, improve the decision-making process, and coordinate the management function.

Team Building. For many years authors have emphasized that the administration and faculty of a school should function as a well-integrated team. Group cohesion is essential for the maintenance of a collaborative, sharing teaching and learning environment. As discussed in Chapters 3 and 4, the open social system facilitates interaction, which is essential for the development of sharing. The principal can lead in the acceptance of the school mission and the attitude of a common fate. The well-coordinated faculty pulls together in a team effort.

Encouraging Social Support. The administrators and members of the faculty experience a variety of stressful problems that can be faced with greater security through mutual support activities and the development of a caring attitude. One way to build a sense of social support among members of the faculty is to encourage self-help groups in which groups of teachers can meet informally and share ideas about particular problems they are experiencing.

Develop Group Skills in Decision Making. If members of the administrative and teaching staff (with the appropriate participation of students) participate in making decisions, they are more likely to buy into the results. The field of group dynamics has made enormous contributions to the skills of group processes. (Some of the leadership skills for working with the faculty were reviewed in Chapter 7.) When the skills of group process are used appropriately they build trust, cohesion, and cooperation.

Communicating/Listening/Hearing. Establishing effective communication may well be the most important leadership function in the development of a teaching and learning environment to maximize achievement. Most theorists assert that an organization cannot function well unless effective communication is established. School principals will not develop effective communication if they take refuge in the office and fail to

---

[12]*See* Wendell L. French and Cecil H. Bell, Jr., *Organizational Development,* 2nd ed. (Englewood Cliffs, N.J.: Prentice-Hall, 1978).

initiate communication with and among members of the faculty. One principal who habitually stayed in his office became known by the faculty and students as "the ghost." One act of communication often overlooked in importance is listening. In conversations with members of the faculty and students, the educational leader must listen intently and, above all, hear. Some leaders pretend to listen, but the faculty soon learn that they do not hear.

Visible Leadership. Sometimes referred to as wandering-around supervision, the suave, skillful principal who is out of the office and around the school in the monitoring function sends a message of caring and involvement. The high visibility reinforces the development of a supportive environment. Rutherford reported that a teacher in an effectively managed school commented that the principal was "always around."[13] However, the highly visible principal must be viewed as positively supportive, helpful, and caring. If the principal is perceived as an ogre that is demeaning and negative, the teachers hope that the principal will stay away from them and spend the whole day in the office. Visibility is not the entire condition; what the visible principal does in the walk about is also critical.

Laughing About It. Many authorities in organizational development emphasize the importance of using humor to defuse stressful situations. Humor can disarm irate feelings. Moreover, if used correctly, humor becomes contagious and can become a part of the faculty climate to reduce stress and anxiety. On the other hand, humor can be very destructive when used to belittle, degrade, or embarrass people.

Staff Development Center

Staff development centers are being utilized in schools and school systems to maintain the instructional strength of the faculty. A well-planned center is staffed by persons skilled in arranging small and large group conferences, workshops, and other aids to the improvement of instruction. A professional library is included. The efficiently organized centers symbolize the commitment of the school and school district to improving the teaching and learning environment. If a district-wide center is not established, the principal and faculty should consider establishing a school-based center. The resources of regional educational agencies are available to schools in many small school districts. The faculty may not want to restrict their activities to one physical location of a center, so variation in locations of professional activities may be possible.

[13]William L. Rutherford, "School Principals as Effective Leaders," *Phi Delta Kappan* (September 1985), pp. 31–34.

The reason for the establishment and use of a staff development center should be determined early in the process of building together a concept of a teaching and learning environment. The objectives must be determined by those who will be involved. The center may be developed for the purpose of helping teachers from various subject areas share ideas to coordinate better their instructional activities so that subjects compliment each other, decreasing the possibility of piecemeal instruction. Starting with this objective, the center can grow into varied activities to improve the teaching and learning climate of the school.

The exchange of ideas among members of the faculty is emphasized in staff development centers. However, this should not become a place to shoot the breeze. The discussion group works best when it is well-planned and five to eight teachers meet with a specific topic or topics.

Professional libraries are an essential aspect of staff development centers. Moreover, administrators and faculty should share information from journals, books, film, and other sources. A principal who knows that a teacher has a certain limitation can share information that pertains to that problem. But the information should not be sent just to that teacher; it should be shared with all members of the faculty with the hope that the teacher with the limitation will benefit most.

Outside resource persons should be appropriately involved in the operation of a staff development center; university and state department personnel often can be of much assistance. The center provides an ideal opportunity to consider the results of research conducted by colleges and universities.

The center will not be productive, at least for long, without the leadership, administration, and guidance of interested and enthusiastic leaders. If a competent staff is not assigned to the center, it will not be very successful in the development of a teaching and learning environment.

Improving Through Planning

Improvements in the teaching and learning environment of the school seldom happen by chance, but are the results of a planning process. Throughout this text, we have emphasized the critical need for a school faculty to have a vision of what the school is becoming. The vision grows out of a formal or informal planning process. Planning and decision making are intertwined—good planning is good decision making.

A variety of approaches to planning are used for improving the teaching and learning environment of the school. Accurate assessment of where we are provides a base for planning. System analysis is one approach that provides a central structure around which ideas for change can be organized. It begins with defining goals and ends with the achievement of those goals. Planning techniques are used to facilitate system analysis.

Nominal Group Technique (NGT) for planning has five steps: (1) generating ideas, (2) recording ideas, (3) clarifying ideas, (4) discussing ideas, and (5) ranking ideas by significance and establishing a priority list of ideas to be pursued, by consensus decision. As indicated previously, if teachers are involved in the process, they will be more inclined to buy into and implement the decisions.

A chart for planning change and evaluating change is very helpful, and is sometimes referred to as a modified Gantt chart. It depicts the orderly steps in the plan and the tasks to be completed. It can be a very good instrument for detailing plans. An example is shown in Figure 9–1.

The Projected Program chart and Evaluation Design Summary Chart depicted in Figure 9–1 include the evaluation plan for planning and implementing a staff development plan for the program. The same kind of plan should be developed for each objective in each component of the program.

The Projected Program includes the objective, activities for accomplishing the objective, and some mention of the evaluation. The particulars of the evaluation are shown in the Evaluation Design Summary Chart. The items on the Evaluation Design Summary Chart correspond to the items in the Projected Program, that is, item II.a. in the summary chart corresponds to item II.a. in the projected program.

The Evaluation Design Summary Chart includes identification of the objective; measurement instrument(s) needed, with the name/type of instrument, date the instrument is to be completed, and the baseline for the data; and data collection procedures, such as the target individual or group, projected date for completion, and who will be responsible for seeing that the objective is completed. With this kind of plan the evaluation of the expected outcomes of the program is very evident and the procedures for determining when and to what extent the objectives are accomplished are very explicit.

Program Evaluation Review Technique (PERT) is another planning technique that can be very useful in establishing steps toward change in the teaching and learning environment. PERT is a flow diagram that includes activities and events, presented in sequential order, showing the logical sequence of events by which goals can be accomplished. It also shows interdependence and interrelationship of the events. An example of a PERT chart is shown in Figure 9–2.

The flowchart depicted in Figure 9–2 is for a reading program that was funded by the U.S. Department of Education. The chart displays the activities and events for the first year of the program. Everything in the chart flows from the box in the upper left-corner, which is the project

PROJECTED PROGRAM

OBJECTIVES	ACTIVITIES	EVALUATION
II Major Objective a. The Project Coordinator will plan and implement a continuing staff development program on reading. The entire staff will spend at least one-half day per month during the program year in staff development activities. This objective will be completed when the written plans have been accepted by the Evaluators, the program has been conducted, and staff members' attendance records are on file in the Project Coordinator's office.	a. A staff training timetable will be developed and will include meeting time, place, and date. When possible, the specific topic for the in-service will also be included. b. Staff members will be informed at least one week in advance what the staff development program will be. c. A monthly attendance record will be kept on each participant. d. Provisions for absences and makeup sessions will be made, determined by the Project Coordinator.	The Evaluators will evaluate the continuing staff development program plan. Staff members will evaluate each monthly session.

EVALUATION DESIGN SUMMARY CHART

PERFORMANCE OBJECTIVE	MEASUREMENT INSTRUMENTS			DATA COLLECTION PROCEDURES		
	Name/Type of Instrument	Date Instrument to be Completed	Baseline Data	Target Group	Scheduled Date(s)	Person Responsible
II. Staff Development a. Staff Development	Curriculum Guide	8/30/88	Staff Evaluation	Selected Members of Project Staff	Monthly	Evaluators
b. Staff PreService	Written PreService Plan	8/15/88	Staff Evaluation	Project Staff	8/30/88	Project Coordinator

Figure 9–1 Sample of Evaluation Design

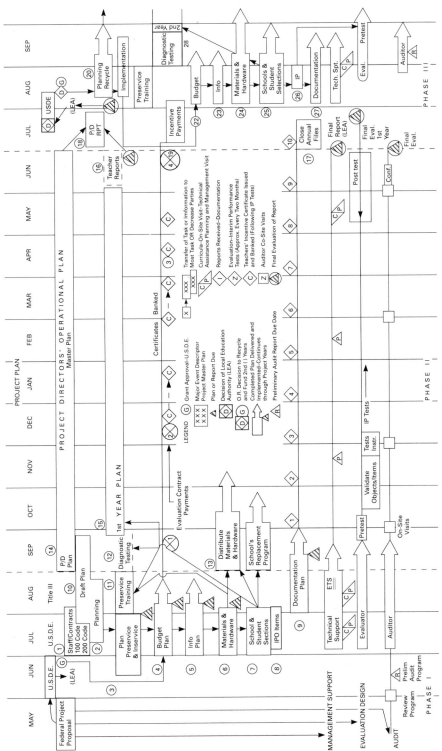

Figure 9–2   Flow Chart.

proposal. The proposal was very comprehensive and included explicit details of all activities and events on the chart.

Phase I on the chart includes time periods from May through September and includes the writing of the project proposal, determination of management support, development of evaluation and audit design, staff planning, preservice and in-service planning, budget and information planning, pupil and staff selection, school site selection, support personnel selection, material and hardware selection, pretesting, and other such preliminary functions. Phase II includes the implementation and operation of the reading program. Phase III includes such activities and events as posttesting students, closing out the program year, and planning for the second year of operation. The flowchart illustrates how all the events of a program can be sequenced and displayed in one compact document.

CHAPTER TEN

The Principal as Supervisor

The development and strategies of supervision will be discussed in this chapter, and some concepts of leadership and social change discussed in previous chapters will be applied to the principal's role as supervisor of the instructional program. The present discussion builds on the teaching and learning environment that was considered in Chapter 9.

Supervision is the means by which leadership is provided for improving the teaching and learning environment of the school. The principal is responsible for providing that leadership. In a very broad sense, the purpose of supervision is to improve the instructional program, and anyone who practices it assumes a supervisory role. Supervisors are defined in the 1987 ASCD Yearbook as "those who have the word in the title, but also principals, superintendents, department heads—all those whose responsibilities include helping other staff members improve their performance."[1]

---

[1]"Supervision," *Working Copy of Association of Supervision and Curriculum Development Yearbook Committee* (Alexandria, Va.: Association of Supervision and Curriculum Development, 1987).

THE NEED FOR SUPERVISION

As we have discussed repeatedly, the school faculty is a social system in interaction with other social systems. Systems vary in openness and closedness, synergy, innovativeness, and other characteristics. The supervisory process is an intervention function to help develop a faculty system that optimizes the opportunity for student achievement. It involves work with individuals and groups of teachers.

One need for supervision is to prevent the tendency toward disorganization, which in systems language is known as entropy. Interventions in, or inputs to, the system are necessary to move the faculty toward openness, because, if left alone, all systems move toward static equilibrium and closedness, which results in an increase in entropy. As discussed in Chapter 4, some schools and school systems maintain impermeable boundaries to resist inputs that promote change; disorganization and randomness eventually result, leaving the school instructional program unproductive and irrelevant.

The principal as supervisor must intervene in the school social system through a variety of approaches and techniques. Strong leadership is essential. The approaches and techniques discussed in the following sections are illustrative of numerous techniques that the principal may use. In the process of employing these techniques the principal must use feedback to determine the effectiveness of the approaches and techniques. As a word of caution, the principal can never be absolutely sure that a given set of techniques used with a faculty will produce the expected changes in behavior. In systems terminology this is the principal of equifinality, where different results are realized from similar techniques and similar results from alternative techniques. Thus there may not be one best approach or set of techniques that the principal should use for all situations. As stated previously, the principle of equifinality supports the contingency (or situational) theory of supervision.

APPROACHES TO SUPERVISION

There have been many approaches to supervision in the schools. The approach that is popularly used at any particular time seems to be determined by trends in society. When there is an ideological swing nationally with a conservative bent, the approach tends to be toward management and inspection. During societal swings to more liberal leanings, a more humanistic, teacher-oriented approach is evident. Presently, the most prevalent approach seems to be management.[2]

---

[2]Jon Wiles and Joseph Bondi, *Supervision: A Guide to Practice,* 2nd ed. (Columbus: Charles E. Merrill, 1986), p. 3.

Taking into account the cultural factors and societal dictates, Alfonso, Firth, and Neville summarized the general propositions of supervision.

1. Supervision as a process is represented in the role performance of supervisors who are responsible for the efficiency and the effectiveness of the organizational system or component to which they are assigned.
2. Supervisors function in formal organizations that are typically complex arrangements for the achievement of particular goals. These formal organizations reflect larger sociocultural system. Supervisory arrangements and services thereby also reflect the sociocultural conditions.
3. The nature of the organization in which the supervisor performs will have a direct bearing on the combination of supervisory skills and performance that is needed if the supervisor is to guide the organization to its goals.
4. The complexity of a formal organization as well as the production system that characterizes it are factors that contribute to the definition of needed supervisory conditions and services.
5. Supervisors in educational organizations are conceived as being primarily responsible for the improvement of instruction. Their effectiveness, in large part, must be seen in terms of the overall accomplishments of the students in relationship to the agreed-upon goals of the school program.
6. Supervisors across organizations have need to demonstrate competence in areas of management, human relations, and the technical aspects of the organizational unit within which they work. The correct combination of these competence areas is called the skill-mix. This mix can vary, depending upon the cultural setting, the nature of the organization, the production system, and the organization's goals.
7. Supervisory performance in educational organizations has tended to concentrate on role expressions that emphasize the human relations and management dimensions. It is in the technical skill area where educational supervisors have been remiss. This may be the result of a lack of competence in the technical areas or the press and demands of managerial and human relations.[3]

The foregoing propositions were written with the responsibilities of those in the position of supervisor in mind. Since most principals are considered to be supervising principals, the concepts can be applied equally well.

Inspection as Supervision

The earliest forms of supervision were inspections. An authority figure would periodically visit teachers and inspect to see that they were doing what they had been commissioned to do. In the earlier days, this function was performed by board members or trustees. Later, as schools grew in size, this function was performed by principals or other adminis-

---

[3]Robert J. Alfonso, Gerald R. Firth, and Richard F. Neville, *Instructional Supervision: A Behavior System* (Boston: Allyn & Bacon, 1975), pp. 11–12.

trators. Inspection was not usually for the purpose of helping teachers to improve. If they were not performing as expected, they were warned; and if there was no subsequent change in their performance, they were replaced.

Traditional Supervision

Traditional supervision is also centered around determining if teachers are performing as expected. Principals, in their supervisory roles, observe teachers to determine if they are teaching in a predetermined way and if they are presenting predetermined subject matter.

Traditional supervision is based on the assumption that someone in authority knows what should be taught and how best to teach it. There is usually a preconference between teacher and principal before the classroom observation. The principal and teacher come to a common understanding as to what subject matter will be presented and how it will be presented. The objectives of the class to be observed are also discussed at the preconference.

The principal records what the teacher and students are doing during the observed session, including such happenings as set, instruction, closure, active participation, monitoring, and adjusting. The teacher is then rated on effectiveness of performance. In follow-up visits, the principal evaluates the teacher on how well the teaching was modified to conform to the suggestions for improvement. The observation process is repeated throughout the year(s).

Laissez Faire Supervision

Weak or lazy principals often adhere to laissez faire supervision, which means that they do not do any effective supervision. The lame excuse often used by such principals is that teachers know how to teach, so they should be left alone to do their thing. Little effort is made to assist teachers in their individual performances. Also, little effort is expended to assist the teachers in working together toward establishing and accomplishing common goals. Laissez faire literally means *leave them alone*. Teachers will almost unanimously agree that laissez faire supervision is the least desirable type of supervision. The uncertainty that goes along with it is unsettling, to say the least. The sad truth is that this lack of supervision can be found in schools throughout the country. Laissez faire principals are not highly respected because they provide little leadership for improving the teaching and learning environment of the school. The lack of performance by principals who practice laissez faire supervision is not only unprofessional, it is unethical. It cheats the students as well as the teachers. As was discussed in an earlier chapter, principals should visit teachers simply to let them know that someone cares about how they do their jobs. There are also many other reasons, discussed in this chapter and elsewhere in this book, why principals should not just "leave teachers alone."

Participative Supervision

Participative supervision is based on the assumption that teachers can and should help to decide what they teach and how to teach it. With the help of a principal who is effective in orchestrating participation and cooperation among faculty members, participative supervision can be very effective. Participative supervision is effective only to the extent that it is practiced in a democratic atmosphere.

Participative supervision requires mutual trust between teachers and between teachers and the principal. The lines of communication must be open both horizontally and vertically, and everyone involved should be given opportunities to share in making decisions at all levels. The formal and informal organizations discussed in earlier chapters must come into play and must support each other.

Jealousies must be kept to a minimum. The prevailing atmosphere should be such that if one person succeeds, everyone in the school gains a degree of success. Therefore, close interpersonal relationships should be maintained among all those involved, especially among teachers, and between teachers and principal. Hoy and Forsyth wrote, "In sum, team-work, cooperation, sharing, group loyalty, responsibility, trust, and high performance goals are typical of the participative system."[4] They also contended, as did the authors in an earlier chapter, that in order to get improvement one must get change. The principal can responsibly promote positive change through participative supervision. The principal's participative role in promoting change is complicated by conflicts with the principalship role as an administrator striving for harmony. Clearly, the conflicting roles pull at the individual placed in the position to act as both administrator and supervisor.[5]

There are many approaches to supervision that the principal may take; these approaches range from very autocratic to democratic. No given technique will work best for a particular principal in any school. As mentioned earlier, the general prevailing approach is influenced to some extent by social trends; however, individual direction is dictated by the combination of ability and personality of the principal and the cultural climate of the school—the contingency theory of supervision. In the long

[4]Wayne K. Hoy and Patrick B. Forsyth, *Effective Supervision: Theory into Practice* (New York: Random House, 1986), p. 174.

[5]Hoy and Forsyth, *Effective Supervision*, p. 174.

run, the best approach is for the principal to provide leadership that will permit teachers to work together in a nonthreatening, high-expectation climate of constant improvement where they can realize their accomplishments themselves.

SUPERVISORY STRATEGIES

A number of interacting social systems will have to be considered by principals who are interested in planned program improvement. For instance, the central office regime and the community power system are suprasystems of the school. Within the school there are subsystems such as student and faculty cliques. The various interacting social systems attempt to survive, and one obvious necessity for their survival is the maintenance of group norms. There is a crystallization of behavior, interaction patterns, and activities within the systems and a tendency toward equilibrium. Because the systems exchange matter and energy, a revolutionary change in one system is likely to affect the system with which it interacts.

For example, a new principal who abruptly demands a change in the teaching of science prior to checking it out through the central office regime may experience some repercussions from outside the school. There may be powerful forces in the community, such as research-based industries who have a special interest in promoting some of the sciences because of their special workforce needs. Therefore, change in the teaching of science may be in conflict with some community demands. When faced with demands from the central office or industry, officials may have to explain why methods of teaching science are being changed. The supervisory strategy of the principal must include the fact that educational improvement is not an isolated decision for the principal and teachers to make. Failure to recognize this factor has caused many attempted instructional improvements to fail.

Why Change?

As mentioned earlier in Chapter 8, the reasons for and the process of change are vitally important to principals in their roles as supervisors and leaders. It is tempting to jump on the bandwagon of popular movements that may turn out to be fads. The way in which some principals proceed indicates that they have given little thought to such questions as *Why do we want change?* and *For what purposes are we attempting to provide leadership in program development?* The need for change that brings improvement in schools is obviously great, but change for the sake of change will not serve the students, community, or national interests. By casual examination of conditions one may point to grave deficiencies in educational programs. Yet, to insist upon the trial of numerous untested practices without reference or purpose involves risks to the students that are hardly worth defending. Therefore, principals are responsible for ascertaining whether the changes they are promoting are in the best interest of the students. In order to do this, principals must engage in the clarification of educational goals and evaluate the degree to which they are reaching these goals.

Strategies for Organizing Effective Teaching

Huge amounts of money are spent each year on in-service training of teachers in the use of new instructional methods and materials. Failure to commit some of these funds to the improvement of the organizational climates in which the new methods and materials are supposed to be used makes this a very inefficient strategy. With greater attention and commitment of resources to improving leadership and social climate, the strategy for instructional improvement would be more effective. For example, the teaching of mathematics will not be improved greatly by introducing a few new concepts to teachers and, at the same time, leaving them in an undesirable climate for practicing effective teaching. Too much attention has been given to the piecemeal in-service training of principals and teachers at the expense of planning for the overall improvement of the teaching and learning environment and leadership. One restraint in this regard is the categorical aid policies of state and federal governments that prevent the use of funds for many needed programs in leadership development.

Improving the School Climate

Principals, in their roles as supervisors and change agents, should attend to questions for improving the organizational climate of the school and possibly its suprasystems. The job of the principal in improving the teaching and learning environment goes further than encouraging the adoption of new techniques for teaching mathematics and other subjects. Principals must include in their supervisory plans the improvement of the social system within which mathematics is taught. How can the organizational climate be improved as a means of facilitating the change and improvement of instruction?

Miles proposed, in a 1960s study that is still relevant, a concept of organizational health as associated with the process of change.[6] He contended that organizations have differing degrees of health and advocated applying health concepts of the organism to the social system. Principals,

[6]Matthew B. Miles, "Planned Change and Organizational Health: Figure and Ground," *Change Processes in the Public Schools* (Eugene: The University of Oregon, Center for the Advanced Study of Educational Administration, 1965), pp. 11–34.

according to this concept, have a responsibility for the induction of organizational health that is conducive to program development.

As discussed in Chapter 9, Halpin and Croft pointed to the great significance of organizational climate.[7] Their study provided descriptions of several different climates of schools. Obviously, just fumbling around with a new method of teaching or a different curriculum design without attention to the organizational climate of the school would be a self-defeating supervisory strategy.

Appropriate Use of Strategies and Approaches

Attainable goals must be defined in order to develop successful supervisory strategies. Techniques and processes for reaching these goals must also be planned. A *strategy* is a supervisory plan for improving education. The supervisory techniques used in the plan should fit into a conceptual design of leadership and change. The strategy must also take into account the state of the social systems within which improvement is desired. These points will be illustrated.

One of the goals may be to improve instruction in the language arts. To deal with this problem effectively, consideration must be given to the social systems and the process of change discussed earlier. One major concern in planning for change in the teaching of language arts will be whether the social system of the school is more closed than open. What is the leadership structure of the system? Assume that one technique employed in the overall strategy will be an institute for language arts teachers. What conceptual idea of change underlies the use of an institute? The institute technique relies upon the input of information as a basis for changing the internal state of the social system. The mere input of information, however, may not appreciably affect the tension in the system. A closed system may necessitate more varied techniques, including the input of matter (such as new teachers) as another process of opening up the system with resulting change.

Our point in providing this example is that the techniques used must be selected with a conceptualization of the group as a social system; only in this way will the teachers significantly change the practices of teaching language arts. The overall strategy involves the effective use of processes and techniques to move the system (teachers of language arts) from one social position to another, and also requires that the principal use proper change procedures. Such traditional techniques as workshops, faculty meetings, research, and institutes may be used as parts of the strategy to unfreeze the system and move it to another position of crystallization.

[7]Andrew W. Halpin and Donald B. Croft, *The Organizational Climate of Schools* (Chicago: The University of Chicago, Midwest Administration Center, 1963).

As previously mentioned, supervisory strategies should be employed for a well-defined, defensible purpose. Attention to the development of internally consistent, effective, and ethically defensible strategies for program improvement is of great importance in supervisory leadership. It enhances the supervisory leadership of the principal and faculty leaders.

There are several conceptual approaches that can be employed by the principal. Some techniques, such as the workshop, rely upon the group-dynamics approach, which attempts to redistribute power in the social system as a means of producing openness to new ideas and practices. The efficiency expert view is perhaps best represented in the expert-type survey wherein outside experts are engaged to study and make recommendations. In spite of humorous stories about "experts," the principal should not overlook their possible contributions. Other approaches would emphasize direct inputs to the system. For instance, teachers who already believe in the ideas and practices desired may be employed as advocates. Teachers who rigidly oppose change for improvement may be reassigned; however, this would be an extreme move that should only be employed after all positive attempts to involve them have failed.

Another approach might be to establish a research and development agency that is relatively independent of the regular line of authority as a stimulant to improvement and change. Large business corporations use this approach successfully by establishing laboratories that are free to develop ideas. The projects developed in the laboratories are tested and implemented in the operational part of the business. Likewise, school systems would do well to establish a think tank as a developing and testing system that is rather independent of the recurring administrative emergencies. It could eventually contribute a great deal to the improvement of educational programs, such as language arts, mentioned earlier.

WHAT SHOULD PRINCIPALS DO IN THEIR ROLE AS SUPERVISOR?

Numerous authorities have written extensively about the tasks of supervisors. When is a principal performing a supervisory role? There is no distinct line between the roles of principals as supervisors and their other administrative duties. Many functions performed by principals can be labeled as supervisory in nature; those roles will be discussed in this section.

Involvement with Teachers in Instruction

Principals should be closely involved with teachers in instruction. In fact, the principal should become a functional member of the instructional team. Some of the tasks of the principal, however, are somewhat different from those of the teacher, one of which is observation of the teacher and the instructional process.

Successful visitation and observation of instruction is based on a set of conditions to observe. An important condition is the tone or climate of the classroom. What are the students' attitudes toward the teacher, classmates, school, and learning? Of supreme importance is how well the students are motivated to learn, as it determines the difference between a teacher and a presenter. If the teacher can motivate students to learn, the rest of the teaching task is routine; the teacher only has to provide access to the resources for learning.

Through observation the leader can also determine whether teachers have planned for the unique learning needs of students. Are the objectives and activities selected based on the needs of the students or, since pages 34 through 36 were covered yesterday, are pages 37 through 39 in the textbook the basis of the lesson? Are the objectives and activities compatible? Have the teachers given serious consideration to why the subject is being taught? Is the material used in instruction timely? Relevant? Is the teacher appropriately varying the methods among lectures, large and small group activities, and independent study? Are appropriate instructional resources being used, such as projectors, computers, calculators, films, filmstrips, hands-on materials, television, and resource persons? Observation of instruction will assist in discovering ways in which in-service education activities can be provided for the improvement of instruction.

Classroom visitation should not only be used to identify problems, but also to reinforce the good practices of teachers. It is easier to build on strengths than weaknesses. If the strengths of teachers can be identified during observations and emphasized during conferences, teachers can sometimes overshadow the weaknesses and eliminate them. For example, if an elementary teacher is strong in teaching art but weak in teaching arithmetic, the teacher may, with help, learn to combine the two and strengthen both components.

Observations should also be used to help the effective teachers get better; the good teachers are often the ones most ignored. Since those teachers perform well on their own, many principals do not give them much support; yet good teachers can, with help, get better. In fact, they can make much more progress than poor teachers, and that progress can have greater effect on improving the quality of instruction in the school than the slow progress of the less-effective teachers.

To be effective, principals must develop a sense of trust and rapport with teachers. Teachers should believe that the principal is there to help them and that improving the instructional program is a mutual task shared with the principal. Above all, information should not be used in any way to harm anyone. A principal cannot discuss weaknesses discovered in an observation with another teacher in a derogatory way and hope to be successful in helping that teacher. If the principal is to be successful in helping teachers in the observing and counseling process, there must be an unspoken bond of trust and support between the teachers and the principal. If a trusting relationship has been developed it is much easier to approach problems. One procedure for discussing identified problems with teachers is to begin with the commendable things that were identified during observations, move to any suggestions for improvement, and end on a positive note about other good practices observed.

Some of the classroom observations should be formal and for an extended period of time—one or two hours. Other observations should be shorter in duration. When the right kind of trust has been developed, the principal should be able to visit throughout the school without being formal about it. The feeling will develop that the principal is a part of the teaching team whose presence is desired in the classroom.

Meeting the Needs of Teachers

There have been many studies supporting the principal's supervisory role in meeting the needs of teachers. Marks, Stoops, and Stoops stressed this point concerning the needs of teachers on and off the job. They contended that if teachers are to be effective, the off-the-job needs of a good standard of living, family, social life, recreation, sexual fulfillment, financial security, community recognition, and reputation must be met. They listed as on-the-job needs egotistic accomplishment, feeling important, feeling whole, skill, program completion, autonomy, security, and job advancement. Friendship, identification, and teamwork were discussed as on-the-job social needs.[8] Marks and associates believe that the performance of teachers can be enhanced greatly by providing for these needs. Obviously, the principal cannot personally provide for all of these needs. However, the principal may be able to open some doors of opportunity through which teachers can achieve their own gratifications. The principal can and should directly influence need gratification in such areas as recognition, feeling of self-worth, autonomy, and so on, since these higher-order needs are the motivators.

Principals have a responsibility for providing not only for the individual needs of teachers but for universal roles within the organization as well. Purkey and Smith stated, "An academically effective school is distinguished by its culture: a structure, process, and climate of values and

[8]James R. Marks, Emery Stoops, and Joyce King-Stoops, *Handbook of Educational Supervision: A Guide for the Practitioner* (Boston: Allyn & Bacon, 1971).

norms that channel staff and students in the direction of successful teaching and learning."[9]

Other Supervisory Roles and Tasks

Lucio and McNeil contended that instructional supervisors must be statesmen "able to give direction beyond merely ministering to the organization's equilibrium."[10] There are numerous roles that principals play in their capacity as instructional supervisors. They must successfully perform activities such as evaluating results of innovations, organizing materials, interacting with members of the community, assisting in determining learner needs and providing for the development of proper personal qualities of all involved. Principals perform these activities to help teachers adjust their behavior in a way that will be compatible with the organizational goals. Lucio and McNeil also emphasized the importance of moving the neutral individuals in directions that are compatible with the overall goals of the schools. The principal must communicate and coordinate these goals if they are to be attained.[11]

Ritz believed that in order to achieve the established goals of the school, principals must perform both formal and informal tasks. Curriculum development, in-service planning and classroom observations are examples of some of the formal tasks. Assisting teachers to solve personal problems, facilitating better interpersonal relationships among staff members, and protecting faculty members from undue criticism are examples of the informal tasks.[12] Gwynn supported this contention, and was very concerned about the mental health of teachers. He believed that accomplishing this condition was a prerequisite to attaining a desirable teaching and learning environment.[13]

Young and Heichberger were concerned about protecting children from incompetent teaching. They contended that to do this principals must assist teachers in administering the curriculum and maintaining maximum effectiveness in instruction.[14] Leithwood and Montgomery supported these purposes. They believed that student learning is influ-

[9]Stewart C. Purkey and Marshall S. Smith, "Too Soon to Cheer? Synthesis of Research on School Effectiveness," *Educational Leadership,* 40 (March 1982), 69.

[10]William H. Lucio and John D. McNeil, *Supervision: A Synthesis of Thought and Action,* 2nd ed. (New York: McGraw-Hill, 1969), p. vi.

[11]Lucio and McNeil, *Supervision: A Synthesis.*

[12]William C. Ritz and Jane G. Cashell, "Cold War between Supervisors and Teachers?" *Educational Leadership,* 38, No. 1 (October 1980), 77–78.

[13]John M. Gwynn, *Theory and Practice of Supervision* (New York: Dodd, Mead, 1969).

[14]Manes M. Young and Robert L. Heichberger, "Teachers' Perceptions of an Effective School Supervision and Evaluation Program, *Education,* 96, No. 1 (Fall 1975), 10–19.

enced indirectly by teacher growth, and that the role of the principal is to facilitate that growth.[15]

The importance of human relations in supervision has been emphasized by many authorities in that discipline. Perrine argued that both cooperation and good human relations are needed to improve the teaching and learning environment. He cited many components in the literature that were related to effective supervision. Two of the major components found were the provision of technical expertise and humanistic interaction with teachers.[16] Guild and Garger also stressed the importance of good human relations. They stated that "education is a people business"[17] and that the role of the principal is to determine common goals and work with others within the organization. A principal must also promote a positive climate, high morale, and open communication in the institution. Glickman concurred that the role of the supervising principal is a crucial one in developing human relations. He emphasized the team concept involving the whole staff. He also stated that supervisors can create more effective schools by

1. Enhancing teacher belief in a cause beyond oneself and the four walls
2. Promoting the teacher's sense of efficiency
3. Making teachers aware of how they complement each other in striving for common goals
4. Stimulating teachers to plan common purpose and actions
5. Challenging teachers to think abstractly about their work[18]

Supervisory Tasks

Doll suggested that those in the position of supervisors should experiment in problem solving. He further encouraged working toward lasting results through being cooperative and task-oriented. He recommended the following set of principles to guide the work of supervisors.

1. Work with people, not over them.
2. Show that you too desire to improve.

[15]Kenneth A. Leithwood and Deborah J. Montgomery, "The Role of the Elementary School Principal in Program Improvement," *Review of Educational Research,* 52 (Fall 1982), 309–39.

[16]Walter G. Perrine, "Teacher and Supervisory Perceptions of Elementary Science Supervision," *Science Education,* 68 (January 1984), 3–9.

[17]Pat Burke Guild and Stephen Garger, *Marching to Different Drummers* (Alexandria, Va.: Association for Supervision and Curriculum Development, 1985), p. 5.

[18]Carl D. Glickman, *Supervision of Instruction: A Developmental Approach* (Boston: Allyn & Bacon, 1985), p. 21.

3. Help the people with whom you work know you and know each other.
4. Help teachers enjoy a variety of in-service experiences.
5. Work with both individuals and groups.
6. Recognize that some people improve more slowly than others, both in a general sense and in specific activities.
7. Use problem solving as a means to improvement.
8. Help teachers feel free to improve.
9. Keep channels of communication open.
10. Use status with great care—you can be a threat or impediment.
11. Be sensible and modest in expectations, doing well that which you under-take.[19]

Harris also presented a list of tasks for supervisors. He listed those tasks under three different categories: preliminary tasks, operational tasks, and developmental tasks. Developing curriculum, providing facilities, and providing staff were listed in the preliminary category. Organization for instruction, orienting staff members, providing materials, relating pupil services, and developing public relations were listed in the operational category. The developmental category included the tasks of evaluation of instruction and arranging for in-service education. The core elements of effective supervision were evaluation of instruction, curriculum development, materials development, and staffing.[20]

Mosher and Purpel contended that since supervisors were expected to do so many tasks, defining their roles was very difficult. They emphasized that those in supervisory roles should lead in developing curriculum, teaching, assisting beginning teachers, supervising teachers in numerous subject areas, and evaluating teachers in addition to performing administrative and clerical tasks. They emphasized, however, that the primary task of the person in a supervisory position was to provide leadership in improving the teaching and learning environment.[21] Eye and Netzer believed that the supervisor should stimulate, originate, coordinate, analyze, evaluate, and synthesize and that the major task of supervision is that of "influencing situations, persons, and relationships for the purpose of stimulating change that may be evaluated as improvement."[22]

---

[19]Ronald C. Doll, *Supervision for Staff Development: Ideas and Application* (Boston: Allyn & Bacon, 1983), pp. 125–26. This list appeared originally in Ronald C. Doll, "Our Orbits of Change," *Educational Leadership,* 17 (November 1959), 102–05.

[20]Ben M. Harris, *Supervisory Behavior in Education,* 3rd ed. (Englewood Cliffs, N.J.: Prentice-Hall, 1985).

[21]Ralph L. Mosher and David E. Purpel, *Supervision: The Reluctant Profession* (Boston: Houghton Mifflin, 1972).

[22]Glen G. Eye and Lanore A. Netzer, *Supervision of Instruction: A Phase of Administration* (New York: Harper & Row, 1965), 39.

COOPERATIVE SUPERVISION

Professionally mature principals work toward creating a school atmosphere in which, when their work is done, the teachers will say "We did it ourselves." As discussed in earlier chapters, there is enough expertise in any school to have an outstanding school if the expertise can be effectively shared. As a supervisor, the principal's responsibility is to see that the expertise is shared through cooperative supervision.

Providing leadership for cooperative supervision, however, is like walking the proverbial tightrope. Too much attention given to any one teacher can spell disaster. Cooperative supervision requires a truly cooperative effort in which everyone has a chance to share. It would be rare indeed to find a single teacher in a given school who did not have some expertise from which the rest of the faculty would not benefit. It is the principal's responsibility to assess individual capabilities and plan ways of having the expertise shared.

Faculty Meetings

Faculty meetings can be a good place to initiate cooperative supervision. Meetings devoted to sharing would certainly be a welcome relief from the boredom experienced in many faculty meetings where the typical agenda consists of announcements and admonishments. The meetings could be devoted to concerns such as

1. Goal setting
2. Teachers working in small groups on topics that are of interest to them
3. Brain storming
4. Sharing ideas for resources and materials
5. Sharing information about students
6. Sharing information about the community
7. Planning in-service activities
8. Evaluating in-service activities
9. Following up on in-service activities
10. Sharing successes and failures and soliciting suggestions for dealing with the problems
11. Discussing ideas for improving the climate of the school
12. Planning strategies to deal with concerns, such as the current political, educational, cultural, and economic conditions that affect the school
13. Exchanging information across disciplines or grades
14. Sharing ideas and activities
15. Studying administrative problems and sharing possible solutions with the principal

This is certainly not an exhaustive list; it is limited only by the willingness of the principal to involve all concerned individuals in the improvement of the school and its atmosphere.

Teachers Observing Teachers

The principal should arrange for selective observation by encouraging different teachers to observe other teachers. How does this work? The principal notes strengths and weaknesses of the various teachers during observations. The strengths and weaknesses are matched with those of other teachers. For instance, one teacher who is strong in discipline and weak in creativity may be matched with one who has just the opposite traits, then each is allowed to visit the other to observe classroom techniques. If the two are compatible, they may work together over a period of time and help one another to solve their respective problems. Other teachers may be matched for observation and sharing based on areas of strengths and interests. How are teachers freed to work with one another in this way? It takes a bit of planning and ingenuity on the part of the principal and the teachers. A substitute teacher can be employed or the principal may take a teacher's class occasionally to allow time for peer observation. Aids or volunteers, under legal supervision, may also be used for this purpose.

Action Research

Mention the word *research* and many teachers immediately get a vision of "ivory tower stuff" that "sounds good in theory but will not work." Most teachers are reluctant to get involved in action research, but it is a very effective cooperative technique for improving the teaching and learning environment. Research not only provides new knowledge to the existing body, it can have a positive effect on the school environment. Teachers, working cooperatively, can enhance their self images and, at the same time, develop knowledge about better methods of teaching.

Action research is more specific and structured than one usually finds in a regular cooperative effort between teachers. Definite, standardized steps must be followed for the research to be effective. The principal or a teacher with research interest, skills, and orientation can provide leadership for the project by following the necessary steps.

1. Determining the problem
2. Specifying the problem explicitly so that all can understand
3. Specifying some possible causes of the problem
4. Developing the hypotheses

5. Planning and implementing necessary activities
6. Developing or selecting the tests
7. Gathering and organizing the data
8. Interpreting the data
9. Evaluating the results of the activities
10. Generalizing the findings to other teachers

Action research can be used effectively in most schools without undue burden if it is well planned. Using the language-arts illustration mentioned earlier provides a simple example of how this research can be implemented. Assume that the fifth- and sixth-grade teachers express an interest in this approach to find a better way to teach language arts. They have now identified the problem. They may hypothesize that another specified approach will yield significantly better results. Some teachers can use the standard approach for a semester or year while others use the experimental approach. Students will be tested and their scores compared. The study can be further refined by having the teachers reverse their methods and teach the same children for a semester, then have the test results further analyzed and compared. Teachers who are involved in a research project are more likely than others to take action based on the research findings. This is a very elementary example of how action research can be a part of cooperative supervision. Action research holds great promise for improving schools where teachers are willing to use it.

Workshops

Workshop is a common term used to describe teachers, principals, or both getting together and working on a common interest. Workshops can be system-wide or confined to one school. More than one school or school system may get together and have workshops of common interests. The most successful workshops are those that are initiated by the teachers and principals involved. Workshops may be conducted for teachers, principals, or for the two groups combined to consider a common interest topic.

Some of the more popular workshops for principals have been built around simulated situations in which they attempt to solve commonly identified problems. The simulations help principals deal with problem situations in a setting away from their own real world. A simulated setting is less threatening than the real day-to-day problems that principals face on the job; therefore, they do not feel as much stress in their performance. They can be more objective because they do not have to live with the consequences of their decisions. Workshops also provide them with an opportunity to see and hear how other principals deal with the same problems and situations. Simulations are only one of many ways to conduct workshops for principals.

Topics for teacher workshops are limitless. The workshops should be planned around teachers' interests. For instance, one of the authors assisted in conducting a series of workshops for teachers during a three-year period. The workshops were designed to introduce elementary teachers to the learning center concept; they were "make and take" workshops, ranging in length from one to three days. Teachers were provided with all the materials and patterns for making centers like the ones displayed. Some of the teachers spent the entire time making learning centers; others traced the patterns on newspaper and took them home to complete; some even photographed each of the centers and used the pictures later for ideas for centers. The centers displayed were all developed from ideas submitted by classroom teachers from throughout the United States. The make and take workshop is only one of many ideas of the kinds of workshops that are of benefit to teachers. That particular learning center workshop was described here to emphasize that the hands-on type workshops are, usually, of most interest to teachers.

Interest Groups

Few concerns are of interest to an entire school faculty or to the teachers in an entire system. There are mutual concerns that can be the subject of study groups. Like workshops, study groups should be based on teacher and principal interests. For instance, teachers interested in improving the sequence of mathematics from grades 1–12 may form a study group to deal with that concern. Likewise, kindergarten and first-grade teachers may form a study group to deal with the transition from kindergarten to first grade and how it can best be made. Discipline as a study-group topic is always of high interest. Current topics are also a popular basis for a study group, such as the AIDS crisis and drug problems in the schools. Study groups may be formed as a result of a school-wide interest. For instance, the faculty members in a school may be interested in how to deal with the situation of a student with AIDS. A small volunteer study group can be formed to develop guidelines for dealing with the situation. Opportunities for forming study groups to improve the teaching and learning environment of the school are limitless. The wise use of study groups can be a great asset to principals in their roles as supervisors.

Effective principals use group supervision techniques. They depend on coordinating the knowledge and expertise of faculty members to provide for the improvement of the teaching and learning environment of the schools.

SUPERVISION AND THE INDIVIDUAL SUPERVISED

Group supervision is effective, but it is not adequate for taking care of all of the supervisory responsibilities of principals. Each individual in the school (students, teachers, and support personnel such as secretaries, custodians, guidance counselors, nurses, and cooks) must receive individual attention. Teachers, especially, must receive individual attention if they are to continue to develop professionally, and they must continue to develop professionally if the school is to continue to improve. As discussed in Chapter 4, a school that is not improving is experiencing the maximization of entropy and is in a state of deterioration.

Classroom Observations and Follow-up Conferences

Classroom observation with the follow-up conference is one of the most popular formal methods of individual supervision. The classroom observation and follow-up conference have traditionally been devoted to identifying the teacher's strengths and weaknesses. The idea is to encourage teachers about the things they are doing well and to offer suggestions on how to improve the observed weaknesses. The follow-up technique has much value and is used widely, but it has one inherent weakness: Often the advice for overcoming the weaknesses is unsolicited. A general rule in life is to offer advice only when someone asks for it. Otherwise, the effort is usually wasted because unsolicited advice is seldom heeded. The wise principal will cultivate a working relationship with each teacher that is nonthreatening so that the teacher will be receptive to advice.

Wood suggested several questions that principals should ask themselves as they observe the teacher and plan the follow-up conference.

1. Can you identify the lesson objective in terms of what the students will be able to do as a result of the lesson? If not, what might you say to the teacher?
2. Do the activities and follow-up work seem related clearly and directly to the objective?
3. If students are reading orally, are they stumbling over more than two or three words on a page? If so, what could you say to the teacher?
4. If teacher-corrected work is handed back, do you see more than two or three red marks on a page for any student?
5. Do you see some provision for getting work checked soon after it is finished?
6. If corrected papers are visible, do you see some with specific comments from the teacher, rather than just grades or check marks?

7. Do practice activities and homework assignments seem to be of reasonable length?

8. If appropriate, did the teacher use some kind of oral or visual modeling?

9. If some students seem to show evidence of poor understanding during the lesson, what provision is made for helping them?

10. Were most students engaged in on-task activities most of the time? Did the teacher try to involve many in the lesson, or only a few?

11. Did the teacher take time to praise both effort and success?

12. Did the teacher make it clear that the students would be held accountable for assigned work? How?

13. Did the teacher check for understanding after assigning tasks or giving directions? If there was lack of understanding, did reteaching follow?

14. Did the feeling and emotional climate in the room seem pleasant and relaxed? Did the students feel free to question or contribute ideas?

15. Did you see examples of "calling out" behavior? If so, how did the teacher respond?

16. Did you see the teacher use relevant examples to relate the lesson to the students' own lives and interests?

17. If students needed to be corrected for behavior, was this done without overreaction from the teacher? Without undue embarrassment or humiliation of students? If not, was there a reason?

18. Did the lesson show evidence of advanced planning and prior organization? Did it progress without stops and jumps? Were books and materials ready and accessible?

19. Did the teacher allow wait time after asking questions, to allow students time to think of and phrase an answer?

20. Did you see the teacher dignify an incorrect response by giving the student an opportunity to respond correctly a short time later?

21. Could you identify an introductory activity that created a mental set or provided a focus for the lesson? If there was none, could you see some reason that it was unnecessary?

COMPLEX THINKING

22. Did the teacher ask questions requiring students to think at levels more complex than the recall of information?

23. Did students who finished assigned tasks early appear to have productive ways to spend their time?

24. Were "housekeeping" chores and transitions between activities accomplished without confusion or waste of time?

25. Did you see actual teaching during the lesson, as opposed to doing assignments or self-directed activities? If there was no teaching, was there evidence that it had taken place at another time?[23]

Wood further advised that not all lessons would contain all of the elements mentioned here and that there were other questions that

[23]Phyllis J. Wood, "A Checklist for Instructional Supervision," *Education Digest,* 47 (April 1987), 46–47.

should be considered concerning the observation and follow-up conference.[24]

Ideally, the observation of individual teachers should be coordinated with the outcome of group activities, such as workshops and study groups. The observations should support the development of individual teachers in conjunction with group support systems, so that the entire instructional program can be enhanced.

Individual problems are often problems shared by many faculty members. With the tendency for teachers to be isolated in their classrooms, many of them do not know that their concern is a common problem that could be worked on as a group. The principal can discover this by observing individual teachers.

One of the better situations for classroom observation and follow-up conference is when teachers invite the principal to observe. The teacher may have something for the principal to see. Or, the teacher may have a problem with which the principal can help. In either case, the principal and teacher should discuss the situation to be observed beforehand, and plan for the time and approach. The postconference can then be used for advising and reinforcing the teacher's confidence.

In a situation in which the teacher is having problems, video taping the observation can be a very valuable aid. The principal tapes what the teacher and children are doing for approximately one half-hour. The video tape is then played back to the teacher as soon as possible. Usually, the principal does not have to do very much commenting during the playback. Most teachers can point out their own classroom strengths and problems. Often teachers are amazed at how well the students are working; sometimes there is just the opposite reaction.

New teachers need a great deal of help. Their success or failure as teachers often hinges on how much attention and help they get from the principal. The principal should have a planned sequence for classroom visitation with time built in for impromptu visits. Teaching and the school social system are strange to new teachers; they need a lot of help and understanding in becoming familiar with the entire situation. A principal who does not give attention to a first-year teacher and recommends dismissal at the end of the year should be the one to go. Such action is inexcusable since dismissal is a very serious matter and should have sound reasons behind it.

The teacher and principal together should plan the individual classroom observations. The purposes should vary according to needs and should not be restricted to rating or correcting the teacher. The observation varies significantly from the mere inspection.

[24]Wood, *Digest,* p. 47.

CLINICAL SUPERVISION

Clinical supervision is a term currently in vogue to describe a sequence of events for classroom observation and follow-up. Cogan described clinical supervision in terms of stages.[25]

Establishing the Teacher-Supervisor Relationship. The supervising principal's first tasks are to establish a positive working relationship with the teacher, to help the teacher understand clinical supervision including its sequence of events, and to apprise the teacher of the new role of the principal. These tasks should be accomplished before the principal actually begins the observations.

Planning with the Teacher. The lesson or unit is planned cooperatively between the principal and the teacher. The objectives and activities for both the teacher and students are planned in detail. The plans also include specific expected outcomes, possible problems to be encountered, materials and hardware needed, teaching strategies, processes of learning to be utilized, and plans for feedback and evaluation.

Planning the Strategy of Observation. The principal plans the objectives and processes physical and technical arrangements for the observation. The teacher is given explicit information regarding the principal's functions as an observer. As the teachers become more experienced, they assist with planning the observation strategies.

Observing Instruction. The principal observes the teacher and records data.

Analyzing the Teaching/Learning Processes. Both the teacher and the principal analyze the events of the class. They do this separately at the beginning, and as they get more comfortable with the process they do it together.

Planning the Strategy of the Conference. The principal develops the strategies, plans, and alternatives for the conference. As they get more comfortable with the clinical supervision procedure, the principal and teacher may plan the conference together.

The Conference. The principal and teacher confer about the events in the class.

[25]Morris L. Cogan, *Clinical Supervision* (Boston: Houghton Mifflin, 1973).

Renewed Planning. The teacher and principal together decide what action is to be taken as a result of the findings of the observation. They make plans concerning what classroom behavior the teacher will continue and what to change. The cycle then starts over again as the principal and teacher begin to plan the next lesson or unit to be observed.[26]

Smith and Andrews recommend that clinical supervision be carried one step further to include central office personnel in the process. The principal goes through the same process as the teachers. A supervisor from the central office works with the principal in providing assessment and assistance throughout the clinical supervision process. Smith and Andrews recommend a calendar with three phases for a modified approach: (1) the preschool goal setting conference, (2) the collection of school based data during the school year, and (3) an analysis and evaluation at the end of the school year.[27] They also suggest several steps for clinical supervision, beginning with an initial conference between the principal and teacher, followed by a conference between the supervisor and principal. The principal and supervisor together observe a teaching episode after which each analyzes the lesson. Then the supervisor observes as the principal confers with the teacher. As the last step in the process, the supervisor debriefs and confers with the principal.[28]

Clinical supervision can be a very useful tool, but it should not be overworked. Taken to extremes it can become another traditional method of inspection and dictation in which the teacher is observed and then told how and what to teach. Many times a less formal manner of intervention would be more effective for the principal to use in assisting the faculty.

Informal Observation

Peters and Waterman, in their well-known book *In Search of Excellence,* coined the familiar phrase "Management by Wandering Around" (MBWA).[29] Good relations with teachers can be accomplished by wandering around the building in an informal manner. A principal can do many little things to earn status with the teachers. The principal may take a teacher's class for the last fifteen minutes of the day, so that the teacher can keep an important personal appointment. The principal may wander by a teacher's classroom door, discover that the teacher is having a

[26]Cogan, *Clinical Supervision.*

[27]William F. Smith and Richard L. Andrews, "Clinical Supervision for Principals," *Education Leadership,* 45, No. 1 (September 1987), 36.

[28]Ibib, p. 37.

[29]Thomas J. Peters and Robert H. Waterman, Jr., *In Search of Excellence* (New York: Warner Books, 1984), p. 122.

particularly frustrating day, and take the teacher's class for half an hour. Helpful wandering around pays big dividends when the principal asks for assistance and support from the teachers, and it promotes an atmosphere of caring and sharing that can permeate the entire school.

APPROACHES TO INSTRUCTION

In preparation for the supervisory role, the principal should understand the basic approaches to instruction. This is not to say that the principal will be as expert in all fields of study as the master teachers in those fields. There is no greater bore than principals who believe that they are the ultimate authority about instructional methodology. The attitude should be that the teachers are the professionals in their fields, but they will realize improvement with the involvement and support of the principal. Yet all of us know that less experienced teachers may need suggestions about other approaches to teaching; therefore, the principal should be informed about learning theory.

Most theories of learning are based on competing theories of psychology, which in turn are based on competing philosophical systems. For example, the philosophy of existentialism supports phenomenological theories of instruction and learning. The traditional mental-discipline theories of the mind support classical humanism and Herbartianism (apperception). The overview presented by Bigge illustrates the interrelationship of theory of learning, psychological systems, philosophical values, and so on. The overview is presented in Table 10–1.

The reader will note that an internal consistency exists among theory of learning, psychological system, conception of human nature (that is, philosophy), basic transfer of learning, and emphasis in teaching. For example, the S-R (stimulus-response) theory of connectionism of Thorndyke assumes that the learner is passive and is manipulated to learn by the skilled teacher. On the other hand, the Gestalt, or field theory, emphasizes the student as an active participant in the process.

The school principal needs these background insights about the nature of competing learning theories as a basis for observing instruction. Although teachers may be eclectic in their theories of how students learn, they will favor one theory. Great dependence on the programmed sequence of information such as small units, drill, and reinforcement of learning units would indicate a faith in behaviorism. On the other hand, if the teacher leans toward a cognitive theory like Lewin's field theory, step-by-step or drill is less prevalent, and the student is on patterns or wholes rather than parts. The modern humanist approach to teaching, based on

TABLE 10–1. Theories of Learning.

THEORY OF LEARNING I	PSYCHOLOGICAL SYSTEM OR OUTLOOK II	CONCEPTION OF HUMANKIND'S MORAL AND ACTIONAL NATURE III	BASIS FOR TRANSFER OF LEARNING IV	EMPHASIS IN TEACHING V	KEY PERSONS VI	CONTEMPORARY EXPONENTS VII
Mental discipline theories of mind substance family						
1. Theistic mental discipline	Faculty psychology	*Bad-active* mind substance continues active until curbed	Exercised faculties, automatic transfer	Exercise of faculties of the mind	St. Augustine J. Calvin C. Wolff J. Edwards	Many Hebraic-Christian fundamentalists
2. Humanistic mental discipline	Classical humanism	*Neutral-active* mind substance to be developed through exercise	Cultivated mind or intellect	Training of intrinsic mental power	Plato Aristotle	M. J. Adler Harry S. Broudy R. M. Hutchins
3. Natural unfoldment or self-actualization	Romantic naturalism or psychedelic humanism	*Good-active* natural personality to unfold	Recapitulation of racial history, no transfer needed	Negative or permissive education centered on feelings	J. J. Rousseau F. Froebel Progressivists	P. Goodman J. Holt A. H. Maslow
4. Apperception or Herbartianism	Structuralism	*Neutral-passive* mind composed of active mental states or ideas	Growing apperceptive mass	Addition of new mental states or ideas to a store of old ones in subconscious mind	J. F. Herbart E. B. Titchener	Many teachers and administrators
S-R (stimulus-response) conditioning theories of behavioristic family						
5. S-R bond	Connectionism	*Neutral-passive* or reactive organism with many potential S-R connections	Identical elements	Promotion of acquisition of desired S-R connections	E. L. Thorndike	A. I. Gates J. M. Stephens
6. Conditioning with no reinforcement	Classical conditioning	*Neutral-passive* or reactive organism with innate reflexive drives and emotions	Conditioned responses or reflexes	Promotion of adhesion of desired responses to appropriate stimuli	J. B. Watson	E. R. Guthrie
7. Conditioning through reinforcement	Instrumental conditioning	*Neutral-passive* or reactive organism with innate reflexes and needs with their drive stimuli	Reinforced or conditioned responses plus stimulus and response induction	Successive, systematic changes in organisms' environment to increase the probability of desired responses	C. L. Hull	B. F. Skinner K. W. Spence R. M. Gagné A. Bandura

TABLE 10-1. (Continued)

	THEORY OF LEARNING I	PSYCHOLOGICAL SYSTEM OR OUTLOOK II	CONCEPTION OF HUMANKIND'S MORAL AND ACTIONAL NATURE III	BASIS FOR TRANSFER OF LEARNING IV	EMPHASIS IN TEACHING V	KEY PERSONS VI	CONTEMPORARY EXPONENTS VII
Cognitive theories of Gestalt-field family	8. Insight	Gestalt psychology	*Neutral-active* being whose activity follows psychological laws of organization	Transposition of generalized insights	Promotion of insightful learning	M. Wertheimer K. Koffka	W. Köhler
	9. Goal-insight	Configurationalism	*Neutral-interactive* purposive individual in sequential relationships with environment	Tested insights	Aid students in developing high-quality insights	B. H. Bode R. H. Wheeler	E. E. Bayles
	10. Cognitive-field	Field psychology or positive relativism	*Neutral-interactive* purposive person in simultaneous mutual interaction with psychological environment, including other persons	Continuity of life spaces, experience, or insights	Help students restructure their life spaces—gain new insights into their contemporaneous situations	K. Lewin E. C. Tolman J. Dewey G. W. Allport A. Ames, Jr. R. May	E. L. Deci M. L. Bigge J. S. Bruner D. Snygg M. Deutsch S. Koch

Pages 10–11 from *Learning Theories for Teachers* by Morris L. Bigge. Copyright © 1982 by Harper & Row, Publishers, Inc. Reprinted by permission of the publisher.

phenomenological, or perceptual, psychology, places the feelings and concerns of students equal to the material being presented.[30]

Should the principal encourage teachers to adopt a general theory of how students learn and develop? The answer to this question is difficult, because teachers are comfortable with different instructional approaches and students learn by different methods. For example, some educationally mentally retarded students might benefit from methods not appropriate for above-average students. The authors believe, however, that the principal should engage the faculty in intensive consideration of how students learn and develop. We would hope that this discussion will result in more commonality of instructional processes, which should provide greater student satisfaction in learning. This effort should also help to avoid far out methods of teaching. For example, we would hope that none of the teachers would perceive the student as an inanimate object to be filled with irrelevant, unrelated facts. Finally, the faculty and students will benefit from the raising of consciousness about the importance of instructional methodology.

Principals should never forget that all administrators should be the facilitators of a process and not another obstacle to be circumvented in the exercise of one's duties or responsibilities. Too often principals become one more impediment to an effective teaching and learning environment; or, just as paralyzing to the process, they are perceived in this role.

Supervision has evolved into something besides this very strict definition: No one has super vision or should be expected to meet this narrow requirement; it is only through the cooperative effort of all the parties involved that effective teaching and learning will be achieved. Principal supervisors of the process should never expect miracles unless they are willing to pull one off themselves.

---

[30]Myron H. Dembo, *Teaching for Learning: Applying Educational Psychology in the Classroom,* 2nd ed. (Santa Monica: Goodyear, 1981), p. 351.

CHAPTER ELEVEN

Providing Adequate Library Materials and Instructional Technology

Many years ago Chester I. Barnard introduced the notion of effectiveness (nonpersonal or technical) and efficiency (personal need disposition) dimensions of management. Numerous theorists have used other terms to express the arbitrary division of the principal's function into knowledge of intervention in the social system and technical knowledge of the means of production.

Although the technical and personal dimensions cannot be separated except on an arbitrary basis, Chapters 11 through 16 lean toward the technical aspects of school operation. Chapters are devoted to discussing an adequate library, school law, the use of computers (e.g., scheduling a high school), personnel administration, student personnel administration, and the administration of school plant facilities. As we mentioned in the preface, Chapter 17 is a source chapter for the entire text.

Most of us are familiar with the swing of the pendulum in education. For many years we spoke of the instructional materials center; however, the term *library* or *library media center* is currently used in the literature. The principal must be concerned about maintaining an effective library, its supply of materials, and state-of-the-art technology. The instructional program of a school should, literally and figuratively, revolve around the library. The library facility, the materials, and the technological devices should all complement one another. The American Library Association and the American Association of School Libraries have established standards for school libraries. To be effective these standards are to be considered as the essential requirements for libraries of educational institutions.

GUIDELINES AND STANDARDS OF THE AMERICAN LIBRARY ASSOCIATION

The American Library Association regularly publishes revisions in standards and guidelines for libraries. We believe that the administration and faculty of the school should be familiar with these standards and guidelines; moreover, attention should be directed toward actually meeting these standards.

History of School Library Standards and Their Uses

Standards were first established and published for secondary school libraries by the National Education Association and the American Library Association in 1920. These two groups subsequently developed and published standards for elementary school libraries in 1925. The standards determined the philosophical framework on which the nation's schools were to establish acceptable libraries. They established guidelines for allocation of space, numbers of books, periodicals, and other holdings. They also suggested the qualifications and functions of the school librarian and differentiated between school librarians and public librarians.

The American Association of School Librarians prepared, and the American Library Association published, new library standards in 1960. The 1960 standards covered changes that had taken place in libraries. The librarian had become aligned with the instructional functions of the school, and the library had been expanded to include audiovisual materials. During the 1960s the libraries became what was described as media centers. The new name reflected the expanding role of the library in providing far more than books and periodicals for student use.

New standards were again published in 1969. Those standards emphasized the librarians working as part of the instructional team in the schools. They were to help with analysis of student needs, developing teaching strategies that would utilize the new technology and materials. The standards stressed the librarian's role in assisting in developing student skills in viewing, listening, and reading.

In 1975, a new set of standards emphasized the systems approach to providing media services. The library programs were designed to meet objectives of the school system as well as the individual school libraries.

The 1975 publication was designed to provide guidelines as well as standards. It addressed the needs of the school library programs being supported by the district-level media program. "Through these standards, the role of the media program changed from a support service to an integral part of the total instructional program of the school."[1]

The 1988 publication reflected the change from an emphasis on standards to guidelines. In fact, the publication title did not include the word standard. The new publication includes some quantitative information, but, for the most part, it provides "...guidance for planning and evaluating new and existing programs."[2] Rapid changes in the state-of-the-art of information transfer discourage efforts to establish standards for libraries. The earlier standards served their purpose well, but the changing times have, on the whole, rendered their value minimal.

The Principal's Role Related to the Library

The 1988 guidelines also deal with the role of the principal's responsibilities for the school library.

> The principal, working under the district superintendent, is the primary instructional leader in the school. Principals must be knowledgeable about resource-based learning and the importance of the school library media program. The principal is responsible for communicating the expectations for the school library media program to all the staff and for assuring that the school library media specialist serves as a member of the teaching team. Working together with teachers and the school library media specialists to set clear goals and provide methods of evaluating progress, the principal can facilitate the full integration of the school library media program into the curriculum.
>
> As the chief building administrator, the principal ensures that the school library media program has adequate resources to carry out its mission and provides the necessary clerical help to allow the library media specialists to serve a professional role. The principal also supports that role by structuring the use of the library media center flexibly and allowing time for planning and curriculum work. In addition, the principal supports inservice activities that help teachers understand the use of varied information resources and how new technologies contribute to increased learning. The principal encourages the development of relationships with other community agencies so that teachers use material and human resources within the community, as well as those of the school library media center, in structuring learning activities for their students.[3]

[1] American Association of School Librarians and Association for Educational Communications and Technology, *Information Power: Guidelines for School Library Media Programs* (Chicago and Washington: The Associations, 1988), pp. v–vii.

[2] *Information Power*, p. x.

[3] *Information Power*, p. 22.

Thus these guidelines call upon the school principal to provide resourceful leadership in making the library an important resource for the development of a school of quality. However, school principals face very different situations in the supervision of library services. They may enjoy strong financial and human resources in providing adequate library media services, but in many small elementary schools the full-time services of library media specialists are not provided. The "make-do" situations will challenge all of the leadership resources that the school leader can muster. The resources of public libraries may be used to supplement the inadequate school collection. Volunteer staffing may be possible along with sources from private funding. Leaders finding themselves in these situations should press the board of education and the public to underwrite adequate library media services. Even in these reprehensible situations the principal must, with the cooperative participation of the faculty and community leaders, set goals and use leadership strategies to move the school and the school district toward quality library media services.

The administrator of the school is responsible for some recurring leadership tasks in coordinating and improving the effectiveness of the library. As Anderson suggests, whether excellence in education is achieved may well depend upon how well these tasks are performed.[4] One recurring task is the collection of instructional materials and equipment that are relevant to the instructional program of the school. The library should not become a warehouse for irrelevant printed materials and antiquated equipment. Preventing this requires the constant audit or weeding out of the collection and the purchase of relevant materials and equipment.[5] Policies must be established for the development and operation of the library, requiring the cooperation of the principal, library specialist, and members of the faculty.

Funds must be available for purchases. The positive and resourceful leadership of the principal in the budgeting and funding process is essential. We often hear persons speak of the expense of providing library media services, but the investment in the education of children and youth is nominal when the alternatives are considered. The question here is whether the school will be able to offer resources that are critical to the instructional program of the school.

Establishing a network of faculty participation is a recurring task in the well-functioning library. The support and leadership of the principal and of the staff are imperative. The librarian is directly responsible for the administration of the center; however, supervision and support are needed

---

[4]Pauline H. Anderson, *Library Media Leadership in Academic Secondary Schools* (Hamden: The Shoe String Press, 1985), p. 1.

[5]D. Phillip Baker, *The Library Media Programs and the School* (Littleton: Libraries Unlimited, 1984), pp. 98–99.

from the administration of the school. Delaney stated that the principal's support is essential in the operation of a library of quality.[6]

One of the critical appointments is the selection of a library specialist that has leadership ability in the development of the program to insure correct staffing, scheduling, policy development, managing, instructing, collecting materials and equipment, cataloging and processing, and so on. The librarian should have professional know-how, leadership ability, tactfulness, skill in setting priorities, and managerial finesse in working with the faculty and students.

Much of the success of the library in achieving a central place in the instructional program of the school depends upon the genuine cooperation and leadership of the principal and librarian. Strategies should be planned and initiated to utilize fully the resources in the instructional program. The quality of cooperation and leadership of the principal and librarian will set the tone to show that the library is the single most important nonhuman resource in the school.[7]

BEYOND THE STANDARDS AND GUIDELINES: WHAT LIBRARIES ARE, COULD BE, AND SHOULD BE

Principals need to be aware of the standards established for libraries; they must also remember that standards, important as they are for establishing and maintaining effective libraries, should only serve as guidelines. Standards, and even compliance with them, will not insure an effective library. If all the recommended standards have been met and not many people are using the library effectively, then the service is not adequate.

To deviate from the standards or guidelines for a good cause can be a very productive venture. Traditionally, the problem of most librarians is that they have stuck too closely to what was considered to be the ultimate end of accomplishing a good service by severe adherence to standards or quantitative guidelines. The image of librarians as only concerned with the number of books on the shelves instead of the number off the shelves and in use is, unfortunately, often close to reality.

Another point to consider about library standards: They are revised periodically as previously described, but because of the rapid changes taking place in the dissemination of information systems and the lengthy period of time it takes to prepare standards, they can easily become outdated. Librarians should be given the authority to operate their libraries using their professional knowledge and experience.

[6] Jack J. Delaney, *The Media Program in the Elementary and Middle Schools* (Hamden: The Shoe String Press, 1976), pp. 97–98.

[7] Anderson, *Library and Media Leadership*, p. 8.

Educational Possibilities Using Technology

Libraries are undergoing a great and distinctive transition period. Changes, especially in technology, are taking place that have rendered many traditional libraries inadequate. If an information delivery system could be changed at will in order to use the latest technology available, the formats of materials offered at school libraries could be changed with ease. With the existing technology now available to libraries, there is no reason why a student with a computer hooked to the library by telephone should not be able to get information that heretofore was available only in the physical facilities of large libraries.

Recent developments in the transfer of information puts public school libraries in a precarious position. The general public is accustomed to seeing information on television transmitted live from the farthest corners of the earth or from outer space and wonders why this rapid delivery of information is not available in the public schools. It is possible, but expensive, unless there is pooling of resources and better provisions for orderly and cost-effective ways of providing the services. With proper planning and cooperative efforts between schools and school systems, the state-of-the-art library discussed here could be feasible for most schools.

The rest of this chapter will be devoted to some of the technological advances available in library services. Principals need to be familiar with them and how their use can improve the distribution of information in their schools.

Modern Circulation Systems

Many schools are still using the traditional library circulation system that is done by hand. However, a growing number of schools are beginning to modernize their circulation system. Book Track may be one of the more popular computerized circulation systems. Books can be checked in and out by using a bar code in much the same way that grocery and other stores process articles at the checkout counter. Book Track also does many other things, such as keeping detailed records of overdue books, automatically recording outstanding fines, and recording the number of books a particular individual has checked out. The system was developed by two librarians who later sold it to a publishing company. Therefore, the computerized circulation system can be bought. The main thing to look for when purchasing a computer software circulation system is what is referred to as *stability;* that is, does the publisher provide the users with updates of the program? The stability service should cost approximately one hundred dollars per year—the cost is usually about ten percent of the cost of the software package.

The cost of the circulation system computer software package depends on what it is expected to do. If the circulation system is expected to do inventory, reporting and recording of certain information, as well as provide for the circulation of books and other materials, it will naturally cost more. There are also companion products available for card cataloguing. With Book Track, not only would the circulation system do the checking in and out of library books and materials, but the card catalog would also be computerized. There are companion products available for virtually automating the whole operation of the library. It takes several modules of a program to accomplish this, and the program is somewhat expensive, but if the school can afford it and the librarians want it, it is well worth the cost and effort.

Librarians, with some technical help, could also design their own computerized circulation system after investigating the software available and making an inventory of their needs. Whichever way is chosen, the librarian must be satisfied with the system selected and have the support of the principal for its implementation. Any system, no matter how modern, is inadequate if it is not used. In order to develop a program that will be used, a cooperative effort by the principal, teachers, and librarians is required.

Information Access Products

The full text of most magazines is available commercially on microfiche. Microfiche are available on small films that take very little space to store. They must be read using a machine called a microfiche reader, which displays the information from the film taken of the periodicals onto a screen. It is very easy to search through the pages of periodicals by simply moving the machine focus on the film.

Reader printers for microfiche are also available. These machines perform the same function as the regular reader but will also print copies of selected pages or articles. The user can take information directly from the screen or get a printout of selected pages. The reader printer enables the user to search rapidly for articles in periodicals and print out any that need closer scrutiny.

The microfiche system, with readers and printers, is a very effective space saver in the library. The same information that would take much library space to house if the actual copies of the periodicals were stored can be housed in trays of small films.

Microfiche is increasingly used in school libraries, contrary to what is happening in industry and government. Those sectors are rapidly moving to electronic CD-ROM and other devices that are faster and more efficient but cost-prohibitive for most schools. Perhaps in the future this advanced process will also be utilized in the schools.

There are commercially produced microfiche, such as the New York Times products, the News Bank, and the Information Access Products, three of the many commercially produced programs that are available on microfiche that can be obtained by school libraries.

Nonprint

The term *nonprint,* used widely in libraries, refers to anything in the library that is not printed material. There is, however, some controversy as to what is considered to be nonprint. The microfiche storage system is one of the questionable items.

Some of the nonprint such as filmstrips and records are being used less than they once were. Video and audio tapes have replaced much of the traditional type of nonprint. Cassette tapes are much easier to store, retrieve, and use. They are also practical because many students have their own cassette players that they carry with them, which cuts down on the number of players needed and allows for tapes to be checked out routinely.

A word of caution about the acquisition of nonprint: While the library should provide materials and services that are not outmoded, some prudence should be exercised when purchasing new products that generally are expensive. One should allow for some testing time, a period during which the new product or equipment can be considered for acceptance by the users.

Information Delivery Service

There are information delivery services, such as CompuServe, that provide very good information to libraries. CompuServe is a comprehensive database for electronic transfer of information. The service is far too comprehensive to discuss in detail here, so it will only be mentioned briefly to make the reader aware of its availability. Among the services provided by computer hookup are shopping and airline reservations. The cost is determined by the amount of connect time. School libraries can obtain information such as that contained in the Academic American Encyclopedia by using this service. They can also hook up to other utilities such as the Bibliographic Retrieval Services, which provides instant bibliographic information by topic.

Other electronic services can be accessed by computer for no charge except for the phone connection in some states. There are others that can be accessed, for no charge, by an 800 telephone number. TeleNet and TimeNet are two services that require little cost. Some of these services will only run on certain brands of computers, such as IBMs™ or IBM-compatibles. However, some have reconfigured their service to operate on Apple™ or Apple-compatible computers as well.

Time magazine offers a computerized program that is an example of the electronic services that are available to schools. Its NewsQuest program was developed to teach students to locate and reference facts. Students can locate information rather than just memorize facts. This program is especially effective for use in social studies. Each week, *Time* sends the participating schools computer data disks which contain questions for students to answer. Some of the answers are found in the magazine; others are found in a variety of sources, such as library materials and television programs. The disks can be copied so that students can take them home. The responses are reported back to *Time*, which has an answering service that records them. Students can even be rewarded by getting on the *Time* honor roll if they answer all of the questions.[8]

State-of-the-Art Information Systems

Penniman discusses, in an article entitled "Tomorrow's Library Today," the challenge confronting libraries at present.

> Libraries are challenged on a variety of fronts in terms of their role and function. While technology is advancing at an incredible pace, our ability to absorb and use the technology in an essentially human endeavor, i.e., information transfer, is still limited. The library as an institution is on the brink of becoming either crucial or superfluous, depending upon strategies selected by library leaders within the very near future.[9]

Penniman, Director of Libraries and Information Systems Center at AT&T Bell Laboratories, describes the AT&T Library Network, which would probably be the optimum for most schools but also portrays other systems that are currently available.

Penniman advocates three methods of packaging and delivering information: the physical facility, the electronic equipment, and the human facilitator. He recognizes that these three components are merging and that information should be easily transferred from one to another. A brief description of the system advocated by Penniman, including the identification and use of technologies currently available, follows. The purpose is to utilize components readily available in a different approach, not to develop a new system.

Penniman suggests an access station for shelving current journal literature, references, and selected hard copy. He recommends that shelving be located so that patrons have access to the material for browsing and

[8]Interview with Koleta Tilson, Librarian (Sullivan Central High School, Blountville, Tennessee, February 1988).

[9]W. David Penniman, "Tomorrow's Library Today," *Special Libraries*, 78, No. 3 (Spring 1987), 95.

that the distribution of these materials be accommodated by a local charge-out mechanism.

According to Penniman, access to local and remote databases can be "provided by an online information storage and retrieval system running on a local computer with storage." Access to "records should be via search keys built from selected fields within each record....At least two terminals capable of querying these databases should be available in the access station, one for patrons and one for staff, and a hardcopy printer should be accessible from either terminal."

Penniman suggests that school libraries have access to Library Network databases, which are located at a national center. Information via this Network can be downloaded to local databases in the libraries of selected schools. There are also commercial databases that can be accessed by local schools.

According to Penniman, access to one or more of the existing bibliographic utilities should also be considered, with dialup access available from at least one of the terminals in the access station. "At a minimum, the access station should be capable of receiving copies from one external 'super' source (such as UMI, Information Store, or ISI), as well as other traditional libraries." The option to transmit material directly to the access station by facsimile transmission should be available.

Access to human assistance provided by a trained reference lib-rarian or information specialist at the access site should be available. In addition, access to remotely located reference specialists, skilled in selected areas, should be provided by both telephone and computer terminal and be available to either the access station staff or directly to the patron.

Minimal space is needed to house the functions just described. Penniman states that:

> Commercially available, fabricated library structures can satisfy these requirements and lend themselves to installation in atriums and other areas where heavy staff traffic would assure wide exposure to the information services. Where more austere environments are required, there are packaged designs developed to place an access station within an existing room of 300 to 400 square feet.[10]

State-of-the-art information systems allow for more ready and greatly expanded amounts of information to be stored and accessed by library users. School libraries would be greatly enhanced by availability of state-of-the-art equipment and information systems such as the one described by Penniman.

---

[10]Penniman, "Tomorrow's Library Today," pp. 202–4.

OTHER TECHNOLOGY USED IN SCHOOLS

Message System

Messages can be sent throughout a school on television monitors located at strategic points that flash messages of current interest during the school day, requiring only a software package that costs approximately fifty dollars, a small computer such as an Atari, a sending machine, and the proper hookup. Up to two hundred messages can be recorded and repeatedly sent to the monitors, resulting in a very inexpensive operation for an excellent internal communications service.

Artificial Intelligence

What is often referred to as artificial intelligence is being developed at a staggering speed. For instance, Texas Instruments has developed what they call a Julie Doll, a mechanical doll that can respond to conversation. It operates by responding to voice print. It can even recognize who is speaking if the person's voice print has been programmed in beforehand. She will respond to any conversation that has been programmed into her. Research and development in this kind of artificial intelligence has great possibilities for change in the schools. Robotics are being accepted and used in many segments of society, and their use will increase at a rapid pace. There is good reason to believe that they will make their presence known in schools in the near future.

Scanner

Many schools now have machine scanners that are used primarily for scoring tests. The test scorer can return the raw-score test results within minutes after the test is completed, allowing the teacher to give students almost immediate feedback on how they did on the test and providing for timely corrective action.

Correct test answers are programmed into the machine by the answer key, and all student test responses are then scored against the correct answers. Test answers are recorded on answer sheets by the students, and the teacher then runs the sheets through the scanner to receive almost immediate data concerning the results.

The scanner can do far more than score the tests. Among other things, it can do item analysis of the tests; establish individual student norms, a class roster of norms, and frequency distributions of percentile ranks; and count ballots and tabulate surveys.

CHAPTER TWELVE

Understanding School Law

Since a number of legal questions arise from the operation of a school, school principals need some understanding of school law. Under what conditions may the principal or teacher be liable in tort for injuries? What legal authority does the principal have in controlling the conduct of pupils? What are the sources of legal controls over the school? These are but a few of the legal questions of importance for principals. The information in this chapter deals with school law as it applies directly to the duties and responsibilities of the school principal. It is not intended to be an extensive coverage of the law; we recommend a rigorous course in school law for that purpose.

The educational leader must be clothed with both legal and group-based authority to act. Some principals may try to mix legal authority with actual power and become too impressed with their legally prescribed authority, but they should not always exercise all the legal authority they possess. For example, the school principal has legal authority to assign pupils to a certain teacher's classroom, even though the parents object to the assignment. That authority, however, does not unequivocally solve the question of actual authority for pupil assignment. As discussed in Chapter 5, the principal functions within the spectrum of the community power structure. Suppose the principal assigned the children of the chairman of the school board to a particular teacher over the objections of the parent. Would that be wise? Does the mere possession of legal authority to assign pupils give the principal actual power to act in such cases? The principal may assume the attitude that he has the authority, legally, to assign pupils and may steadfastly exercise the authority and refuse to change the assignment. If the parent should institute court action, the decision of the principal would probably be upheld. Nevertheless, the principal may have forgotten that officially prescribed authority does not necessarily give one charismatic authority. The principal may find that the battle has been won but the war has been lost when reappointment is considered the following year. In fact, this situation may lead to a tangled web of school and community problems that adversely affects the teaching and learning environment of the school. Some persons believe that legality is based on morality. In the case just stated, can the principal make a fair and just decision without endangering the prospects of being reappointed?

One must never confuse legal authority and power with real social power and authority. England had legal authority to pass the Stamp Act, but the process created a revolutionary behavioral problem and lost a colony. The central theme of this book is to emphasize the fact that the school principal is involved with very difficult problems of behavior. By having the weight of law as support, the principal does have certain legally prescribed authority to act, but this authority does not diminish the problem of behavior. In fact, legality may sometimes complicate the behavioral problems. There is an old principle of law saying that no legislative body can pass and have enforced a law that is not acceptable to the people regardless of its merits. The fifty-five mile-per-hour speed limit on interstate highways in this country, which was imposed nationally in the mid-1980s, is a good example of a law that could not be enforced because people did not believe in and adhere to it. As a result, the law was soon amended. Similarly, the state legislatures often pass strict laws to improve the schools, but find actual improvement as a result of the laws elusive.

The principal, therefore, should not study law as a means to deal with the basic leadership problem with groups. As discussed in Chapter 7, the leader must have both legally prescribed and group-based influence. Some maliciously autocratic administrators have manufactured "laws" to prevent teachers from taking action. These people learned that to say something was against the law was enough to deter action, although this is less possible with modern teachers, many of whom are well educated and knowledgeable about laws and who have access to resources such as leaders of teachers groups versed in teachers' rights. Furthermore, the regulations of most school boards are now written and published for all to see, and through the influence of professional groups, teachers are less prone to follow the leadership of demagogues.

The comments in the preceding paragraphs are not intended to imply that school law is not important to behavior. Authorities on school law point to instances in which serious problems of behavior have arisen because principals did not have knowledge of the law. Numerous community hassles could have been avoided completely if school officials had known about the laws involved. Serious problems such as strip searches of students have arisen because the principal was either ignorant of the law or ignored it.

Knowledge of school law is important to the principal, just as knowledge of the law is important to all citizens. Unlike most other citizens, however, educational leaders need to know the law for reasons beyond being able to defend themselves and exercise their rights. For example, we aspire to produce students who are law-abiding citizens. Principals and their faculties should certainly attempt to observe the demands of the laws underlying our democratic society, and should not knowingly or through ignorance flaunt the basic intent of law. Paradoxically, this may be happening more in the issues of religion and prayer in the schools than for any other reason. In some isolated, rural communities religious exercises are still practiced even though they have been declared unconstitutional by the U.S. Supreme Court.

DECENTRALIZED SOURCES OF CONTROL

The administration of education in most European countries is typically centralized under a minister of education in the national government. Persons familiar with the centralized system find the control and administration of schools in the United States somewhat confusing. The organization and control of education in the United States are functions of the various states; the U.S. Constitution contains no reference to education.

Education was traditionally considered to be a function of the state by virtue of the Tenth Amendment to the Constitution, which reads, "The Powers not delegated to the United States by the Constitution, nor prohibited by it to the States, are reserved to the States respectively, or to the people." Yet, through action of the Supreme Court, the states are limited in their operation of schools by the Constitution. Moreover, the Congress has from time to time passed significant acts influencing the organization and administration of schools. Authorities have suggested for many years that the general welfare clause of the Constitution gave the federal government authority to pass legislation affecting education. During the 1960s and 1970s federal participation in the administration of education increased. Some members of the Congress have even given serious thought to seeking an amendment to the Constitution to permit prayer and Bible reading in the schools.

State constitutions usually include a statement relative to the responsibility of the legislature to provide a uniform system of public education in the state. The concept of local control of education has been emphasized so much that many citizens mistakenly assume that education is a function of local government, yet local school districts and the governing boards thereof are creatures of the state legislature. The districts may be altered at will or abolished completely by the legislature as long as the action is constitutional. Most states have established a state board of education that has the power to establish rules and regulations to administer the state program of education. A state agency, usually referred to as the state department of education, with a state commissioner or superintendent as the administrative official, is in charge of the state program.

Local school districts have been established in the states for the administration of education. The board of education in each district is given rather broad powers to establish policies controlling the organization of schools in the district.

SOURCES FOR THE DETERMINATION OF THE PRINCIPAL'S LEGAL STATUS

In consideration of the legally prescribed controls over the typical school, the principal must look to several sources. Through the process of litigation in the courts, decisions are constantly being made concerning the organization and administration of schools. The decisions of the supreme courts of the states and of the Supreme Court of the United States are constantly creating laws that influence public education. Court decisions have been rendered about most areas of school administration; consequently, court decisions constitute one important source of law of which the principal should be cognizant.

Legislated laws are another important source of school law. Laws passed by the Congress have increasingly influenced the operation of public schools. For example, since the 1950s the Congress has been very active in the passage of laws governing the civil rights of students, teachers, and the handicapped. These laws have placed significant restrictions on how a school is administered. Most schools take advantage of various provisions of both state and federal legislation that provide financial support for school improvement.

The state legislature passes massive numbers of statutes governing the organization and administration of education. Principals should give special attention to the state statutes that apply to the areas in which they are administrators. Most states provide for the printing of the statutes governing education, and they are made available to school personnel. Principals have implied obligations by law, even though the state statutes may not specifically name them as being responsible for carrying out certain provisions of it. Furthermore, statutes under civil law affecting the operation of schools may not appear under the codification of educational statutes; nevertheless, certain laws governing public health and safety may include the administration of schools. Restricting attention to the school code would overlook the great body of other law generated by the courts that can affect public education.

Principals are expected to familiarize themselves with the state and local school board rules and regulations. The regulations of the state board and policies of the local board of education have the effect of law. Regulations with regard to the state accreditation of schools are examples of state regulations with which the school principal and staff should be familiar. State regulations affect school operation in the areas of curriculum, teacher personnel, buildings and grounds, student personnel, finance, and other areas of educational administration. The authorities in local school districts should make copies of the state board of education rules and regulations available to school personnel. The policies of the district board of education should also be available to school personnel. Traditionally, the problem of obtaining up-to-date written policies of the board has arisen in some school districts. However, in most school districts, the principal will find written copies of the board of education policies available.

In addition to the official sources that describe their legal status, principals should consult current publications in the field. Numerous books that deal with different aspects of principals' legal status have been published. Principals may want to subscribe to a regularly published yearbook on school law or to other types of subscription services dealing with recent developments in school law. Many journal articles also deal with the different aspects of school law.

Laws affecting the administration of public schools are in a state of development and change. For example, one could point to the dynamics of change relative to the political activities and rights of teachers, and the issues of collective bargaining.

The area of legal foundations of education is not something that is definite and that fits into a neatly arranged package. After completing a university course on school law, one student stated that he had learned the valuable lesson that one can never assume that any one law or regulation will be true of all school districts. The law defies the definitiveness often ascribed to it for various reasons, one being that it is continually changing. Court decisions are constantly being rendered that often provide new interpretations and even reversals of earlier decisions. Many decisions simply raise numerous other unanswered legal questions. Legislative statutes are also in a state of development and change. There are many "iffy" kinds of so-called legal principles created by the courts for which the legal expert can only presume an interpretation. Law is an area that is alive and developing and one in which the educational leader must keep up-to-date.

The purpose of this chapter is to point out that knowledge of school law is imperative for the school principal. Because numerous volumes have been written to inform school administrators of legal principles, only a few of the areas of law that affect the school principal will be discussed here.

CONSTITUTIONAL FOUNDATIONS

Almost all court decisions and legislation that impact upon public education have their origin in six amendments to the Constitution. The first ten amendments are popularly known as the Bill of Rights. Another provision in the Constitution which is significant to teachers and other education personnel is Article 1, Section 10, known as the Contracts Clause, which is important when the guaranteed rights concerning tenure, retirement, and other contractual benefits may be questioned or threatened.[1]

The Tenth Amendment

The Tenth Amendment to the Constitution establishes the fundamental responsibility of the state for establishing and maintaining a system of public education. Since education is not mentioned in the federal Constitution, it is interpreted as one of the powers reserved for the state. On the basis of the Tenth Amendment, therefore, local boards of education, although elected or appointed locally, are state officials, and actually an extension of the state legislature. State legislatures have plenary (complete) powers subject only to constitutional restrictions. Since schools are state functions, the principal acts as an agent for the state. Because one of the purposes of the Bill of Rights was to regulate the police power of the states, the behavior of principals is interpreted in the light of exercising the police power of the state when acting as its agents.[2]

The First Amendment

In recent years, perhaps no constitutional amendment has been argued as frequently and vehemently as the First Amendment. The First Amendment ensures, among other guarantees, that "Congress shall make no law respecting an *establishment* of religion or prohibiting the *free*

---

[1]Floyd H. Edwards, "School Law for Classroom Teachers and Principals" (unpublished paper presented to Upper East Tennessee Educational Cooperative Educator's Inservice, October 30, 1987).
[2]Edwards, "School Law."

exercise thereof." Principals would be well advised to apprise themselves of the ramifications of the amendment and to keep abreast of court rulings based on this part of it. The rulings concerning prayer and Bible reading in the school based on this part of the amendment should be of particular interest to principals. There are two clauses based on the First Amendment with which the principal should be vitally concerned: the establishment clause and the free exercise clause.

The Establishment Clause. In 1962 the Supreme Court ruled in *Engle v. Vitale,* 370 U.S. 306 (1952), that use of the nonsectarian prayer composed by the New York State Board of Regents and recommended to be recited daily in the New York public schools, violated the "no reestablishment" clause even though the prayer was denominationally neutral and its observance on the part of students was voluntary.

In 1963 the Supreme Court handed down another major church-state decision in the case of School District of *Abington* v. *Schempp,* 374 U.S. 203 (1963). At issue in the Schempp case was the validity of a Pennsylvania law requiring the reading without comment of ten verses from the Holy Bible at the beginning of each day. The Court reaffirmed the principle that government may *not* "aid one religion, aid all religions, or prefer one religion over another." The Court held that the morning exercises in question were intended to advance religion; hence, there was a violation of the first-amendment command that government maintain neutrality, neither aiding nor opposing religion. As in the *Engle* v. *Vitale* case, the Court held that the voluntary nature of the exercises was no defense to a challenge under the no establishment clause. In the *Mozert* v. *Hawkins County,* 827 SW 1058 (1987) case, a group of parents and their attorneys argued that the Holt Series teaches a religion, which they labeled as secular humanism, thus violating the establishment clause. The judge in the lower courts ruled in favor of the parents. On appeal, the Sixth Circuit Court of Appeals did not uphold the parents' claim and reversed the decision of the District Court.[3] The case was appealed; however, the Supreme Court refused to hear the case, letting stand the decision of the Appeals Court. Similar tests of the establishment clause will, no doubt, be brought to the courts in the future and principals would be well advised to stay apprised of the outcomes.

None of the court decisions just cited or on record prohibit individual prayer or Bible reading, only that which is conducted by an agent of the state, such as a principal or teacher, and on a state-owned site or building.

The Free Exercise Clause. The Supreme Court has ruled that individuals have an absolute right to hold and advocate any religious view they

[3]Edwards, "School Law."

choose. The right to *act* on those beliefs, however, is not absolute. The state must demonstrate a "compelling interest" in order to regulate or restrain behavior. That compelling interest was not demonstrated when the Court ruled that students of the Jehovah's Witnesses could not be required to violate their religious beliefs by standing and saluting the American flag. On the other hand, courts have consistently upheld the state's compelling interest in requiring that children be immunized against communicable diseases or when giving needed medical treatment, even if such immunization and treatment are against the individual's religious scruples.[4]

The Equal Access Act.   In 1984 the Congress passed the Equal Access Act permitting *secondary* school students in public high schools, which have a limited open forum, to conduct religious meetings. The Act means that any high school that permits students to participate in other clubs and organizations must not deny equal access or fair opportunity to students who wish to have a meeting of religious context within that limited open forum. There can be no sponsorship of the meeting by the school, the government, or its agents or employees, and such a meeting must not substantially interfere with the orderly conduct of educational activities within the school. Nonschool persons may not direct, conduct, control, or regularly attend activities of these student groups. The Supreme Court, in 1986, in *Bender* v. *Williamsport Area School District,* 106 S.Ct. 1326 (1986), reinforced the essence of the Equal Access Act.[5]

Moment of Silence.   Several state legislatures have passed moment-of-silence acts. Most of these acts have been or will be challenged in the courts. In hearing these cases, the court tries to determine if the legislative intent of moment-of-silence statutes violates the Establishment Clause of the First Amendment. Based on the intent of the law, in *Wallace* v. *Jaffree,* U.S. 472 (1985), the Supreme Court ruled an Alabama moment-of-silence law unconstitutional.

Religious Pageants and Displays.   State and federal courts have given different answers to the question of whether schools can present Christmas plays. In *Lynch* v. *Donnelly,* 465 U.S. 668 (1984), the Supreme Court ruled that the expenditure of public funds for a Christmas display, including a Nativity scene, did not violate the establishment clause. It is generally believed that traditional Christmas programs will probably be upheld if challenged.

[4]Edwards, "School Law."
[5]Edwards, "School Law."

Invocation and Baccalaureate Services. Lower courts have been divided on the issue of invocations and baccalaureates, and the Supreme Court has not ruled on it. It is questionable whether invocations in schools will be allowed by the courts. However, if a baccalaureate ceremony is held off-campus and attendance is optional, the practice would probably be upheld.

SEARCH AND SEIZURE

The Fourth Amendment protects individuals and their homes from arbitrary search by the police in the absence of a warrant issued upon probable cause. The Fourth Amendment states in part, "The right of people...against *unreasonable* search and seizures shall not be violated, and no warrants shall be issued but upon probable cause." The warrant must be based on probable cause, which is defined as "reasonable grounds of suspicion, supported by sufficient evidence to warrant a cautious person to believe that the individual is guilty of the offense charged."[6]

Students, too, have Fourth-Amendment rights but not to the same degree as adults under probable cause. The concept of "reasonable suspicion," which is a lower level of due process than is "probable cause," holds in cases of student search and seizure as long as the search and seizure is carried out by school officials and no law officials are present. In some states it is the law, and in others it is recommended, that if contraband drugs are confiscated they must or should be turned over to local law officials. In such cases, principals should demand a receipt specifying exactly what is turned over to the law officials.[7]

School officials have much more flexibility to proceed with searches and seizures when dealing with students under the reasonable suspicion umbrella than do the police when dealing with adults under the reasonable cause limitations. If law officials are called in for search and seizure in cases concerning students, then the higher order of due process, called probable cause, must prevail. Furthermore, as is the case when dealing with adults, evidence gathered when dealing with students in an unconstitutional manner may not be admissible in criminal prosecution under the exclusionary rule.

The classic Supreme Court case which upheld and strengthened principals' rights to search students and seize contraband was *New Jersey v. T.L.O.*, 105 S.Ct. 733 (1985). The case involved the search of a female student's purse by an assistant principal who found her in a smoke-filled bathroom (establishing reasonable suspicion) and asked her to empty her

[6]Martha M. McCarthy and Nelda H. Cambron, *Public School Law: Teachers' and Students' Rights* (Boston: Allyn & Bacon, 1981), pp. 307–8. Reprinted with permission.
[7]Floyd H. Edwards, "School Law."

purse on a desk. When she complied, not only was tobacco found, but also drug paraphernalia and other suspicious items, which led the assistant principal to suspect drug dealing. The student was suspended and she sued the school officials on the basis of an unreasonable search. The Supreme Court upheld the search as constitutional and adopted a standard for determining the legality of school searches. The Court said that if school officials have reasonable grounds for suspecting that the search will turn up evidence of the student violating the law or the rules of the school, and if the scope of the search is reasonable in relation to the situation, the search may be conducted.

The following guidelines for school principals will help to avoid legal confrontations.

1. A search warrant must be obtained if police officials are conducting a search.
2. Both students and parents should be informed that searches can and will be conducted when necessary.
3. Before a search is ever conducted, school personnel should ask the students to volunteer any evidence of contraband in their possession.
4. The person conducting the search should do so in the presence of another staff member.
5. There should be absolutely no strip searches or mass searches.
6. All searches should be based upon reasonable belief that some illegal material is present.[8]

Strip Searches.   Strip searches have generally been ruled by courts to be completely beyond the authority of the schools. School officials would be well advised, in the absence of particularized suspicion of a student, to refrain from strip searches.

Locker Searches.   Courts have almost uniformly agreed that school principals have broad authority to perform locker searches. School lockers are the property of the school system, and school officials retain the authority to search them in cases when there is reasonable suspicion. Boards of education should establish school policy about locker search, and this policy should be publicized in student handbooks and other school media that help students become aware of the policy.

Thomas J. Flygare reported that the Supreme Court did not rule on some important issues in the search and seizure controversy.

> The Court refused to decide whether evidence obtained in an unconstitutional search of a student by school officials is admissible in criminal and juvenile proceedings. The Court refused to address the question of whether a student has "a legitimate expectation of privacy in lockers, desks, or other

[8]McCarthy and Cambron, *Public School Laws*, pp. 307–8.

school property provided for storage of school supplies." The Court declined to comment on searches conducted by school officials "in conjunction with or at the request of law enforcement agencies." The Court did not decide whether a school official needs "individualized suspicion" as a basis for conducting a search of a student's belongings.[9]

It seems that the Supreme Court has merely postponed any major decisions regarding the constitutionality of searches and seizures.

Use of Sniffing Dogs to Detect Drugs.   Generally, the use of trained dogs to sniff out drugs in student lockers and automobiles has been upheld by the courts. Having a sniffing dog check lockers on a regular and frequent basis is questionable. Since the classic case of *Doe* v. *Renfrow,* 451 U.S. 1022 (1981), the use of sniffing dogs to detect drugs on the bodies of students has been prohibited. The courts ruled in that case that sniffing of students in the absence of individual suspicion was too intrusive.

DUE PROCESS

The Fifth Amendment states that no person shall "be deprived of life, liberty, or property, without due process of law." The Fourteenth Amendment guarantees that no *state* shall deprive any person of life, liberty, or property without due process of law, nor deny to any person within its jurisdiction the equal protection of the laws.

Due process is an elusive concept and process. Its exact boundaries are difficult to define, and its content varies according to specific factual contexts. Whether the Constitution demands a particular right depends upon complex factors.

A student has the right to some elements of due process. Certain procedures must be followed by principals before any rights can be taken away from students. Peterson, Rossmiller, and Volz reported that these procedures include the following:

1. A clear, written statement of charges
2. A right to be represented by counsel and to be informed of this fact
3. A reasonable period of time for preparation of a defense
4. The right to present evidence on one's own behalf, including the calling of witnesses
5. The right to confront and cross-examine witnesses in most situations
6. The right to a hearing before an impartial tribunal[10]

[9]Thomas J. Flygare, "High Court Approves Searches of Students but Ducks Many Tough Issues," *Phi Delta Kappan,* 66 (March 1985), 504–5.

[10]Leroy J. Peterson, Richard A. Rossmiller, and Marlin M. Volz, *The Law and Public School Operation* (New York: Harper & Row, 1978), p. 345.

In regard to teacher's rights, McCarthy and Cambron put forth some guidelines to be followed when assessing them.

1. A teacher is entitled to due process of law prior to dismissal when a property or liberty interest exists.
2. A property interest is created through tenure, implied tenure, or contract.
3. A liberty interest may arise if the dismissal action imposes a stigma or damages the teacher's reputation.
4. At minimum, due process requires that the teacher be provided with notice specifying reasons for dismissal and an opportunity for a hearing at which to present evidence and confront witnesses.
5. All procedures specified by statute or contract must be followed in the dismissal process.[11]

Elements of Substantive Due Process

Substantive due process is less precise than procedural due process. It is highly discretionary but embraces the spirit of the need for fair treatment of all people, including students. In other words, substantive due process focuses on *what* the law requires, and procedural due process focuses on *how* it is implemented.[12] Following are some of the elements of substantive due process.

Reasonableness. Schools are always bound by the requirement that their rules and regulations be reasonable (*Burnside* v. *Byars,* 363 F.2d 744 (1966).

Proportionality. Schools are responsible to ascertain that punishment given a student for violation of a reasonable rule is proportional to the transgression (*Lee* v. *Macon County Board of Education,* 190 F.Supp. 307 (1972).

Fair Warning. Students have the constitutional right to be guided by rules that are specific enough so that the ordinary person can know and do what is expected (*Kelly* v. *Metropolitan County Board of Education of Nashville,* 292 F.Supp. 485).

Equal Application. The equal application requirement sets limits on the discretion of school officials to single out individuals for treatment that is not applied to others. Equal protection of the law is guaranteed by the Fourteenth Amendment, which permits school officials to exercise discretion, but they must be fair. The *in loco parentis* status of teachers and

[11]McCarthy and Cambron, *Public School Law,* p. 114.
[12]Floyd H. Edwards, "School Law."

principals allows them some discretionary power to act on individual cases and still stay within the equal application limits. The principal has a greater discretionary power than do teachers concerning equal application or varying from it, which has been granted by statute, school board policy, and custom.

Equal Protection. Equal protection from state police power is also guaranteed by the Fourteenth Amendment. Supreme Court Justice Fortas, in delivering the landmark *Tinker* v. *Des Moines,* 393 U.S. 503 (1969) decision, stated that "It can hardly be argued that neither students or teachers shed their constitutional rights at the schoolhouse door." There are some sensitive areas of equal protection concerning discrimination about which principals should be especially concerned. Race is an especially sensitive area.

Care should be taken to show statistical evidence that there is not a disproportionate number of suspensions or expulsions of minority students. Gender is another special concern. Unequal treatment of girls and boys must be avoided. Finally, treatment of students from different social classes and ethnic groups is another delicate matter under equal protection. Special attention must be given to equal treatment for the poor, underprivileged, and politically powerless students as compared to consideration for all others.

TORT LIABILITY

Any discussion of school law would be incomplete without consideration of the liability of teachers and administrators in legal actions involving damages for tort. A tort is a civil (not criminal) wrong that causes personal injury or property damage and for which courts may provide monetary compensation. An understanding of this area would certainly help administrators and teachers gain increased appreciation of their responsibility to exercise prudent judgment in protecting the well being of pupils. In some instances teachers can be particularly careless in the supervision of pupils. In such instances, the teachers are liable for action involving damages. Since principals are ultimately responsible for all actions in the schools, this situation also puts them at great risk.

The "reasonable man" theory prevails in consideration of whether a tort has been committed. Was an action taken that a reasonable person under similar circumstances would, or would not, have taken? In order for an individual's action to be considered a tort, Peterson, Rossmiller, and Volz have established four conditions that must be shown to exist.

1. A duty or obligation requiring one to conform to a certain standard of conduct so as to protect others against unreasonable risk
2. A failure on one's part to act in a manner which conforms to the standard of conduct required
3. Injury to another caused by one's failure to act in the manner required
4. Actual loss or damage to the person or interest of another as a result of the injury

They also contend that once a tort has been legally established, the person claiming the injury must prove three things.

1. The defendant had a duty to protect the complainant against unreasonable risk of injury.
2. The defendant breached the duty, that is, failed to protect the complainant from injury.
3. The breach of duty by the defendant was the proximate cause of the complainant's injury.[13]

McCarthy and Cambron cited three major categories of tort actions: negligence, intentional torts, and strict liability. Negligence is the failure to comply with an acceptable standard of care. Intentional torts are those that were "committed with the desire to inflict harm, and include assault, battery, false imprisonment, trespass, and defamation." Strict liability is the injury of a person because of the "creation of an unusual hazard."[14]

Negligence is a concept that is closely associated with the law of torts. Negligence is defined as the "failure to exercise the degree of care for the safety and well-being of others that a reasonable and prudent person would have exercised under similar circumstances."[15] It is the responsibility of the plaintiff to prove negligence, but the amount of compensation is always decided by the courts.

Negligence

Negligence is the most common tort, and the question of neglect often arises in schools from the teachers' and principals' alleged breach of some duty of care owed the students and their parents. A few examples are cited here. In one elementary school, the teacher left a group of sixth-grade students unsupervised. While he was out of the room, two students were horseplaying and one broke the other's thumb. In another example, a

---

[13]Peterson, Rossmiller, and Volz, *The Law*, p. 252.

[14]McCarthy and Cambron, *Public School Law*, p. 147.

[15]Peterson, Rossmiller, and Volz, *The Law*, p. 152.

teacher sent a boy on an errand off the school grounds and across the street. The child was injured when hit by a car while crossing the street. In yet another incident, a kindergarten student drowned in a stream of water at the edge of the school ground after slipping away from the teacher. Let us assume that in each of these three incidents the parents instituted action against the teacher involving damages for tort. In each case the teacher may be charged with negligence. What is likely to be the significant test of negligence in each of these cases? In every case, the test of reasonableness will be applied. In other words, would the actions taken by the teachers be that of a reasonably prudent person? If the behavior of the teachers is considered to be substandard as compared to that of the reasonably prudent behavior of others, the teachers are likely to be held liable. Another test of negligence is foreseeability. Again, if a reasonably prudent person would have foreseen that the teachers' behaviors in the examples might very well lead to injury, then the teachers will likely be held as negligent.

Foreseeability. The principle of foreseeability is particularly important for principals. Presumably, the test of foreseeability for kindergarten would be different from the test for a high school class. Ordinarily, a prudent person would provide closer supervision for kindergarten children than for high school students. In the example given of the kindergarten child drowning, the teacher would be expected to provide close supervision, considering the existing hazard of the stream of water near the playground. Such close supervision of high school students would not be expected since it is reasonable to assume that they would have learned to avoid that kind of hazard.

Connectibility. There are other factors in addition to foreseeability that contribute to charges of negligence. For example, connection must be established between the alleged negligence of the teacher and the cause of the incident. The courts may also rule that the person contributed to his own injury. If the court finds that the pupil contributed to his own injury in the absence of adequate supervision and the exercise of caution by the school, the court may find evidence of contributory negligence.

Thoughtless or Lazy Acts. School principals and teachers often thoughtlessly commit students to situations that might be the basis of negligence in court. Some of these cases are often the result of thoughtlessness or even laziness. For example, the principal who sends a student after a package of cigarettes for a visiting dignitary may end up in double jeopardy. There is a risk of student injury and of being charged with breaking the law that prohibits minors from purchasing tobacco products. Another source of concern is the supervision of elementary students on the playground. Teachers are sometimes observed to be lax in the supervision of playground activities. It is not unusual for a teacher to stay in the classroom while the students are playing on the playground just outside the room. While the teacher may very well be able to observe the student activities, it is unlikely that the courts would uphold this as reasonable supervision.

Playground. The playground and playground equipment should be of particular concern to principals. Written safety rules and rules of conduct for the playground should be disseminated, and playground equipment should be kept in a good state of repair and inspected regularly. If there are hazards that cannot be corrected at the school level, they should be reported in writing to the central office along with a request for corrections.

Care about safety in the school and on the school ground is necessary to avoid and protect against accidents or incidents of possible liability. In one case, a third grader was molested by a thirteen-year-old male student on the school grounds. The teacher and principal found out about it, but elected not to inform the parents of the incident. The court ruled that the principal did have an obligation to notify the parents of the incident. However, the appellate court left the dispute over the liability up to the trial court.[16] In another case, an eighth-grade student was injured by a seventeen-year-old student who had been retained three times and had a history of problems. The incident took place on a day when the substitute teacher was out of the room. The substitute was not found liable because she could not have foreseen that the incident might take place. The court decided that the principal should have taken some action against the student's conduct at an earlier time since that action might have prevented the incident from taking place.[17]

Field Trips. Field trips are not a legal problem per se; however, the participating teachers and the principal are required to provide for the safety of the students. Special precautions should be taken in order to minimize circumstances that could result in injury to students and, thus, liability. The following are some safeguards established by one state in regard to school-sponsored field trips.

1. Always plan in advance. This is crucial in proving that safeguards were provided to students.
2. The school authorities must be informed of the intent to take a field trip.
3. Parents should be informed in advance of the field trip.
4. The site of the field trip should be inspected for any possible hazards, and students should be informed of them.

[16]Perry A. Zirkel and Ivan B. Gluckman, "Is a Principal Liable When One Student Injures Another?" *Principal,* 66 (May 1987), 44–47.

[17]Zirkel and Gluckman, "Is a Principal Liable?"

5. There should be an ample number of adult supervisors.
6. Special dress or equipment should be used when necessary.
7. Safe transportation is a must. The use of private vehicles is oftentimes not permitted and, at the very least, should be discouraged.
8. Permission of the controllers of the site of the field trip should be obtained in advance.[18]

Usually, principals are not held liable for negligent actions of teachers and other employees under their supervision; however, there are situations in which they can be. For example, a principal can be held responsible for the negligence of an incompetent subordinate if the person was known to be incompetent and was recommended by the principal for employment anyway. Likewise, if a principal knows about an incompetent and negligent teacher under his supervision and does not try to correct or dismiss the person, the principal may be held responsible in the case of litigation involving negligence on the teacher's part. Likewise, principals can be held liable for their failure to establish proper rules and regulations for pupil safety.[19]

Many of the educational professional organizations have developed insurance that will pay the liability for legal damages in the case of tort. Even for the most careful and cautious principals, this insurance is recommended. It may, however, increase the probability of being sued.

CONTROL OF PUPIL BEHAVIOR

There is no dispute over the fact that the school principal has the right to control student conduct. However, the way in which conduct and punishment are perceived has changed drastically in recent years. The courts have always expected punishment to be reasonable regarding the wrong committed, but the term *reasonable* has evolved into meaning quite different things to different people. The rights of pupils are considered to be almost the same as those of adults.[20] Principals clearly have authority to make and enforce reasonable rules of pupil conduct within the limitation of board regulations, statutory provisions, and constitutional requirements. Because of their responsibilities, principals have a right to stand in place of the parents (*in loco parentis*) while the students are under their jurisdictions and may regulate student behavior accordingly.[21] However,

---

[18]*School Law Workshop: New Education Laws In Tennessee* (Nashville, Tenn.: School Boards Association, 1985).

[19]Peterson, Rossmiller, and Volz, *The Law*, p. 276.

[20]Peterson, Rossmiller, and Volz, *The Law*, p. 345.

[21]Jacob Fox, "The Power of the Principal to Establish Rules and Regulations on Pupil Conduct," in Reynolds C. Secty (ed.), *Law and the School Principal* (Cincinnati: W. H. Anderson, 1961), pp. 38–39.

principals should not become carried away with their authority and act on the premise that they really have as much freedom to discipline students as do the parents. Custom dictates otherwise; moreover, the actions of the Supreme Court have restricted the authority under the *in loco parentis* doctrine.

Punishment

Principals have a legal right to punish students for misbehavior. Unless prohibited by statute or board policy, they can do so by corporal punishment, suspension, in-school suspension, expulsion, or detention halls. There are certain principles, however, that govern the punishment, especially corporal punishment.

Corporal Punishment. Some states and school systems prohibit corporal punishment altogether; others require that corporal punishment be administered only under certain conditions, such as having a witness present. The principal should inspect the rules and regulations of the board and legislative statutes concerning the use of corporal punishment.

Where corporal punishment is not expressly prohibited by statute or regulation, the courts have upheld the right of teachers and principals to administer it. The courts have held that teachers and principals stand *in loco parentis.* In all instances, the punishment must not be unreasonable. Principals should keep in mind that what is reasonable may vary in different communities and states.

As indicated in Chapter 15, corporal punishment on a regular basis is not a desirable means of controlling pupil behavior. Just because the principal may be legally clothed with authority to employ corporal punishment does not mean that the profession condones its frequent use. The fact that the right to use corporal punishment has been upheld by the courts should be viewed as a yardstick of the ends to which school officials may exercise authority to control pupil conduct.

Suspensions. Principals are vested with authority to suspend pupils but not with the authority to expel them. Suspension is the short-term denial of school attendance; students may be suspended when the violation is not of the "magnitude to warrant expulsion."[22] Usually, the principal is legally permitted to suspend pupils for a specified number of days, but denied the authority to suspend students sequentially for the same violation. The courts have been contradictory concerning whether due process is required in suspension cases. The Supreme Court ruled, in the case of *Goss* v. *Lopez,* 419 U.S. 565 (1976), that a minimum of due process is

[22]Fox, "Power of the Principal."

required for suspension for even a short period of time. The Court felt that a suspension of any kind can damage a student's reputation with fellow students as well as with the teachers at the school. As a result, students do have the right to due process under the Fourteenth Amendment. At the bare minimum, the following requirements must be met in cases of suspension:

1. The student must be notified either orally or in written form of the violation and the punishment for the offense.
2. The student must be given the right "to refute the charges before an objective decision maker."
3. The evidence must be explained to the student as to why the need for suspension has been proved.[23]

Expulsion. Expulsion is usually the prerogative of the school board. Expulsion means the denial of school attendance for a period of more than ten days. The following conduct is grounds for expulsion: using violence, stealing or vandalizing, causing physical injury to someone, carrying a weapon, using or possessing intoxicants, failing to comply with rules on a repeated basis, or engaging in any criminal activity.[24]

In most cases the length of the expulsion cannot last for more than one academic year. However, if the offense occurs toward the later portion of the school year, expulsion may carry over into the next academic year.

In cases where expulsion may be involved, students are given the right to due process under the Fourteenth Amendment. The courts have determined that at least the following conditions of due process must be followed:

1. Written notice of the charges, the intention to expel, and the place, time, and circumstances of the hearing, with sufficient time for a defense to be prepared
2. A full and fair hearing before an impartial adjudicator
3. The right to legal counsel or some other adult representation
4. The opportunity to present witnesses or evidence
5. The opportunity to cross-examine opposing witnesses
6. Some type of written record demonstrating that the decision was based on the evidence presented at the hearing[25]

Detention. Detention is a common punishment for students. The courts seem to approve of this type of punishment, but it also has limitations imposed on it: Parents must be informed of the detention if it takes place after school hours; students need to be told of the time for which they

[23]McCarthy and Cambron, *Public School Law,* pp. 289–90.
[24]McCarthy and Cambron, *Public School Law,* p. 207.
[25]McCarthy and Cambron, *Public School Law,* p. 288.

will be detained, and this right should not be violated; detention cannot interfere with transportation; students cannot be denied access to food services during this time; and school officials must never be alone with a student. Teachers who want to detain a student must do so only with administrative approval.[26]

Control of Pupil Behavior off School Property. Principals often receive complaints from parents and citizens concerning pupil behavior while the pupils are on their way to and from school. If students misbehave on the way to or from school, principals usually have the right to punish them for misbehavior. Unless otherwise limited by statute or board regulations, the principal clearly may punish pupils for any misconduct while they are walking between the home and school or even after the children have already been home if the incidents can be shown to be school related. For example, if a pupil meets a teacher on Saturday morning and uses abusive language because of some incident that has happened at school during the week, the child can be legally punished for that act after returning to school. If the conduct of pupils after school hours adversely disrupts or produces insubordination toward official authority in the school, the principal has legal precedence to punish or otherwise restrict pupil behavior after school hours.

Warnings. School officials have recently been confronted with the issue over the necessity of *Miranda* warnings to miscreant students. The warnings were so named because of a decision of the Supreme Court in *Miranda* v. *Arizona*, 384 86 S.Ct. 1062, 16 L.Ed.2d 694 (1966). The warnings must inform the students of the following:

1. The right to remain silent
2. The right to know that anything the accused says can be used against him in court
3. The right to the presence of an attorney
4. The right to an appointed lawyer prior to questioning if the accused is indigent[27]

These warnings are nothing more than safeguards that can be used to protect school officials.

In some instances, school officials have the option of providing or disregarding the *Miranda* warnings. However, school officials are legally required to give them under the following conditions: when there is a

---

[26]*School Law Workshop: New Education Laws in Tennessee* (Nashville, Tenn.: School Boards Association, 1985).

[27]Perry A. Zirkel and Ivan B. Gluckman, "*Miranda* Warnings," *Principal* 66 (January 1987), 51–52.

criminal offense, when there is custodial interrogation, and when a law officer conducts the questioning.[28]

The control of pupil behavior is one of the most persistent and consistent problems facing principals. It is one that changes as the times change, and the law must do so accordingly. The law clearly gives authorization for the establishment of reasonable codes of conduct in order to protect students' rights and in order to provide students with the best possible teaching and learning environment.

Emergencies. Despite careful planning for the safety of the pupils and staff of the school, there will be numerous instances of injury and sudden illness. How should these emergency cases be handled? Principals should work with their faculty members when planning for emergencies. The handling of emergencies is considerably easier in schools that have trained nurses to head a first-aid program.

Teachers and principals should not treat an injured or ill student unless an emergency exists. An emergency is said to exist only when "the decision to secure medical aid cannot safely await the decision of the parent."[29] Teachers and principals can render first aid that any reasonable or prudent person would under similar circumstances. The courts ruled in *Guerrieri* v. *Tyson*, 147 Pa. Super. 239, 24A.2d 468 (1942), that teachers have no right to treat any injury or diseases when an emergency does not exist. Only parents have this right and officials can not exercise their *in loco parentis* authority except in the case of emergencies.

DISCRIMINATION

The equal protection clause of the Fourteenth Amendment requires states to treat groups of individuals equally in classifying them. Discrimination is forbidden; particular persons cannot be favored over others. Individuals can be grouped reasonably, but unreasonable classifications are not permitted. Unreasonable groupings include grouping by race, sex, handicap, ethnic origin, and personal appearance.

Acts and Court Cases Concerning Discrimination. The Rehabilitation Act of 1973 prohibits discrimination of handicapped persons. It assures them the right to an education. Title VI of the Civil Rights Act of 1964 prohibits discrimination in educational opportunity of persons based

[28]Zirkel and Gluckman, "*Miranda* Warnings."
[29]Peterson, Rossmiller, and Volz, *The Law*, p. 277.

on race, color, and national origin. Title IX of the Education Amendments of 1972 prohibits the same type of discrimination based on sex. These are just a few of the many provisions concerning discrimination.[30]

In the case of *Plessy* v. *Ferguson,* 163 U.S. 537 (1896), which had no direct relationship to education, the doctrine of separate-but-equal was ruled constitutional. It allowed for much discrimination between races in the schools. However, in the 1954 landmark case of *Brown* v. *Board of Education of Topeka,* 347 U.S. 483 (1954), the court ruled against the separate-but-equal policy and that separate school facilities were inherently unequal. Subsequently, the Supreme Court ruled that they must desegregate.[31]

School Athletics. The courts have generally agreed in recent years that there has been widespread sex discrimination in school athletics. Athletic activities of males have been favored over those of females. The courts seem to use the following criteria in ruling on these cases:

1. If team competition is available for boys, it should also be available for girls.
2. In noncontact sports, if there is no team for girls, they may compete for positions on the boys' team.
3. If there are teams for both, courts tend to respect the separation of the sexes for athletic activities.[32]

Married or Pregnant Students. Until recently, married students, especially married females, were not allowed to participate in extracurricular activities in most schools in this country, and pregnant students, until recently, were excluded from regular classes as well as extracurricular activities, but this has changed in recent years. The courts now protect the rights of married and pregnant students to attend regular classes and to participate in activities.[33]

Discrimination Concerning Teachers' Salaries. Discrimination of salaries based on the sex of the teachers is prohibited. The courts have upheld, in most instances, that equal work merits equal pay regardless of the sex of the individual performing it. One issue in the schools that has not yet been finally resolved is that of pay for coaches. It appears that pay for male coaches in school athletics still exceeds that of female coaches. Principals should be alerted that this will probably be a matter of concern for them in the future.[34]

[30]Patricia A. Hollander, *Legal Handbook for Educators* (Boulder, Colo.: Westview Press, 1978), pp. 53–54.

[31]Louis Fischer and David Schimmel, *The Rights of Students and Teachers* (New York: Harper & Row, 1982), p. 261.

[32]Fischer and Schimmel, "Rights of Students," p. 274.

[33]Fischer and Schimmel, "Rights of Students," p. 285.

[34]Fischer and Schimmel, "Rights of Students," p. 294.

Hiring and Firing. Two of the greatest responsibilities of principals are recommending the hiring and firing of teachers. Principals would do well to establish and abide by very strict rules in each process. In hiring and firing, neither ethnic origin, race, sex, religion, creed, or handicap can be a factor. Firings are especially troublesome for principals. Principals should never recommend that someone be fired during a time of anger, on the spur of the moment, for reasons not specified by the policy manual, because the employee is disliked, without authority, or if it is enjoyable.[35]

The school system is required to establish an affirmative action program to prevent discrimination in the employment or termination of employees. The program should include specific guidelines regarding the recruitment, screening, and recommendations for appointment of all personnel. As long as these guidelines are followed and the best qualified candidate is employed without reference to race, sex, ethnic origin, and so on, the school district has met its obligation concerning discrimination.

In the case of *Verniero* v. *Air Force Academy School District N. 20,* 705 F.2d 388 (1983), a female teacher alleged that she was discriminated against in the selection of administrators. The case illustrates that sex discrimination is not easily proven, since Verniero lost the case. The courts found no discrimination in any of the processes.[36]

A general policy of fairness should be followed by principals when hiring and firing personnel. Both practices should be done with much care.

Assignment of Teachers. The assignment of work loads for teachers is usually done by the principal of the school. The principal matches teacher expertise and areas of certification with the classes to be taught and extra duties. Effective principals are usually able to make these work assignments with few problems. Assignment of teaching and other responsibilities can be troublesome, however, if improperly handled. Even with the most careful attention some teachers will be discontented with their assignments. It is, of course, preferable to handle assignments of teachers without the force of law, although it is not always possible. In most cases where teachers have challenged their work assignments, the courts have not ruled favorably for them. In the case of *McGarth* v. *Burkhard,* 131 Cal. App.2d 367, 280 P.2d 864 (1955), male teachers were assigned six nonteaching activities that included supervising ball games off school grounds. The court held that the assignments did not violate the teachers' contracts and ruled against the teachers. In another case, *Blair* v. *Robstown Independent School Dist.,* 556 F.2d 1331 (5th Cir. 1977), the Fifth Court of

[35]"The Hiring and Firing Process," *The School Law Newsletter,* 13 (Fall 1986), 552.

[36]Perry A. Zirkel and Ivan B. Gluckman, "Sex Discrimination in Choosing Administrators," *Principal,* 64 (September 1984), 51–52.

Appeals held that to refuse nonteaching activities constitutes insubordination and reason for denying renewal of contract.

The work assignments must be related to the teachers' subject matter fields or the duties normally expected of them. For example, teachers would not be expected to perform custodial services as a requirement for fulfilling their contracts. They can, however, perform those duties under a separate contract.

Local school boards have the discretion for assigning teachers to individual school buildings. While it is advisable in most cases to assign teachers to the buildings they desire, cases such as *Matthews* v. *Board of Education,* 198 Cal. App.2d 748, 18 Cal. Rptr. 101 (1962) and *Maupin* v. *Independent School Dist. No. 26,* 632 P.2d 396 (Okla. 1981), make it abundantly clear that teachers have no common-law rights to be assigned to specific buildings. In the case of transfers from one school to another, school boards are bound to follow their own school board rules concerning transfers.

In summary, principals, with authority from the school board, have the legal right to assign teachers in their schools to teaching and other duties, within the limits of the contracts. School boards have legal authority to assign teachers to particular school buildings.[37]

TEACHERS' RIGHTS

The courts have generally held that teachers have essentially the same legal rights as any other citizens. Teachers today do not have any more rights than they ever had under the Constitution, but they are exercising their rights more, and are increasingly testing those rights in courts of law, a fairly recent phenomenon. Teachers have rights—more than we are able to discuss at length in this chapter. A few of the more important rights with which principals should be familiar will be mentioned and briefly discussed.

Speech and Academic Freedom. The Supreme Court ruled in *Pickering* v. *Board of Education,* 391 SW 563 (1968), that teachers must be allowed to speak in the community without fear of reprisal. The Court allowed that teachers are the persons in the community most likely to have "informed and definite opinions."

Teachers are given the right to speak and to exercise academic freedom under the First Amendment. The majority of court decisions have allowed teachers to use methods and materials that are relevant to an

---

[37]E. Edmund Reutter, Jr., *The Law of Public Education,* 3rd ed. (Mineola, N.Y.: The Foundation Press, 1985), pp. 462–63, 526–27.

academic subject. The courts have ruled, however, that teachers do not have total freedom when it comes to what can be used or said in class. The courts do not protect incompetency or the use of materials or methods that are irrelevant to the subject matter being taught. Religious or political indoctrination is also prohibited.

In a teacher's attempt to prove denial of freedom of speech under the First Amendment, the Supreme Court has stated:

1. The plaintiff-teacher has the initial burden to show that the conduct under question was protected under the First Amendment
2. The plaintiff-teacher next must show that the protected conduct was a substantial or motivating factor in the board's decision not to rehire the teacher
3. The burden then shifts to the defendant-board to show that it would have reached the same decision in the absence of the protected conduct[38]

Teacher's Private Life. The teacher's private life has always been a matter of public concern. Teachers are expected to serve as role models with higher standards than some other individuals. Cases censoring teachers' morals are especially sensitive. Whether a school board can dismiss a teacher for immorality hinges on the circumstances surrounding the conduct. The following circumstances are important when considering cases of this type: Was the conduct personal or private? Was the conduct likely to become public knowledge? Did the conduct involve students?

The case of *Morrison* v. *State Board of Education,* 82 Cal. Rptr. 175 (1969), held that a teacher cannot be dismissed simply because of immoral conduct that a community finds improper. The immoral conduct must affect a teacher's ability to teach before dismissal is warranted.

In cases involving immoral conduct with students, courts are very strict with the teachers involved. Whether the conduct was made known publicly at the time seems to have little bearing on the outcome of the court decision. If there is sufficient evidence to prove that a teacher engaged in immoral conduct with a student, dismissal of that teacher is almost always upheld.[39]

Teachers' Rights to Freedom of Religion. Teachers have been required to do such things as teach Sunday school and go to church, which has been found to be unconstitutional and a denial of teachers' rights.

Teacher Tenure. Tenure is a right afforded teachers after they have met the requirements of the school. Tenure is defined as "a contract of

---

[38]Fischer and Schimmel, *Rights of Students,* pp. 234–35.
[39]Hollander, *Legal Handbook,* p. 162.

continuing employment between an individual and an institution." There are usually three ways to obtain tenure:

1. Formal granting procedures
2. De facto tenure
3. Operation of a statute[40]

Tenure laws differ from state to state, but they all basically contain the same elements: Teachers must be given timely notice if dismissal is being considered; they must be given a statement of the charges; they must be given the right to a fair hearing, and the right to refute evidence. The tenure statute places the burden of proof for dismissal on the board of education. There are three reasons for which tenured teachers can be dismissed: incompetence, immorality, and insubordination.[41,42]

Equal Employment Opportunities.   Principals must take great care when recommending employment that they do not discriminate against someone because of race, creed, color, appearance, handicap, marital status, or other such conditions. In other words, interviewing must be done in a nondiscriminatory way. Essentially the same questions must be asked of all the candidates for the position or the principal risks charges of discrimination. The questions may only relate to the candidate's qualifications. For instance, candidates cannot be asked if they are married, have children, or other such personal questions.[43]

Drug Testing.   A very great concern regarding teachers' rights is the question of drug testing. Many states have implemented requirements that employees be tested for drugs. If the tests prove to be positive, the employees are usually released. The courts have not yet settled the issue as to whether this testing impinges on Fourth-Amendment rights, which protect against unwarranted searches. In the cases that have been brought to court, the courts have ruled that mass drug testing is illegal. The only way a school system may conduct a drug test is when there is reasonable suspicion that an employee has been illegally using drugs.[44]

[40]E. Edmund Reutter, Jr., *Schools and the Law* (Reston, Va.: National Association of Secondary School Principals, 1981), p. 62.

[41]Perry A. Zirkel and Ivan B. Gluckman, "Teacher Termination," *Principal,* 64 (March 1985), 52–53.

[42]"Hiring and Firing," *Newsletter,* p. 123.

[43]Perry A. Zirkel and Ivan B. Gluckman, "Drug Testing," *Principal,* 66 (March 1987), 54–56.

[44]Floyd G. Delon, *Administrators and the Courts: Update 1977* (Arlington, Va.: Educational Research Service, 1977), p. 3.

Infectious Diseases. The Supreme Court ruled in *Arline* v. *Nassau County,* 107 S.Ct. 1123 (1987), that a teacher who had been terminated with an infectious disease (tuberculosis) could return to the classroom in that school system after there was no longer a danger of spreading the disease. The Court held that Section 504 of the Rehabilitation Act of 1973 prohibited discrimination against her because she had an infectious disease that was no longer contagious. The decision is expected to weigh heavily on cases concerning acquired immune deficiency syndrome (AIDS).

Confidentiality of Student Records

The Family Educational Rights to Privacy Act (FERPA) has to do with the confidentiality and correctness of students' records. Under this act, students and parents of minors are permitted to inspect and have copies of items in their respective records. They are also allowed to question the contents of the records. In cases of errors, the inaccuracies must be expunged from the records.

The contents of students' records may not be disclosed to outsiders except in certain situations. Teachers may have access to students' records if the information desired is related to educational needs. The individual may give written permission for outsiders to review the records or documents may be accessed by court order. Principals should monitor the use of students' records very carefully to ascertain that the requirements of FERPA are met.

PRINCIPALS' RIGHTS

Principals do have certain legal rights as well as responsibilities. However, the courts have been much slower in determining the rights of principals than they have been in determining those of teachers. For example, most principals hold tenure only as a teacher, not as a principal. They have frequently been excluded from job-protection concepts such as academic freedom and contracts. In some states they are not allowed to be members of teacher organizations. Comparatively speaking, principals have few and undefined rights; nevertheless, they do have some important rights.

In 1972, a federal district court ruled concerning the rights of principals:

> This court does not think that there need be the same vigilant protection when an administrator is involved as may be necessary when a teacher is. The need for teachers to have freedom in what they teach arises from the

very heart of the First Amendment. The workshop of the administrator, however, is not the classroom but the office and the conference room. His primary duties are to coordinate, delegate, and regulate, not to educate.[45]

The idea that the administrators serve at the pleasure of the governing body and do not enjoy all of the rights of teachers is changing. Most administrators now have the security of a contract. Some of the contracts are for three to five years, at the end of which time the administrators are evaluated. Principals thereby have some job security. If a principal does not have a contract and is dismissed, no due process or reason for dismissal is in order; however, if the principal does have a contract, then due process is necessary. Due process is also necessary if the dismissal will place a stigma upon the reputation of the principal and any future employment.[46]

Principals can legally be dismissed. In the case of *Yielding* v. *Crockett Independent School District,* 707 F.2d 196 (1983), the principal was dismissed based on his overall low performance. The court upheld this decision based on long periods of complaints from coworkers and the ignoring of repeated warnings from the superintendent. In another court case the court did not uphold the dismissal of the principal. The case of *Rust* v. *Clark County School District,* 683 P.2d, 23 (Nev. 1984), involved a principal's earned leave time. He had planned for a year to go to Europe to visit his son for two weeks who was a missionary there. Just before it was time for him to leave the board passed a new policy denying such leave. The principal went anyway. The board fired him for insubordination. The court held for Rust, and determined that the board's new rule was not reasonable in the face of the situation.

Principals have some rights of privileged communication. For example, they have the freedom to make statements about teachers or pupils as long as they do so with good intentions of furthering the purposes of the school. The principal, of course, should use this privilege cautiously, and always uphold professional standards in the exercise of privileged communication.[47]

[45]Delon, *Administrators and the Courts.*

[46]"Hiring and Firing," *Newsletter,* pp. 134–35.

[47]Jennifer W. Teague, "School Law: It's the Principal's Responsibility to Know" (unpublished, Fall 1987). (Some of the research on which this chapter is based was completed by Teague.)

CHAPTER THIRTEEN

Computers as Aids to Principals

Traditionally, historians have recognized two eras in the development of the United States as a nation. The first period was an agricultural one, followed by the industrial age. Historians and futurists contend that we are now entering a third wave, which they have labeled the information age. They also contend that computers and related technology have been primarily responsible for hastening us into this period. Schools, in response to the demands of society, are being computerized. The principal is responsible for providing the leadership for this new emphasis.

The pace of change in the information age is much more rapid than it was during the preceding ones. Schools must respond more quickly, which means that school administrators must move with a sense of urgency to computerize the schools in order to keep pace with technology and the demands of society.[1]

In some respects, the computerization of schools has also occurred in stages. First, a few large, complex school systems were computerized. Second, computers were used in varying degrees for instructional purposes. Finally, computers are now being used in almost all school districts,

---

[1]J. Allen Watson, Sandra L. Calvert, and Vickie M. Brinkley, "The Computer/Information Technologies Revolution: Controversial Attitudes and Software Bottlenecks—A Mostly Promising Report," *Educational Technology*, 27, No. 2 (February 1987), 7–11.

at varying levels, for both instruction and administration. While computer use is now common in most school districts, educational institutions seem to be lagging behind many of the other institutions, especially retail and manufacturing, as well as government, in widespread computer use.

THE PRINCIPAL AND THE COMPUTER

The extent to which principals are involved in computer use in schools varies, depending on the personal interest of the individual and on the emphasis given to computers in the school system. Principals should become involved with computers, if for no other reason than to be able to provide leadership in computer use. There are other good reasons, however, for principals to become familiar with computer use. Computer skills provide a great deal of credibility for the principal with teachers, students, administrators, and members of the community. Principals who have knowledge of and use computers are usually perceived as leaders; they are seen as being on the cutting edge of what is going on in education.

Huntington contends that "The use of the computer can greatly reduce your paperwork and make you infinitely more efficient." For example, he found that it takes 15–30 seconds to suspend a student when the suspension letter is already recorded electronically on the computer, whereas it used to take up to 30 minutes on a typewriter.[2] A principal with a computer and printer in the office and the skills to operate them can save much time and produce what is needed much more efficiently.

It is accepted practice for principals to use computers—for that matter it is accepted practice for top administrators in any organization to use computers. For example, executives who would never have been caught using a typewriter find it perfectly acceptable to use the computer for word processing.

SELECTING COMPUTERS

How does a principal decide what computer hardware is needed? The process begins by making a "use list" of the things for which the computer will be used. Every school will need to do word processing, so that should be the first item on the list. The extent of the word processing to be done will determine the type of machine needed. For example, if the word

---

[2]Fred Huntington, "Using a Microcomputer in the Principal's Office," *Thrust for Educational Leadership,* 14, No. 1 (September 1984), 19, 31, 33.

processor will only be used to write letters, a relatively small computer will suffice. If you are going to send the same letter to numerous people and want a personal touch, you will need a larger, more powerful machine to do the merging of letters with names and addresses. To determine the capacity of spread sheets, you need to know if they will be used to manage a small budget, or for record keeping of more complex projects. When the list of uses is made, it must also indicate the complexity of the tasks. A spreadsheet sufficient to handle the book-keeping for the internal accounting of a small school may not be adequate for handling the entire financial structure of a large secondary school.

Salespeople at computer outlets can be helpful, but one must keep in mind that they are there to sell computers and may not be familiar with the needs of a particular school. A reputable dealer, however, will try to assess the needs using the list of applications mentioned before. The more thorough the list of anticipated use, the easier it is going to be to select the right computer. It is a good idea to visit several computer stores before deciding on one with which to deal. One can get an education on computer use from the demonstrations of different brands. One thing that should not be assumed is that the more expensive machine is necessarily the best and that the less expensive computer is the worst choice. Keep in mind that computers may be put out for bid and that the lowest bidder who meets the specifications may get the order; therefore it is very important to specify exactly what is needed.

The amount of money available will determine to a great extent which computer can be purchased; when figuring the cost of computers do not forget the cost of the accessories. When pricing computers ask for a total price of all peripherals and software that are needed for functions described on the previously mentioned use list. For example, if the machine will be used for word processing, which it probably will, word-processor software will be needed. A printer will also be needed for printing copies. Some computers come with a complement of software, such as the Disk Operating System (DOS), and others do not. The principal should know the particular needs of the school to make sure that the computer, peripherals, and accompanying software are what is needed.

It is usually a good idea to look at future use when selecting a computer. For example, networking with other computers may not be an immediate need but may be required in the future. Used computers, like used cars, do not bring much on trade-ins; therefore, the principal would be wise to invest a bit more at the outset to provide for future use. One can be assured that whatever computer system is selected will be on sale next week and an announcement made that it is being replaced by a new improved model! There will always be faster, larger or better computers that make us wish we had waited just a month longer to select one. There are a few things to look for when choosing a computer, such as power, memory, disk storage, and speed.

Power

At least a 16-bit computer should be considered if the machine will be used for administrative purposes. While 8-bit machines are prevalent in many schools for instructional purposes, they are too slow to handle the administrative tasks in most schools. The 16-bit is also preferable since most programs available for school administration purposes require this power level. Connors and Valesky describe the power of a microcomputer in terms of memory, storage, and speed.[3]

Memory. A microcomputer to be used for administrative purposes by school principals should have no less than 256K (K is the symbol for thousands of bytes) and 640K is preferred. It is preferable that the machine have the capacity to be expanded in the future in order to provide for more complex needs. As the software expands to make the computer more versatile and easier to use, it also requires more memory just to hold the programs. An increased amount of K, or capacity for memory, adds relatively little to the cost of most microcomputers; therefore, it is suggested that the inclusion of additional memory capacity is worth the small added expense. In fact, it is generally acknowledged that the more memory capacity a computer has, the better a purchase it is.[4]

Electronic Storage. The computer only stores information while it is turned on. When the computer is turned off, it loses all of the information that is presently showing. Therefore, the information has to be stored by some other means. The programs, such as the word processor or the accounting program, are already stored on a disk. Programs are either stored on a *floppy disk* or on a *hard disk.* The floppy disk looks something like a miniature phonograph record and stores information in the same way. The hard disk works in a similar fashion but is different in that it is permanently installed in the machine. The disks store information that can be retrieved later in the same way that a phonograph record does.

Many programs are prepared commercially and only need to be loaded into the machine. They can be loaded by inserting a floppy disk each

[3]Eugene T. Connors and Thomas C. Valesky, "Using Microcomputers in School Administration," *Phi Delta Kappa Fastback,* No. 248, 1986.

[4]Connors and Valesky, "Using Microcomputers in School Administration."

time the program is to be used, or they can be loaded from a permanent hard disk (if the computer has a hard disk). The programs tell the computer to do the work and how to do it. Here again, the program information for whatever program one desires to use must be loaded into the computer each time it is turned on. The computer only stores in memory programs when it is activated. The programs themselves are stored on the disks and must be retrieved each time the machine is turned on. Incidentally, it is highly recommended that the computer used by the principal for administrative purposes have a hard disk drive of 20-megabyte capacity. Without a hard disk, the operation is slowed considerably by the operator having to insert and change programs that are on floppy disks.

Most new microcomputers use 5 1/4-inch or 3 1/2-inch floppy disks. The computer selected for administrative use by the principal should have at least two disk drives. If the machine has a hard disk drive, it should have at least one floppy disk drive, but two are preferable. Files on hard disk need to be backed up, or copied, daily on floppy disks. If for some reason, such as a power surge, the data on the hard disk are destroyed, the same data will be safely stored on the floppy disk.

Information is produced and stored electronically in the computer when it is activated. A combination of computer, program, and operator is required to process the information. For example, to produce a letter the word processor program must be loaded into the computer and the words keyed in by the operator. By using the proper commands the information can be sent directly from the computer to the printer and the printer will produce the letter. The information can be stored on a disk (floppy or hard) and used at a later time.

The computer will save information onto a disk for future use. That disk is called a *data disk*. The data disk is similar to a note pad in some respects; it can be written on and stored. The data disk is very important because many documents that can be used repeatedly or altered and reused can be stored on it, which saves the principal much time and helps with producing better documents. Storage will be discussed in greater detail later in this chapter. The capacity to store information is one of the great advantages of using a computer.

Speed. Speed is one of the major reasons for using a computer. The suspension letter mentioned earlier saved the principal much valuable time that could be used for other important matters. Usually, the more powerful the machine, the greater is the speed. When selecting a computer pay careful attention to the speed.[5]

[5]Connors and Valesky, "Using Microcomputers in School Administration."

PERIPHERALS

Peripherals that are essential to the most effective use of the computer include monitors and printers. Again, purchasing decisions must be made based on the use list compiled by the principal and faculty. Many different printers and monitors with different capabilities are on the market.

Monitors

The monitor is a special television set made for displaying the information to be produced by the printer. The monitor displays information as it is being put on the machine. It will also display stored information on command (information that has been retrieved from a data disk). A monitor especially designed for computers is preferred; however, most regular television sets can be used for this purpose. Color or monochrome monitors are usually preferred.

Printers

Printers are required for producing written copies of what has been produced on the computer. There are many models, types, and brands of printers on the market. The printer should be selected with much care because it can create serious problems. Most problems that occur when trying to print a document lie with the printer. It is either not capable of doing the desired task, or it is not compatible with the computer. The right printer, however, has the potential for providing printed documents that achieve very satisfying results.

We recommend that the printer selected for school administrative purposes have a long carriage to accommodate fourteen-inch computer paper and that it be capable of producing letter-quality print. It should have speed capabilities that eliminate unnecessary delays in producing documents.

Printers are available that produce print in different ways. The daisy-wheel printer operates much like a typewriter and produces nice, letter-quality print; however, it has limited capabilities to produce satisfactory work in graphics and designs. It is also slower than some of the other printers. The dot matrix is the most commonly used printer. It is fast and relatively easy to use. It also is very good for producing graphics, designs, and various kinds of print. It has limitations in achieving quality print, but these printers are now being improved so that a 24 or more pen printer head will produce very fine quality print. The laser printer works something like a copying machine and produces excellent results. One of its limitations is that it is relatively expensive. The ink-jet printer sprays ink on the paper to produce the print. It is very good for multicolored prints. Its limitations are that it is relatively expensive and has not been tested in everyday use.

There are other peripherals that are necessary for carrying out some functions of the computer, including plotters, buffers, and modems.

SELECTING SOFTWARE

Software purchases for administrative purposes make up approximately 25 percent of the cost of a computer system, so their acquisition should be approached with care.[6] When the first microcomputer was installed in the office of one of the authors, and software was purchased for it on the advice of an "expert," the software required 64K of memory. The machine only had a 48K capacity, so the expensive software could not be used on that machine. As a matter of fact, most of it was never used.

There is a wide variety of software on the market. It sometimes seems impossible to select the proper kind. Often neophyte users become so confused that they leave the selection to the dealer, which is a mistake. Principals should be actively involved in the selection of software because they are responsible for its use. There are some things that principals should look for in selecting software.

Requirements. Principals should be familiar enough with their computers to determine if the software requirements are compatible with the configuration of the machines. The requirements are usually listed on the cover of the software. The information presented usually includes a list of the computers on which the software will run. Memory requirements of the computer are also usually listed on the software cover. There may be other things to check; for example, if the software produces graphics and the computer does not have the capability of running graphics, that feature will not work.

Features. What are the intended uses of the software? What are the needs? The list of needs suggested earlier will serve well here. Selecting features would be an appropriate area in which to employ a specialist in software programming as a consultant. However, the consultant will rely heavily on the list of needs for computer use when determining which software to select. The principal must know enough about the needs to explain them in some detail. For example, if the same letter is to be sent to 300 different people, software that will merge names and addresses with the letter will be required. That kind of information will help the consultant in recommending which software to select.

[6]Joseph Shearn, "How to Buy Administrative Software," *Principal,* 66, No. 5 (May 1987), 38–39.

Manuals. Manuals that accompany the programs are very important. Some of the manuals are very explicit, whereas others are very vague. A great deal of time will be spent when first using the software packages in pouring over the manuals. The user manuals must be clear and concise. They must direct and show by illustration the various procedures necessary for guidance through the system. There are very helpful books on the market that are very explicit on many of the major programs. Those books are commonly referred to as "Using..." books. They tend to be more helpful than some of the more technical manuals.

User Support. There is hardly a doubt that one can get through any new computer program without pushing the wrong button or misunderstanding a procedure. Often the operator is certain that there is something wrong with the program, computer, or both. That is possible, but usually it is an error on the part of the operator. When selecting software packages, consideration should be given to what kind of help will be available when these errors occur. The manual should be checked to see if it provides information on correcting errors in procedure. Most good programs will also have a toll-free number at which a consultant can be called to help with the problem, a very important consideration when selecting software packages.

Resource Persons. Other individuals who are using software packages under consideration can be a great help in the selection process. They can provide information on the strengths and weaknesses of particular programs. One caution should be taken when consulting other users: Those familiar with only one program may overrate it because of their unfamiliarity with the merits of other programs. Those users, however, can be helpful after a program is installed, and can be a ready source of information when problems arise.

The state of the art in software development is changing swiftly. Programs are getting more sophisticated and easier to use. Care during the selection process can result in providing the most service for the least cost.

WORD PROCESSING

The most common use of microcomputers for school administration is word processing. Before the microcomputer, word processing in schools was done mostly by typewriter. It still is in many schools. Word processing was commonly referred to as typing before the microcomputer. *Word processing* simply means putting printed matter on paper as can be done with a typewriter; yet the word processor can do much more than the typewriter.

Information can be typed on the computer in the same way that it is typed on a typewriter. The printed matter is stored electronically in the computer and appears on the screen of a monitor or television set. The information is usually stored and then printed when the document is complete. There are a few programs that will allow for printing while typing, but this option is usually used for filling out forms. There are major advantages to displaying the information on-screen before printing it: The information can be rearranged or corrected before it is printed; information can be moved from one place to another; and text can be changed, deleted, or added to with ease. In other words, editing changes can be made before the document is ever printed. If after the document has been printed changes are desired, this can be easily done by accessing the filed document, making the changes, and reprinting the document.

Word processors are used most frequently for routine letters and memos. The letter or memo is printed, sent out, and never used again. However, other letters and memos are sent out regularly. These can be stored and used repeatedly. If they require alterations for subsequent use, that can be done easily by retrieving the information and altering it before it is printed. For example, if a standard letter is sent home when students are absent from school, that document can be stored and used repeatedly. It is a simple matter to change the name and address so that the letter is personalized.

Merging.   Quite often principals will have the need for a mass mailing of letters. For example, a principal might want to send original letters urging support for a booster's club. The letters will be more effective if they are original prints and personalized, that is, not duplicated copies, and they have a name and address and other personal references in the letter. The names and addresses of all those to whom the letters are to be sent can be typed into one file and the text of the letter into another. The better word processing programs will, with the proper commands, merge the names, addresses, salutations, and personal references with the text of the letter and send the letters, one by one, to the printer, which will produce original documents.

The merging function will also usually print envelopes for mailing letters from the same list of names and addresses in the merge file. The merge file can also be used for routine letters reporting student absences and discipline problems to parents, good conduct reports, and such matters.

Spell Check.   Many word processing programs have spell checkers built in, but separate spell checkers can be purchased for those word processing programs that do not. The spell checker does just that—it checks the spelling of a typed text. Spell checkers have built-in dictionaries, usually containing from 70,000 to 100,000 words. When properly activated with the text on the screen, the checker works its way through the text, checking the spelling of each word against the spelling in the dictionary. It stops at each misspelled word and each word not in the dictionary. It will allow for the misspelled word to be replaced by a properly spelled word from the dictionary or for typed corrections for words not in the dictionary. The checker works very swiftly. A lengthy document can be checked for spelling in just a few minutes. The spell checker assists in eliminating misspelled words and even most typographical errors.

Word processing is not only used for letters and memos but is very valuable for processing reports and all other documents that the principal must prepare. Word processors have features for preparing documents, such as numbering pages and footnoting.

The word processor is a very important tool for a school principal. It assists in preparing written documents faster and more efficiently than they can be prepared on a typewriter, and it provides for easy corrections and alterations. Sending communications to parents and other citizens with misspelled words is prevented with the use of a word processor.

FILE CREATION AND MANAGEMENT

Files are essential in schools. In fact, many of them are required by one agency or another. Others are not required but still essential for creating the best management system and learning environment. Stored information, used appropriately and timely, can greatly increase learning opportunities for students. We know of one elementary principal who provides the teachers in his school with valuable information on their respective children by retrieving stored information from the microcomputer and printing it for the teachers to use when making decisions about how to help individual children. For example, he will give a teacher a printout of information on how a particular student is currently performing, based on grades and other reports. That printout will include a comparison of how the student is performing as compared to his or her potential, based on information such as achievement tests scores, past performance, and attitude ratings. An example of one of those printouts is included in Figure 13–1 (the names shown are fictitious). In previous discussions we have emphasized the significance of continuous evaluation of pupil progress as one aspect of educational excellence. The computer is a very useful system for processing and printing out data that are useful in the continuous monitoring of student progress.

The computer stores information electronically just as information is stored in file cabinets. The greatest difference is that the information is much more easily stored and retrieved. It also occupies must less space.

Homeroom: Karen   Grade: Third   School Year:

NAME	HR	IQFL	RDL	POT	PRRD	PRMA	RD %	MA %	TRD	TMA	TLI	BBA	R	S	LT
Alden, J. A.	3A	107	12*	2.89	-.59	.81	37	79	2.3	3.7	3.0	3.0	W	F	s
Baird, E. A.	3A	097R	14	2.62	.48	2.18	63	94	3.1	4.8	3.8	3.8	W	F	D
Beckford, I. J.	3A	094F	13	2.54	.36	1.96	57	72	2.9	4.5	3.3	3.5	W	F	S
Bricker, G. A.	3A	079	13*	2.13	-.47	.17	48	40	2.6	2.3	1.0	1.9	B	M	D
Brownell, I. N.	3A	088F	14	2.38	-.52	.32	56	53	2.6	3.2	2.0	2.3	W	M	F
Buck, M. A.	3A	084F	12*	2.27	-.03	.93	35	68	2.3	3.2	1.1	2.2	B	M	D
Cannon, J.	3A	101	11*	2.73	-.73	-.03	25	53	3.0	2.7	1.6	3.1	W	F	F
Childress, M. L.	3A	102F	13	2.75	-.25	1.75	60	91	3.0	4.5	3.1	3.5	B	F	s
Cyrus, E. A.	3A	007F	14*	2.08	-.02	1.12	28	68	2.1	3.2	2.7	2.2	W	F	F
Daniel, L. B.	3A	078F	13	2.11	.39	.59	43	53	2.5	2.7	1.6	2.6	B	F	s
Dennis, A.	3A	087F	14	2.35	1.05	2.15	70	91	3.4	4.5	3.0	3.6	W	M	F
Durell, B. J.	3A	081F	13	2.19	.71	.21	57	44	2.9	2.4	0.3	1.8	B	F	H
Dyan, D. M.	3A	120	14	3.24	3.66	3.56	96	99	6.9	6.8	6.2	6.6	W	M	Tr
Egan, M. L.	3A	085F	11*	2.30	-.60	0.00	10	39	1.7	2.3	0.2	1.4	B	F	D
Evans, A. T.	3A	123F	13	3.32	-.52	1.28	53	93	2.8	4.6	2.5	3.2	B	M	D
Fox, J. J.	3A	117	13	3.16	-.36	1.04	54	88	2.8	4.2	1.7	3.1	W	F	s
George, M.	3A	095F	13	2.57	-.14	1.04	51	78	2.7	3.6	2.6	2.6	W	F	F
Gibson, R. O.	3A	088	14	2.38	1.32	1.02	74	74	3.7	3.4	2.6	3.2	W	M	s
Irvine, J. K.	3A	079	11*	2.13	-.43	-.13	09	32	1.7	2.0	0.9	1.5	B	F	Tr
Lambertti, D.	3A	086F	12*	2.32	-.43	1.02	74	74	3.7	3.4	2.6	2.2	W	F	F
Locis, Z. T.	3A	086F	12*	2.32	-.02	.68	37	62	2.3	3.0	1.3	2.2	W	F	D
McClosky, J. B.	3A	082R	13	2.21	-.02	.68	37	62	2.3	3.0	1.3	2.2	B	M	Tr
AVERAGES		92.8		2.51	.31	1.03	53	76	2.88	3.54	2.94	3.1			

TLI average: 1.6

Legend

NAME	Names appear in alphabetical order but can be arranged in any sequence desired. (i.e. I.Q.'s from highest to lowest.)
HR	Homeroom assignment for the coming year. (Can be changed or reassigned by changing this column to 3B or 3C.)
IQFL	Students' most recent I.Q. and free or reduced lunch qualification.
RDL	The level at which the student is currently performing in the Macmillan reading series.
POT	Potential. An expected level of performance computed by multiplying the student's I.Q. by the year and month in which the achievement test is given. (Read as grade equivalent score.)
PRRD	Potential relative to the actual reading score. (Subtract the potential from the actual grade equivalent reading score.)
PRMA	Potential relative to the actual math score. (Subtract the potential from the actual grade equivalent math score.)
RD %	Reading percentile score. (Used to determine Chapter I eligibility.)
MA %	Math percentile score. (Used to determine Chapter I eligibility.) NOTE—We will be adding Language Arts to this category during the next school year.
TRD	Total reading score, in grade equivalent, from the Stanford-Binet Achievement Test.
TMA	Total math score, in grade equivalent, from the Stanford-Binet Achievement Test.
TLI	Total listening score, in grade equivalent, from the Stanford-Binet Achievement Test.
BBA	Basic battery score, in grade equivalent, from the Stanford-Binet Achievement Test.
R	Listing of race.
S	Listing of sex.
LT	Listing of the teacher who taught this student the previous school year.

FIGURE 13–1. Student Progress Printout

The computer files also provide for much more versatility in retrieving the data based on the information needed, allowing for ready access to information when it is needed.

There are certain common data that are usually filed in student files. Each child's name, address, date of birth, phone number, and student number are usually part of the student's personal file. There may also be other records, such as health, attendance, schedule, test scores, and grades. If the information is properly filed in the computer, any or all of this information can be retrieved at will.

If the proper program is used and the proper data are filed, information can be stored in many different ways. For example, information may be needed on all students who were born between October 1 and November 30 of a particular year. That information can be easily retrieved if it has been properly filed. Figure 13–2 is an example of a useful printout.

There are many database (file) management computer programs on the market. If principals know what they want to file and retrieve, the selection of a proper program is relatively easy. Programs do, however, differ in complexity and in the ways they can be formatted. A program

STUDENT LIST

STUDENT NUMBER & NAME		SEX	RACE	GRADE	BIRTH DATE	DAYS MISSED	ACTIVE
25701	Abbott, M.	M	W	6	11/29/74	20	Y
25753	Ayers, A. R.	F	W	6	05/19/75	2	Y
25754	Blasky, K. D.	F	W	6	04/29/74	0	Y
25031	Blazquez, C. H.	M	W	6	11/02/74	3	Y
05310	Blitch, J. E.	M	B	6	11/24/73	4	Y
25723	Cameron, M. A.	M	W	6	08/05/75	1	Y
25755	Chance, V. M.	F	W	6	08/12/75	4	Y
25655	Collins, J. O.	M	B	6	12/15/74	0	Y
25048	Cuffie, M. D.	F	W	6	08/05/75	10	Y
25757	Dodd, T. T.	F	W	6	01/10/75	9	Y
25082	Dunham, N. I.	M	W	6	08/13/74	3	Y
25707	Eberst, J. T.	F	W	6	07/10/75	13	Y
25708	Ferguson, M. E.	M	W	6	04/20/73	6	Y
25829	Hackett, W. D.	M	H	6	04/15/74	9	Y
25709	Jones, D. E.	F	W	6	05/24/75	19	Y
25121	Latimer, K. R.	M	W	6	01/07/75	0	Y
25124	Lawson, M.	M	W	6	10/07/75	3	Y
25711	Martin, S. E.	F	B	6	08/13/76	7	Y
25662	Neidigh, E. A.	F	W	6	07/31/73	1	Y
25713	Rainey, R.	M	W	6	05/06/74	0	Y
25715	Rockwood, N. C.	F	W	6	06/09/75	1	Y
25243	Smith, D. E.	M	W	6	04/15/75	9	Y
25297	Smith, G. T.	F	W	6	07/22/72	0	Y
25287	Thomas, R. B.	F	W	6	11/23/73	2	Y
25766	Todd, J. C.	F	W	6	01/01/73	4	Y
25235	Udell, H.	M	W	6	06/21/75	6	Y
25672	Valley, M. P.	F	B	6	09/18/75	8	Y
25668	Vander, L. M.	M	B	6	02/19/74	6	Y
25721	Waters, E. A.	F	W	6	01/18/75	2	Y
25768	Wicks, W. E.	F	W	6	03/02/75	1	Y

FIGURE 13–2. Student Information Printout

that allows the operator to set up the information anywhere on the monitor is preferred for school purposes. By using the keyboard and screen, a desired form can be designed. It can then be saved on a diskette for future use.

There are often different files kept on students. Some filing programs will provide for information from one file to be merged with information from another file; others will not. It depends on specific needs as to which type of program is used. The programs that do not allow for merging data from file to file are less complex and easier to use; conversely, the programs that allow merging are more complex and more difficult to use.

SCHEDULING

Scheduling was one of the earliest uses of computers in school administration. Its potential as a time saver was realized early. The computer can do in minutes what would take hours to do by hand. It can tell almost instantly which classes are filled; it can also tell which students chose more than one class scheduled for the same period.

According to Connors and Valesky, "Most scheduling programs for microcomputers require entering the following data: student demographics, student course requests, a list of valid courses, teacher data including any courses that require specific rooms." The programs will then "produce the following reports: section, teacher, and course lists; individual student schedules; student course requests; class lists; student schedule matrices for scheduled and nonscheduled students; and room-conflict matrices."[7]

There are different approaches to scheduling students by microcomputer. Three of these approaches will be discussed briefly here.

One approach to scheduling is to do what is generally referred to as *automatic* scheduling. Automatic scheduling requires the following steps.

1. During preregistration students choose the courses they wish to take. No period or teacher is designated at this time.
2. The preregistration requests are loaded into the computer.
3. A total request listing indicating how many students desire each course is generated by the computer.
4. Given teachers, time, and rooms available, the principal or his designee makes the master schedule. (Some scheduling programs have the ability to create the master schedule. The primary disadvantage of a computer generated master schedule lies in the inability of the computer to consider individual teacher's desires, such as "planning period after lunch" or "all three English classes in consecutive periods.")
5. The master schedule is loaded into the computer.

[7]Connors and Valesky, "Using Microcomputers."

6. The computer fits the student course requests into the master schedule. (One good test of the quality of the scheduling program is the number of nonscheduled students.)
7. The computer prints a list of scheduling conflicts and nonscheduled students.
8. The person responsible for making the schedule adjusts the master and individual student request, and the scheduling program is rerun until a minimum number of conflicts remain. The students with conflicts are then hand-scheduled.
9. Schedule cards are printed, as are class rosters and other necessary documents.
10. The schedule files may be updated if students drop or add classes.[8]

Arena-style scheduling is another approach that can be utilized on microcomputer. The major steps in this process are as follows.

1. Steps 1–4 are essentially the same as the first four steps for automatic scheduling.
2. Instead of loading the master schedule into the computer and scheduling students, blank class rosters are printed and a copy of the master schedule is given to each student.
3. Students make out their own schedules, enter their names and student numbers, and return them.
4. A gymnasium or some other large open space is used for the arena. Each subject has a station in the arena. Students bring their schedules and sign up for the classes.
5. After all students have been through the arena, the rosters are entered into the computer and the master schedule on the computer is built from the rosters.
6. Schedule cards and class rosters are printed.
7. The schedules may be updated if students add or drop classes.[9]

A third method of computer-assisted scheduling is essentially like the arena style except that the computer does the running from station to station. The student can do the entire operation at one location.

There are advantages and disadvantages to each of the three methods. Some are listed here.

1. Automatic scheduling is probably the easier of the three methods from the principal's point of view.
2. Automatic scheduling is probably the least desirable from the student's viewpoint because the students have little control over their schedules.
3. Arena scheduling requires a great deal of careful planning, the cooperation of the entire faculty and staff, and efficient execution of the scheduling plan.
4. Arena scheduling allows the students a greater amount of control over their schedules. When conflicts arise, students work them out with the help of teachers and counselors.

[8]Charlie Joe Allen, "Scheduling Students by Computer" (unpublished, Fall 1987).
[9]Allen, "Scheduling Students by Computer."

5. The third style combines the best features of automatic and arena scheduling. Students work out their schedule with the assistance of a counselor, whereas the computer adds their courses to the master schedule and checks for conflicts.
6. The third style requires that scheduling be spread over several weeks, since counselors must talk with all students.
7. The third type of scheduling also requires a more powerful computer.[10]

There are other programs available that use an optical scanning device for preregistering students. The scanning device provides the reports necessary for making a master schedule. The programs have special features that will provide for

1. Twenty-eight courses per student
2. Labs and other unusual meeting times such as Tuesday/Thursday classes or sections meeting more than once a day
3. Determination of study-hall needs
4. Automatic study-hall and lunch assignments
5. Automatic homeroom assignments
6. Quarter-year courses
7. Maximum and optimum enrollment
8. Prioritized students
9. Prioritized courses and sections
10. Editing student schedules at the keyboard
11. Course and section linking
12. Balancing section enrollment
13. Fifteen periods per day
14. Five or six day week[11]

Most medium and large school districts have computer scheduling systems established. If your school system is not scheduling by computer, getting started requires a lot of work. In the long run, however, it saves much time and is far more accurate. Copies of a student schedule and a teacher enrollment summary that have been produced by computer scheduling are included in Figure 13–3 and Figure 13–4, respectively.

ATTENDANCE REPORTS

The computer is an excellent tool for keeping attendance records. Attendance can be taken in all classes at the beginning of the first period of the day. The names of those students who are absent can be entered into the

[10]Allen, "Scheduling Students by Computer."

[11]"The Administrative Answer" (Concord, N.H.: Applied Educational Systems Software), p. 6.

```
                        **  REPORT CARD  **                    1986/1987

STUDENT NAME . . . .                      STUDENT NUMBER . . . 860694
ADDRESS  . . . . . . 611 PINE RIDGE RD    CLASS YEAR . . . . . 10
CITY,  STATE,  ZIP .                      SEX  . . . . . . . . M
COUNSELOR  . . . . .                DORIS PHONE  . . . . . . . 282-5224
```

COURSE	SUBJECT	PERIOD	TEACHER	MKP4	MKP5	MKP6	AB6	COM6	SAB2	EXM2	SEM2
813 11 01	FRENCH II	01		75	80	83	1			4	65	77
321 22 02	BIOLOGY I	02	WELL	71	76	67	1			4	74	72
919 34 03	HEALTH	03	ORDWELL	89	81	86	1			6	82	85
114 41 04	ENG 10 S I	04	RED	84	74	83	0			5	83	81
225 51 05	ALG I	05	RONTS	88	85	85	0			3	74	84
519 64 06	GEN BUSINESS	06	SANT	93	93	92	0			3	92	93

```
GRADING SCALE: A = 94-100 B = 86-93 C = 75-85 D = 70-74 F = 50-69
MRS. PITTS WILL HELP WITH THE PLANNING OF YOUR SCHEDULE FOR NEXT YEAR.
APPOINTMENTS ARE AVAILABLE APRIL 21-23 FROM 1:30-9:00 P.M. CALL 926-8911.
```

```
                        STUDENT SCHEDULE        1986/1987

STUDENT NAME . . . .                      STUDENT NUMBER . . . 860001
ADDRESS  . . . . . . 1507 E CHILHOWIE AV  CLASS YEAR . . . . . . 10
CITY,  STATE,  ZIP .                      SEX  . . . . . . . . . M
COUNSELOR  . . . . .               CAROL  PHONE  . . . . . . . . 929-7477
```

COURSE	SUBJECT	PERIOD	+------ REGISTERED -------+			ROOM	TEACHER
			TERM	DAYS			
			1 2 3 4 5 6	A B C D E F			
				M T W H F O			
210 11 01	PRE-ALG	01 X X X		X X X X X		S240	ELLIS
312 21 02	BIOLOGY I	02 X X X		X X X X X		S219	WELL
112 31 03	9TH ENG COMP I	03 X X X		X X X X X		S251	ORDWELL
614 41 04	AUTO BODY B1	04 X X X		X X X X X		V201	SELL
923 51 05	DRIVER ED	05 X X X		X X X X X		V112	SMITH
922 61 06	HEALTH	06 X X X		X X X X X		S307	JONES

```
ABEL          CHAD       A
```

FIGURE 13-3. Student Schedule

computer, and the computer will generate an absentee list. The absentee list can be duplicated and distributed to all teachers by the beginning of the second period. At the beginning of the second period and each subsequent period, only the names of students who are not in class and whose names do not appear on the absentee list are sent to the office. The attendance teacher will know that the students whose names are on this

TEACHER ENROLLMENT SUMMARY

10/13/87

CRS	SEC	SES	PER	TEACHER NAME	ROOM	COURSE NAME	OFFERED 123456	OFFERED ABCDEF MTWHFO	FEES	MAX	ENR 1	2	3	4	5	6
131	41	04	04	CALLIE	S265	11TH ENG LIT B	XXX	XXXXX		28	21	21	21			
132	21	02	02	CALLIE	S265	11TH ENG COMP I	XXX	XXXXX		35	29	29	29			
132	24	02	02	CALLIE	S265	11TH ENG COMP I	XXX	XXXXX		35				25	25	25
132	34	03	03	JACKIE	S256	11TH ENG COMP I	XXX	XXXXX		35				30	30	30
132	44	04	04	JOAN	S263	11TH ENG COMP I	XXX	XXXXX		35				21	21	21
132	51	05	05	DORIS	S262	11TH ENG COMP I	XXX	XXXXX		35	25	25	25			
132	52	05	05	CALLIE	S265	11TH ENG COMP I	XXX	XXXXX		35	19	19	19			
132	54	05	05	CALLIE	S265	11TH ENG COMP I	XXX	XXXXX		35				23	23	23
132	61	06	06	DORIS	S262	11TH ENG COMP I	XXX	XXXXX		35	23	23	23			
132	64	06	06	GWEN	S258	11TH ENG COMP I	XXX	XXXXX		35				23	23	23
133	11	01	01	JUDY	S260	11TH ENG LIT I	XXX	XXXXX		35	25	25	25			
133	14	01	01	JUDY	S260	11TH ENG LIT I	XXX	XXXXX		35				15	15	15
133	21	02	02	JOAN	S263	11TH ENG LIT I	XXX	XXXXX		35	27	27	27			
133	24	02	02	JOAN	S263	11TH ENG LIT I	XXX	XXXXX		35				25	25	25
133	31	03	03	JACKIE	S256	11TH ENG LIT I	XXX	XXXXX		35	27	27	27			
133	32	03	03	JOAN	S263	11TH ENG LIT I	XXX	XXXXX		35	19	19	19			
133	34	03	03	JOAN	S263	11TH ENG LIT I	XXX	XXXXX		35				17	17	17
133	41	04	04	JOYCE	S264	11TH ENG LIT I	XXX	XXXXX		35	32	32				
133	54	05	05	JUDY	S260	11TH ENG LIT I	XXX	XXXXX		35				29	29	29
133	64	06	06	JUDY	S260	11TH ENG LIT I	XXX	XXXXX		35				32	32	32
134	51	05	05	JUDY	S260	11TH ENG COMP C	XXX	XXXXX		35	25	25	25			
134	61	06	06	JUDY	S260	11TH ENG COMP C	XXX	XXXXX		35	21	21	21			
135	54	05	05	DORIS	S262	11TH CHALL ENG	XXX	XXXXX		35				24	24	24
135	64	06	06	DORIS	S262	11TH CHALL ENG	XXX	XXXXX		35				21	21	21
140	31	03	03	GWEN	S258	12TH ENG COMP B	XXX	XXXXX		23	27	27	27			

FIGURE 13-4. Teacher Enrollment Summary

CRS	SEC	SES	PER	TEACHER NAME	ROOM	COURSE NAME	OFFERED 123456	ABCDEF MTWHFO	FEES	MAX	ENR 1	ENR 2	ENR 3	ENR 4	ENR 5	ENR 6
140	64	06	06	MYMA	S261	12TH ENG COMP B	XXX	XXXXX		23				16	16	16
141	34	03	03	GWEN	S258	12TH ENG LIT B	XXX	XXXXX		23				24	24	24
141	61	06	06	MYMA	S261	12TH ENG LIT B	XXX	XXXXX		23	18	18	18			
142	14	01	01	JOYCE	S264	12TH ENG COMP I	XXX	XXXXX		35				24	24	24
142	24	02	02	JOYCE	S264	12TH ENG COMP I	XXX	XXXXX		35				23	23	23
142	31	03	03	JUDY	S260	12TH ENG COMP I	XXX	XXXXX		35	25	25	25			
142	41	04	04	JUDY	S260	12TH ENG COMP I	XXX	XXXXX		35	20	20	20			
142	54	05	05	JOAN	S263	12TH ENG COMP I	XXX	XXXXX		35				18	18	18
142	61	06	06	ANNE	S251	12TH ENG COMP I	XXX	XXXXX		35	16	16	16			
143	11	01	01	JOYCE	S264	12TH ENG LIT I	XXX	XXXXX		35	25	25	25			
143	21	02	02	JOYCE	S264	12TH ENG LIT I	XXX	XXXXX		35	29	29	29			
143	34	03	03	JUDY	S260	12TH ENG LIT I	XXX	XXXXX		35				19	19	19
143	44	04	04	JUDY	S260	12TH ENG LIT I	XXX	XXXXX		35				18	18	18
143	51	05	05	JOAN	S263	12TH ENG LIT I	XXX	XXXXX		35	23	23	23			
143	64	06	06	ANNE	S251	12TH ENG LIT I	XXX	XXXXX		35				14	14	14
144	14	01	01	DORIS	S262	12TH ENG COMP A	XXX	XXXXX		35				31	31	31
144	24	02	02	MYMA	S261	12TH ENG COMP A	XXX	XXXXX		35				29	29	29
144	31	03	03	CALLIE	S265	12TH ENG COMP A	XXX	XXXXX		35	18	18	18			
144	34	03	03	MYMA	S261	12TH ENG COMP A	XXX	XXXXX		35				23	23	23
144	41	04	04	JOAN	S263	12TH ENG COMP A	XXX	XXXXX		35	21	21	21			
144	61	06	06	CALLIE	S265	12TH ENG COMP A	XXX	XXXXX		35	19	19	19			
144	64	06	06	JUDY	S313	12TH ENG COMP A	XXX	XXXXX		35				6	6	6
145	11	01	01	DORIS	S262	12TH ENG LIT A	XXX	XXXXX		35	29	29	29			
145	21	02	02	MYMA	S261	12TH ENG LIT A	XXX	XXXXX		35	29	29	29			
145	31	03	03	MYMA	S261	12TH ENG LIT A	XXX	XXXXX		35	26	26	26			

FIGURE 13-4. Continued.

list have probably cut a class. Corrections for students who arrived late can be made in the computer file at the end of the day.

A big part of attendance reporting is mandated by the state departments of education, such as school registers and end-of-year reports. Monthly and yearly attendance reports in the format required by the state can be generated from computer files.

There are some commercial programs on the market for attendance reporting that have some very good features. For example, the programs will provide for

1. Personalized letters: Imbed over 20 variables to create a personal letter to any group of students or parents you must notify—students with specific number of days absent, for example
2. End-of-year reports providing such data as total aggregate enrollment, average daily attendance (ADA), average daily membership (ADM), and percentage of perfect attendance
3. User-defined descriptive categories: You define up to 10 categories with 20 subcategories each to classify your student population (bus route, town of residence, and ethnic group are examples); end-of-year reports can be produced for each of these categories
4. User-defined daily attendance codes (15) to tailor attendance information to your school's reporting needs
5. Attendance reports listing full or half-day absence
6. Daily course cutting report listing student, teacher, course, and period
7. Student's year-to-date attendance record printed or on the video
8. Automatic transferal of attendance summaries to each student's scholarship report
9. Entry and withdrawal dates assigned to the entire school, if desired
10. Automatic calling: Call parents of absent students using a prerecorded message; the system notes the outcome of call and records a response from the parent[12]

AUTOMATIC CALLING

The computer can assist in automatic calling of parents about their respective children. Either an internal or external calling device is needed to support the computer with these calls. The peripheral is commonly called an *automatic telephone computer robot*. The voice message is recorded by the school principal or a designee. The voice message is not altered in any way by having passed through the computer. It does not sound like a computer talking, but conveys the natural voice of the sender.

How does the system work? The principal or designee creates a student phone directory on a diskette at the beginning of the school year. The messages

[12]The Administrative Answer," p. 6.

are recorded to fit the occasion. Each day a parent is to be called, the name of the student is typed in. The computer, assisted by the device, will call the home phone number. The time for the call to be made must also be set in the machine. At the proper time, the computer will activate a telephone and make the call. The message is then delivered. Some of the devices will also record a reply by parents. The devices can record calls that are answered or unanswered, redials, and busy signals. They can also make a written record of the calls and the subsequent followup.

McGinty stated that

> Administrators are using dialers to get messages to parents quickly—everything from when report cards are coming home to the date of the next PTA meeting. But administrators agree, the most effective use of these systems is in contacting parents of absent students. Across the country, school systems using dialing systems report they are effective in improving average daily attendance.[13]

Automatic calling has been very effective in increasing attendance in most of the situations when it was used for that purpose. Cleaton reported that when automatic calling was used to call parents whose children were absent at Taft High School in New York City, attendance increased by approximately 10 percent.[14] Attendance rose from 78.8 percent to 86.4 percent at DuSable High School and from 80.5 percent to 85.8 percent at Tilden High School in Chicago when automatic calling about absences was instituted.[15] One Florida school had a 59 percent reduction in truancy during the first three months of automatic calling about absences. A California school reduced absences by 52 percent during a three-month period, saving more than $36,000 in possible lost revenue.[16] Helm found, in a year-long study of elementary, middle, and high schools, that students whose parents were automatically called concerning absences had much better attendance records than did students whose parents were not called.[17]

[13]Tony McGinty, "Tracking Truants with Automatic Dialers," *Electronic Learning* (January 1985), p. 24.

[14]Stephanie Cleaton, "Computers to Be Used to Snitch on Students Who Play Hooky," *New York Voice* (September 10, 1983).

[15]"Schools Using Robots Against Absenteeism," *The New York Times*, February 18, 1986.

[16]Graham Hartwell, "Computerized Phone System Successfully Reduced Truancy," *School Business Affairs* (May 1984), p. 26.

[17]Carroll M. Helm, "The Effects of Administrative Uses of Computer Assisted Telecommunications on School Attendance" (Doctoral Dissertation, East Tennessee State University, Dec. 1987), pp. 73–77.

GRADE REPORTING

There are several excellent grade-reporting systems software packages on the market. They provide capabilities for reporting letter grades, number grades, or both, and much more. They will also produce course weights (for honor rolls, GPA, and such), course tracks, honor rolls, semester exam scores, final exam scores, teacher comments, and much more. Some other special features include reporting class attendance on report cards, cumulative grade-point averages, homeroom assignments, and personalized letters to parents.

There are other helpful functions of grade reporting software packages. They will produce

> student lists by school or year of graduation, grade level lists, teacher lists, course catalogues, report card comment lists, homeroom lists, honor rolls, rank in class based on GPA, alphabetized grade point averages, students with failures, incompletes, or withdrawals; frequency grades distribution by teacher or department, summary attendance; and teacher verifications.[18]

INTERNAL BOOKKEEPING

Records of internal finances can range all the way from a few hundred dollars to several hundred thousand dollars, depending on the size of the school. Very small schools may do as well keeping the records by hand as managing them on the computer. If they do manage them by computer, they can be satisfactorily maintained on a ledger produced by the spreadsheet on a word processor. The larger schools with vast amounts of internal money will need a more complex program. VisiCalc and Lotus 1, 2, 3, are probably the most commonly used programs for this purpose. These programs will handle records of purchases, expenditures, and income very nicely. They will also handle the great variety of accounts in the larger schools, and store and produce the proper documents of the bookkeeping and accounting system.

COMMUNICATION BETWEEN COMPUTERS

Information can be shared by microcomputer users through the use of communication networks. There is a great range of possible use, from local hookups to worldwide networks. Computers can be linked among a small group of users in the same building, or they can send and receive messages

[18]"The Administrative Answer," p. 6.

to and from great distances. The communication among computers within a building is called local area networking (LAN).

Local Area Network

A LAN is a system of linked computers in which the various machines may access one another and share resources. A LAN allows two or more computer users to share printers, storage devices, and other computer equipment. In a network, cables physically link the microcomputers and the other types of computer equipment. However, the physical link must be within the limits established by the network hardware. Figure 13–5 conceptually depicts one way that microcomputers, peripherals, and a mainframe may be linked on a LAN.

Items of importance regarding LANs are

1. Each microcomputer on the network may use shared peripheral devices, such as printers, plotters, and mass-storage devices.

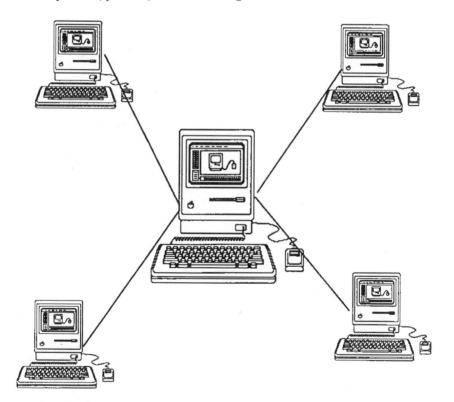

FIGURE 13–5. Local Area Network

2. In a network, at least one microcomputer is designated as a file server. The file server manages communication and the sharing of peripheral devices. The file server must have a hard disk and is usually the most powerful computer in the network.

3. A network may contain more than one file server. The second file server might be another microcomputer in the LAN or it might be a mainframe computer in the central office.

4. Microcomputers not physically linked with the LAN may access the network via the telephone system; however, a modem and appropriate software must be utilized.

5. Currently some brands of computer and software products are not compatible with other brands, but software exists that may allow files to be transferred from one to the other.

6. Special attention must be given to software to insure compatibility with the LAN.

Many schools are beginning to use LANs to enhance communication, facilitate efficiency, and improve office automation. For example, the computer with the hard disk (the file server) may be located in the secretary's office. Smaller microcomputers located in the offices of the principal, guidance counselor, bookkeeper, and three teachers could all be on the LAN. With the proper hookups and software, all could use the peripheral equipment located in the secretary's office. All could also possibly be using the same word processor that is stored in the memory of the file server computer. All of the users could retrieve information stored on the file server and share information with one another.

The LAN in a particular school could be linked with a mainframe computer in the central office by telephone line, which requires a modem. (Caution: Dial-up telephone ports on a mainframe computer greatly increase the risk of hackers breaching security and gaining access to confidential files). Having a telephone link can be a very useful service—it saves time and provides for greater efficiency in record keeping and retrieval of information. A local school could store teacher and student records in the central office mainframe and add to or retrieve them as needed. It could also provide central office personnel with ready access to information. For example, information required for teachers' record books could be stored and retrieved for the monthly and annual reports that must be made to the state departments of education.

External Communication

External networks can be established by using telephones to connect computers almost anywhere. For example, if a school needs to share information with other schools in the system or even across the state or nation, it can be done via use of computer and telephone line. External hookups require that each computer on the network have a special software package and a modem. A modem converts data at the sending computer so that it can be sent on the telephone to the receiving computer and converts it back at the receiving computer so that it can be entered into the machine. In other words, it modulates at the sending end and demodulates at the receiving end. External networks are the type that would usually be established by schools. There are other means of establishing networks that are beyond the scope of the discussion in this chapter. Why would a school need to be on an external network? A school and six others in the state may be operating a special experimental program in experiential teaching of Biology II. They may need to share information with ease and at will. The external network is ideal for that purpose.

Electronic Bulletin Boards. There are literally thousands of electronic bulletin boards in this country. They are used primarily for the exchange of information and are usually special-interest networks. Anyone with the proper equipment can set one up with relative ease. Most can be set up or accessed at little or no cost. A user needs a computer, a telephone, the proper software, and a modem. The user can send and receive messages. Use of the electronic bulletin board is a very efficient way for schools to exchange information.

National Networks. There are several commercial network services available. Most of them require a subscription for an initial fee and an hourly rate for services. The information services store vast amounts of data that can be accessed by subscribers. The user is usually required to key in descriptors of the kind of information desired. The computer at the service center searches the files and sends all directly related information to the descriptors. ERIC is one of the services used in education that can be very useful, especially in keeping principals and their staffs informed on current happenings in education.

Electronic Mail. Electronic mail is very valuable when there is a need to send information quickly. It allows one person to send a message to another by computer and telephone. The sender records the message electronically in the computer using a computer-based mail system. The computer is programmed as to whom the message is intended. The message is stored until the receiver, at a preselected time, retrieves the information. The information may be displayed on the monitor, printer, or both.

Research. The computer offers an excellent opportunity for manipulation of data in research about various aspects of school administration. For example, schools often conduct public-opinion polls. Computer programs are available to generate a random sample for the survey. The instrument used can be prepared for easy transfer of the data to the computer; moreover, the computer can be programmed to generate numerous configurations of opinions (such as opinions classified by age, area of residence, male, or female) that would take many hours by hand. The computer might also generate information data concerning the production of different instructional practices that would be helpful in making curriculum decisions. The computer uses in action research could be very helpful in improving schools.

Computers have moved from the category of being a luxury to that of a necessity. They are used almost everywhere. Communication systems such as the telephone have been computerized for a long time; calls all over the world are handled by computers. Computers check our health conditions and produce our bank records. A visit to the local dealer of used car parts (junkyard) will reveal that the inventory is recorded on computer. Computers are being used by the lowest to the highest level personnel in organizations. Principals, to be most effective, must see that their schools take full advantage of the services that can be provided by computers.

CHAPTER FOURTEEN

The Personnel Function

Very basic to successful practice in the principalship is knowing how to motivate teachers and other personnel to (1) work diligently at the performance of tasks essential to the school mission, (2) observe those professional standards of task performance supported by research and accepted by the school faculty, and (3) complete the tasks on set schedule. The principal's primary task is to motivate teachers to do what needs to be done, assist them in the performance of their tasks, and maintain a schedule of when it needs to be done. The foregoing is the focus of practically all of this text; however, this chapter also concerns the principal's tasks of (1) planning for the improvement of the personnel of the school, (2) recruitment of teachers, (3) selection of teachers and non-certificated personnel (4) orientation and placement of new teachers, (5) the evaluation of personnel, and (6) contract management.

Personnel tasks are administered very differently among the school districts in the nation, and so the principal's role varies among school districts. For example, in very large school districts a large staff exists in the central office to assist in the recruitment, selection, and placement of teachers among the schools of the district. In those districts the principal's tasks in recruitment are minimal, and probably consist of selecting from a pool of teachers who have been recruited and screened for possible employment. Yet in many of the smaller districts of the nation, the principal is given authority to recruit, screen, and recommend employment to the superintendent and board of education. It is regrettable that in a few school districts political appointments are still practiced by some members of the board of education.

NEEDED: A PERSONNEL LEADERSHIP VIEW

As discussed in Chapter 3, the principal should begin with a personally accepted theory or concept for the administration of personnel. Otherwise, the principal's behavior will very likely be inconsistent, and a loss of leadership will be suffered. We have insisted previously that the leader who is blown about by the wind will experience loss of influence. Since accepting a general theory of management is so critical to consistency, we will again discuss briefly the alternative concepts or approaches to managing personnel.

Since the early 1900s, management theory has been influenced by several eras: the traditional era, the transitional era, and the systems era and beyond.[1] As discussed previously in Chapters 5 and 6, the contingency theory of management is supported by systems theory, and loosely coupled theory is currently a topic of discussion in the literature.

The Traditional View of Managing Personnel

Traditional management theory, which was in vogue until the 1930s, was very heavily influenced by the theories of Frederick W. Taylor.[2] In the theory known as scientific management, Taylor emphasized (1) time and motion studies, (2) piece-rate payment, (3) management control over the means of production, and (4) scientific analysis for the most efficient means of work. In combination with the concept of bureaucratic organization, which was founded by Weber[3] and further developed by such scholars as Gulick and Urwick,[4] the traditional concept of management emerged as the dominant theme in educational administration.

Very briefly, if scientific management were applied, teachers would be paid on the basis of the productivity of their students, most probably as measured by a standardized achievement test. Ms. A would receive the

[1]Ralph B. Kimbrough and Michael Y. Nunnery, *Educational Administration: An Introduction*, 3rd ed. (New York: Macmillan, 1988), pp. 251–335.

[2]Frederick W. Taylor, *Shop Management* (New York: Harper & Row, 1911).

[3]Max Weber, *The Theory of Social and Economic Organization*, trans. A. M. Henderson and Talcott Parsons, ed. Talcott Parsons (New York: Free Press, 1964).

[4]Luther Gulick and L. Urwick, eds., *Papers on the Science of Administration* (New York: Institute for Public Administration, 1937).

normal or average payment or raise in salary if her first-grade pupils achieved at exactly the second-grade level at the close of school. Ms. A's salary increase or decrease would depend upon how many percentage points the children's standardized scores were above or below the national norm for the test. The principal would decide which instructional processes the teachers should use, based on scientific analysis including time and motion studies, used to find the best instructional techniques at the lowest possible per-pupil cost. If scientific management were applied, the teachers would have to agree to perform their tasks as specified by the principal before they could be employed.

The school would be organized according to Weber's bureaucratic model, which includes (1) the enforcement of rules of pupil and teacher conduct, (2) hierarchy of authority from the principal down, (3) impersonality, and (4) specialization. The teachers, who are highly specialized to perform specific tasks, would be promoted in rank up the career ladder based on personal competence, not on political or personal consideration. The climate of the school would be strictly business, no-nonsense, with little time devoted to consideration.

The teachers and noncertificated personnel would be paid very well; in fact, Taylor always offered those in his experiments higher wages than the accepted payment for labor. The principal might, for example, be authorized to raise the salaries of teachers willing to participate fully in the process. Efficiencies would result from greatly increased productivity. Taylor assumed that everyone was motivated by money. Given the correct control and management processes, he assumed that workers (or teachers) would work harder for more pay.

The Transitional Era

During the 1920s some writers, notably Mary Parker Follett, emphasized the need for greater attention to the human side of management.[5] An important turning point in the rejection of scientific management began in 1923 with the beginning of the noted Western Electric studies under the direction of Elton Mayo. Mayo and his associates began their experiment using traditional assumptions; however, they soon discovered that the traditional views did not explain how the workers were motivated.

Certain psychological and social factors, not piece-rate payment, were critical to worker motivation. Morale was believed to be associated with worker output. Experiments with boys' clubs by Lewin, Lippitt, and White further cast doubt on the efficacy of autocratic control of personnel.[6]

[5]Mary Parker Follett, *Creative Experience* (New York: Longmans, 1924).

[6]Kurt Lewin, Ronald Lippitt, and Ralph White, "Patterns of Aggressive Behavior in Experimentally Created Climates," *Journal of Social Psychology,* 10 (May 1939), 271–99.

Continued development of the field of group dynamics further emphasized that, rather than being perceived as checkers to be moved about at the will of the school principal, teachers were human beings capable of self-motivation, creativity, and willingness to assume responsibility.

As discussed in Chapter 7, the relationship-oriented school principal works diligently to create a personnel climate marked by good human relations and high morale. The principal assumes that, given good human relations and high morale, teachers will be self-motivated to work hard, will exercise creativity in task performance, and will be accountable for the educational development of students. Teachers are well-educated professionals who know more about their specialties than does the principal; consequently, the principal's role is to create a climate and provide the services and resources that are the most appropriate for the teachers to practice their profession.

The Systems Era

By the 1960s many authorities in the fields of management had all but abandoned the human-relations view, which was thought to neglect the structural side of personnel administration. The development of general systems theory, which is the focus of this text, soon emerged as a dominant theme for research and development. The model by Getzels and Guba is illustrative of the application of systems theory to school administration (see discussion, Chapter 4).[7]

General systems theorists assume that the whole is greater than the sum of its parts, whereas scientific management is an atomistic approach that focuses on the parts. As we have demonstrated throughout this text, the systems-oriented principal thinks in terms of individual teachers as interactive in social systems, both influencing and influenced by the interacting systems. Concentrating exclusively upon parts, wholes, structure, or the human side to the exclusion of the systematic whole leads up blind alleys in attempts to understand school operation. In the process of interaction teachers develop norms of just how much they should teach and how much students should learn in a school year. Parents and students then absorb these learning norms, which become their expectations of acceptable performance by a process resembling osmosis. The norms become fixed in the system and have great influence upon motivation and productivity. In cooperation with the faculty, the principal's task is to intervene in the system to bring about fundamental changes in those norms that result in low student achievement. A primary consideration in leadership is to develop a

[7]Jacob W. Getzels and Egon G. Guba, "Social Behavior and the Administrative Process," *School Review,* LXV (Winter 1957), 423–41.

system with very high standards or norms of production by which the tendency toward entropy is arrested.

The application of systems theory may also lead to the contingency concept of leadership and management. The contingency theory has implications for the placement of principals in social situations as well as within the actual leadership practices used in the school. For further discussion of contingency theory, please return to Chapter 4.

As discussed in Chapter 5, what is referred to as loosely coupled theory began to attract the attention of some authorities during the 1980s. Unlike the fully joined bureaucracy, much independence or autonomy exists among the administrative units of loosely coupled systems. For example, loosely coupled theorists contend that principals have limited influence over what goes on in classrooms. For this reason, the loosely coupled system is often referred to as an organized anarchy. If this concept is accepted, the principal will have limited opportunity to influence the classroom system. Attempts to control the education process via bureaucratic structure prove futile because teaching is not a fully coupled process. The teacher is the focus of control of the process.

Time for Personal Decision

The school principal should make a personal decision regarding the conflicting concepts of personnel management, probably the most important decision the principal will make, because it has implications for (1) investigating the existing management policy before accepting a contract, (2) keeping on course in the face of very difficult decisions, and (3) facilitating the establishment of working relationships with the faculty. If you know that you have a personality consistent with the humanistic view, you may want to engage in very serious thought before accepting a principalship in which your predecessor was a task-oriented person that was well received by the faculty. There is a question concerning how much you may be able to "fake" a task orientation before your true leadership persuasion emerges, usually in critical decision situations. Moreover, you may not be able to persuade the faculty to follow your style of leadership.

RECRUITMENT AND SELECTION OF PERSONNEL

The most direct route to an excellent school is to locate, recruit, and employ excellent teachers. However, one seldom has an opportunity to employ an entirely new faculty; even if this opportunity is provided there is no assurance that the recruitment and selection processes will result in excellent teachers in every position. Also, if a principal lacks leadership, faculty performance may adjust accordingly and an excellent faculty can become just an average faculty. Nevertheless, an effective method for the selection of faculty members is essential.

Some Observations About the Process

Before discussing some of the nuts and bolts of the recruitment and selection process, let us consider the fundamental importance of the process. The principal usually exercises leadership in or through the school social system, which consists of formal and informal groups having norms, sentiments, established relations, patterns of interaction, leadership hierarchies, and so on. The central office probably expects the principal to exercise more influence on the system than it exercises on the principal. That authority is the essence of leadership.

The selection of teachers and other personnel of the school provides a very effective means of intervention in the system. Is the object to select teachers who will fit in with the existing system, or is the aim to select new teachers who may further challenge the status quo and minimize the effects of entropy? The answer to this question is contingent on the condition of the school. Many schools that are located in relatively isolated rural areas are loaded with native-born teachers who tend to lock in an antiquated educational system where entropy is maximized. The authors have visited many such communities in which a kind of community brainwashing has occurred, so that school leaders maintain the status quo, reluctant to keep pace with the larger society.

Whether the school is a closed or open system has implications for the establishment of an orientation program for new teachers. The social systems of schools are very adept at propagandizing, persuading, and encouraging new teachers to accept the established way of doing things, and this is where the informal organization of the school is at its best in influencing school policy. Sometimes coercion may be used, especially with beginning teachers. The so-called big buddy system is tailor-made for the continuance of the existing system equilibrium and maintenance of the status quo. After all, the primary aim of most orientation programs is to insure that the beginning faculty member behaves consistently with the accepted norms, goals, interaction patterns, and customs of the social system.

The main point of this discussion is that, in the selection and orientation of faculty members, the principal and faculty may set up conditions that either freeze or unfreeze the system. The process of change and improvement within a school may be facilitated through the selection of persons who can make certain new inputs, especially if the system is willing to give the new arrivals support.

Educators often value low teacher turnover; however, a sizable turnover at any one time may signal an opportunity to select teachers who can complement the system that is desired by the principal and faculty. On the other hand, too much teacher turnover year after year can be detrimental because then the system may lack continuity or become so loaded with inputs and so open that it cannot survive.

When viewed in the light of potential impact upon the social system of the school, the recruitment and selection of teachers take on added significance. But the effect upon the school social system is not the only reason for attaching great importance to staff recruitment and selection. We often pass a building with a comment such as "That is Hill Valley Middle School." Such a statement is inaccurate. The Hill Valley Middle School is the structured social system of administrators, teachers, students, and noncertificated personnel who are working together to carry out the educational mission. The teacher is the heartbeat of that system. The most competent principal in the society will fail with a staff containing too many incompetent teachers. Excellent teaching will make the principal look very good to the community and board of education.

The selection of personnel, however, is not restricted to teachers. The counseling staff and other support personnel are essential for a good school. Much energy should also be invested in the selection of nurses, custodians, lunchroom workers, and other service personnel.

The problem of recruiting and holding excellent teachers is affected by the socioeconomic level of the community. Principals in the low socioeconomic neighborhoods of inner-city schools experience greater difficulty attracting teachers than do principals in upper-economic-status suburban communities. Moreover, a shortage of excellent teachers, particularly in some subject areas, usually exists. What are some suggestions to the principal for the recruitment and selection process?

Recruitment, Selection, and Orientation

Forward-thinking school systems are committed to a strong recruitment and selection process; moreover, as discussed in Chapter 12, they observe legally required affirmative action procedures. In such a school system, the principal will be measurably assisted by central office personnel in the process of selecting good teachers. Through the centralized process of recruitment the principal can make personal needs known and any special competencies desired. Castetter suggests that recruitment and screening be handled centrally, but that the final selection be decentralized to the individual schools.[8] Variance exists

---

[8]William B. Castetter, *The Personnel Function in Educational Administration,* 3rd ed. (New York: Macmillan, 1986), p. 199.

among school districts concerning the recruitment and selection of personnel. Regardless of the recruitment and selection processes employed, the principal, with the appropriate participation of the faculty, should have the final choice of those recommended by the superintendent to the board for appointment. As discussed in Chapter 12, the assignment of work load is usually the prerogative of the principal.

Castetter recommends, and many contracts require, that opportunity be given for transfers and promotions within the school system.[9] However, in some school systems incompetent teachers are constantly shuffled among unsuspecting principals, so that no one principal has to be in the uncomfortable position of bringing charges for dismissal. As soon as these teachers wear out their welcome in one school, the principal makes plans to pawn them off on another, a practice that occurs often enough for the principal and the faculty to review thoroughly any person seeking a transfer.

Fundamental to the selection process is the development of clear understandings of what kind of teacher is desired for each position open in the school. Following pet whims or hunches must be avoided. Teaching competency or the high potential for excellent teaching should be prime considerations. However, the contribution that the applicant can make to the improvement of the faculty, such as committee work and school service, should also be emphasized. Can the applicant meet the specific demands of the position? These and other considerations furnish a basis for judgment by the principal and colleagues.

The collection of data regarding each applicant is a significant step in selection. Usual sources of information are application forms, transcripts, letters of recommendation, results of examinations, and interviews. Yet almost any suave person can put together a good set of papers (they are known in the business as paper hangers), and interviews have been repeatedly found to be an invalid means for selection. The principal and members of the advisory committee should contact persons who know the applicant through the use of telephone or personal visits, particularly if the applicant is under serious consideration. Telephone and travel charges are low compared to the cost of an incompetent teacher.

New members of the faculty should be provided a welcome and an orientation to the school. As discussed previously, this is not for the purpose of completely co-opting the new teachers to the existing system, but to acquaint them with the nature of services available and to provide any services that will make their first days a welcome experience. Beginning teachers especially will need greater assistance and possibly very close supervision during the first months of service.

[9]Castetter, *Personnel Function*, p. 207.

EVALUATION OF PERSONNEL

The principal will have the task of evaluating teachers, and this can be a very frustrating responsibility. Since these evaluations may be used as a basis for promotion and the results may affect a teacher's psychological needs (such as self-esteem), their results can be destructive. Negative evaluations of certain teachers may create very strong feelings and discord among politicians, board members, teacher organizations, educational leaders, and other citizens. Teachers sometimes view evaluation of their work as arbitrary and dehumanizing, yet community leaders and other citizens believe that the evaluation of teachers is the primary process through which accountability is assured. The frustrating aspect of teacher evaluation is heightened by the lack of an objective means for the evaluation process. Much research about the personnel evaluation process has failed to find an objective approach that is satisfactory, because we are dealing with a complex social system in which there are unknown variables related to student achievement.

School districts seeking merit differentials in salary have followed various schemes such as student ratings, use of outside professional ratings, self-ratings, colleague ratings, committee evaluations, and so on. The most common procedure is to employ a rating instrument that features items thought to measure competencies. In some instances the district office adopts an instrument and decrees that the principal shall rate each teacher, an approach filled with difficulties for the principal. Other school systems have provided salary differentials based upon a point system in which points are awarded for a variety of activities, some of which may have little relevance to the classroom.

Castetter identified five models for the evaluation of teaching: (1) common-law, (2) goal-setting, (3) product, (4) clinical-supervision, and (5) artistic.[10] The common-law approach is a high administrator–low teacher participation model. The principal and the teacher participate in the goal-setting model. Goal setting may be somewhat consistent with management by objectives (MBO), in which the teacher and the principal negotiate specific objectives and review the progress toward their goal. The product model places emphasis on the achievements of students within a time frame; standardized achievement tests may be used to measure productivity. The clinical-supervision model places emphasis on collegiality with the primary aim to increase teacher competence. Those preferring the artistic model accept teaching as an art that is not subject to objective measurement. Thus creativity in the teaching art is not well served by the establishment of objectives.

[10]Castetter, *Personnel Function*, p. 323.

The common-law approach is not preferred by the authors, because of the possibility of arbitrarily rating teachers, resulting in little motivation of teachers to improve their competency. This traditional procedure of "doing it to someone" can really be a very dehumanizing experience for teachers as well as for the conscientious principal.

Product evaluation is loaded with insurmountable problems. It ignores the obvious impact that the socioeconomic levels of communities have on student achievement. Moreover, student groups will vary more than a standard deviation difference in their aptitude for learning. The classroom is a dynamic system in which many variables uncontrolled by the teacher affect scores on a standardized test. The cause-and-effect relationships in classrooms are very difficult to establish and may result in the phenomenon known as equifinality (see Chapter 4); that is, the same teaching processes used with five matched groups of students by the same teacher may produce statistically different results, or in another trial, similar test scores may result from the use of different methods of teaching. Finally, to judge a teacher's competency entirely on the basis of student test scores would be like holding a physician accountable for whether patients live or die rather than basing accountability on whether standard medical procedure was performed. The product approach ignores the existence of interacting systems.

The authors favor a participatory model in which the administration and teachers establish the bases for evaluation. We believe that administrators should also receive annual evaluations. The first step in successful evaluation is to agree on a plan for evaluation and the performance areas to be included, probably a district-wide endeavor. The development of the plan should be followed by a series of in-service training meetings for teachers and administrators to assure proper implementation.

The actual evaluation process in the school should include a preevaluation conference (or conferences) between the principal and each teacher to be evaluated. Conferences permit further communication about the evaluation process and remove some doubts concerning the efficacy of the process. At the appropriate time the teachers complete a self-evaluation, which is followed by a meet-and-confer appointment to review and discuss the principal's evaluation. Upon agreement between the teacher and the principal, the evaluation may be properly processed and placed in the teacher's file. In the event the principal and teacher fail to agree, a process usually exists, such as a bargained contract, for resolution of the disagreement.

THE DECISION TO DISMISS A TEACHER

After doing everything humanly possible to help a teacher become competent, the principal is sometimes faced with the prospect of dismissal. Our job as administrators demands that we dismiss those teachers who are keeping children and youth from having a first-class education. We must use every strategy and technique at our disposal to help the ineffective teacher become an excellent teacher. Yet every principal will have to make the decision to initiate action for dismissal in some cases. Every situation is different; consequently, numerous reasons for dismissal occur, including incompetency, unethical behavior, emotional disability, and so on. In cases of gross immorality and moral turpitude, the decision is easy—suspension followed by the initiation to dismiss. However, these decisions in the absence of gross failures of character are often frustrating.

The most soul-searching feeling of frustration happens when a fine young man or woman tries very hard to become a good teacher but continues, with all the professional development assistance we can provide them, to experience failure. In one case a young man was experiencing continuous discipline problems in his fifth-grade classroom. Over a period involving many hours, the principal and teacher isolated the problems and planned changes in behavior to overcome them. The teacher was able to intellectualize his difficulty but continued to lapse into behavior that caused serious disruption and loss of instructional time. For example, he was never able to avoid those classroom behaviors, discussed in Chapter 9, that resulted in disorganization verging on anarchy.

As much as the principal wanted to see the young man succeed, he could not allow his feelings to deprive the students of good teaching. The decision had to be made to remove the young man from a situation in which he was suffering constant embarrassment and misery. In this particular case, the young man talked through the situation with the principal and decided that he should pursue another career. Perhaps in another case, and under different circumstances, the principal could have transferred the teacher out of a bad situation, and the teacher might have been able to correct his errors; however, in this particular case a transfer was not indicated.

The cases that test the principal's character are those in which the incompetent teacher refuses to recognize that a problem exists, cases when unilateral action is necessary because the teacher in question refuses to admit failure. Before taking action the principal must see that all legal requirements are met. Legalities are discussed in Chapter 12; however, in addition to what we have written, the principal should consult the superintendent, the resident attorney for the school district (if available), and/or the board attorney. The basis for dismissal must be thoroughly documented. The documentation must be recognizable evidence in a court of law. The case may be lost if past evaluations of performance indicate competency. One must remember that the most incompetent teacher in the school may know of parents who will testify that the accused was a good teacher in whose class their children learned. Many of these situations test the character and courage of the principal. The principal should be prepared for recriminatory actions, including political action to attempt to remove the head of the school, one reason why the principal must enjoy a power base in the community, as we discussed and recommended in Chapter 6.

CONTRACT MANAGEMENT

Collective bargaining began in the private sector. During the 1960s the industrial model for the collective bargaining process had become accepted in many local school districts. By 1965 six state legislatures had passed statutes authorizing collective bargaining in the public sector. Including those states that have meet-and-confer legislation, over thirty states have some form of statute for collective negotiations. Even in those states not having such legislation, school districts may practice a form of collective negotiation. Where negotiated contracts are authorized by law, school principals are responsible for the administration of the contract, because they have the most direct contact with teachers.

In the beginning of collective bargaining, school boards and superintendents were not very knowledgeable about the process, and some mistakes were made. One grievous mistake was to leave school principals out of the negotiations. The result was specific language in the contract that seriously eroded the principal's authority to administer the school. Thus principals in those situations were responsible for administering a contract that they had no part in negotiating. In some school districts the principals organized and demanded negotiated contracts to protect their positions. Through experience this has been remedied by including principals in the process. As a result, principals can better perform their primary responsibility in this area: namely, the administration of the contract.

The contract may include specific constraints upon the authority of the principal in carrying out administrative tasks. For example, the contract may specify that a school council be appointed to meet with the principal at specified times, such as once each month. Other specified restraints may deal with the evaluation of teachers, special duty assignments, and classroom observation.

The first step in contract administration is to become informed about the contract, including the intentions in the language of the specific provisions. Second, the contract must be willingly accepted in good faith without any display whatsoever of anti-union feelings. Third, the principal should be consistent in administering the specific provisions of the contract.[11] Otherwise, the matter of trustworthiness in leadership arises, and the principal will lose influence. Moreover, the principals who have too many grievances may not receive very favorable ratings from the central office.

[11]Kimbrough and Nunnery, *Educational Administration*, p. 518.

Under collective bargaining each building has a union representative or building steward. If a teacher has a complaint, the principal will be visited by the building steward concerning the matter. The frequency of steward visits may be a good criterion of the climate of the school. One would expect a great many visits from the steward and more formal grievances if the climate is in an unhealthy state, but few complaints in a genuine social climate.

CHAPTER FIFTEEN

Administration of Student Personnel

Recurring student personnel task areas include grading, reporting to parents, grouping for instruction, cumulative records, attendance, guidance, and discipline. The performance of tasks in these traditional areas is becoming increasingly complex, and during the 1970s some additional tasks were added. For example, because of the growth of crime in schools, the principal must assume increasing responsibility for student security. Tasks in the administration of exceptional education have been added. The growth of forces in the society that are counteractive to the education process, such as the competition of television, teenage employment after school, increased divorce rate, and the drug problem, has complicated tasks in student personnel.

Nevertheless, the authors believe that achieving a school of quality is dependent on a well-administered student personnel program. If a student climate conducive to high educational achievement is achieved and is coupled with enthusiastic teaching, the school will probably achieve its goal of excellence. On the other hand, even the highest quality of teachers in existence cannot succeed in a climate marked by fear, insensitivity to delayed rewards, or student behavior best described as chaos.

DEVELOPING OPTIMUM STUDENT DISCIPLINE

Throughout this text we have emphasized that the principal should invest leadership in the development of a climate conducive to high educational achievement. Most students, parents, and teachers correctly expect the administration to develop and maintain an orderly, caring, trusting school climate. Given such a milieu, students will succeed admirably and the school faculty will be rewarded in many ways for its effort. The tragedy of so many drop-outs from schools will be curtailed, much to the benefit of the society. On the other hand, a school that deteriorates into a blackboard jungle, inhabited by an uncaring administration and faculty and a student body having low expectations of itself, will probably fail to offer the quality of education the students deserve. The authors believe that the development of a desirable school climate (or culture) combined with efficient methods to cope with disciplinary problems will result in student conduct consistent with the attainment of educational excellence.

Objectives for a Climate Conducive to Learning

The school faculty and the administration need to concur on an orderly conceptual climate for optimum student learning. This concept can be translated into specific objectives for the administration of student personnel. Because conditions and student needs differ, some variation in the climate will be evident for different schools; no one "ideal" can be universally applicable for all schools. In the following sections of this chapter we discuss what we believe to be some general characteristics of a climate that will assist the faculty and students in maintaining student discipline. All personnel of the school must be united in the effort to create a desirable climate.

Acceptance of Delayed Rewards. From the first grade through the senior year in high school, students must learn and accept the self-discipline of delayed gratification. The school's reinforcement of this concept is basic to a productive climate. As most mature adults know, the process of learning involves much expenditure of energy and time. In fact it can be painful, especially when students would rather be partying with their friends. Yet all of us must learn that in most instances gratification extracts a personal sacrifice, and that the reward for such sacrifice is seldom immediate. In their daily contact with students, teachers and school administrators should emphasize delayed rewards as a value.

A Caring Relationship. Students should perceive that the administration and faculty care about whether they learn and develop into productive citizens. A caring attitude is very motivating. Students are not fools;

they know whether the administration and the faculty are sincere. Through regular evaluation, the administration and faculty can gauge how well this concept is being realized.

Trust. The social climate for students should have trust as a foundation quality. Krajewski, Martin, and Walden correctly stated that "establishing trust is to be trustworthy."[1] The establishment of trust begins with students viewing the verbal and overt behavior of the administrative staff and faculty as trustworthy. Trust is a two-way street: If the faculty members expect students to trust them, they must express trust in students. Mutual trust is not an immediate response, but over a period of time it can be achieved. Students must learn, of course, that some behavior does not deserve the trust of the faculty, but trust must underlie the relationship of the faculty with the great majority of students. Some of the worst-disciplined schools are those in which trust is lacking, and the climate deteriorates into a "cat and mouse" game. In this game the school principal or faculty member playing it always loses, and ultimately so does everyone else.

High Expectations of Achievement. The prevailing norm among students should be to do their best at every school activity. Members of the faculty should have high expectations of themselves and of the students—if anything is worth doing, it is worth doing well. Most students will respond positively to challenge. A challenge for high achievement supported by quality teaching, parental support, and necessary resources is associated with educational excellence.

Assuming Personal Responsibility. Within the everyday conversations of society are truisms that relate to individual responsibility, one of which is, "You can take a horse to water but you can't make him drink." If the students do not assume personal responsibility for learning, most of our efforts to motivate them will be misdirected. Learning to assume personal responsibility for solving problems and for educational development is one of the great lessons of life. Learning this lesson is time consuming and often painful. Yet, if a callous attitude prevails among the faculty, such as "we're presenting the facts; it's up to you to learn them," one may expect a greater degree of failure for the school. The objective is to develop a climate in which students are accountable for their own educational development, not a teach-me-if-you-can climate.

Helping Students Meet Their Needs. Achieving adulthood is a problem-filled, challenging task that requires much help from parents or

---

[1]Robert J. Krajewski, John S. Martin, and John C. Walden, *The Elementary School Principalship* (New York: Holt, Rinehart, and Winston, 1983), p. 25.

guardians, teachers, and others. Humans have an unusually long dependency. Within their school experiences students encounter a wide range of problems about which administrators, teachers, coaches, guidance counselors, and other school personnel may be helpful. Key words in this helping relationship are listening, accessibility, empathy, caring, and referral. The resources of the professional counseling staff should be employed in the establishment of a helping relationship.

Personal Security. The feeling of personal safety is one of our most basic needs. Despite great efforts to quell its relentless growth, crime in and outside the schools continues to be intolerably high. Student fear of bodily harm creates great anxiety. If the school climate is one of fear for safety, the success of the instructional program is in doubt. Securing student safety is a problem in all communities, but is particularly acute in many inner-city schools. With their chained entrances (which are probably illegal), security checks at the doors, and hall monitors equipped with walkie-talkies, some high schools in high-crime areas appear to be more like prisons than educational institutions. Yet from the authors' experience these prisons are perceived by students as havens of refuge from the drug pushers, extortionists, rapists, and other ruffians out on the streets. In a well-monitored school the students can experience some feeling of safety because the streets on the way home produce the greatest anxiety.

Maintaining Discipline

As the daily logs in Chapter 17 indicate, the principals were frequently involved in solving disciplinary problems. Moreover, discipline usually leads the list of concerns that parents express about schools. Burns wrote that the existence of an inadequate school culture is the reason discipline remains a problem in many schools. He contended that schools with poor discipline were characterized by (1) lack of adequate teacher accountability for monitoring student behavior, (2) inconsistency in enforcement of school rules, (3) students uninformed about expected behavior, (4) teachers who perceive that the administration will not support them, and (5) timidity in dealing with hard-core discipline cases.[2]

Assuming that the administration and faculty of the school have been successful in establishing a healthy student climate approximating the one described in the previous section, one can be confident that maintaining acceptable discipline will be more easily accomplished. The student social system supportive of those climate norms will be a powerful influence in

[2]James A. Burns, "Discipline: Why Does It Continue to Be a Problem?" *NASSP Bulletin*, 69 (October 1985), 1–5.

the control of disruptive behavior. Yet, given the best possible school climate, a policy to deal with student misbehavior is necessary, and requires that the school faculty make public through a variety of means those behaviors expected of students. Even in the most democratic situations, rules of conduct are essential. Otherwise the situation may degenerate into one in which the rules are made to fit the situation—the worst possible exercise of arbitrary authority. The establishment of rules of conduct should be based on the participation of the faculty and student body. If students have a part in making the rules, they are more likely to buy into their observance and enforcement. Tanner emphasized that the school faculty should invest much energy in training students how to act.[3] Any behavior contrary to expectations constitutes misbehavior and is subject to some process of correction.

Traditional methods for correcting student behavior include (1) corporal punishment, (2) reprimands, (3) staying after school, (4) enforced duties, (5) suspension from school, (6) in-school suspension, and (7) expulsion from school. This list in no way exhausts the variety of correctional measures used in schools. Increased use of in-school suspension is used with some success, wherein the culprits are confined to a study room—out of communication with other students, a form of solitary confinement—to complete course assignments. The use of corporal punishment is a controversial corrective measure; regrettably, it is still practiced in those states and school districts in which it is legal and expected by a majority of parents in the community.

The corrective method used is probably secondary to the style and timing in which it is employed. If punishment is given in anger and without expressions of caring and counseling, even the most extreme punishment only breeds resentment and widespread problems of discipline. Kounin and Gump found that alternative techniques used by classroom teachers to control student behavior had different *ripple effects* on other students in the classroom,[4] consistent with the theory of social system discussed previously. When a student is disciplined, others are also affected. The ripple effect goes throughout the student body and affects the climate of the school. If the corrective measure is viewed as cruel and unfair, the act of disciplining one student is destructive to administrator and faculty relationships with all other students. Some of the worst-disciplined schools the authors have observed were headed by an aloof principal who felt a responsibility to use severe punishment. The school principal or assistant principal who is viewed as deliberative, fair, just, and compassionate—but

---

[3]Laurel N. Tanner, *Classroom Discipline* (New York: Holt, Rinehart, and Winston, 1978), p. 7.

[4]J. S. Kounin and P. V. Gump, "The Ripple Effect in Discipline," *Elementary School Journal,* 59 (December 1985), 3.

tough—is more successful than the vindictive or vicious chastiser in correcting misbehavior. Throughout each discussion of school discipline by the administration and faculty, one aspect should be to focus on the question, *What are we doing that might precipitate student misbehavior?*

The objective in student discipline is to correct misbehavior; the means used is primarily to focus the student's attention on the problem. All mature adults have learned the painful lesson that they are responsible for their own behavior. If we do not learn this lesson, we may go through life with the character disorder of blaming everyone in our circle of influence for our own shortcomings and making everyone around us miserable.

As discussed in Chapter 12, due process must be observed in such serious matters as expulsion from school. We believe that the spirit of due process should underlie all corrective measures, even in the use of those measures reserved for minor offenses. In all cases the object is to allow time for the counseling process to be used in helping the misbehaving student correct unacceptable behavior. The actual dread of punishment combined with the helping relationship should open up the communication necessary to accomplish this goal.

Educators are learning, however, that a school of quality cannot be achieved in the "blackboard jungles" that have been, in some instances, allowed to develop and exist. A reasonable amount of order and discipline is essential. Moreover, despite all of our efforts, some ruffians in every school cannot be taught self-control. Regrettably, some form of remunerative structure (usually by the name of alternative school) should exist to which these students can be assigned; otherwise we sacrifice the motivated students for those whose primary aim is to disrupt the school. Those who engage in criminal activity (drug pushers and extortionists) must be swiftly removed from the premises and prosecuted to the full extent of the law. Within recent years some of the blackboard jungles have used this approach and have been transformed into very productive schools.

COUNSELING AND GUIDANCE SERVICES

Maintaining a good student climate for learning is facilitated by a well-organized and administered program of guidance and counseling services. According to Myrick, school guidance activities are carried out with four approaches: (1) crisis intervention, (2) the remedial approach, (3) the problem preventive approach, and (4) the development approach. Crisis guidance is reacting to a critical behavior by a student in which the welfare of other students may be threatened, such as a physical fight, use of illegal drugs, or when a student threatens someone with a weapon. Remedial counseling involves helping students deal with certain deficiencies in their personal lives or in their studies. Preventive guidance includes anticipating and preventing problems, such as teen-age pregnancy, use of illegal drugs, and excessive absenteeism. The objective in developmental counseling is to develop the skills and attitudes that help students do well in school.[5]

Professional guidance counselors are needed for the coordination of guidance functions; however, members of the administrative staff and teachers serve a very important role in the guidance program. The classroom teacher is usually the initial contact of students for help in educational and personal problems. Numerous authors have expressed the opinion that good teaching is good guidance. The Teachers As Advisors Program (TAP), for example, is designed to coordinate the efforts of teachers in the total guidance program of the school.[6] The key to effective guidance is the establishment of a helping relationship.

The guidance process is carried out through a variety of techniques. Individual counseling plays a major role in the process. Small-group (ten students or fewer) counseling is also a significant part of the process. Group counseling has the advantage of helping students to work together and builds reinforcement networks to deal with personal problems. Not to be overlooked in the guidance process is the use of large groups. Much may be accomplished through student assemblies coordinated with classroom guidance. Even in the larger political system, leaders address problems by "jawboning" to influence the system, a technique that should never be overlooked as a means to influence the development of a better school learning climate. If the efforts of administrators and classroom teachers are coordinated with the objective to develop a better school climate, the combined power of persuasion will greatly influence student behavior.

Our concern with personal guidance tends to crowd out the importance of vocational guidance. The staff of the school should not let that happen. Students need help on this aspect of their lives; therefore, much energy should be expended in guidance activities to provide information to students about life after formal education.

EVALUATING AND REPORTING PUPIL PROGRESS

As discussed previously, continuous monitoring of pupil progress is a characteristic of the effective inner-city elementary schools not found in less effective schools. There is little reason not to assume that the same

[5]Robert D. Myrick, *Developmental Guidance and Counseling: A Practical Approach* (Minneapolis: Educational Media Association, 1988), pp. 11–16.

[6]Myrick, *Developmental Guidance*, p. 61.

may be found in studies of effective and low achieving middle, junior high, and senior high schools. Continuous evaluation of student progress includes (1) giving each student immediate feedback about the progress being made, (2) assisting the faculty in monitoring how well the instruction is progressing, and (3) providing a basis for reporting unusual conditions to parents before it is too late.

In those subjects in which immediate feedback is provided, the instructor seldom experiences a serious lack of student motivation. For example, in learning to type the student has immediate feedback. With each speed test, it is apparent how the skill is being acquired. In some academic subjects, this kind of feedback may take weeks and the result can be deadening. Everyone who invests much energy in an activity, whether in Algebra I or the 100-yard dash, is concerned with how much progress is being made, whether changes are necessary, or whether, in the long run, another pursuit is advised. Without continuous evaluation and feedback the system can lose much energy.

The collection of data is an essential step in the evaluation process. Some conventionally used techniques include standardized tests, teacher-made tests, commercial norm-referenced tests, observation, and so on. Standardized achievement tests are widely used and provide feedback useful to students, parents, and school personnel. But the limitations of standardized tests should be thoroughly understood by all persons using them. Norm-referenced tests may not be consistent with the objectives of the school in which they are used; moreover, what they are designed to measure is very limited in scope. If scores on standardized tests are overemphasized, classroom teaching will inevitably flow toward "teaching to the test," particularly if the results are used as a part of teacher evaluation. The system of evaluation should include a balance of norm-referenced tests, teacher-made tests, criterion-referenced tests, recorded observation of student behavior, and samples of student work. As discussed in Chapter 13, the computer can be of much assistance in accumulating, merging, and dispensing information about students that can be very useful to teachers, parents, and students in evaluating individual pupil progress.

Need for a Policy on Promotion

School policy is needed for the promotion and retention of students, and it should be cooperatively developed with the faculty. Many studies have shown that the threat of failure does not motivate and that nonpromotion does not usually result in better performance. On the other hand, the adoption of a continuous promotion policy may contribute to student perceptions of low academic expectations, which is counteractive to the establishment of a climate of high expectations of student performance.

Since numerous in-school, out-of-school, and personal conditions may contribute to failure in courses, the first step in the promotion or nonpromotion process should be to help each student remove conditions contributing to lack of success. The school assists by continuously monitoring student progress. Yet everything the faculty can do will not prevent the failure of some students to meet the expected standards of performance. An explicit policy must be developed and accepted by the faculty to guide in whether marginal students should be retained or promoted.

Given the right school climate, retention because of low performance may sometimes contribute to personal growth. Moreover, there has been a strong public reaction to "social promotion." The authors believe that the principal and faculty should be conscious of the specter of educational malpractice. The noted Peter Doe (fictitious name) case was in reality an educational malpractice action. Peter Doe received a high school diploma, but his parents learned later that he was functionally illiterate, even though he had received passing grades throughout all of his school experience, was of normal intelligence, attended school regularly, and was not a disciplinary problem. For many years leaders in school districts have complained about high school graduates that are functionally illiterate, producing a serious credibility gap for educators with the public. Educators were, for the most part, slow to respond to complaints of educational malpractice. Many state legislatures have responded with a variety of minimum-competency tests that must be passed to receive a high school diploma. It was by their inaction that educators lost control over the evaluation process.

A promotion policy is needed for the school district and for the individual schools. The policy should spell out explicitly the grounds for promotion and nonpromotion. It should not contain language consistent with the concept that promotion and eventual graduation from high school is a matter only of attending school with little or no reference to academic achievement. One of the duties of the school principal is to see that parents and students thoroughly understand the policy.

Reporting to Parents

Every conscientious parent has some anxiety concerning how well their children are doing in school, particularly during the early years of elementary school. The normal "pulling away from Mom" during the middle and secondary school years does not dampen parental concern; young people learn not to express their own anxiety so overtly. Administrators and teachers at all levels of schooling have heavy responsibilities to report pupil development to parents as succinctly as possible. The traditional report card with its A, B, C, D, and F symbols has been roundly criticized by professional educators for many years, and a variety of substitutes have been tried. Nevertheless, in most of the school districts, parents feel that they understand the traditional symbols, and so the traditional report card is a mainstay for reporting pupil progress. All of the tampering with traditional reporting, including the use of narrative statements, has not diminished parental expectations for letter grades.

Based on their extensive review of literature about the best means of reporting pupil progress, Kingston and Walsh reached the following generalizations: (1) report forms should not use marks in evaluation of attitudes and pupil conduct in content areas; (2) there is some support for the use of teacher comments of student strengths and weaknesses on report forms; (3) schools should use samples of the pupil's work supplemented by explanatory notes by the teacher; (4) report forms should not be too comprehensive in the range of behavior covered and reported on; (5) dual reporting is advantageous, in which two marks are given—a mark in terms of the group norm and an additional mark in terms of the child's own progress or growth; (6) informal letters, telephone calls, and parent-teacher conferences enhance the reporting system; and (7) a system that uses several techniques for reporting is superior to a system that relies on a single technique.[7]

Many schools, especially elementary schools, substitute a narrative description of pupil progress for the traditional letter-grade marks. Sometimes the letter grades are combined with narrative comments. The problem with exclusive use of narrative reporting is that teacher comments may fall into foolish or even irrational statements, such as a fifth-grade teacher's remark, "Johnny far exceeds his ability." Comments are also made that anger parents. If narrative comments are used, teachers should participate in much in-service preparation for their construction. Otherwise, the process tends to degenerate into meaningless platitudes or in statements that create bad home-school relations.

The best means of reporting pupil progress is the well-planned, skillfully conducted conference with parents and guardians. On the other hand, if these conferences are not well planned and administered, the parents will go away more confused than ever and probably with heightened anxiety. Much in-service planning time should go into planning for and conducting parent-teacher conferences. In preparation for each conference the teacher should compile a folder of information to share with the parents including such things as sample teacher-made tests, standardized achievement tests, written exercises, charts, recordings, and other material about the progress of the student. Planning, preparing, and organizing these materials into a coherent unity must precede the parent-

[7]Albert J. Kingston and James A. Walsh, "Research on Reporting Systems," *The National Elementary Principal*, 45 (May 1966), 36–39.

teacher conference. Especially important is the oral explanation of the kinds of instructional materials, tests, and instructional activities used with the student. For example, in explaining standardized test results, the teacher can make use of a test manual to explain how the test was constructed. A sample teacher-made test can be examined item by item to demonstrate the student's strengths and limitations. Parents should be encouraged to ask questions and otherwise enter into the conference.

Guidelines should be developed for conducting parent conferences. Teachers inexperienced in parent conferences should be given some dry runs by conducting trial conferences with experienced teachers, followed by critiques. The telephone should be used to follow up conferences and for initiating continuous contact with parents. Having telephones readily available to teachers for use in communicating with parents is a very good approach to linking the resources of the home and the school in the educational development of students.

As mentioned previously, before the student reaches senior high school, growth in independence becomes accelerated and shows a healthy maturing process. The regularly scheduled parent conferences, so useful in the elementary grades, may be more difficult to schedule and may even disappear from general practice in the secondary school. Nevertheless, informal contacts, telephone discussions, and the use of innovative ways to communicate with parents should be pursued during the teen years. The school should not use them as an excuse for not communicating with parents.

ATTENDANCE, STUDENT RECORDS, AND FOLLOW-UP SERVICES

School districts usually develop basic policies and procedures to deal with student attendance and the maintenance of student records. Within those guidelines, the principal is accountable for the maintenance of student records and regular attendance for the school center.

Admission of Students

As discussed subsequently, where compulsory attendance laws exist the school district must conduct a school census preparatory for the enrollment of pupils in elementary school for the first time. The principals at all schools must have projected enrollment data to prepare the school schedule for the coming year.

Since some parents are very anxious to enroll their child before the child reaches the age requirement, the elementary school principal must be concerned with the age qualification of children when enrolling them in kindergarten and first grade. The state statutes vary on the minimum age requirements for admission to the elementary school. All school principals must see that regulations and statutes concerning inoculations for contagious disease are enforced.

Intensive planning for the registration process is necessary. Nothing can be more frustrating than a tangled, disorganized, bungled registration followed by a defective schedule. The result is the loss of many days of instruction, not to speak of the devastation of faculty and student morale and of good school-public relations. Registration procedures are particularly pressing at the senior high school where a complicated schedule and large numbers of students and teachers are involved. The process of scheduling is discussed in Chapter 13. Although computers have greatly simplified the problem of registration, the computer can only be as successfully used as the data entered, or it becomes a garbage-in–garbage-out process. The principal must have very accurate student data and plans for registration available for the process of enrolling students in school.

Regular Attendance and Dropout Prevention

Several administrative tasks are involved in keeping regular attendance. The school system must conduct the school census to identify children of school age, particularly important for compliance with state compulsory attendance laws. But even in the absence of compulsory attendance provisions, these census data are needed for educational planning. Daily attendance reports must be prepared for the school center, including records of excused or inexcusable absence from school. The principal feels pressured to maintain high levels of attendance at the school, especially if state financial reimbursement is tied to attendance in the school district. Also, good attendance is believed to be associated with good administration. Every school must have a system for dealing with tardiness, the unauthorized leaving of school grounds, and other control measures in school attendance.

The dropout problem continues to be a crucial one for many schools, particularly in low socioeconomic areas of the school district. The problem contributes to many of the ills of society and causes those who withdraw before graduation from high school to be educationally disadvantaged. Dropping out is one of the contributing factors to functional illiteracy; it is most certainly a contributing factor to the inability of some persons to obtain and keep jobs, and may be a factor in the high incidence of crime. The school principal should lead the faculty in developing procedures to prevent dropouts.

In considering means to deal with attendance and dropout problems, we must return to the significance of a school climate conducive to educational development. If the school is an interesting, challenging, caring place that meets the needs of students, students will be motivated to attend regularly and to stay in school through graduation. As discussed in the section on discipline, however, even in the schools with the best climates, some students will be absent without valid reason, and others will arrive late to school. Inevitably, some will want to drop out of school; hence a system must be in place to deal with those cases.

The first step in dealing with truancy is to keep adequate records by using a system of accounting for unauthorized absences. Secondly, someone must continuously monitor attendance and attempt to identify potential dropouts. Finally, a procedure for encouraging regular attendance must be in place that involves finding the cause of absenteeism and doing something to remove the problem. Since these are complicated and time-consuming procedures, someone must be placed in charge of attendance and dropout prevention to address the many variables involved in irregular attendance and to impede, and prevent when possible, the decisions of students to quit school.

The key to controlling dropouts and irregular attendance is the establishment of oversight procedures, based on knowledge concerning which students are most at risk of dropping out of school. Most potential dropouts are not under the effective control of their parents. Most parents of students who quit school are not involved with their children's education, and many of them may even have a resentful sour grapes attitude toward the value of education. Children from low socioeconomic homes are much more likely to quit school than are children from middle and upper socioeconomic families. Students at risk of quitting school usually demonstrate irregular attendance, which is usually the first indication that the decision to quit school may be impending. Substandard achievement and frequent disciplinary problems may also be indications of students at risk of dropping out.

Educators have pointed to the expectations of the middle class as being very different from those of children from lower socioeconomic homes. However, the authors believe that much writing in this area is based upon speculation. There are simply too many variables involved to make sweeping generalizations. For example, children who do not progress well in their studies and who seldom experience success will find many excuses for not attending school. If the parents of such children are not personally involved in their children's education, irregular attendance followed by the decision to quit school may not be far away. Personal conflicts within the school contribute to irregular attendance, low achievement, and finally the decision to drop out. Each case must be dealt with individually and conscientious effort should be made to help the student correct the problems contributing to the decision to withdraw from school. Well-organized and administered oversight procedures to control irregular attendance and prevent dropouts should be accompanied by remedial intervention processes. Attempts should be made to help parents become more involved in their children's educational progress; programs should be in place to help students correct achievement deficiencies; and guidance and counseling processes should be available to help students adapt to the school setting.

The increased incidence of divorced parents has accompanied unauthorized "parentnapping" of children from school; consequently, the school must maintain strict procedures for the removal of students from the school. As a part of this control process, the classroom teacher must be kept informed about the possibility that a student might be taken from the school without authorization.

Maintaining Student Records

Keeping permanent student records is another time-consuming task for which the principal is accountable. Fortunately, the use of computers has replaced the manual process of recording and storing cumulative records, eliminated the need for filing space, facilitated the retrieval of individual student records, and reduced the laborious process of handwritten records.

The use of computers has also brought new administrative concerns about unauthorized access to student records by hackers. Englade warned about the problem and about the responsibility of administrators to adopt procedures to prevent computer piracy.[8] Students who are enamored by the computer and who view unauthorized entry into systems as a personal challenge may not realize the seriousness of the situation. Unauthorized entry to school records is a crime, and students should be warned about the seriousness of such behavior.

As discussed in Chapter 12, the confidentiality and accuracy of student records must be maintained. The Family Education Rights to Privacy Act, the so-called Buckley Amendment, restricts the accessibility of student records and provides for the removal of inaccuracies from them.

Follow-Up Services

Based on the observation of the authors, few schools maintain adequate follow-up records and services. Most follow-up records of senior high schools revolve around how many graduates attend college and college reports about the performance of graduates. But what about the many high school graduates who do not go to college? What services does the school provide for students beyond graduation? What are the follow-up programs of elementary schools? Of middle and junior high schools? Without follow-

[8]Ken Englade, "Here's How You Can Be Safe Instead of Sorry about School Computer Crime," *The American School Board Journal* (July 1984), pp. 26–28.

up interests in the elementary, middle, and junior high schools, a serious articulation problem often exists. The principal of an elementary school, for example, should interview a sample of former students about their first year in middle or junior high school to identify ways in which the elementary school can better assist in this transition. Likewise, the middle and junior high schools should regularly collect follow-up data about former students.

The need for follow-up services is very critical in the senior high school. Someone on the high school staff should be assigned responsibility for these services. Most of the complaints offered for not having first-class follow-up studies and services involve lack of financial resources, an unfounded excuse. Somehow schools find a way to fund other programs, some of which we believe have lower priority than follow-up services.

A good follow-up program results in the collection of data about graduates that are essential in the development of the instructional program. What occupations are entered by the graduates? What suggestions do the graduates have for the instructional program? What are the five- and ten-year graduates doing? How do they feel about their elementary, middle, and high school programs?

The senior high school should maintain a placement service for graduates, and it should not be limited to helping graduates enter college. Graduates need many job-hunting, college-locating, and personal services that many high schools may not be providing. Those entering the job market after graduation need assistance in locating gainful employment and in changing jobs.

ORGANIZING STUDENTS FOR INSTRUCTION

The board of education makes decisions concerning the organization of school centers. The principal and faculty of these centers, consistent with school board policy, group students for instruction. The grouping of students for instruction is an area marked by much controversy.

Organization of School Centers

Traditionally, the school centers were organized into the 8-4 plan of instruction, consisting of 8 years of elementary school and 4 years of high school. By the 1950s the 6-3-3 (or K6-3-3) plan had become predominant, especially in school districts experiencing large increases in enrollment. In the 1960s the middle school concept began to grow in popularity, resulting in several variations such as 5-3-4 and 4-4-4. However, numerous combinations are now found among school districts, such as 6-3-3, 6-2-4, 8-4, 5-3-4, 7-5, 6-6, and 4-4-4. Why are so many configurations found? In too many instances the answer is determined by economics, which means choosing the most economical plan for housing students. For example, one very economical answer to the traditional 8-4 plan was to build a new senior high school and turn the old high school building into a junior high school. If the district continued rapid population growth, the pattern was repeated. The action was consistent with the views of educators interested in extending the high school experience downward. For some school districts the enrollment pressures on the 6-3-3 arrangement could best be met by reducing the size of the elementary school and utilizing the excess capacity at the senior high school—the 5-3-4 plan. Middle school plans were readily supported by educators who were discontented with the evolution of the junior high school into a "little brother" of the senior high school.

External pressures have influenced many decisions concerning school centers. Desegregation plans have been implemented, such as pairing, clustering, and magnet schools, to facilitate racial integration in the schools. The alternative school movement has grown in popularity, and much interest has been demonstrated in freedom-of-choice plans. As a consequence of these movements, many school districts have all but abandoned the concept of the neighborhood school. These changes may complicate the principal's task of communicating with parents.

Classification and Grouping of Students

Almost every conceivable means of grouping students for instruction has been proposed and tried. Student classification has been a source of much controversy among educators. One encounters arguments for and against ability grouping, age grouping, heterogeneous grouping, team teaching, self-contained classroom, departmentalization, interest grouping, needs grouping, graded school, nongraded school, and so on. The need for some plan for grouping is obvious. The principal and faculty must divide instructional responsibility for the 720, 1500, or 3500 students that are enrolled in the elementary, junior high, middle, or senior high school. The problem is complicated by the fact that students have a great range of backgrounds, interests, capacities, motivation, and growth patterns. Grouping by achievement alone will result in great differences in interests, social backgrounds, motivation, and so on.

Unfortunately, in many schools the grouping used is based more on administrative convenience than on the placement of students where they will best achieve. For example, the graded school using chronological age as the primary criterion for placement is a lock-step organization that can be very inflexible for the different learning rates of students. Likewise, ability grouping can sentence some students to a life of underachievement. For example, the students of one junior high school were grouped by ability.

One of the students in one of the lower ability groups consistently performed above the group in which he was placed. When his beginning teacher announced this good news and requested that the student be moved to a higher ability group, the head of the department objected vehemently and asserted, "You ought to know that those 'Z' students cannot compete with the students in the higher I.Q. group." The principal also vetoed the idea. The student was defrauded of the right to be challenged to excel because of an implanted administrative convenience.

If, as we have emphasized, the school monitors student progress continuously, and this is a factor in placement, the grouping procedure of the school should be flexible. The goal is to group students where they can best achieve. The authors believe that the school should epitomize system openness in the grouping of students. The reader will recall from the discussion in Chapters 3 and 4 that entropy is arrested in the open system. Therefore, the authors strongly endorse flexibility in the grouping of students.

The principal and faculty should always remember that they did not select the students, and the students had little to do with selecting them. The faculty should not further complicate this relationship by the adoption of grouping schemes that result in unsatisfactory adaptations of large numbers of students to an inflexible social climate. The primary consideration must be a grouping policy that best facilitates the intellectual development of students.

Most elementary schools, particularly at the primary level, use the self-contained classroom arrangement that calls for one teacher to teach or guide the learning activities of all pupils in all subjects. However, the departmental organization predominates in the middle, junior high, and senior high schools.

The principal is accountable for managing whatever instructional grouping plan is adopted by the school or school system and for developing an accurate and functional school schedule. The scheduling process is discussed in Chapter 13.

Exceptional Education Programs

Students may be considered exceptional for a variety of conditions; however, the term exceptional means that their physical, social, emotional, or intellectual strengths and limitations lie outside what society believes is in the normal range. Schools were concerned traditionally with the exceptionally gifted and the exceptionally mentally retarded children, because the placement of both extremes within what was believed to be "normal" instructional groups made teaching more difficult. Within the last three decades there has been strong political pressure to declare a wide variety of educational exceptionalities, including the physically disabled, educationally mentally retarded, the gifted, the emotionally disturbed, visually handicapped, speech impaired, hearing impaired, and others. The clamor to have the public schools provide special programs for the variety of exceptionalities resulted in passage by the Congress of Public Law 94-142 in 1975. Often referred to as the "civil rights act" for handicapped students, the law has had much influence upon the management of schools.

Public Law 94-142 provided that handicapped children (1) be provided with free and appropriate education, (2) be given the right to due process and equal protection, and (3) be grouped for instruction with nonhandicapped students to the extent possible (the mainstreaming provision). Needless to say, all school principals realize the challenge involved in the identification, evaluation, and assignment of these students. Yet the authors are just as concerned that all "normal" children be given the same intensive evaluation and placement services.

We believe that the spirit of identification, evaluation, and placement of students usually present in exceptional educational programs should epitomize the processes in the assignment of all students to instructional groups. Yes, let all educators declare a civil rights act for each and every student enrolled in the school. The intensive evaluation and instructional processes in the area of special education for the handicapped are good educational processes for every student. The educational guidance and counseling program participated in by each member of the administrative staff and faculty should be dedicated to this proposition. Through continuous evaluation and flexibility in the placement of students, much can be gained toward achieving a school of quality and equality.

ADMINISTERING STUDENT ACTIVITY PROGRAMS

Citizens have disagreed for decades about the need for extracurricular (or cocurricular) activities. Attending school can be a rather dull, stark experience without a well-planned program of student activities. Marano pointed to the need for an activities program to (1) help students learn how to assume leadership roles, (2) provide experience in self-government, (3) give recognition to individuals and groups, and (4) provide physical and social recreation.[9]

Unfortunately, when student activities are mentioned most citizens immediately think of the senior high school activity program and its emphasis upon competitive sports, clubs, dramatics, and social events. Yet the better administered elementary schools also have programs rich in student activities. Obviously, the nature of student activities offered among elementary, middle, and senior high schools is different. However,

[9]Rocco Marano, "Student Activities," *NASSP Bulletin*, 69 (October 1985), 1–2.

elementary schools may offer experience in student council activity, camping and outdoor activities, recreation and intramural sports, music, dramatics, publications, and service activities. Children also benefit from art, dramatic activities, musical activities, and other cocurricular programs.

Many elementary and middle schools make extensive use of camping and outdoor activities, experiences that encourage nature study, crafts, and safety education. Pupil activities also provide an opportunity to learn concepts about conservation, cooperation, and leadership, and permit faculty and students to interact at a level rarely attained in the formal atmosphere of the classroom.

The authors certainly agree with those who condemn highly competitive sports for very young children in elementary school, an activity that has been found to be injurious physically and emotionally for young children and has been widely condemned in much of the media. To force very young children into contact sports activities is the height of absurdity and irresponsibility, although sports and play activities should be sponsored within reason.

By the time students enter the middle or junior high school, activity programs become more extensive and may include more competitive sports. Yet, the urge to emulate the senior high school should be resisted by the administration and faculty. For the most part, sports activities should remain on an intramural basis. Unfortunately, the students of junior high schools have the desire to emulate students in high schools just as the senior high students want to emulate college and university students. Consequently, the school administration and faculty are pressured by parents and students to include activities that should be rejected. For example, senior high students frequently demand the inclusion of social fraternal organizations, and their parents use pressure to have them included among the activities offered. Even though the school officially rejects such requests, they may be carried out on an informal basis in the homes and communities served by the school.

An overemphasis upon student activities, particularly in competitive sports, sometimes develops in the senior high school. Somewhat troublesome are those schools in which the band and sports boosters organizations gain much community influence and power and are able to make demands on the school, such as the appointment of a certain person as coach. Situations like this have led to great faculty and community divisions, which can cause serious personnel problems in a school. The payment of supplements to coaches but not to sponsors of other student activities has always been an issue and is usually an important part of the collective bargaining process. The authors believe that these issues become greatly increased as an overemphasis on interscholastic sports occurs.

Even in those schools having reasonable activity programs, the principals have to appoint a person to administer the student activity program. The development of a calendar or schedule of events becomes very complex; moreover, the overall supervision of activities requires that someone be accountable for coordinating the program.

Beginning in the 1980s, many educators and public leaders became concerned that high schools and colleges were overemphasizing sports programs and that student athletes were being exploited; hence Rule 48 was passed by the NCAA in an attempt to correct the situation. The rule placed restrictions upon colleges to prevent them from recruiting athletes who could not achieve a minimum score on an entrance examination. In addition, several states passed no-pass–no-play statutes in an attempt to correct the overemphasis upon sports.

We began this discussion by embracing student activities; however, we are patently opposed to the instances when interscholastic sports take priority over academic subjects. That imbalance shows irresponsibility on the part of everyone connected with the administration of educational programs. The reader will recall our emphasis in a previous chapter upon keeping the real, educational goals as the basis of operation. Those situations in which wild, irresponsible emphasis upon sports have occurred are illustrative of goal displacement, and in such schools the principal and faculty have lost sight of the purposes for which the school was organized.

CHAPTER SIXTEEN

Operation of School Plant Facilities

The influence of school plant facilities upon the human system is often overlooked by school administrators. Unfortunately, some of the ancient ideas of stoicism that favored learning to bear physical pain and grief underlie the traditional belief that too much physical comfort may not motivate students to learn. Yet according to Castaldi, evidence indicates that the opposite is true; the provision of attractive, comfortable, and functional school plant facilities facilitates the learning process.[1]

Anyone visiting schools has experienced the overheated, stuffy classrooms that produce drowsiness, which is not conducive to learning. School facilities may even be hazardous to the health and safety of students. One of the tasks of school administrators is to oversee the development of optimum environmental conditions for the instructional process and for the health and safety of students and staff. Regular surveillance of the school plant facilities by the school principal is required.

[1]Basil Castaldi, *Educational Facilities: Planning, Modernization, and Management*, 3rd ed. (Boston: Allyn & Bacon, 1987), p. 231.

THE INTERFACE OF THE HUMAN
AND PHYSICAL SYSTEMS

Research about the interaction of persons with the physical environment inside buildings has revealed some valuable lessons for educational leaders. Consider, for example, the influence of color upon emotions. Those conducting research on the effects of color on humans have found that when persons were placed in a room decorated in red, there was an increase in blood pressure, respiration rate, heartbeat, blinks, and other evidence of a change in mood. On the other hand, a room decorated in blue precipitated a calming influence and feelings of serenity. Green produced different moods, a calming effect on some and a disquieting influence on others. The authorities are divided on the influence of green; consequently, in her article about the influence of color, Kane referred to green as a masquerader.[2] Some authorities, however, contend that different shades of green provide the soothing effect of a forest.

The nature and arrangement of furniture can become symbols of differences in leadership and power. A principal's office that is large, well-furnished, and somewhat inaccessible to the traffic flow is a symbol of power and influence. According to Korda, the arrangement of furniture in the office may also symbolize power. The most powerful symbol is to locate the desk in front of a window, somewhat forward in the office, so that the visitor is separated from the principal by the desk.[3] If the principal thirsts for power *over* rather than power *with* the faculty and staff, the desk, chair, and other furniture should be larger and more ornate than that in any other office in the building. If power *with* the faculty is desired, the symbols of power should be avoided. The furniture should be arranged to minimize the distance between the principal and visitors to the office.

Evidence presented by Bowers and Burkett suggests that a relationship may exist between student behavior and school buildings having different age of construction. They found that the old school in their sample was characterized by lower student achievement, more incidences of illness, and more discipline problems.[4] An important consideration in this study, however, was that no conscious effort had been made to refurbish, modernize, replace outdated furniture, or color coordinate the rooms in the

[2]Leslie Kane, "The Power of Color," *Health*, 14 (July 1982), 35.

[3]Michael Korda, *Power: How to Get It and How to Use It* (New York: Ballantine Books, 1975), pp. 232–33.

[4]J. Howard Bowers and Charles W. Burkett, "Relationship of Student Achievement and Characteristics in Two Selected School Facility Environmental Settings" (paper presented at the 64th Council of Educational Facility Planners, International Conference in Edmonton, Alberta, Canada, October 1987).

older building, suggesting that the problem may not be the age of the building but the diligence of the administration to maintain and modernize the old facility.

To summarize, the condition, maintenance, and design of school plant facilities influence the human system. The attitudes of teachers, students, and parents are influenced by a school building with aged paint peeling off the ceiling and walls, unsanitary toilets, unkempt floors, leaking roofs, and outdated furniture that is much in need of repair. Such a building can effect a demoralizing atmosphere where an educational leader is attempting to develop the climate necessary for a school of quality. The immediate signal is that this is a school in which the administration, the faculty, and perhaps the community do not care. Unsanitary conditions cause the spread of disease and illness, depriving students of many days of instruction, and substitute teachers must be called frequently to replace regular teachers who are ill. Those days are all but lost to productive instructional activity. One might also expect that such an unkempt school facility would have numerous hazards to the safety of students and faculty.

PHYSICAL APPEARANCE AND SAFETY

The school plant facilities and grounds must be properly maintained and physically attractive. In large school systems the central office staff may be accountable for the maintenance of the site and facilities. However, this does not absolve the principal of accountability and leadership with the central staff in seeing that the facilities are properly maintained, attractively decorated, and functional. For example, the principal, or person on the school staff so designated, must regularly survey the school plant and work with the central office personnel in the maintenance process. The administrative staff and faculty must be always alert to any conditions that might be hazardous to the safety of pupils. Castaldi wrote that "The school principal is the key person in the school district responsible for the operation and maintenance of the school building to which he [or she] is assigned."[5] He stated that the principal is functionally responsible even though many of the services may be under the administration of the central office.

In the large comprehensive high school or middle school, the responsibility for preventing conditions that can contribute to injury is very complex. For example, in the senior high school hazardous conditions in the shops are of special concern. Science laboratories must be well supervised and kept in first-rate repair. All chemicals should be kept in safe

[5]Castaldi, *Educational Facilities*, p. 363.

containers under lock and key. Teachers, especially those who are not qualified to teach science but who sometimes substitute in this area, should be instructed in safety measures. The condition of athletic facilities and grounds must be surveyed regularly and maintained to be free of safety hazards. Since most educators are not specialists in safety, someone expert in the field should be consulted to review the facility and assist in the development of a checklist for regular review. Safety specialists will note problems that might be overlooked by school administrators and teachers. For example, the average observer may not consider the importance of seeing that all electrical machines are grounded.

In the elementary school, the principal is accountable for offering greater supervision of student activities. As discussed in Chapter 12, elementary school pupils cannot be expected to exercise the care that one might expect of older students or adults. The condition, location, and use of play equipment are of great concern. The equipment should be regularly inspected for safety and repaired or replaced when necessary. If play equipment is improperly located, such as in lines of heavy traffic, negligence may be a factor in case of injury.

The states require school administrators to hold fire drills. Because there is always the possibility of fire, they should be held on a regular basis and closely supervised by teachers and administrators. The practice drills should be evaluated for purposes of improvement. The school plant facilities should be surveyed for fire hazards. The storage of chemicals and cleaning supplies present a special concern. Storage areas should be inspected regularly for the possibility of spontaneous development of fire.

OPERATION OF THE SCHOOL FACILITIES

Some of the several tasks in the operation of school plant facilities include (1) maintaining an optimum thermal environment for the educational processes, (2) maintaining the attractiveness of the plant and grounds, and (3) custodial services. Even though some or all of these services may be administered on a district-wide basis, the school principal is responsible for seeing that the work is performed satisfactorily.

A Thermal Environment to Facilitate Achievement

Several things are to be monitored in maintaining an optimum thermal environment to maximize learning conditions in the school. For most classrooms a constant temperature should be maintained between 70 and 75 degrees Fahrenheit. In older schools having original heating equipment, maintaining optimum temperature will be difficult.

One must consider humidity in relation to temperature in attempting to maintain an optimum thermal environment. The humidity of the room may vary with the temperature. Some authorities suggest that humidity should be kept around 50 percent in the classroom, ±10 percent. The temperature may have to be lowered or raised for comfort if the humidity is not within a desirable range. However, maintaining desirable humidity involves more than comfort. Inadequate humidity control leads to health problems, including more colds and other communicable diseases. Extremely low humidity may lead to dryness and cracking of the nasal passages, precipitating serious nosebleeds and other complications, not to speak of the discomfort involved.

If the school is not equipped with air conditioning, ventilation of the classrooms is essential. Improperly ventilated rooms produce stale and odor-ridden classrooms, which are not conducive to maximum productivity and may constitute a health hazard as well. If the school is equipped with modern thermal equipment, control of temperature, ventilation, and humidity is simplified.

Authorities contend that optimum thermal conditions cannot be maintained unless automatically controlled heating, ventilation, and humidifier equipment is installed. They point to the fact that the human organism is not sensitive enough to undesirable variations in thermal conditions to maintain optimum physical conditions. For example, the students and teachers in an overly heated and stuffy classroom may be completely unaware of the condition because the human organism is not immediately conscious of gradually changing conditions. School authorities should work with the board of education and other leaders in the community for the installation of modern equipment to maintain optimum year-round physical conditions. Many school districts are providing year-round air conditioning, which will become even more necessary if the school year is lengthened or year-round operation of the schools becomes a reality.

Adequate illumination must be maintained in classrooms and other instructional facilities. Unfortunately, a large number of schools were built during the 1950s and 1960s according to architectural fads rather than for adequate illumination and the maintenance of an optimum thermal environment, best illustrated by the "glass houses" that were built in many school districts following World War II. Large amounts of glass create problems of air currents, temperature control, lighting glare, and other problems related to the control of thermal conditions. Drapes and blinds have been used in these buildings in attempts to correct the situation; however, the control of illumination is extremely complicated because of changing sunlight during the day.

If the principal is assigned to an old building that has not been refurbished, the artificial lighting present may be inadequate. A light meter should be used to check the system. Authorities differ concerning the foot-candles needed. Some contend that 50 foot-candles are an absolute minimum, whereas 70 foot-candles are recommended by other authorities. Uncontrolled natural lighting can become a problem because of too much window space. Too much illumination may be present in areas near the windows. As mentioned previously, changing natural conditions, such as clouded conditions mixed with bright sunlight, greatly complicate the control of illumination of rooms unless window covering is employed. Some lighting engineers contend that optimal illumination can be provided only by the elimination of all natural light in the building. However, the fuel shortage during the 1970s, coupled with high rising costs, resulted in a return to buildings that could be ventilated.

The principal should assist the faculty in the control of lighting conditions in the classroom and provide resource help and equipment necessary for control of illumination through the use of draperies, blinds, and replacement of additional artificial lighting equipment. Otherwise, years may pass before inadequate lighting conditions are brought to the attention of the board of education.

Numerous other problems are associated with providing a satisfactory classroom environment for learning. Acoustical treatment has been necessary for the classrooms of some schools. Often the speech intelligibility of instructional areas can be improved with inexpensive equipment and the installation of carpeting. Outside and inside sources of excessive noise may be a problem. In some schools the bandroom or shop areas may be located too close to other instructional areas.

Acoustical treatment can solve many noise problems. Color is a factor that must be considered in providing an optimum physical environment for instruction. If the furniture and equipment in older buildings have never been replaced, the principal should seek the assistance of the central administrative staff and board of education in completely replacing the furniture and possibly refurbishing the entire school plant.

Maintenance and Attractiveness

Every effort should be made to provide an attractive school and instructional area. As discussed previously, care should be given to selecting colors that are not disquieting to teachers and students. Some of the older schools were painted in a very dull color that did not contribute a comfortable warmth or aesthetic quality. If the school has not been redecorated for some time, the newly appointed principal should attempt to have the building redecorated before the beginning of school. Redecorating could do much to signal the beginning of a new and more productive era.

Teachers should be encouraged to maintain attractive classrooms. A tangled, disheveled room can produce negative influences on the attitudes, expectations, and behavior of pupils. Through the cooperation of pupils, teachers, and other staff, the principal can be very successful in maintaining the attractiveness of the school plant facilities. The cooperation of all can be realized by discussion and persuasion: "Now that we have a beautiful building and school grounds, let's all pitch in and keep it that way." The key is to remove any smear, damage, or mark when it occurs before negative encouragement takes hold. For example, the custodians should never leave any graffiti found on the toilet walls—immediate removal is essential.

Areas needing the attention of maintenance personnel should be noted and reported. Someone should be responsible for following up reports of maintenance needs to be sure that repairs are made without fail; otherwise, conditions may exist for months before corrections are made.

Custodial Services

Adequate housekeeping processes provide for the health and safety of occupants, help provide an optimum climate for instruction, and preserve the condition of the buildings. School facilities must be kept sparkling clean. When the faculty, students, and other citizens of the community walk into a facility that is exceptionally clean, the result is a lift to their spirits. The reason this is not true of all schools is because the custodial services are not well organized and supervised, inadequate financial support is available, and the custodians may not receive training to perform the required services.

The principal should not assume that the custodians know how to clean. Without training, some custodial personnel would rather use deodorants in the toilets in an attempt to cover up one bad odor with another obnoxious odor. Smelly toilets filled with deodorants in an attempt to cover up uncleanliness is unacceptable. By using proper cleaning practices, deodorants will be neither necessary nor desirable.

School floors may be ruined by improper cleaning and waxing agents. Specialists in housekeeping practices are located in state departments of education and some colleges and universities. Training programs should be provided for custodians, and someone should be assigned the responsibility for overseeing the process in the school.

The organization and supervision of well-trained custodians are essential to keep the school plant facilities and grounds in good condition. Standards must be set and maintained. The custodial staff must know for what and to whom they are responsible. Through study and analysis of the areas to be cleaned and normal expectations in an eight-hour day, the principal can divide labor and fix responsibility among the custodial staff.

According to Finchum, there are numerous variables to be considered in determining the personnel needs for custodial services.[6] The size, condition, and stage of development of the school site are important factors. Another consideration is the age, type of construction, design, size, location, and mechanical system of the school building or buildings. Whether automatic cleaning equipment can be used or is used will affect the number of personnel required. General climate conditions also influence the custodial services needed.

There are too many variable conditions among school plant facilities to arrive at a simple formula for the allocation of custodial personnel. Some authorities suggest that the work load for custodial personnel be established through the use of time-and-motion studies. Other writers have suggested a rule-of-thumb estimate of about one custodian for eight teachers; however, Castaldi suggests that too many different conditions may exist among different schools for a simple answer.[7] A few of the conditions that influence a decision are whether it is an old or a new school, amount of use, size of site, condition of the building, area of the building, and so on. Through adequate supervision and cooperative planning with the custodial staff, reasonable estimates can be made concerning the size requirement of the staff.

Not to be overlooked in this discussion is the great contribution that custodians make to the educational process through their interaction with students and staff. They should be selected on the basis of their ability to relate to and enhance a positive attitude toward the school as well as their ability to maintain the buildings and grounds. Custodians are motivated by the same forces and conditions that motivate all other members of the school staff. They are to be respected and held in high esteem for the contributions they make. If the students and faculty show disrespect by deliberately making extra work for them (such as by leaving paper indiscriminately about the school or throwing chewing gum on the floor), low morale will be created among the custodial staff. Yet if the custodians are respected as members of the total staff of the school, they will make a very valuable contribution to the educational process.

THE ADMINISTRATIVE OFFICES

The administrative suite of a modern high school houses numerous facilities to serve the students and faculty. Among these in the typical high school are the principal's office, assistant principals' offices, reception area,

---

[6] R. N. Finchum, *School Plant Management: Administering the Custodial Program,* U.S. Department of Health, Education, and Welfare, Office of Education, Bulletin 1961, No. 4 (Washington, D.C., 1961).

[7] Castaldi, *Educational Facilities*, p. 399.

guidance and counseling offices, teachers' workroom, deans' offices, conference rooms, office for the activities director, secretarial work spaces, vault, clinic, and storage areas. The administrative suite for an elementary school is usually smaller and may not include offices for deans and activities directors. Well-organized administrative offices provide the initial entry into a well-served school. The principal's office will likely be the first contact for parents and other citizens visiting the school. As discussed in Chapter 6, the principal's office must express courtesy and helpfulness in all telephone conversations and with all visitors to the school.

The administrative suite should more properly be perceived as the leadership unit or service suite; it should be accessible to the faculty and other members of the staff, and it should function as a leadership and coordination center for the improvement of instruction and for service to faculty and students. Members of the faculty and staff should be involved in the use and arrangement of the administrative suite. Cooperative studies should be conducted by faculty committees to examine the flow of activity in relation to the arrangement of the office, noise, adequacy of communication, location of facilities and equipment, adequacy of equipment, and other conditions in the leadership area.

Furnishing and Appearance of the Office

Some school principals resist providing well-furnished administrative suites because they fear public criticism. Traditionally, school offices have been very austere in appearance. Yet visitors to the school may judge the quality of the school by the general appearance, cleanliness, and furnishings in the offices.

If a newcomer to a town is selecting a dentist, physician, or lawyer, the extent to which an office indicates success in a given profession can be influential. A dingy, dirty, impoverished appearance would not be a symbol of success. To the businessperson, an impoverished principal's office will probably send a message of undesirable business standards. Therefore, the furnishings and decoration of the administrative suite should be equal to the better-equipped offices in the district. This is not to say that the furnishings should be exceptionally ornate, because that would and should lead to public criticism.

Providing an attractive, comfortable leadership area facilitates the development of an instructional program of quality. For example, an attractive office facilitates teacher conferences, meetings with students and parents, and discussions with leaders in the community. A pleasant conference room helps to make teacher planning enjoyable, as opposed to the dreary feeling one gets from an ill-equipped, unattractive, noisy meeting area.

The furnishings and appearance of office areas in older schools may need improvement. Even in newer schools, the planners may not have directed attention to the arrangement and appearance of the office suite. In many instances offices have very poor color schemes and lack such accessories as drapes and curtains. Refurbishment, with the addition of draperies, carpeting, replacement and rearrangement of furniture, and improved illumination can work miracles in an otherwise very drab office area. Attractive, comfortable furniture and chairs should be provided and are relatively inexpensive in comparison to the instructional costs of educating students.

CHAPTER SEVENTEEN

Days in the Life
of Principals

This chapter is devoted to giving the reader an idea of what a day in the life of a principal is really like and providing some simulations for decision making. We give actual accounts of activities in elementary, middle, and secondary schools. The schools are located in communities ranging from rural to inner-city. The situations presented in this chapter are real accounts recorded by principals, with fictitious names used to protect their anonymity and that of their schools.

Too often, students of school administration complain, "It is all right to talk about how to be a principal, but how can we know about the real world of the principal?" The contents of this chapter are intended for students to read and discuss how it *is* in the real world of being a principal. Each of the school principals agreed to keep a daily log of their activities and to write vignettes of unique problem situations they have faced.

Since the schools involved are located in socioeconomic settings ranging from very low to very high and from rural to inner-city, no attempt will be made to explain thoroughly the school settings. Students will have to extrapolate from their own experiences and try to imagine the school settings from the information that is presented.

The first part of the chapter gives the principals' accounts of activities and situations recorded by them. Students may make analyses, and in some instances, decisions about the events. We suggest that the class form study groups to analyze the logs of activities.

PRINCIPAL A

Principal A is principal of Elmwood Elementary School in a city with a population of 45,000 located in the Appalachian area of the Southeastern United States. Elmwood is a Chapter 1 school serving the lowest socioeconomic section of the city. The building was constructed of brick in the 1940s; therefore, it is relatively old but clean and spacious with a large gymnasium. The enrollment is approximately 400 students in grades K–6 at any one time. The population fluctuates since there is a great deal of mobility of families in the community.

The school system is perceived by educators to be relatively progressive, and open to change and improvement. The central office regime welcomes innovation if the ideas are supported by thoughtful rationale. Principals are free to express disagreement in a constructive manner.

The financial base is average in the region for a system of this size, yet the financial support exceeds that of most school systems in the immediate area. Teachers' salaries are not the highest in the area, but higher than in many other school systems.

The faculty and staff consist of 18 regular classroom teachers, 1 physical education teacher, a part-time nurse, 1 secretary, and 7 teachers' aids. Special-education students are all housed in another elementary school in the system. The district does not provide an assistant principal, counselor, or other staff.

Principal A is a white middle-aged male. He is a long-time resident of the area and formerly a very respected band leader at the only high school in the system. He is known as a very hard-working principal who spends long hours at school before and after school. He has a very deep concern for the well being of students and teachers, and is committed to quality education. He has served as principal of Elmwood Elementary School for 8 years. What follows is an actual account of Principal A's activities in this school on two selected days.

Tuesday

7:00 Arrived at school early. It is Election Day, and the school is a voting place for this community.

7:00 Checked on students who arrived early. (Parents who go to work early leave their children at school. There is no one here when they arrive but the custodian. They are allowed to sit in the auditorium if they have a special permit that relieves the school of responsibility.)

7:10 Checked the voting area to ascertain that it was ready.

7:20 Consulted with the custodian to see that all was in good order. Discovered that there were not enough tables as previously used since they are now being used by the students in the writing-to-read program. Helped the custodian set up makeshift tables for the election commission officers.

7:30 Supervised buses unloading.

8:00 School day began.

8:05 Morning announcements, moment of silence, and flag salute.

8:10 Spoke with a student who was on in-school suspension concerning the arrival of her parents to discuss plans for improvement. The student had been caught stealing from a teacher assistant's desk. The offense was serious enough to ask for a parent conference. The student will be on in-school suspension until the parent arrives for the conference.

8:30 Met with the second-grade faculty members to discuss items that are appropriate to the second-grade curriculum and organization. Today's agenda included items concerning completion of basic skills, retaining of students, and the mid-term progress reports. (Each grade level faculty meets twice each six-week period to discuss and plan their procedures and activities.)

9:30 Went to a district meeting of the elementary school principals.

12:30 Returned to school and visited with some of the people who were coming to the school to vote.

1:30 Completed the payroll report and took the copy to the central office.

1:45 Picked up the payroll for the certificated personnel and returned to school.

2:00 Stuffed the paychecks into individual envelopes in accordance with the guidelines of the negotiated contract. Delivered the sealed envelopes, with the checks enclosed, to the individual teachers.

2:30 Met with a student from the university who was enrolled in a class which required that she test three students for reading ability. Explained that she needed to obtain parental permission before testing the students.

3:00 School dismissed—supervised loading of buses.

3:20 Worked in the office doing reports, answering mail, and making phone calls.

4:00 Went home.

7:00 Worked for a couple of hours on self-improvement plan.

Wednesday

7:30 Arrived at school.

7:32 Checked on early students.

7:40 Opened the office and turned on all of the equipment (intercom, copying machines, computers).

7:42 Put together daily announcements from notes.

7:45 Supervised unloading of school buses.

8:00 School opened.

8:05 Morning announcements, moment of silence, and flag salute.

8:10 Spoke with the student on in-school suspension.

8:20 Completed work on agenda for today's faculty meeting. There were several items that had come out of the principals' meeting that were added to the agenda.

8:45 Ran copies of the agenda for the faculty meeting and placed them in the teachers' boxes.

9:00 A teacher brought a student to the office for being rude, disrespectful, and unruly. This was the fifth visit to the office for the student for the same offense. After exploring several alternatives the student was suspended for three days.

9:30 Left for a Principals' Study Council Steering Committee meeting at the State First District Office.

11:30 Returned to school.

11:35 A lunchroom supervisor brought a student to the office for discipline because of his use of inappropriate language in the lunchroom. The student had never been sent to the office before for discipline. He seemed very frightened and was let off with a warning. (Discipline is not usually a great problem at this school, and to have three such problems of this magnitude referred to the principal's office in such a short time was unusual).

11:50 Had lunch while discussing self-improvement plans with a teacher.

12:30 Met with the father of the student suspended the day before. He was in agreement with the punishment and asked us to send homework for the days that the student would be out of school.

1:00 Called the home of the student who had been caught stealing and given in-school suspension. The mother was surprised since she had never been given the letter of suspension that was sent home with her daughter. The mother apologized and said she would be here to discuss the matter as soon as possible.

1:30 Returned phone calls, opened mail, and attended to office duties.

2:00 Had a meeting with the librarian and her supervisor for a summative conference on evaluation.

2:45 The mother of the girl who had been caught stealing arrived and had a conference with the teacher.

3:00 School dismissed—supervised loading of buses.

3:15 Faculty meeting. The agenda included items regarding dates for events at the end of school year, Basic Skills Test completion, kindergarten registration, Stanford and Basic Skill testing, in-service credit, proper supervision of students, coming dates of importance and options of summer in-service.

4:15 Worked in the office.

5:15 Went home.

7:00 Down-loaded information from network services on the computer. The information was related to current happenings in education.

Problems and Issues for Discussion

The authors reiterate that this is only two of many days in the life of a principal; consequently, sweeping generalizations about the behavior of Principal A are somewhat speculative. Yet, assuming that these two days are typical of most days in Principal A's life, what comments could be made about his role? What balance was indicated between instructional leadership and other administrative duties? Was he having to assume responsibilities that should be shouldered by other community agencies? What does this short period of time indicate about the organization of the school? Does the school need additional staff, such as a counselor or assistant principal? How should the adequately staffed school be organized? Is the social system of the school implicit in the activity log? Are legal problems indicated? What other observations might be made about the situation?

PRINCIPAL B

Principal B is principal of an elementary school in a school system similar to Principal A's. This school is in the highest socioeconomic section of the city, and is one of two elementary schools in the city that real-estate salespersons almost never fail to mention when they list a dwelling for sale.

The building was built in the 1960s. It is a campus-type building and well maintained. It has a large gymnasium, is located near the center of the highest socioeconomic dwelling area in town, and houses grades K–6.

This school has a rather stable student population of approximately 350 students. There are 17 classroom teachers, 1 physical-education teacher, a part-time nurse, 6 teachers' aids, and a secretary, but no assistant principal.

Principal B is in his fifth year of service in the school. He is a white middle-aged male, and was previously principal of another school in the same school system. He is highly respected by the teachers. Many parents of children in the school boast that he is the best principal in town. He shows great concern for the welfare of students and teachers. He also is very devoted to maintaining and improving the teaching and learning environment of the school and spends long hours in that quest. The following events are actual occurrences recorded by this principal during a school day.

Wednesday

7:35 Briefly studied the list of items that needed attention the previous day but were carried over. Added several things that needed to be accomplished today.

7:38 Had a conference with a fifth-grade teacher who is coordinating our efforts for both the school and a system-wide science fair. We discussed type and number of awards that should be given, and how they should be financed. We also discussed opening the school one night so working parents could view the projects.

7:57 Reviewed my notes from the previous-night PTA meeting. Added two items to my list of things to be done.

8:02 Received a note from the parent of a third-grade student. The mother was very upset because she contended that a boy had kicked her daughter three times for simply rubbing his head. The girl did have several bruises on her leg.

8:03 Received a copy of a petition being circulated in our town. It asked that the "Family Life" portion of our recently adopted Health Curriculum Guide be dropped. Several parents of students at our school are actively working for the repeal of this planned project.

8:20 Talked with the boy and girl involved in the kicking incident. The boy maintained that the girl had pulled his hair and admitted kicking the girl, but only once. Their teacher indicated that the girl had also tripped over a chair in the classroom and that the bruises were in the same area that showed on her leg.

8:35 Conferred with the chairman of the Southern Association of Colleges and Schools (SACS) visiting committee (interim accreditation visit). We discussed his committee's commendations and recommendations.

9:00 Met a student from a local university who was to observe both kindergarten and third-grade classes. Asked the secretary to take her to the rooms where she was expected.

9:05 Ate a snack with the SACS visiting committee.

9:10 Toured the classrooms with two members of the SACS visiting committee. We discussed strategies and management systems and viewed student work.

10:50 Helped the secretary to enroll a new kindergarten student. This required my going to the cafeteria to insure that the child received a free lunch today.

11:05 Had a conference with a teacher to discuss problems a child was having. After a lengthy talk, I decided to change the child to another class.

11:50 Talked with a parent whose child has been sick. Made arrangements to get her assignments sent to her.

12:00 Had lunch at the central office building and heard the report of SACS team's visits.

1:35 Returned to school and received a call from another principal about two students who had recently moved from his school to this one. We also discussed the SACS report.

1:40 Sent a "read and route" sheet (announcement sheet taken from teacher to teacher by a student). This one was to thank the staff for their efforts concerning the PTA program the previous evening and for their efforts in preparing for the SACS committee visit. It also alerted them to the petition that was being circulated about the family life curriculum component.

1:55 Helped the secretary decide which portions of a child's permanent record should be sent to another school.

2:05 Returned a call to another principal. Discussed the SACS report and the petition regarding family-life curriculum objectives.

2:16 Directed an election commission representative to the voting machines.

2:17 Returned a parent's call. He requested that I give a message to a Boy Scout representative who was scheduled to be in the building later that day. Asked the secretary to deliver the message.

2:18 A faculty member asked to leave school early for a medical appointment, and I granted the request.

2:20 Helped the secretary change the type cartridge in her typewriter.

2:23 A fourth-grade teacher and I questioned several students about a video-game cartridge missing from a locker. Following the conference, I searched one child's locker and his desk but did not find the cartridge.

Called the mother of the suspected child and asked her to help by looking for the cartridge at home—she was very cooperative but did not find the cartridge.

3:05 Phoned the parent of the child who was changing from one class to another, and she was in agreement with the change.

3:40 Thanked the cleaning crew for the appearance of the building and relayed the positive comments received from the SACS committee.

3:42 Left for home.

Thursday

7:15 Arrived at school and turned on all equipment.

7:35 Checked and updated list of items needing attention during day.

7:37 Returned a motivational tape that belonged to a staff member.

7:38 Wrote a thank-you letter to people who had donated two computers to the school.

7:50 Had a brief conference with a teacher regarding the best way to handle some situations evolving from the family-life curriculum stand.

7:53 Received a call from an instructional aide whose daughter had just been involved in an automobile accident. Made adjustments for her absence for the day.

7:55 Continued the conference with the teacher about the family-life curriculum.

7:57 Received a call from the parent of the child who was changing classrooms and discussed the best way to make the change.

8:00 School day began.

8:00 Notified the teacher that worked with the aide whose daughter was in the accident that the aide would not be here today.

8:01 Began to file the SACS materials.

8:05 Received a call from another principal regarding a transportation problem.

8:13 Had a conference with a bus driver who referred three boys for discipline problems on the bus.

8:22 Compiled another announcement sheet to be sent around to the teachers concerning the next staff meeting.

8:30 Had a conference with another teacher about the family-life curriculum. This teacher had mixed feelings about the program and had many friends outside of school who opposed the subject.

9:00 Talked with the boys who were reported as misbehaving on the bus and told them that I was sending a letter to their parents and that any further misbehavior would result in their not being allowed to ride the bus.

9:20 Had a conference with a teacher about a new student and discussed several apparent academic problems and procedures for securing free bus transportation for the child.

9:35 Talked with a music teacher and made arrangements for the chorus to perform at the senior citizens' center.

9:40 Wrote a letter to parents of the boys who had problems on the bus and gave the letters to the secretary.

10:15 Ate some ice cream and cupcakes that were sent by a class that was having a party.

10:20 Had a call from another principal in the system and discussed the SACS report and asked about the funding formula for the yearly magazine orders.

10:30 Walked through all classrooms once and some of them twice.

11:30 Completed forms required by the system to document student and teacher behavior.

11:45 Received a call from a principal asking to borrow equipment.

11:53 Wrote application for several days' vacation and sent the form to the assistant superintendent.

11:55 Completed a job reference for a girl who did student teaching here last year.

12:00 Watched the office while the secretary was at lunch and during the time found some paper for a second-grade class, took temperatures of three students, answered the telephone twice, and checked a child for head lice.

12:15 Secluded myself in my office and had lunch.

12:30 Continued to file SACS information.

12:45 Worked on clearing desk and filing.

12:55 Reviewed proposed changes in School Board Policies and sent several notes to committee representatives.

1:20 Had a conference with the school's committee chairman for the end-of-year celebration and discussed ideas and methods of financing the activities.

1:25 Signed reading awards for one class.

1:28 Discussed with the parent of the child who had the video cartridge stolen yesterday that every effort had been made to recover the item.

1:35 Had a conference with the teacher to whom a child would be transferred.

1:45 Had a conference with a comprehensive development class teacher about which achievement tests should be used with her students.

1:58 Attempted to locate the school's spotlight to lend to a local church.

2:07 Checked copies of permanent records of several students to insure that proper documents were being sent to other schools.

2:15 Was notified of a possible tuition violation by a teacher who believed that a false address may have been given so that the student could attend school without paying out-of-city tuition.

2:26 Helped a teacher repair the scales so that students could be weighed and measured.

2:40 Began investigating the tuition situation and, after reviewing several sources of information, referred the matter to the central office and requested a home visit by an alternative teacher.

3:35 Went home.

Problems and Issues for Discussion

The record of events in this school in an affluent neighborhood emphasizes that there are problems even in the best of schools. Some of the problems are different, some are not so different. What could this principal do to prevent some of these situations from developing into problems? What are the situations that might lead to serious problems? What do you think of the tone of this school? What do you think of the leadership of the principal? Is the attention given to management and leadership appropriately distributed? If not, what changes would you suggest? What events took place during these two days that were positive and could be built upon?

PRINCIPAL C

Principal C is head of the only high school in a town of approximately 20,000 people. There are approximately 1000 students with about an 80:20 percent white and black racial mix. The town is located in a primarily farming community and has two relatively large manufacturing plants.

The central office regime is considered to be relatively open to change for improvement and generally supportive of the principal and school. Funding, while still relatively high in the area, has dropped some lately, attributed to the fact that a school board member died who was considered to be high in the community power structure.

The school building was built in the 1960s, is in good repair, and is clean and well kept. Football and basketball are high priorities of the townfolks; therefore, the playing field and gymnasium are high building priorities. Winning athletic teams are more the rule than the exception.

The school has had some occasional drug problems; however, these problems seem to be under control at the present time. Racial problems have been a source of concern from time to time.

There are 54 teachers in the school. The faculty, taken as a whole, is considered to be a very good faculty with most classes being taught by teachers certificated in their respective areas.

Principal C is a white middle-aged male who came up through the ranks, beginning as a mathematics teacher in the junior high school. He has been in the system for 20 years and has been principal of the high school for the last 14 years. He is well respected by students, faculty, community members, and the central office regime. He has his detractors, a condition not unusual for a stern disciplinarian, as he is considered to be. He holds a doctorate in educational administration. Events listed here are actual recordings of happenings during a selected two days in the life of this principal.

Monday

7:35 Arrived at school.

7:40 Two teachers came into the office to discuss a matter concerning some students.

7:50 Went to the English Department to discuss observation of classes by a student from a local college.

8:00 The school day officially begun.

8:05 A senior boy came in to discuss with me his concern about the process of determining GPA, class rank, and honor graduates [this problem is presented in the simulations section]. He is an honor student. He was specifically concerned about an exchange student and a student from a private church school with only one semester at the school who qualified as honor graduates. [See simulations section of this chapter for greater details.]

9:00 A senior girl (handicapped and in a wheelchair) came in to talk about building deficiencies for handicapped students.

9:15 Discussed with one of the assistant principals the problems raised by the two students about eligibility to be an honor graduate and poor access to upper-level rooms by handicapped students.

9:30 Took a call from the school system's artist-in-residence about a trip that is being planned to Washington, D.C. for a group of students.

9:40 Worked on preparation for the faculty meeting the next day.

10:10 The assistant principal came in to discuss a meeting he had with the police chief about a traffic problem in the back parking lot.

10:20 Talked with a student who was sent to the office for not dressing out for P.E. class—she was a recent transfer from Michigan and said she kept forgetting to bring her gym clothes.

1:35 Called the superintendent and discussed the problem of honor graduates and class ranking of seniors and transfer students from nonaccredited schools. There are five students tied for number one with a 4.0 GPA and two tied for the number-two position. The number-two students cannot understand why they occupy number six and seven positions in class rank when the transfer student did not earn the number-one ranking at this school.

11:00 The guidance counselor came in to discuss the problem about ranking and honor graduates that had been raised by students earlier in the day. She was in sympathy with the complaining students—maybe too much so.

11:05 Took a call from a local business asking me to send information for a fund drive on student-type school spirit items.

11:10 Continued the discussion with the counselor.

11:30 Lunch

12:10 Returned to office, opened the mail, and made final preparations for faculty meeting the next day.

1:00 Took a call from a principal of a local high school regarding a girl who has been suspended from this school for sexual activity on school grounds during lunch—she was trying to enter that school. [See simulations section of this chapter for greater details on this situation.]

1:15 Discussed with one of the assistant principals several pressing matters.

1:50 Took a coke break—had a bad headache.

2:10 An instructor from a local college called—had six or seven students in a secondary curriculum class that needed to observe classes at the school for 10–20 hours.

2:20 Finished opening the mail.

2:40 Signed checks and purchase orders.

2:55 Reviewed an evaluation instrument and process for counselors and librarians.

3:00 School was dismissed. Monitored student and parent automobile traffic and bus loading.

3:15 Had a conference with a teacher about a student problem.

3:40 Returned several telephone calls.

4:10 Reviewed the day's accomplishments and listed things to do tomorrow.

4:35 Left school for the day.

Tuesday

7:30 Arrived at school. There was a parent with a senior girl (not her daughter) waiting to see me. The girl had left home and this lady was letting her live at her house (she also has a daughter in this school) with parental knowledge. She wanted to make me (the school) aware of the situation.

8:00 School officially opened. Made daily announcements over the intercom.

8:10 Reviewed and signed special education documentation forms and records.

8:35 A mother came in to see me and wanted to know why her son was suspended. Sent her to the assistant principal in charge of attendance and discipline.

8:40 Reviewed materials relevant to state monitoring of the special education program.

8:50 Took a telephone call from a lady who supervises the hospitality room at basketball games explaining (at length) why she was not present at the last game.

9:00 During class change, checked with two special-education teachers to verify readiness for state monitoring later in the week.

9:15 Dr. Crawford, from the State Department district office, called to follow up on some questions from me concerning state proficiency tests and distribution of different types of diplomas.

9:25 The counselor came in to discuss the academic situation of a senior girl who has been absent several days following an auto accident and death of her mother.

9:35 The secretary came in to discuss the problem of receiving repeated GED results for the same person who had never picked up the original GED diploma.

9:45 Worked on paper work at my desk.

10:45 Checked the parking lots prior to lunch and found two students trying to sneak off early. They had slipped out of class.

11:20 Contacted a parent by telephone to follow up on a previous complaint about a teacher hurting his daughter's feelings in front of a class.

11:30 Had lunch during which time several students and teachers asked various questions.

12:10 Talked with an assistant principal about a senior boy from Holston Home, a group home for boys, who had been punished for an infraction at the home by not being allowed to perform a school drama production part, which he had earned—very frustrating to the boy.

12:30 Met with a teacher about a student and parent concerning negative feedback about grades.

12:50 Monitored halls during change of classes.

1:00 Came upon a problem in the hall between a senior boy and his ex-girlfriend. He was in a co-op program and should have been at work. Told him to go on where he belonged. He ignored me. I tried repeatedly to coax him into leaving the building, but he still did not go. Took him by the back of the neck and physically took him to the door. His challenge to me created a very explosive situation. Contacted his mother who works nearby. She brought him to my office. I explained what happened, my position, that he must understand who is in charge; and, that when he challenged me, I had no choice but to make sure he understood. She was very supportive of me and reprimanded him very aggressively.

2:45 Took a Happy-Birthday balloon and ribbon to a teacher. I do this regularly for all employees of the school on their birthdays.

2:50 Worked in the office at my desk.

3:15 The chorus teacher came in to discuss plans for next year.

3:30 Talked with both assistant principals regarding a problem at lunch in the field house. Preliminary information shows that a fifteen-year-old girl had sex with two different students in the field house on the previous

Friday. [Further details of this problem are discussed in the simulations section of this chapter.]

3:50 Left school for the day and went home.

6:10 Returned for a home basketball game.

10:10 Left for home after a twelve-hour, twenty-minute day.

Problems and Issues for Discussion

Again, we emphasize that this account represents only two days in the life of Principal C. These days do illustrate, however, how frustrating the life of a secondary principal can become. The log illustrates the difficulty of delegating administrative responsibility to the school staff. It seems that everyone with a problem wants a slice of the principal's time. How can the principal deal with this problem?

PRINCIPAL D

Principal D is a white female and heads a junior high school in one of the ten largest school systems in the United States. There are approximately 1900 students and 74 teachers. The ethnic status is about one-third white, black and Hispanic respectively. The socioeconomic level in the school community is relatively low. Principal D included the following note to one of the authors: "These two days were easy days. Sometimes we have to rush to have paperwork finished at a certain time. Other times we have to break up fights, prevent them, find out about stolen items, and work with police officers to discuss gang activities in the community, etc."

Monday

8:00 Arrived at school.

8:30 Checked the mail from the afternoon before.

9:00 Went to the central office for an Attendance Boundary Committee (ABC) meeting.

9:30 Made an ABC presentation on a minor boundary change.

10:30 Went back to school, read the electronic mail, and worked on calendar activities.

11:00 Talked with a mother whose child had broken a flute and refused to pay for the repair. After the conversation she agreed to pay one-half now and the other half a month from now.

12:00 Had a light lunch and checked the cafeteria monitors.

12:30 Talked to the head custodian about a broken pipe in the kitchen and followed up by asking the secretary to call maintenance.

1:00 Met with a central office official about a minor accident involving a special-education child two years ago. The secretary brought the accident report and the official took the depositions, including one from the teacher who had been present when the accident occurred.

2:00 Talked to a cameraman from Channel 23 about the use of the building for a special program.

2:30 Had a conference with the head counselor about SSAT results and Quipp pretest to prepare students for the Stanford Achievement Test.

2:45 Observed a teacher.

3:45 Went through the mail with the secretary.

4:30 Went home.

7:30 Came back to school for a dropout-prevention meeting.

9:30 Checked with the community school assistant principals to see that classes were conducted properly.

10:00 Went home again.

Tuesday

8:00 Arrived at school.

8:15 Inspected corridors, classrooms, and restrooms to see if they were clean.

8:50 Had a conference with a mother whose child has been recommended for expulsion because of a physical attack on a teacher.

9:30 Checked mail from the day before.

10:00 Made the morning announcements over the P.A. system to stress the importance of attending every class every day and the importance of scoring high on the Stanford Achievement Test.

10:15 Observed a teacher on prescription.

11:15 Organized a workshop for teachers with assistant principal and the area language arts coordinator.

11:50 Checked on a student who fell down on the stairs accidentally. Called the rescue squad.

12:00 The girl who fell had no fractured bones. The attendance clerk called the girl's home and asked the parents to come and pick up the injured girl.

12:30 Had a light lunch.

1:00 Observed a teacher.

2:00 Checked the mail.

2:30 Had a meeting with the student-activities sponsor to check the progress of the Disney World trip.

3:00 Had a conference with the assistant principal for curriculum and head counselor to discuss the master schedule for next school year and to determine the teachers needed for new courses.

3:30 Had a meeting with the PTA president to plan a general meeting to talk with the parents about the bond referendum.

4:00 Checked the dismissal time.

4:15 Conducted a faculty meeting to discuss assertive discipline, report cards, attendance procedures, bond referendum, and the youth fair.

5:30 Went home.

Problems and Issues

Principal D's days appear to be somewhat more routine and less problem-oriented than Principal C's. As already mentioned, she commented to one of the authors that these turned out to be easy days. Most principals have their good and bad days. This account should serve as a ray of hope for those readers who fear the responsibility. The readers might consider several questions about Principal D's behavior, which she described as atypical. What was the balance between fulfilling routine administrative duties and providing instructional leadership? How well did Principal D delegate administrative responsibility? Were there any indications of the school climate? How would you characterize the leadership style of Principal D?

PRINCIPAL E

Principal E heads an inner-city senior high school in a low socioeconomic area in one of the largest metropolitan areas in the country. He is middle aged. He has been principal of the school for three years. He succeeded another male principal of Hispanic ancestry who now works in the central office as assistant superintendent. The principal he succeeded was very effective and left the school in very good shape for his successor.

The school system is in very good financial condition. The central office regime strongly supports the school and its principal. The school district has approximately 250,000 students. There are 2400 students, 96 teachers and 4 assistant principals in the school. There are 11 faculty council members: 5 elected faculty, 5 selected by the union, and 1 building steward. There are adequate numbers of aides, custodians, secretaries and security guards (the corridors and grounds are patrolled by guards).

The school has a racial/ethnic mix of approximately 90 percent black, 1 percent white, with the balance made up of other ethnic minorities. Approximately the same racial/ethnic ratio exists among the teachers and staff. Following is the daily log of Principal E.

Monday

7:00 Reviewed daily calendar, suspension file, and things to do for the day.

7:15 Met with the assistant principal for curriculum to discuss the regional accrediting agency report on accreditation. The report required information about each teacher's area of certification in relation to the subject each is actually teaching.

7:30 Met with the tenth-grade assistant principal to discuss implementation of a new tardy class policy. The security monitors assign detentions to students who are tardy to class using a detention form. Names of students not serving their detentions within 48 hours are placed on an exclusion-from-class list and are given one day on in-school suspension.

7:45 Signed checks for school purchases and reviewed requests for purchases from school personnel.

8:00 Met with the tenth-grade assistant principal, computer teacher, and the attendance counselor to devise a system for a computerized detention-exclusion list. We devised a system whereby the computer will record and delete detentions given and served daily and will generate a daily exclusion list.

8:30 Delivered a welcome address to our Student Leadership Conference. The Student Leadership Conference is a leadership training workshop designed to improve student officer leadership skills.

8:45 Verified and signed the school employees' payroll.

9:00 Had a telephone conversation with the school district's personnel officer about an investigation involving one of our employees.

9:15 Observed an English teacher.

10:00 Met with the new vice-president of the state university about possible linkage between our two institutions. Tentatively agreed to establish a new program in which our honor students could shadow college students on campus.

11:15 Returned the morning phone calls. We use the telephone log—routing phone calls twice a day.

11:30 Met with the assistant principal for curriculum about a possible child-abuse case.

12:00 Supervised part of the lunch period.

12:30 Met with the computer-education department head about a new voice-interaction computer lab for next year.

1:30 Met with the facilitators for a new language-arts program. The program will begin next month. Foundation for Learning, a holistic approach to teaching language arts, will be piloted in our school during the second semester.

1:45 Met with the bilingual department head to discuss a transitional class for our limited-English-proficiency students with little previous formal schooling. A transitional class for these students would allow for teaching the basics of reading and arithmetic at the high school level. It would require district approval.

2:00 Reviewed plans for a community meeting on a school bond issue to be held at our school tonight.

2:15 Met with the test chairperson about a possible change in district policy about testing our limited-English-proficient students on the Stanford Achievement Test.

2:30 Met with the ninth-grade assistant principal about what to do with a continuously disruptive student.

2:45 Inspected the building and grounds with the head custodian. Finalized plans for use of the auditorium for tonight's community meeting.

3:15 Attended the after-school Valentine's dance.

3:45 Returned the afternoon phone calls.

4:00 Read and routed the mail. Also wrote a memo.

5:15 Went home.

7:00 Greeted 400 principals, parents, and community leaders who were attending a meeting at our school.

7:30 Attended the meeting.

10:00 Supervised the building and parking lot after the meeting ended.

10:00 Went home.

Problems and Issues

Principal E's daily log is the last of five logs included in the chapter. At this point the readers might give consideration to a comparison of the logs. Is there an indication of differences in leadership styles among the principals? Did any of the principals demonstrate more emphasis on instructional leadership activities? Should any of the principals consider using the logs to redirect the use of their time?

SIMULATIONS

Following are some problems, situations, and opportunities that the five principals mentioned have encountered. In addition, the authors were given the opportunity to review the entire three-year file of memoranda written by the principal of a large inner-city senior high school. We selected, from this file and from those contributed by four principals presenting activity logs, a number of vignettes that may be used as simulations by college classes and in-service groups. We suggest that these situations be reviewed by individuals who each decide how they would deal with them. The situations should also be considered in small group settings, allowing each small group to decide how they would deal with the situations. Finally, each small group should report their decisions to the entire group and the different small groups should then debate, argue, or justify their decisions.

The reader will need to look back at the earlier brief descriptions of each principal, school, and community in order to get some understanding of the settings in which some of these situations occurred.

PRINCIPAL A

Situation 1

LITTLETON ELEMENTARY SCHOOL
Jonesville, USA

INTERSCHOOL COMMUNICATION

TO: Mr. Ted Belo, Principal
FROM: Ida Regan, Teacher, Grade 6
RE: Information Concerning Suspicion of Shoplifting
DATE: March 21, 1988

This memo is to give you the information requested about three of our students who are suspected by the police of shoplifting. One of the students is in my class. I do have several pencils that this student brought to school the day after the incident was supposed to have occurred. I understand that pencils like that were supposed to have been taken in the shoplifting incident.

I recommend that this case be turned over to the juvenile authorities since the incident happened after school hours and off school grounds. I do not feel that we should concern ourselves with this situation but the decision is yours.

Discussion and Questions For Simulation 1—Principal A Ida Regan's memorandum raises several legal and professional concerns that were discussed in Chapter 12 (such as reasonable suspicion, probable cause, and due process). Also, the question of the school's legal responsibility is involved. Her memo also raises ethical and professional issues of the caring function, prudence, and justice. Should Mr. Belo call juvenile authorities based on the teacher's memorandum? Since the incident happened off school grounds, should he absolve himself and the school of any responsibility? What concern should he show for the welfare of the student? What response would be appropriate for Mr. Ted Belo?

Situation 2

JONESVILLE CITY SCHOOLS
Jonesville, USA

INTERSYSTEM COMMUNICATION

TO: Mr. Ted Belo, Principal, Littleton Elementary School
FROM: Judy Ensor, Elementary Supervisor
RE: Evaluation of Teachers
DATE: March 22, 1988

Thirteen teachers in your school were evaluated by both you and me recently. The results of your and my evaluations of twelve of the teachers were very close. However, you evaluated one teacher much higher than I. The superintendent is very concerned about your evaluation and has asked me to meet with you about this matter.

When I evaluated the teacher she never did have the attention of the students. She also took issue with my low ratings and never did agree with them.

I suggest that you make a development plan for this teacher. I also suggest that you rethink your evaluation. Please let me know of your decision soon.

Discussion and Questions for Simulation 2—Principal A This very direct memorandum from Elementary Supervisor Judy Ensor is a classic example of conflict in authority. Principal Belo is being pressured by Ms. Ensor, presumably with the concurrence of the superintendent, to change his evaluation of the teacher. School principals often are placed in these precarious situations. How should Mr. Belo respond to this memorandum? Why? How would his adherence to Ms. Ensor's demand influence his leadership in the school? What are possible reactions if he rejects her request? Could he seek a compromise or coordinated approach? What are some other illustrations in which the school principal might be pressured by the central office? What are the principal's alternatives when experiencing these situations?

Situation 3

4 Fairway Court
Jonesville, USA 47621
March 22, 1988

Mr. Ted Belo, Principal
Littleton Elementary School
1421 Eakton Highway
Jonesville, USA 47621

Dear Mr. Belo:

I enrolled my daughter in your school last week after moving here from New York City. She is in Mrs. Blevin's fifth-grade class. It appears that my daughter is in very good hands in most respects; however, I have some concerns about what I observed on my initial visit to your school and what my little girl has told me about the activities there.

When I visited Mr. Blevin's room, I saw a King James Version of the Holy Bible on her desk. My daughter also tells me that immediately following the early morning moment of silence her teacher exclaims "In His name we pray, Amen." I have checked with the ACLU about the presence of the Bible and the exclamation. They tell me that both are highly questionable as far as their constitutionality.

I do not want to appear as a *cause celebre* but neither do I want our fine school to be outside the bounds of the law. Would you please investigate this situation and check back with me soon? I will wait a reasonable length of time before I take further action.

Sincerely,
Ralph Faucette

Discussion and Questions for Simulation 3—Principal A As discussed in Chapter 12, the First Amendment to the Constitution guarantees that "Congress shall make no law respecting an *establishment* of religion or prohibiting the *free exercise* thereof...." Issues involving religion and freedom of speech often become very explosive and destructive to school operation. For example, high school principals frequently face problems involving officially sponsored (and unofficially printed) student newspapers. Mr. Ralph Faucette obviously feels that the teacher's practices violate his daughter's constitutional rights. Mr. Blevins may also feel strongly about this issue since he, in all likelihood, understands that there are some risks involved in this situation. From your understanding of the numerous court decisions on this subject, is the teacher in violation of the law? Is Mr. Faucette overly sensitive about the First Amendment provisions? What consideration should be given to Mr. Blevins? Should Mr. Belo take action? If so, what should he do? How should he proceed?

PRINCIPAL B

Simulation 1

222 Quickway Ct.
Banter, USA 37582
March 31, 1988

Mr. John Dixon, Principal
Frickey Elementary School
113 Academy Road
Banter, USA 37582

Dear Mr. Dixon:

I have recently moved into this community and have two children in your school. I have always been highly involved with the PTA of the school my children attend. My concern is that the PTA at your school appears to be fading.

I have asked some other parents about this situation, and they have told me that a small group of parents are in office and have been for the past few years. This group seems to place its members on the nominating committee each year and nominates and elects members from the group as officers. This means that they control the programs and activities of the PTA and virtually exclude parents outside their group.

I am aware that these people are very influential community members and that they have done a great deal for Frickey school. However, if you want participation from the rest of us parents, you will need to do something about this situation. New officers will be elected at the next PTA meeting.

Sincerely,
Rhonda Newton

Discussion and Questions for Simulation 1—Principal B The letter from Rhonda Newton to John Dixon is fairly typical of the leadership demands placed on the school principal. These demands come in a variety of ways and for numerous expressed feelings. In this instance, Mrs. Newton feels that the leaders in the community power structure are dominating the PTA. She probably feels that social discrimination is involved in the control of the PTA. As discussed in Chapter 6, school principals have to provide leadership in the school and community. Mrs. Newton believes that Mr. Dixon should act to make the control of the PTA a more open, democratic process. Whether she is expressing the facts in this case remains to be seen. In a series of steps and anticipated reactions, what should Mr. Dixon do (or not do) as a response to Rhonda Newton's letter? Should he ignore the letter? Collect facts about the situation? Seek to change the structure of the PTA?

Simulation 2

Banter School System
Banter, USA

INTERSYSTEM COMMUNICATION

To: Mr. John Dixon, Principal
Frickey Elementary School
From: Wendell Clark, Assistant Superintendent
Subject: Placement of Students
Date: March 30, 1988

This memo is to call your attention to a potential problem of placing students who will be in the sixth grade in your school for next year. I recall that there was some problem last year with the placements; some parents thought some students got preferential treatment. We are already having inquiries in this office as to how you plan to place students in the sixth grade for next year.

It seems that you have four sixth-grade teachers and word of mouth has it that one of those four is a far superior teacher. You and I have discussed this matter before and decided that that is not necessarily so, but it seems in the perception of most parents involved that she is the "teacher to have."

I am aware that some of your more influential parents will have students in the sixth grade next year. They will almost surely request that their children be placed with this particular teacher.

I believe that you will be making student assignments to teachers for next year in the near future. The superintendent and I would like to know how you plan to handle the situation of placement of students with teachers in the sixth grade.

Discussion and Questions for Simulation 2—Principal B The potential situation anticipated by Mr. Wendell Clark frequently happens in elementary schools. In fact, it is most likely to occur in the first grade, in which one of the first-grade teachers enjoys an unusually high reputation among parents. Moreover, some teachers have perpetuated the practice by recruiting within the attendance area of the school. If allowed to continue unrestricted, the situation can result in social segregation in which the children of influential (in-the-know) parents are clustered in the most popular teacher's classroom. In these situations the principal becomes the point of leadership pressure and politics. If this practice of social discrimination has a history in the school, Mr. Dixon will be subjected to great pressure to continue the practice. As the principal of Frickey Elementary School, how would you respond to Mr. Clark's memorandum? If there is substance to his concerns, what policy would you seek to establish to prevent these situations from occurring in the school?

Simulation 3

LITTLETON ELEMENTARY SCHOOL
BANTER, USA

INTERSYSTEM COMMUNICATION

To: Mr. John Dixon, Principal
From: Della McDee, President, PTA
Subject: PTA Announcement
Date: October 1, 1988

Much thought, effort, and planning has gone into a fun night for the school and community. The corresponding secretary for the PTA has written and duplicated an announcement and sent the copies to school to be sent home to parents and to local businesses. The school secretary noticed some misspelled words. On closer scrutiny, there were several glaring errors in the announcement. What can be done?

Discussion and Questions for Simulation 3—Principal B Sending materials to parents and other citizens that contain the errors indicated can contribute to the lack of credibility with the public. Nevertheless, in this case the announcement in question was prepared for distribution by the hard working (probably very loyal) corresponding secretary of the PTA. It is evident that the PTA president is not going to deal with this situation and she is handing it to you. If you were the principal of this school, what do you believe would be an appropriate alternative?

Simulation 4

Notes of Events of a Problem Situation
for Principal's File
Beginning September, 1988

At the beginning of the school year, I was called to the superintendent's office for a conference. The superintendent had received a letter from a parent of a child attending this school. The letter was protesting the retention of her son in the second grade from the previous year. The letter was well written and claimed that because she and her son lived in the "projects" they were being discriminated against and that she had written her congressman and others in order to get satisfaction. After discussing the matter, the superintendent gave me the discretion of handling the situation and of getting back to him with my decision and with a plan as to what I intend to do about the matter.

I went back to school and talked with the teacher the child had the year before; she did, in fact, seem to be of the "high society" type. In retrospect, she has at times been somewhat disrespectful to some students, especially those from lower socioeconomic families. Maybe the mother has a point.

I sent a letter to the mother saying that the superintendent and I had decided to promote the boy to the next grade because of his size, age, and social development level if the mother would agree to having the child tested by the special education department to determine if there was a learning disability. The teacher, mentioned above, disagreed with this action.

The mother would not sign to have the child tested. In fact, she was most uncooperative. She claimed that we were prejudiced against the child because he was a "bastard."

Considering these circumstances, what action do I take concerning this situation?

Discussion and Questions for Simulation 4—Principal B Nothing seems to disturb parents more than the feelings arising from what they believe to be discriminatory acts against their children. Therefore, the school principal must project fairness, justice, and caring where discrimination might be suspected. Assuming that the anonymously prepared statement left in the principal's file is representative of what had transpired, and if you were the principal, what actions would you take?

Simulation 5

54 Pine Street
Banter, USA
April 12, 1988

Mr. John Dixon, Principal
Frickey Elementary School
113 Academy Rd.
Banter, USA

Dear Mr. Dixon:

I am writing to you to express a concern that I, and several other persons, have about a situation in your school. We know that last year you allowed a volunteer tutor to come to school and work with a student with reading problems (dyslexia). We now understand that you have decided to disallow this practice this year. Why?

The other parents and I can well afford to pay for a tutor for our children and cannot understand why we might be disallowed this opportunity. We will wait a reasonable length of time for your reply before taking further action.

Sincerely,
Ruben Cates

Discussion and Questions for Simulation 5—Principal B What appears, at times, to be an insignificant decision can result in major difficulties. In this case, the principal allowed a tutor who was not a school employee to work with a student during school hours. He had no authority over her, however, she created no problems for him. If the principal allows others in over whom he has no authority and they are not as cooperative as the one mentioned here, he may not be so fortunate. They may create problems. The principal is in this potentially troublesome situation as a result of his previous decision. How can he get out of the situation without creating animosity between Mr. Cates, the other parents and himself? How does he respond to the letter? What immediate action should he take? What action should he take to assure that this problem does not reoccur?

PRINCIPAL C

Situation 1

UPTOWN HIGH SCHOOL
Uptown, USA

INTERDEPARTMENTAL COMMUNICATION

TO: Mr. Gene Fugate, Principal
FROM: Nancy Ann Dick, Guidance Counselor
RE: Determination of Honor Students
DATE: February 29, 1988

We have 235 seniors in this year's graduating class. Thirty-five have honor grades with a 3.5 overall standing. Five of those students have a perfect 4.0 standing.

As you know, we have a policy of giving special honors to five students with the best grades. Since we have five students with perfect 4.0 grade standings, it appears that the decision as to who will get the special honors should be without question. It is not, and this is the problem about which I write.

Two of the five students with 4.0 averages have only been in this school during this, their senior, year. One is a visiting student from Madrid, Spain, who did not have grades from her school back home, so her grade point average is only for one year. The other is a transfer student from a local church school. Some of the other students are complaining that grading was much easier at the church school than here, which may have allowed her to have this high average. They are also complaining that she had already had most of her required courses at the other school and is only taking easy courses here. To further complicate the situation, there are two other students who have been in this school all four years who have a 3.9 average. Naturally, these two students are very concerned about this situation.

I will abide by your decision concerning this matter and will be awaiting your decision.

Discussion and Questions for Simulation 1—Principal C Successful practice as a school principal depends on leadership in decision making about situations as raised by Nancy Ann Dick. The exchange theory of leadership presupposes that every decision made by the leader involves costs and rewards. Leadership behavior that results in too many costs may result in very serious difficulty, including reassignment or revocation of contract. The situation involving special honors is laden with the possibility of costs in leadership. Earlier the authors reviewed several approaches to decision making (see Chapter 7). What are the alternative processes that might be used in making a decision about the special honors for a student's situation? What are some critical steps that should be made in reaching a solution to this problem?

Situation 2

222 Oldham Lane
Uptown, USA
February 29, 1988

Mr. Gene Fugate, Principal
2 Academy Way
Uptown, USA

Dear Mr. Fugate:

I am writing you about a problem that my physically handicapped daughter is having in school. As you know, my daughter June, who just enrolled in your school two weeks ago, is confined to a wheelchair. The doctors have cautioned us to be very careful with her because even a minor injury could be very serious.

Your school building has three floors and June has classes on the second and third floors. I have not been able to convince her to ride the mechanical device you installed on the stairs to transport her from one floor to the other. She says she is terrified of the device, and she refuses to use it. Some of the other students have been carrying her from one floor to the other. The first time they did that, a wheel fell off the wheelchair and almost caused the students to drop her and the chair. I am most concerned for my daughter's safety in this building that is not barrier-free.

I know that you will want to do something about this situation soon. I will be looking forward to hearing from you about the matter.

Sincerely,
Alice Kizee

Discussion and Questions for Simulation 2—Principal C Mrs. Kizee has raised a question with Mr. Gene Fugate about the physical facilities of the school. Did the school meet the demands of state law concerning the education of handicapped students? Moreover, questions arise about the prudence of having students carry her daughter to the second and third floors. This could raise questions of foreseeability and liability for tort (See Chapter 12). Again, Mrs. Kizee's letter demands the immediate attention of Mr. Fugate. Explain in some detail how you as a principal would respond to the letter. What should be some of the immediate actions? What are some longer-range solutions?

Situation 3

UPTOWN HIGH SCHOOL
Uptown, USA

INTERDEPARTMENTAL COMMUNICATION

TO: Mr. Gene Fugate, Principal
FROM: Vernon Stout, Assistant Principal
RE: Student Behavior
DATE: February 29, 1988

This memo is a report of the details that the McKenzie girl gave me about having sex with two boys here at school yesterday. You will remember that you asked me for a written report of this situation.

Melissa is a fifteen-year-old girl who until recently was somewhat obese and lacking in self-confidence. She has recently lost weight and seems to be rather attractive to boys. She has also developed a better self-image. Furthermore, according to all reports, she has become very interested in certain boys in our school.

Earlier this year, she was dating one of the boys and her mother disapproved. Her mother has taken her out of this school twice this year and enrolled her in private schools. During the second stay away from this school, her boyfriend, who was a student here, was sent to a correctional institution. The mother then returned Melissa to this school, thinking that things would be all right with him gone. Since she returned, she has given considerable attention to other boys.

Yesterday she came to see me at the urging of a girlfriend. She reported that she had had sex with two different boys in the field house. She was scared that one of them had hurt her because she was bleeding.

I talked with the two boys. One of them admitted right off that this had happened. The other one denied it at first and later admitted it. He was scared because he was nineteen years old and she was only fifteen.

The two boys are transferring to another school system today. How do you suggest that this situation be handled?

Discussion and Questions for Simulation 3—Principal C This rather sad memorandum from the assistant principal leaves one with a variety of reactions and questions. For example, the McKenzie girl is obviously in need of a caring counseling service. What kind of counseling service is indicated? Should school officials have initiated conferences with Mrs. McKenzie? What should be done with the boys involved? If you were the principal in this situation, what actions would you believe to be prudent and just?

Situation 4

UPTOWN HIGH SCHOOL
Uptown, USA

INTERDEPARTMENTAL COMMUNICATION

TO: Mr. Gene Fugate
FROM: Glenna Goff
RE: One Day Leave of Absence
DATE: February 16, 1988

Enclosed are copies of requests for leave so that I may go to the University to be screened for the Ed.S. program. I prefer to take professional leave since this screening seems to be a professional matter. I know that you explained to me that taking professional leave for this purpose was frowned on by the administration. I hope that you have had time to think about this matter and have changed your mind. I discussed this matter with Carl, my husband, whom you have known since boyhood, and he is adamant about my saving my two personal days of leave to go to a convention with him. I have submitted both forms and you may approve whichever you choose.

Discussion and Questions for Simulation 4—Principal C School principals are frequently pressured to give favors that are outside the bounds of policy and standard administrative practice. In fact, some persons seem to enjoy trying to circumvent conventional practice or challenge existing policy. Should Mr. Fugate approve Glenna Goff's request to take professional leave? If so, what are some possible reactions within the faculty and central office regime? What message does Mr. Fugate send if professional leave is not approved?

Situation 5

INTERSYSTEM COMMUNICATION

TO: All Principals
FROM: Elbert Hoover, Assistant Superintendent
SUBJECT: Decision on Expenditures
DATE: February 29, 1988

Please give me in writing your thoughts about how we will spend the additional monies that have just been allotted to the school system by the city council. This is not a sizable amount of money, so we must plan to get the most from it. It seems to me that we have three logical choices: (1) raise teacher pay, (2) further promote the career ladder, or (3) develop an improved in-service program. I am sorry to rush you, but I need your input by March 5.

Discussion and Questions for Simulation 5—Principal C This short memorandum from Elbert Hoover raises the question of priorities. Although we do not know much about the situation, we are told that the amount of the "windfall" is small. Therefore, one question would be how the scarce resource provided can be used for the most advantage to students, that is, "the most bang for the buck." What criteria would you use to decide among the options provided in the memo? Could you suggest additional options? Should you involve the faculty in your decision process? Write a memo to Mr. Hoover expressing your preference for investing funds.

(Principal D did not submit simulations.)

PRINCIPAL E

Situation 1

DOWNTOWN HIGH SCHOOL
Buena Vista, USA

INTERSCHOOL COMMUNICATION

TO: Mr. Roberto Sanchez, Principal
FROM: Elena P. Howard, Building Representative, Teacher's Union
RE: Teacher Complaint
DATE: March 2, 1988

    Mrs. Maria Herring, a first-year teacher in this school and in the system, has informed me that she was recently evaluated by you. It seems that you evaluated her teaching performance in Biology I and II. The union contract clearly states that a beginning teacher will only be evaluated at one level in any particular subject if this evaluation is to be used in determining if he or she is to be retained.
    It appears that there are several questions about this situation: Are these evaluations to be used in determining if Mrs. Herring will be retained in her present position after this year? If only one of them is to be used, how can you prevent the evaluation of the other class from influencing your decision about retaining her? If neither evaluation is to be used in the decision to retain her in what way will they be used? I suggest that we meet soon with the grievance committee to discuss this matter.

Discussion and Questions for Simulation 1—Principal E As the authors have discussed previously, the principal is the key person in administering the contract negotiated by the board of education and teachers' union. The principal who is negligent in this duty will be subjected to a grievance. Too many grievances against a principal may lead to problems with the central administration. What action should Mr. Sanchez take?

Situation 2

DOWNTOWN HIGH SCHOOL
Buena Vista, USA

INTERSCHOOL COMMUNICATION

TO: Mrs. Verline Daws
FROM: Roberto Sanchez
RE: Confirmation of Conferences Held on February 25 and 26, 1988
DATE: March 3, 1988

On February 23, 1988, I had a conference with you in reference to your job performance as a teacher assistant in the Exceptional Student Program. Mr. Gary Elliott, Exceptional Student Department Head, was also present. I discussed the following incidents:

1. On February 16, 1988, as you were pushing Bernetta Ingram, an orthopedic handicapped student, in her wheelchair toward the elevator, you said to her that she weighed a ton. The student has a weight problem and is very sensitive about it. You admitted saying this and told me that you meant no harm to the student.

2. On February 20, 1988, during the first period you made a derogatory statement about Mr. Athel Carter, Assistant Principal, in front of Mrs. Irene Balt, teacher; Mrs. Joan Little, assistant teacher; and the students in the classroom. You were also talking to Mrs. Little about other matters not related to the lesson. You admitted doing this and told me that you were sorry.

3. On February 20, 1988, during the second period you went to socialize with Mr. Edgar Poe while he was teaching his class. You were on break at the time, but he was not. You admitted this and stated that you were sorry.

4. On February 20, 1988, you left your students unattended while you went to meet Leonard Brett, the UTD Building Steward. I explained that Mr. Brett cannot conduct UTD matters while he is teaching (UTD contract division) and that you must not leave your class unattended.

5. On February 21, 1988, you had a conference with Mr. Fair and Mrs. Balt. Mr. Fair discussed your behavior in the classroom. You expressed your concerns. Everyone felt that the conference had "cleared the air."

I directed you to do the following:

1. Refrain from making derogatory remarks to students, even in jest. I explained how exceptional students often mistake jokes and do feel insulted.
2. Refrain from criticizing an assistant principal or any other employee in front of students. An action like this undermines the administration of the school and creates a negative image of the school in the community.
3. Refrain from interrupting teachers or teacher/assistants while they are working with students.
4. Stay with your classes at all times. If you need to see the UTD Building Steward, do it before or after school hours.

On February 22, 1988, you requested to see me. You assured me that you wanted to help our students and work effectively with the staff in your department. I will have to decide now what action to take if there is the least indication that you have violated any of my directives or any like them.

cc: Mr. Gary Exum, Exceptional Student Department Head
Mr. Leonard Brett, UTD Steward
Mr. William Lockhart, Area Director

Discussion and Questions for Simulation 2—Principal E This memorandum from Mr. Sanchez to Mrs. Daws indicates that he may be contemplating dismissal. Involved are the legal rights of teachers and substantive due process. Yet, beyond these legal standards are other standards of ethics, such as justice, prudence, and use of authority. Based on the memorandum would the violation of any or all of Mr. Sanchez's directives be sufficient grounds for dismissal? Is the implied threat in Mr. Sanchez's memorandum (see last paragraph) prudent? Should Mr. Sanchez seek the signature of Mrs. Daws on the directives? How would you have administered this situation?

Index